INTERNATIONAL STATUS IN THE SHADOW OF EMPIRE

Nauru is often figured as an anomaly in the international order. This book offers a new account of Nauru's imperial history and examines its significance to the histories of international law. Drawing on theories of jurisdiction and bureaucracy, it reconstructs four shifts in Nauru's status – from German protectorate, to League of Nations C Mandate, to UN Trust Territory, to sovereign state – as a means of redescribing the transition from the nineteenth-century imperial order to the twentieth-century state system. The book argues that as international status shifts, imperial form accretes: as Nauru's status shifted, what occurred at the local level was a gradual process of bureaucratisation. Two conclusions emerge from this argument. The first is that imperial administration in Nauru produced the Republic's post-independence 'failures'. The second is that international recognition of sovereign status is best understood as marking a beginning, not an end, of the process of decolonisation.

CAIT STORR is Chancellor's Postdoctoral Research Fellow at the University of Technology Sydney. She is an associate member of the Institute of International Law and the Humanities at Melbourne Law School, and junior faculty with the Institute of Global Law and Policy at Harvard Law School. Her doctoral thesis was awarded the University of Melbourne Chancellor's Prize.

CAMBRIDGE STUDIES IN INTERNATIONAL
AND COMPARATIVE LAW: 150

Established in 1946, this series produces high quality, reflective and innovative scholarship in the field of public international law. It publishes works on international law that are of a theoretical, historical, cross-disciplinary or doctrinal nature. The series also welcomes books providing insights from private international law, comparative law and transnational studies which inform international legal thought and practice more generally.

The series seeks to publish views from diverse legal traditions and perspectives, and of any geographical origin. In this respect it invites studies offering regional perspectives on core *problématiques* of international law, and in the same vein, it appreciates contrasts and debates between diverging approaches. Accordingly, books offering new or less orthodox perspectives are very much welcome. Works of a generalist character are greatly valued and the series is also open to studies on specific areas, institutions or problems. Translations of the most outstanding works published in other languages are also considered.

After seventy years, Cambridge Studies in International and Comparative Law sets the standard for international legal scholarship and will continue to define the discipline as it evolves in the years to come.

Series Editors

Larissa van den Herik

Professor of Public International Law, Grotius Centre for International Legal Studies, Leiden University

Jean d'Aspremont

Professor of International Law, University of Manchester and Sciences Po Law School

A list of books in the series can be found at the end of this volume.

INTERNATIONAL STATUS IN THE SHADOW OF EMPIRE

Nauru and the Histories of International Law

CAIT STORR
University of Technology Sydney

CAMBRIDGE
UNIVERSITY PRESS

University Printing House, Cambridge CB2 8BS, United Kingdom

One Liberty Plaza, 20th Floor, New York, NY 10006, USA

477 Williamstown Road, Port Melbourne, VIC 3207, Australia

314–321, 3rd Floor, Plot 3, Splendor Forum, Jasola District Centre, New Delhi – 110025, India

79 Anson Road, #06-04/06, Singapore 079906

Cambridge University Press is part of the University of Cambridge.

It furthers the University's mission by disseminating knowledge in the pursuit of education, learning, and research at the highest international levels of excellence.

www.cambridge.org
Information on this title: www.cambridge.org/9781108498500
DOI: 10.1017/9781108682602

© Cait Storr 2020

This publication is in copyright. Subject to statutory exception and to the provisions of relevant collective licensing agreements, no reproduction of any part may take place without the written permission of Cambridge University Press.

First published 2020

A catalogue record for this publication is available from the British Library.

Library of Congress Cataloging-in-Publication Data
Names: Storr, Cait, author.
Title: International status in the shadow of empire : Nauru and the histories of international law / Cait Storr, University of Glasgow.
Description: Cambridge, United Kingdom ; New York, NY, USA : Cambridge University Press, 2020. | Series: Cambridge studies in international and comparative law | Based on author's thesis (doctoral – University of Melbourne, 2017) issued under title: Nauru : international status, imperial form and the histories of international law. | Includes bibliographical references and index.
Identifiers: LCCN 2020009166 | ISBN 9781108498500 (hardback) | ISBN 9781108682602 (ebook)
Subjects: LCSH: Nauru – International status – History. | Nauru – Politics and government.
Classification: LCC KZ4796 .S76 2020 | DDC 341.4/2099685–dc23
LC record available at https://lccn.loc.gov/2020009166

ISBN 978-1-108-49850-0 Hardback

Cambridge University Press has no responsibility for the persistence or accuracy of URLs for external or third-party internet websites referred to in this publication and does not guarantee that any content on such websites is, or will remain, accurate or appropriate.

CONTENTS

List of Illustrations   *page* ix
Acknowledgements   xi

Prologue   1

1 International Status, Imperial Form: Nauru and the Histories of International Law   9

   1.1 Introduction   9

   1.2 Nauru as Symptom versus Nauru as Parable   12

   1.3 On Administrative Form: Attending to Practices of Jurisdiction and Bureaucracy   15

   1.4 The Argument: Status Shifts, Form Accretes   24

   1.5 Situating this Book in the Field   26

   1.6 Telling an Administrative Story: Strengths and Limitations   32

   1.7 The Structure of the Book   39

2 From Trading Post to Protectorate, 1888   45

   2.1 Introduction   45

   2.2 1884: the DHPG Pays its First Dividend   46

   2.3 The Reluctance of the Bismarckian Reich   48

   2.4 Hamburg Trading Firms and the Legacy of the Hansa   50

   2.5 Hanseatic Firms in the Pacific   54

2.6 The Reich, Imperial Expansion and the Berlin Conference of 1884   59

2.7 The Concept of the Protectorate   62

2.8 The 'Colonial Protectorate'   65

2.9 The Establishment of German Protectorates   66

2.10 Concern in the Australasian Colonies over German Imperial Expansion   72

2.11 German and British Consular Jurisdiction in the Western Pacific   76

2.12 The Establishment of the German Protectorate of the Marshall Islands   80

2.13 The Legal Structure of the German Protectorate Regime   82

2.14 The Agreement between the Jaluit Gesellschaft and the Reich   84

2.15 The Incorporation of Nauru into the Marshall Islands Protectorate   89

2.16 Nauru's Incorporation into the Marshall Islands Protectorate as a Matter of Law   93

2.17 International Status and Imperial Form: Administration in Nauru   97

2.18 Conclusion   98

3 From Protectorate to Colony to Mandate, 1920   100

3.1 Introduction   100

3.2 Administration of Nauru as Part of the Marshall Islands Protectorate   102

3.3 The Collapse of the German Protectorates and the Assertion of Direct Rule   107

3.4 The Federation of Australia and Taxonomies of British Imperial Form   114

3.5 Agriculture, Phosphate, Labour and Race in the Pacific   119

3.6 The Pacific Islands Company and its Agreement with the Jaluit Gesellschaft   125

3.7 The Right Passed from the Gesellschaft to the Pacific Phosphate Company   129

3.8 The Commencement of Phosphate Operations on Nauru   131

3.9 Nauru, War and Australian 'Sub-Empire' in the Pacific   134

3.10 Internationalisation, the Mandatory Principle and the Peace Treaty   140

3.11 The Nauru Island Agreement of 1919   148

3.12 Incorporation of the Nauru Island Agreement and its Relationship to Article 22   151

3.13 The Transfer Agreement with the Pacific Phosphate Company   154

3.14 The Mandate for Nauru and the Tension between International and Sub-Imperial Status   154

3.15 Conclusion   158

4 From Mandate to Trust Territory, 1947   161

4.1 Introduction   161

4.2 Administration of Nauru as a C Mandate of the League of Nations   163

4.3 Phosphate, Agriculture, Population and Race in the Australian Interwar Period   175

4.4 The Co-Existence of Mandates and Protectorates: the Interwar International   179

4.5 The 'Colonial Question' and the Failing Legitimacy of the League of Nations   182

4.6 The Return to War and the Japanese Occupation of Nauru   187

4.7 The Formation of the United Nations and the Trusteeship Council   191

4.8 Nauru becomes a Trust Territory   197

4.9 Conclusion   201

5 From Trust Territory to Sovereign State, 1968   204

   5.1 Introduction   204

   5.2 Administration of Nauru as a Trust Territory   210

   5.3 Trusteeship, Decolonisation and the South West Africa Cases   217

   5.4 The Nauru Talks: Resettlement, Political Independence and Phosphate   225

   5.5 Independence Day: Nauru becomes a Republic   234

   5.6 The Constitution of the Republic of Nauru   239

   5.7 Conclusion: The Ironies of Nauruan Independence   241

6 After Independence: Sovereign Status and the Republic of Nauru   244

   6.1 Introduction   244

   6.2 *Nauru* v. *Australia* and the Unresolved Question of Rehabilitation   248

   6.3 After Independence: Deployments of Sovereign Status and the Future of Nauru   252

   6.4 Conclusion   259

   Bibliography   262
   Index   290

ILLUSTRATIONS

1 Map of Nauru from Paul Hambruch, *Nauru: Ergebnisse der Südsee-Expedition, 1908–1910* (Hamburg: L. Friederichsen & Co, 1914). Credit: Alamy Stock Images.   *page 7*
1.1 Head Chief Hammer DeRoburt and Minister for Territories Charles Barnes sign the Nauru Independence Agreement, 1967. Parliament House, Canberra. Credit: National Archives of Australia. NAA: A1200, L67643.   15
1.2 Abandoned phosphate cantilever, Aiwo, Nauru, August 2018. Credit: Mike Leyral/AFP/Getty Images.   37
2.1 'Die Südsee ist das Mittelmeer der Zukunft' [The South Sea is the Mediterranean of the Future], from *Kladderadatsch*, 13 July 1884. Credit: Bildarchiv Preußischer Kulturbesitz, Staatsbibliothek zu Berlin.   61
2.2 German map of the Marshall Islands, est. 1884. Credit: Universitätsbibliothek Johann Christian Senckenberg Frankfurt am Main.   74
3.1 Nauruan community with German naval officers, 1896. Credit: ullstein bild/ullstein bild via Getty Images.   107
3.2 Pacific Phosphate Company officers with Chinese labourers, est. 1906–1908. Credit: Image courtesy of the National Archives of Australia. NAA: R32, VOLUME 118/41.   133
3.3 'Pacific Mandates', map published in George Blakeslee, 'Mandates of the Pacific' (1922) *Foreign Affairs* 1, 102. Republished with permission of *Foreign Affairs*, conveyed through Copyright Clearance Center Inc.   156
4.1 Phosphate workings near Number 2 Unit, British Phosphate Commission, April 1923. Image courtesy of the National Archives of Australia. NAA: R32, NAURU 5/502.   169
4.2 North American B-25 Mitchell bomber above Nauru during Japanese occupation. Credit: Seventh Air Force Photo/The LIFE Picture Collection via Getty Images.   190
5.1 Nauru Legislative Council on a visit to Australia during the Nauru Talks. J. A. Bop (chairman), Agoko Doguape, Edwin Tsitsi and Roy Degoreore. Credit: John Patrick O'Gready/Fairfax Media via Getty Images.   229
5.2 The British Phosphate Commissioners (D. J. Carter (NZ) C. E. Barnes (Aus) and Sir Charles Johnston (UK)) with President Hammer De Roburt and the flag of the Republic of Nauru, Independence Day, 31 January 1968. Credit:

Image courtesy of the National Archives of Australia. NAA: A1200, L69077.   239

6.1 His Excellency Hammer DeRoburt, President of Nauru (right) and Queen Elizabeth II. Credit: John Shelley Collection/Avalon/Getty Images.   247

6.2 Satellite image of Australia's Regional Processing Centre, topside, Nauru. Credit: DigitalGlobe via Getty Images.   253

6.3 DeepGreen CEO Gerard Barron and Kenyan delegate Pauline Mcharo, International Seabed Authority, February 2019. Credit: IISD/Diego Noguera (enb.iisd.org/oceans/isa/2019-1/26feb.html).   258

ACKNOWLEDGEMENTS

This project has generated its own global community, real and imagined. It is beyond me to list all those who have contributed to its realisation, and the list that follows will inevitably omit others equally deserving of acknowledgement. To that end I begin by acknowledging that very little is achieved alone. We simply do not always, or in good time, recognise the ways we are supported by others.

This project originated in a brief consultancy I held with the Parliament of Nauru in 2009. Thanks to Cheryl Saunders and Katy Le Roy for suggesting me as a candidate for the role; and thanks to Stella Duburiya, Fimosa Temaki, Tini Duburiya, Barina Waqa, Kristie Dunne and Catriona Steele.

The doctoral research on which this book is based was completed at the University of Melbourne, with the support of an Australian Postgraduate Award from the Australian Department of Education and Training, and a Melbourne Abroad Travelling Scholarship. The conversion from doctoral thesis to monograph was completed at the University of Glasgow, with publication support from the University of Glasgow's Research Excellence Framework Fund. Postgraduate research remains out of reach for many, particularly in the global South, and access to funding support for doctoral research and publication is a privilege I do not wear lightly.

I have been beyond fortunate to receive outstanding scholarly advice throughout the course of this project. My principal doctoral supervisor Sundhya Pahuja walked this path with me from beginning to end, and her acumen and grace have been guiding lights along the way. Co-supervisor Shaun McVeigh has been a steadfast source of intellectual integrity and care. Gerry Simpson and Matthew Craven have both provided wise counsel at pivotal moments in this project's development. Doctoral examiners Antony Anghie and Peter Fitzpatrick provided incisive feedback and advice on converting the thesis into a monograph, as did two anonymous peer reviewers for Cambridge University Press – my sincere thanks to all. Comments on work in progress have contributed enormously to the refinement of this work along the way. Thanks in particular to Anne Orford, Tim Lindsey, Hani Sayed, Martti Koskenniemi, Miranda Johnson, Tim Rowse, Nehal Bhuta and Mai Taha for their time, diligence, and custodianship of the craft. Any errors and shortcomings in the text remain my own.

The Institute of International Law and the Humanities at Melbourne Law School and the Institute of Global Law and Policy at Harvard Law School have been the unofficial homes of this project. The Melbourne and Glasgow communities were fabulous intellectual environments in which to complete this work. Each of these communities has been a source of solidarity and good humour, and I thank my academic and professional colleagues across these institutions for their contributions to keeping these communities alive. In particular, I thank the following for their friendship: James Parker, Jake Goldenfein, Tom Andrews, Sara Dehm, Maria Elander, Anna Hood, Maddy Chiam, Kirsty Gover, Rose Parfitt, Julia Dehm, Adil Hasan Khan, Christopher Gevers, Monique Cormier, Ntina Tzouvala and Olivia Barr; Henry Jones; and at Glasgow, Charlie Peevers, Christian Tams, Anna Chadwick, Akbar Rasulov, Alan Brown, Toni Marzal and Jane Mair.

It is the nature of scholarly work that this book leans heavily on the earlier work of others. I want to acknowledge certain scholars here, if only to illustrate that the real impact of good scholarship escapes contemporary metrics: thanks to Wilhelm Fabricius, Stewart Firth, Peter Sack, Dymphna Clark, Dirk Spennemann, Maslyn Williams, Barrie Macdonald, Nancy Viviani, Christopher Weeramantry, Antony Anghie and Deborah Cass. I would also like to thank Tom Randall and Gemma Smith at Cambridge University Press for editorial assistance and patience along the way; and Kate McIntosh, for expert indexing assistance.

Lastly, my deepest gratitude and love to Tess, Rob, Mick and Pete; to Tom, Alice and Tadeo; to Andrea, Nigel, Monica, Zoë, James and Zoë; and to Miles.

Prologue

In 2009 I was briefly engaged by the Parliament of Nauru as a legal adviser. I joined a team of four Nauruans and four international consultants to formulate a referendum campaign informing the Nauruan people of proposed amendments to the 1968 Constitution. The referendum was the culmination of a lengthy process of constitutional review that had been conducted with United Nations Development Programme funding.[1] In its 2007 Report, the Constitutional Review Commission appointed by the Parliament of Nauru had described what it understood to be the historical factors requiring address via constitutional reform – 'what', in other words, had 'gone wrong' with the Republic of Nauru:

> The failure of institutions due to defective or ineffective laws, including the Constitution and statutes.
> Lack of motivation or incentive to preserve wealth for the future, and account for its management and drawings upon it.
> Absence of machinery for enforcing accountability and transparency, and for punishing breaches.
> Failure of leaders to learn the principles of good governance and elements of the cabinet parliamentary system, and make a commitment to them.
> In planning for improvement in the above areas, a serious shortage of human capital, particularly people with appropriate skills, and accountants and lawyers.[2]

Failure of institutions, lack of motivation to preserve wealth for the future, lack of machinery for enforcing accountability and transparency, failure of leaders to learn the principles of good governance, shortage of

---

[1] Government of the Republic of Nauru and United Nations Development Programme, 'Nauru Constitutional Reform Project', project document, 2008. Available at info.undp.org/docs/pdc/Documents/FJI/00058097_Nauru%20CRC_Prodoc.pdf.

[2] Nauru Constitutional Review Commission, '"*Naoero Ituga*": Report', 28 February 2007, 3–4. Available at paclii.org/nr/other/Nauru_Constitutional_Review_Commission_Report_28Feb07.pdf.

people with appropriate skills. The implication was that the 'failures' of the Nauruan state were to be solved with better institutions, better laws and better training of leaders in the business of governance. To achieve these goals, the Republic required constitutional reform. It also required more 'human capital' – the shortage of which was, in the meantime, to be filled by people like me, paid with UNDP funding. The small Nauruan public service was top-heavy with Australian public servants on secondment from the Commonwealth Treasury, and the Department of Foreign Affairs and Trade.

Armed with comparative constitutional studies of Pacific island states, the Commission had recommended a suite of amendments to bring the Nauruan Constitution in line with 'internationally recognised principles and standards'.[3] Proposed amendments were designed to strengthen the separation of the legislature and the executive, particularly with respect to financial transparency, a notorious issue in the historical management of the Nauru Phosphate Royalties Trust; to recognise at constitutional level the status of customary law as 'continuing to have effect as part of the law of Nauru, to the extent that such law is not repugnant to the Constitution or to any Act of Parliament'; and to introduce social and economic rights into the Constitution.[4] From a human rights perspective, this last recommendation would have made the Nauruan Constitution one of the most progressive in the world.[5]

The Constitution under review had remained unchanged since 1968. It had been drafted over the course of a few months by historian Professor James W. Davidson and Victorian Parliamentary Counsel Rowena Armstrong, in anticipation of Nauru's United Nations-decreed Independence Day of 31 January 1968. Two years earlier in 1966, negotiations between the Nauru Local Government Council and the Australian Department of Territories over the wholesale resettlement of the Nauruan people to Curtis Island in Queensland with some form of self-government, as decreed by the UN Charter provisions on trusteeship, had reached an impasse.[6] The Nauruan delegation, led by Hammer

---

[3] Nauru Constitutional Review Commission, '*Naoero Ituga*', 3.

[4] The 1968 Constitution made no reference to the effect or status of 'customary law' in Nauruan law, although custom was recognised in legislation and frequently applied with respect to land ownership and usufruct. Ibid., 13.

[5] Steven Ratuva, 'The Gap Between Global Thinking and Local Living: Dilemmas of Constitutional Reform in Nauru' (2011) 20 *The Journal of the Polynesian Society*, 241–68 at 244.

[6] Gil Tabucanon and Brian Opeskin, 'The Resettlement of Nauruans in Australia: An Early Case of Failed Environmental Migration' (2011) 46 *Journal of Pacific History*, 337–57.

DeRoburt, insisted that 'self-government' meant international status as a sovereign state, whether on the island of Nauru itself, or on Curtis Island. The Australian Department of Territories, however, would concede no more than status as a municipal council within the State of Queensland.[7]

The UNDP's constitutional review process had commenced in 2004, when the first iteration of Australia's offshore detention regime was in full swing. In 2001 the Commonwealth executive under Liberal Prime Minister John Howard had alighted upon what it labelled a 'Pacific solution' to Australia's 'asylum seeker crisis'. That crisis consisted of the arrival of comparatively small numbers of asylum seekers in the northern territorial waters of Australia, most then from Afghanistan and Sri Lanka.[8] The last detained asylum seekers of the Howard era had been relocated from Nauru to Australia in 2007 with great moral fanfare by the new Labor Prime Minister, Kevin Rudd. When I arrived in Nauru in 2009, the detention centre had been repurposed as a government storage depot. Office supplies were stacked against corrugated iron walls. Weeds grew in the gravel. Offshore detention – yet another ignoble entry in the catalogue of Australian immigration policies – seemed then a brief entry, mercifully consigned to the past. That impression was soon proved wrong. A few years later, in 2012, Australia's 'Pacific Solution' was revived, this time by Rudd's successor as Labor Prime Minister, Julia Gillard. Office supplies were moved back out of the sheds, which were returned to their original function, and renamed 'Regional Processing Centre 1'.[9] Soon there would be an RPC 2, an RPC 3 and an RPC 4, all built and run by Australian commercial subcontractors. Throughout the duration of this project, asylum seekers who arrive by sea in Australian waters as 'unauthorised maritime arrivals' have been detained and sent to Nauru, or to Manus Island in Papua New Guinea, for 'processing' of their asylum claims. Soon after Australia revived its offshore detention regime, a new Nauruan government was elected and Nauru's still-unfolding constitutional crisis took

---

[7] Nancy Viviani, *Nauru: Phosphate and Political Progress* (Canberra: Australian National University Press, 1970), 140–7.

[8] Savitri Taylor, 'The Pacific Solution or a Pacific Nightmare: The Difference between Burden Shifting and Responsibility Sharing' (2005) 6 *Asian-Pacific Law and Policy Journal*, 1–43; and Susan Metcalfe, *The Pacific Solution* (North Melbourne: Australian Scholarly Publishing, 2010).

[9] Peter Billings, 'Irregular Maritime Migration and the Pacific Solution Mark II: Back to the Future for Refugee Law and Policy in Australia' (2013) 20 *International Journal on Minority and Group Rights*, 279–306.

a darker turn.[10] The new executive moved to limit and then effectively cease issuing visas to visitors not engaged directly by detention centre contractors. With dubious pretext, the executive deported the Resident Magistrate and cancelled the visa of the Chief Justice of the Supreme Court, both Australian judges.[11] The time frame of claim processing stretched out to two, to three, to four, to six years. Independently verifiable information on conditions for asylum seekers on Nauru became increasingly difficult to obtain.

Wave after wave of legal challenges to the offshore detention regime have since been mounted, drawing on Australian law, Nauruan law and international law. Legal victories have been few and far between, and the contortions of executive power – in both Australia and Nauru – more frequent. In February 2016 in a case brought by a Bangladeshi asylum seeker, the High Court of Australia accepted the Minister for Immigration and Border Protection's argument, prepared by some of the best legal minds in the country, as to why offshore processing of her asylum claim did not amount to arbitrary detention under Australian law: the Commonwealth of Australia, the Minister argued, does not detain anyone on Nauru. The Republic is a sovereign state; if anyone is detained there, they are detained by the Nauruan executive, not by the Australian executive.[12] The majority of the High Court agreed. Even though the offshore detention regime exists at the Australian government's instigation, with Australian funding under Australian oversight, the regime was held to be run by private contractors, operating under Nauruan sovereign jurisdiction.[13] But back in 2009, in that window between the two phases of offshore detention, the tortuous architecture of Australian immigration law seemed a thing of the past, not the future. Nauru had been left – in extreme foreign debt, without a bank and owing years of back pay to its public servants – to raise revenue in other ways.

Compared to the gravity of these events for the Nauruan community, for asylum seekers and indeed for Australia's international reputation, my brief experience in Nauru is insignificant. Law student from an elite

---

[10] Stewart Firth, 'Australia's Detention Centre and the Erosion of Democracy in Nauru' (2016) 51 *Journal of Pacific History*, 286–300. See also Chapter 6, 'After Independence: Sovereign Status and the Republic of Nauru'.

[11] On the prevalence of foreign judges in the Pacific, see Anna Dziedzic, 'The Use of Foreign Judges on Courts of Constitutional Jurisdiction in Pacific Island States' (2018), PhD thesis, University of Melbourne.

[12] *Plaintiff M68 v. Commonwealth of Australia* (2016) 257 CLR 42.

[13] *Plaintiff M68/2015* at 375.

first-world university takes up a temporary UN-funded position, almost oblivious to the deeper historical and political context in which they are working; hardly news. But the experience troubled me for years afterward. What I had learnt of Nauru whilst on the island was enough only to highlight the contours of my ignorance. Beyond the singsong clichés picked up in my suburban Australian childhood – bird poo island, poor then rich then poor again – I knew next to nothing about the place. A Nauruan boarder in my class at school, there for the first few years of the 1990s then gone. A geography class called 'Our Pacific Neighbours', which in retrospect was a valiant attempt to orient Australian high school students to their planetary whereabouts. In that class, I learnt a little of Nauru's 'squandered phosphate wealth', amid textbook sketches of the Dutch colonisation of Irian Jaya, now West Papua; of the British importation of Indian labourers to Fiji; of Australia's role in the Portuguese handover of Timor Leste to Indonesia in 1976. If I was taught anything about German imperialism in the Pacific, I don't remember it. But I had a German great-grandfather who had left Kiel before World War I, either to escape conscription or join the merchant navy, we didn't know which. I had a grandfather who had fought in the Australian army against Japan in Papua New Guinea during World War II. But these fragments of regional history, and their relation to what I was doing in Nauru, had never arranged themselves into a coherent story.

On the island, I did my underqualified best to do the job I had been hired to do. But it was obvious that the referendum process was regarded with polite distrust, if not contempt, by the Nauruan community. We worked to put together bilingual campaign materials, increasingly aware that the Nauruan team's wary deliberations over how to translate English constitutional vocabulary into Nauruan were surface reflections of the tectonic political tensions they were reckoning with in their lives as a result of their work on the campaign. We attended meetings with 'H.E.' – His Excellency the President, then Marcus Stephen – and with government MPs, trying and failing to divine who was working for the proposed amendments, and who against. I visited the house of the Taiwanese ambassador, who grew green vegetables in his front yard in boycott of the miserable lettuces shipped from Australia for sale in Nauru's old company store, Capelle & Partner. I shared a hotel corridor with a delegation from the Russian Federation, and the reason why soon became apparent: as the referendum campaign got underway, the Nauruan government announced its recognition of the independence of the Georgian provinces of Abkhazia and South Ossetia. A few days later, Nauru expressed gratitude to the Russian Federation for

AUD$50 million in development aid.[14] I ate at the handful of Chinese restaurants on the island, and picked up some of the stories of the British Phosphate Commission's importation of labourers from mainland China in the early twentieth century – but not, it turns out, even the half of it. I was loaned a government car, donated to the Nauruan government as part of Japan's bilateral aid programme. Nauru, I was told with a wink when I picked up the car, voted with Japan in the International Whaling Commission.[15]

Toyota notwithstanding, I preferred to walk. In the early mornings I walked along the beach at Menen, separated from the open ocean by the jagged limestone reef that fringes the island. In the evenings I walked up to topside, Nauru's mined-out central plateau, following the well-trodden paths that weaved through limestone pinnacles and noddy bird carcasses. On Sundays I walked the island's perimeter road, passing unadorned monuments marking Japan's occupation of Nauru during World War II. A fifth of the Nauruan population died during that war, interned on Chuuk Atoll in the Japanese Mandated Islands, now part of the Federated States of Micronesia. The Nauruan community had chosen 31 January as their Independence Day, the date the survivors came home from Chuuk. Clockwise from Parliament House was the cantilever, a gargantuan steel arm hulking out from the beach across the reef to the open ocean. The original cantilever had been built in the late 1920s by the British Phosphate Commission to cart phosphate from topside straight down into the holds of moored ships, to be spread over the farms of Australia, New Zealand and the United Kingdom. Anticlockwise was Anibare Bay, blown out of the limestone reef with dynamite by the Pacific Phosphate Company in the 1910s to create a harbour for the harbourless atoll.

One morning out walking on the beach, I had an uncanny experience. Watching a container ship disappear over the horizon, I lost my balance. In that moment, I realised I had not simply boarded a plane and shifted location in a fixed world; had not simply flown from one point to another. Rather, the world itself unfolded differently from the point at which I stood. The net of relations cast by Nauru over the world created a different international order to the one I knew. The one I knew was already – so I had foolishly thought – alive to the imperialism of European knowledge structures, sensitive to the legacies of colonial violence, aware of the politics of difference. Yet I had arrived in Nauru believing the place was somehow fundamentally out of

---

[14] Reuters, 'Pacific Island Recognises Georgian Rebel Region', *Reuters*, 15 December 2009.
[15] Republic of Nauru, 'Republic of Nauru Defends its Vote at the International Whaling Commission', press release, 28 June 2005.

1 Map of Nauru from Paul Hambruch, *Nauru: Ergebnisse der Südsee-Expedition, 1908–1910* (Hamburg: L. Friederichsen & Co, 1914). Credit: Alamy Stock Images.

joint with the world. Standing on that beach, it no longer made sense to think of Nauru as an anomaly in the international order. As much as Paris and New York and London, as Japan and Germany and Australia, Nauru was what was.[16] It was me that had it all wrong.

---

[16] Doreen Massey describes the world-making effect of imagining space as a surface across which the ignorant discoverer moves: '(c)onceiving of space as in the voyages of discovery, as something to be crossed and maybe conquered, has particular ramifications ... this way of imagining space can lead us to conceive of other places, peoples, cultures simply as phenomena "on" this surface. It is not an innocent manoeuvre, for by this means they are deprived of histories.' Doreen Massey, *For Space* (London: SAGE Publications, 2005), 4.

The referendum campaign failed. The Nauruan people voted overwhelmingly against constitutional change.[17] I left the island in deep disquiet over what I had just participated in, and with a visceral memory of that slip in perception. This book began as an attempt to understand two fleeting impressions that stayed with me following my brief time in Nauru: first, that the disjuncture between the ideals of international status and the actual forms of administrative relation in Nauru had a deep history; and secondly, that the international order one perceives is radically determined by the place in which one stands. The book has ended as a detailed account of how imperial law and administration in Nauru produced the post-independence 'failures' the Constitutional Review Commission identified in its 2007 Report. It is dedicated to the people of Nauru, from one more in a long line of *iburbur* to have washed up on their island.

[17] Ratuva, 'Gap Between Global Thinking and Local Living', 241–68.

1

International Status, Imperial Form: Nauru and the Histories of International Law

1.1 Introduction

This book proceeds from the premise that the Republic of Nauru is not anomalous to the contemporary international legal order but deeply symptomatic of it. The story it tells began as a response to a deceptively simple question: how did Naoerō – a single coral atoll in the Western Pacific, with an area of twenty-one square kilometres, beloved home of the Nauruan people who at the time of independence numbered just over 6,000 – become the Republic of Nauru in 1968, the third smallest sovereign state in the world? It has developed over time into a response to a more pointed question: what might a close reading of the history of imperial administration in Nauru reveal about the continuities between nineteenth-century European imperialism and twentieth-century international law that accounts focusing on the received 'centres' of international legal formation do not? The answer given here takes the form of a narrative of four shifts in the international status of Nauru since the violent incorporation of the island into the German protectorate of the Marshall Islands in 1888, and the changes in administrative form at the local level that accompanied those shifts. The book reconstructs in turn the declaration of protectorate status, the designation of Nauru as a C Class Mandate by the League of Nations in 1920, its redesignation as a United Nations Trust Territory in 1947 and the recognition of Nauru as a sovereign state in 1968. The central argument that emerges is this: as the international status of Nauru shifted from protectorate, to mandate, to trust territory, to sovereign state, what occurred at the level of local administrative form was an accretive process of internal bureaucratisation and external restatement according to the prevailing concepts of the period.

1 NAURU AND THE HISTORIES OF INTERNATIONAL LAW

The book is offered as a contribution to the vibrant cross-disciplinary genre of histories of imperialism and international law. Rejecting from the outset any presumption of Nauru as anomaly, the book constructs a detailed history of the relationship between international status and administrative form in the Nauruan case as a frame through which to redescribe how the international system of sovereign states has developed in continuation of European imperial administrative practices of the late nineteenth century.[1] To that end, this book joins the chorus of voices that have, since the 1950s, challenged the presumption that sovereign territorial statehood is the natural or final vehicle for decolonisation.[2] It seeks to supplement this corpus of analytical tools for diagnosing the continuities between imperial exploitation and the contemporary international order, as a necessary step towards disrupting and dismantling those continuities, and working to support a more expansive concept of decolonisation than that institutionalised in the international legal order of the twentieth century.

Conceptual and intellectual histories of international law that centre the archetypical sites of international law – Versailles, The Hague, New York – and the writings of archetypical jurists – Grotius, Vitoria, Vattel and, more recently, a marginally more inclusive cast of protagonists including Lorimer, Twiss and Schmitt – have tended to dominate the field.[3] This book reflects a growing trend toward treatments of the

---

[1] Anghie's field-defining text proceeds from a similar observation about the significance of Nauru in the history of international law, following the thread into the realm of conceptual history. Antony Anghie, '"The Heart of My Home": Colonialism, Environmental Damage and the Nauru Case' (1993) 34 *Harvard International Law Journal*, 445–506; and *Imperialism, Sovereignty and the Making of International Law* (Cambridge: Cambridge University Press, 2005), 1–2. Orford revives questions of the relationship between international status and administrative form in her adroit analysis of the responsibility to protect concept. Anne Orford, *International Authority and the Responsibility to Protect* (Cambridge: Cambridge University Press, 2011), 189–212. On the significance of the anomaly in imperial development, see Lauren Benton, *A Search for Sovereignty: Law and Geography in European Empires 1400–1900* (Cambridge: Cambridge University Press, 2010), 2.

[2] The statist paradigm of self-determination in international law has always attracted strong critique. See for example Kwame Nkrumah, *Neo-Colonialism: The Last Stage of Capitalism* (USA: International Publishers, 1965); Siba N'Zatioula Grovogui, *Sovereigns, Quasi Sovereigns, and Africans: Race and Self-Determination in International Law* (Minneapolis: University of Minnesota Press, 1996); Vasuki Nesiah, 'Placing International Law: White Spaces on a Map' (2003) 16 *Leiden Journal of International Law*, 1–35.

[3] Randall Lesaffer, 'International Law and its History: The Story of an Unrequited Love' in Matthew Craven, Malgosia Fitzmaurice and Maria Vogiatzi (eds.), *Time, History and International Law* (Leiden and Boston: Martinus Nijhoff Publishing, 2007), 32, 36–7.

historical transition from imperial to international ordering that take seriously the quotidian business of local administration and institutional practice as equally relevant to understanding that history as the conceptual projects of jurists and statesmen.[4] What is attempted here is not an explanation of 'the' history of international law but an illumination of the relationship between conceptual development and administrative practice in the transition from the openly unequal status designations by which European imperial territories were characterised in the late nineteenth century, to the universalisation of the formally equal status designation of sovereign statehood in the mid-twentieth century. The Nauruan story offers one of the more remarkable examples of that transition. This book revisits that history and asks the following questions: resisting as best as possible easy reversion to teleological presumptions about the trajectory of international legal development, precisely *how* did Nauru become a German protectorate, a League mandate, a UN trust territory and then a sovereign state? And how were those shifts in international status reflected in the local administrative structure through which the island was governed?

What follows, then, is a critical redescription of the way in which German, British and Australian empires deployed legal concepts and administrative forms to authorise and maintain structural relations of political, economic and environmental exploitation in Nauru.[5] It is crucial to emphasise from the outset that this is not a Nauruan history as such. It does not purport to represent Nauruan perspectives on, or modes of resistance to, the imperial and international interventions described here. The importance of Nauruan accounts of that history remains paramount. Unfortunately the political circumstances that have endured for the life of this project have effectively prevented those accounts comprising part of this book.[6] The account of European imperial administration offered here

---

[4] Andrew Fitzmaurice, 'Context in the History of International Law' (2018) 20 *Journal of the History of International Law*, 5–30 at 6–7; and Lauren Benton, 'Beyond Anachronism: Histories of International Law and Global Legal Politics' (2019) 21 *Journal of the History of International Law*, 13–16.

[5] On critical redescription, see Anne Orford, 'In Praise of Description' (2012) 25 *Leiden Journal of International Law*, 609–25; and Sundhya Pahuja, 'Laws of Encounter: A Jurisdictional Account of International Law' (2013) 1 *London Review of International Law*, 63–98. On exploitation, see Susan Marks, 'Exploitation as an International Legal Concept' in *International Law on the Left* (Cambridge: Cambridge University Press, 2009).

[6] As detailed in Chapter 6, this project commenced just after the recommencement of Australia's offshore detention regime and the election of the Waqa government of Nauru. These events exacerbated deep political conflicts in the Nauruan community. In

is told not to recentre the perspective it reconstructs but rather to historicise it from the inside out, to trace its logic, its contradictions and silences, and thereby to make it strange.[7] Two conclusions emerge from this account. First, if the issues with the Republic of Nauru that the UNDP Constitutional Review Commission identified in 2007 are accepted – 'failure of democratic institutions', 'lack of motivation to preserve wealth for the future', 'lack of machinery for enforcing accountability and transparency', 'failure of leaders to learn the principles of good governance', 'shortage of people with appropriate skills' – then it must also be accepted that those issues were historically produced by European imperial and international interventions. Secondly, this conclusion illustrates the importance of reckoning with the distinction between 'the' history of international law as the development of an ideal conceptual framework for governing the world, and the irreducibly multiple histories of 'international law' as actually practised in place.

1.2 Nauru as Symptom versus Nauru as Parable

In resisting the presumption that Nauru is anomalous or exceptional to 'normal' processes of state formation, it is crucial not to revert to the 'Nauru-as-metonym' trope that is now habitual in popular accounts of the island. Since the early 1990s, the story of Nauru has routinely been reworked into an exemplar of whichever dystopia preoccupies the moment: as an eschatological parable of impending environmental collapse due to unsustainable practices of resource exploitation; as a parable of economic collapse due to poor governance practices; and more recently, as the dystopic stage in which Australia's offshore detention regime has been set.[8] The common

---

this context, I confined the focus of this book to external administration prior to independence in 1968. See Stewart Firth, 'Australia's Detention Centre and the Erosion of Democracy in Nauru' (2016) 51 *Journal of Pacific History*, 286–300.

[7] Dipesh Chakrabarty, *Provincialising Europe: Postcolonial Thought and Historical Difference*, 2nd ed. (Princeton: Princeton University Press, 2008), 16. Scott urges 'an approach to colonialism in which Europe is historicized, historicized in such a way as to bring into focus the differentials in the political rationalities through which its colonial projects were constructed'. David Scott, 'Colonial Governmentality' (1995) 43 *Social Text*, 191–220 at 214.

[8] Examples include Carl N. McDaniel and John M. Gowdy, *Paradise for Sale: A Parable of Nature* (Berkeley and London: University of California Press, 2000); Naomi Klein, *This Changes Everything: Capitalism versus the Climate* (London: Penguin Group, 2014), 161–9; John Connell, 'Nauru: The First Failed Pacific State?' (2006) 95(383) *The Round Table*, 47–63; David Kendall, 'Doomed Island' (2009) 35 *Alternatives Journal* 1, 34–7;

elements of these 'Nauru-as' parables will now be familiar to many. Tiny coral atoll, around twenty-one square kilometres in area, in the Western Pacific south of the equator; smallest state by area and population, after the Vatican and the principality of Monaco. Strip-mined for phosphate under the control of Australia, Britain and New Zealand from the early 1920s to the late 1960s, when Nauru gained independence. High GDP per capita throughout the 1970s and into the 1980s due to the nationalisation of the phosphate industry, followed by economic collapse in the mid-1990s due to florid mismanagement of trust funds.[9] A series of national revenue-raising schemes from the unconventional to the bizarre throughout the 1990s, including money laundering, passport sales and erratic clientelism; and from the early 2000s, self-interested complicity as a rented site in Australia's offshore detention regime.[10]

The Nauru-as parable is recycled so regularly in popular discourse that it creates an impression that there is nothing more to say. But Nauru is not a parable of future collapse, or an island dystopia. It belongs in the contemporary moment, in the international order, in the global environment. The motivation of this book was to find a way of narrating the imperial administration of Nauru that takes seriously the contemporaneity of Nauru and Versailles, of Nauru and The Hague – of Nauru and New York – as sites of international legal formation. The island was incorporated into the German protectorate of the Marshall Islands in 1888 under a contractual arrangement between the Bismarckian Reich and a Hanseatic trading company from Hamburg, the Jaluit Gesellschaft. It was designated as a C Class Mandate of the British empire by the League of Nations in 1920, and administered by Australia pursuant to a tripartite agreement between the United Kingdom and its then Dominions of Australia and New Zealand. Nauru was redesignated as a UN Trust Territory under

---

Martin McKenzie Murray, 'The Dysfunction of Offshore Detention on Nauru', *The Saturday Paper*, 27 August 2016; Stephen Charles, 'Our Detention Centres are Concentration Camps and Must be Closed', *The Sydney Morning Herald*, 4 May 2016; *The Economist*, 'Paradise Well and Truly Lost', *The Economist*, 20 December 2001; and Tony Thomas, 'The Naughty Nation of Nauru' (2013) *Quadrant*, 30–4.

[9] Rowan Callick, 'Conmen's Paradise', *The Australian*, 19 January 2007.

[10] Jon Henley, 'Pacific Atoll Paradise for Mafia Loot', *The Guardian*, 23 June 2001; Glenn R. Simpson, 'Tiny Island Selling Passports Is Big Worry for U.S. Officials', *The Wall Street Journal*, 16 May 2003; Joy Su, 'Nauru Switches its Allegiance back to Taiwan from China', *Taipei Times*, 15 May 2005; Michael Koziol and Michael Gordon, 'UN Slams Australia's Regional Processing Centres in Nauru', *Sydney Morning Herald*, 7 October 2016.

Australian administration by the United Nations in 1947 and gained sovereign status in 1968 – after the Australian Department of Territories had attempted to resettle the entire population of Nauru in Queensland as Australian citizens, as a cheaper alternative to remedying the severe environmental damage caused by phosphate mining and handing over self-government.[11]

Reconstructing these shifts in their own time and place turns a mirror on the transition from the European imperial order to the contemporary international legal order, revealing an aspect of that transition that might otherwise be hard to see. Critical treatments of the concepts foundational to that transition – including concepts of protection, mandate, trust and sovereignty itself – are now well established in the field, and include contributions from historians, and from scholars associated with the Third World Approaches to International Law (TWAIL) movement.[12] This book seeks to add to that literature by tracing how the development of these concepts related to changes in local administrative form in the Nauruan case. Taking this view, the transition from nineteenth-century imperial administration through to the universalisation of the statist paradigm of self-determination in the later twentieth century does not unfold as a conceptually driven process. It unfolds rather as an iterative process of experimentation in imperial administration, driven by commercial and geopolitical imperatives and often only retrospectively and thinly justified through reference to international legal concepts. The implication is not that the particularities of the story of the Republic of Nauru should be overlooked in order to make it serve as a universal diagnosis of the continuities between imperial and international ordering. It is rather that if the distinction between international status and administrative form is taken seriously, shifts in international status toward political independence are better understood as marking not the end but the beginning of the process of decolonisation.

---

[11] Nancy Viviani, *Nauru: Phosphate and Political Progress* (Canberra: Australian National University Press, 1970), 141–55. Christopher Weeramantry, *Nauru: Environmental Damage under International Trusteeship* (Oxford: Oxford University Press), 265–305.

[12] Key texts include W. Ross Johnson, *Sovereignty and Protection: A Study of British Jurisdictional Imperialism in the Late Nineteenth Century* (Durham: Duke University Press, 1973); Gerrit Gong, *The Standard of Civilization in International Society* (Oxford: Oxford University Press, 1984); Anghie, *Imperialism, Sovereignty and the Making of International Law*; Andrew Fitzmaurice, *Sovereignty, Property and Empire, 1500–2000* (Cambridge: Cambridge University Press, 2014).

1.1 Head Chief Hammer DeRoburt and Minister for Territories Charles Barnes sign the Nauru Independence Agreement, 1967. Parliament House, Canberra. Credit: National Archives of Australia. NAA: A1200, L67643.

1.3 On Administrative Form: Attending to Practices of Jurisdiction and Bureaucracy

The attention to administrative form in this book draws upon two theoretical traditions. The first addresses concepts and practices of jurisdiction, and the second, concepts and practices of bureaucracy. The way in which these traditions are being drawn upon is explained here in turn. Dorsett and McVeigh describe 'jurisdictional thinking' as 'giv(ing) us a distinct way of representing authority' through attending to the forms that law takes, as a question precedent to the content of that law.[13] In this sense, jurisdictional thinking is better understood less as a theory of law than as a sensibility that attends to the practices of authorisation that

---

[13] Shaunnagh Dorsett and Shaun McVeigh, *Jurisdiction* (Abingdon and New York: Routledge, 2012); Shaunnagh Dorsett and Shaun McVeigh, 'Questions of Jurisdiction' in Shaun McVeigh (ed.), *Jurisprudence of Jurisdiction* (Oxford: Routledge Cavendish, 2007), 3–18.

precede the articulation of law.[14] Jurisdictional thinking thus emphasises aspects of law as a socio-political phenomenon that are often relegated within the discipline to introductory paragraphs on the 'history' of a particular area of law, or otherwise to the deceptively dry realm of procedural law. These include the ritualised behaviours, the forms of words and the symbolic vocabularies that mark out the legal from other registers of socio-political conduct.[15] In Dorsett and McVeigh's treatment, jurisdictional thinking thus reveals the way in which the 'abstractness and immateriality of law is greatly exaggerated'.[16] Attentiveness to jurisdiction requires paying attention to conflict at the thresholds across which the political becomes legal, and to the material forms those thresholds take.[17] Jurisdictional thinking is therefore particularly useful to the study of the transition from nineteenth-century imperialism to twentieth-century international law. It directs attention to the nature and volume of the work of authorisation that has been done at the edges of European imperial expansion. This book makes no claim regarding the construction of authority, legal or otherwise, for those upon whom imperial law has been imposed. It seeks rather to trace carefully in the Nauruan case the construction of legal authority – imperial and then international – for those who have presumed to impose it. This move is echoed in Benton's call to make 'legal politics' an object of analysis in the history of international law, to expand the field's traditional focus on concept and doctrine.[18]

As Orford has argued, the nature of the work done to authorise the transition from nineteenth-century European imperial rule to twentieth-century international law has been largely administrative.[19] Orford's particular concern in this respect has been the relationship between the shift during the formal decolonisation movements of the 1950s and 1960s towards administration as a mode

---

[14] Sundhya Pahuja, 'Laws of Encounter: A Jurisdictional Account of International Law' (2013) 1 *London Review of International Law*, 63–98.

[15] Dorsett and McVeigh, *Jurisdiction*, 24–5; Shaun McVeigh and Sundhya Pahuja, 'Rival Jurisdictions: The Promise and Loss of Sovereignty' in Charles Barbour and George Pavlich (eds.), *After Sovereignty: On the Question of Political Beginnings* (London: Routledge Cavendish, 2011), 97–114.

[16] Dorsett and McVeigh, *Jurisdiction*, 5–6.

[17] Ibid., 11–12.

[18] Benton, 'Beyond Anachronism', 3.

[19] Orford, *International Authority and the Responsibility to Protect*, 4–5; Anne Orford, 'International Territorial Administration and the Management of Decolonization' (2010) *International and Comparative Law Quarterly*, 227–49.

of international governance and the expansion of international executive authority, retrospectively justified through the development of the responsibility to protect concept. The contemporary field of global administrative law, proceeding from Kingsbury, Krisch and Stewart's influential assertion that 'much of global governance can be understood and analysed as administrative action', has traced the post-Cold War phase of this phenomenon.[20] The treatment of administration in this book is not concerned, however, with perfecting or legalising the sprawling range of contemporary global practices that could be classed as administrative.[21] It is concerned with locating the instantiation of an administrative form of rule in the late nineteenth century in a particular imperial location, and following its development through into the period of sovereign statehood.[22] Klabbers makes a similarly patterned intervention within the framework of intellectual history, pulling the frame back in time and arguing that 'functionalism in international institutional law was already by and large in place when the "move to institutions" took off in earnest after World War I, and was born out of an encounter with colonial administration'.[23]

However, this book seeks to offer a history of administrative practice, rather than a conceptual history of the rise of functionalism. In order to do so, it turns to Max Weber's account of bureaucratisation and the significance of bureaucratic rationalisation to European modernity. A number of histories of twentieth-century international law have drawn from Weber's account of bureaucratisation to account for the advent of international organisations and their expanding jurisdictional remit.[24] Weber's career as a scholar spanned the period covered in the first two chapters of this history, from the early 1880s to his death in 1920, shortly after the Versailles settlement that Weber himself, as expert adviser to the

---

[20] Benedict Kingsbury, Nico Krisch and Richard B. Stewart, 'The Emergence of Global Administrative Law' (2005) 68 *Law and Contemporary Problems*, 15–61. See also Benedict Kingsbury, 'The Concept of "Law" in Global Administrative Law' (2009) 20 *European Journal of International Law*, 23–57.

[21] Orford, *International Authority and the Responsibility to Protect*, 203–5.

[22] On 'imperial locations', see Martti Koskenniemi, 'Less is More: Legal Imagination in Context – Introduction' (2018) 31 *Leiden Journal of International Law*, 469–72.

[23] Jan Klabbers, 'The Emergence of Functionalism in International Institutional Law: Colonial Inspirations' (2014) 25 *European Journal of International Law* 645–75 at 648. Sinclair pulls the time frame forward to World War II in Guy Fiti Sinclair, 'Towards a Postcolonial Genealogy of International Organizations Law' (2018) 31 *Leiden Journal of International Law*, 841–69.

[24] Guy Fiti Sinclair, *To Reform the World: International Organizations and the Making of Modern States* (Oxford: Oxford University Press, 2017), 10–15.

German delegation, vehemently opposed.[25] Weber had trained as a lawyer, completing his academic and his legal professional training concurrently.[26] Weber's legal training lent ballast to his sociological account of the role of law in the modern European state.[27] His sociology of law proceeded from his definition of modern legal authority as constituted not by objective democratic legitimacy but by 'legitimised' or 'legitimate' domination.[28]

Given Weber's politics – discussed further below – the ambivalence here between 'legitimised' and 'legitimate' domination is still a matter of contemporary debate. What is less controversial is that for Weber, legality itself was the type of legitimised domination that characterised the European modern condition.[29] His treatment of legal authority was at odds with the 'liberal' legal thought of his time, which tended to project a democratic ideal dependent on the Rousseauian concept of voluntary consent as the foundation of legitimate rule.[30] According to Weber, the authority of the modern European state – as a 'relation of men dominating men',[31] supported by means of violence – was upheld by 'belief in the validity of legal statute and functional "competence" based on rationally created rules'.[32] It followed that in order to describe legal authority as an

---

[25] Marianne Weber's seminal hagiography was first published in 1926. Marianne Weber, *Max Weber: A Biography*, trans. Harry Zohn (New York: John Wiley, 1975). See also H. H. Gerth and C. Wright Mills (eds.), *From Max Weber: Essays in Sociology* (Abingdon and New York: Routledge, 2009), 3–31; and Stefan Eich and Adam Tooze, 'The Allure of Dark Times: Max Weber, Politics and the Crisis of Historicism' (2017) 56 *History and Theory*, 197–215 at 203.

[26] Gerth and Mills (eds.), *From Max Weber*, 10–12.

[27] Weber's student, Max Rheinstein, extracted the lengthy chapter on the sociology of law included in the posthumously published *Economy and Society*. Max Rheinstein (ed.), *Max Weber on Law in Economy and Society* (Cambridge, MA: Harvard University Press, 1954). See also Panu Minkkinen, 'The Legal Academic of Max Weber's Tragic Modernity' (2010) 19 *Social and Legal Studies*, 165–82.

[28] Rheinstein (ed.), *Max Weber on Law in Economy and Society*, 8–9, 333–7; Weber, 'Politics as a Vocation' in Gerth and Mills (eds.), *From Max Weber*, 78–9; Duncan Kennedy, 'Disenchantment of Logically Formal Legal Rationality, or Max Weber's Sociology in the Genealogy of the Contemporary Mode of Western Legal Thought' (2004) 55 *Hastings Law Journal*, 1031–76 at 1038–9. Thomas considers the interpretive effect of the various translations of Weber's term *Herrschaft* into English in Chantal Thomas, 'Max Weber, Talcott Parsons and the Sociology of Legal Reform: A Reassessment with Implications for Law and Development' (2006) 15 *Minnesota Journal of International Law*, 383–424 at 418.

[29] Rheinstein (ed.), *Max Weber on Law in Economy and Society*, 322–8.

[30] Thomas, 'Max Weber, Talcott Parsons and the Sociology of Legal Reform', 420.

[31] Weber, 'Politics as a Vocation', 78.

[32] Ibid., 78–9.

historical phenomenon, one looked not to principles of democracy, monarchy or theism but to practices of legitimisation. In this sense, Weber's account of law is not dissimilar to the rendering of jurisdictional thinking given above, in directing attention to the practices of legitimisation that occur prior to the law being given content, rather than focusing exclusively on the content of that law.[33]

For Weber, the bureaucratic rationalisation of public and private power was as fundamental to the emergence of European modernity as the capitalist mode of production and the democratic state.[34] Weber defined modern bureaucracy by a set of characteristics: fixed and official jurisdictional areas ordered by rules; the fixed distribution of authority to give commands, and the fixed hierarchical distribution of activities as official duties; the primacy of written documents or 'files'; the separation of public official activity from private activity; and the development of expertise in the execution of official activity.[35] This shift towards bureaucratic form was common to both 'public' and 'private' organisations of authority. 'Bureaucratic authority', in the sense of public administration, and 'bureaucratic management', in the sense of corporate hierarchy, were therefore facets of the same modern phenomenon.[36] The development of a money economy that allowed the regular payment of wages to officials was a necessary but not sufficient condition for the emergence of bureaucracy, as the initial stages of bureaucratisation were dependent on the security of income payable to officials, which enabled the separation of official service as an exclusive vocation.[37] The emergence of 'modern mass democracy' was another necessary condition, although Weber's understanding of 'democracy' is not consistent with the contemporary liberal connotations attached to the term.[38] For Weber, 'democratisation' was synonymous with the depersonalisation of authority and its attachment to public offices, and is thus more akin to the contemporary notion of the 'rule of law'.[39] There was therefore no necessary

---

[33] Dorsett and McVeigh, *Jurisdiction*, 10–12.
[34] Weber, 'Politics as a Vocation', 82; Thomas, 'Max Weber, Talcott Parsons and the Sociology of Legal Reform', 393–6.
[35] Weber, 'Bureaucracy' in Gerth and Mills (eds.), *From Max Weber*, 196–8.
[36] Ibid., 196, 214–15; Weber, 'Politics as a Vocation', 91. Weber submitted his doctoral thesis on the history of trading companies to the University of Heidelberg in 1889. See Gerth and Mills (eds.), *From Max Weber*, 9–10.
[37] Weber, 'Bureaucracy', 204–9; and 'Politics as a Vocation' 80 et seq.
[38] Thomas, 'Max Weber, Talcott Parsons and the Sociology of Legal Reform', 401; Gerth and Mills (eds.), *From Max Weber*, 38.
[39] Weber, 'Bureaucracy', 224–6; Kennedy, 'Disenchantment of Logically Formal Legal Rationality', 1039.

contradiction in Weber's schema between democratic government and autocratic rule.[40]

The account of imperial administration in Nauru constructed in this book owes much to Weber's theory of bureaucratisation. For Weber, democratisation and bureaucratisation had occurred in tandem in Western Europe, and the tension between them defined European modernity: the former depersonalised political power and levelled traditional status-based power relations; the latter produced organisational complexity that favoured hierarchy and the development of expertise.[41] Once instantiated, bureaucratic organisation tended to prevail as a means of administering authority, due to its comparative efficiency or 'technical superiority' in executing authoritative command. At the same time, consonant with Weber's notion of elective affinity, officials themselves tended to justify their power through reference to objective ideals, in order to maintain that power. Once established, bureaucracy thus proved incredibly hard to dismantle: for Weber, 'where the bureaucratization of administration has been completely carried through, a form of power relation is established that is practically unshatterable'.[42] 'Bureaucratisation' therein referred to the qualitative intensification of bureaucratic activity once established, rather than quantitative increase in the scope of tasks.[43] There was thus a contradiction in the parallel emergence of 'mass' democracy and bureaucratic organisation of the state in modern Europe. What tended to occur in response to democratic pressures on authority was change in the identity of the persons in office, but not shifts in the power relations institutionalised in bureaucratic form.[44] For Weber, the dual rise of democratisation and bureaucratisation amounted to the 'societalising' of relations of domination.[45]

Weber's corpus continues to pose challenges for scholars of Western social theory.[46] His written work is both ponderous and deeply

---

[40] 'Of course one must always remember that the term "democratization" can be misleading. The demos itself, in the sense of an inarticulate mass, never "governs" larger associations; rather, it is governed, and its existence only changes the way in which the executive leaders are selected', Weber, 'Bureaucracy', 225.
[41] Rheinstein (ed.), *Max Weber on Law in Economy and Society*, 220; Thomas, 'Max Weber, Talcott Parsons and the Sociology of Legal Reform', 399–400.
[42] Ibid., 228.
[43] Ibid., 214.
[44] Ibid., 230; 'Politics as a Vocation', 82.
[45] Weber, 'Bureaucracy', 228.
[46] Richard Swedberg, 'The Changing Picture of Max Weber's Sociology' (2003) 29 *Annual Review of Sociology*, 283–306. Andrew Zimmerman, 'Decolonizing Weber' (2006) 9 *Postcolonial Studies*, 53–79.

ambivalent about its own objects of analysis. His personal politics, embedded in the centripetal forces of the Wilhelmine Reich, defy easy categorisation in contemporary terms.[47] Roth identifies an irresolvable tension between nationalism and cosmopolitanism at the heart of Weber's ambivalence about European modernity.[48] Zimmerman has more recently declared without equivocation: 'Max Weber was an imperialist, a racist, and a Social Darwinistic nationalist and these political positions fundamentally shaped his social scientific work'.[49] The extent to which such judgements serve historical understanding is a matter of debate.[50] Despite or perhaps because of their normative ambivalence, the concepts and terminology that Weber developed to describe European modernity proved foundational to the discipline of sociology, and have taken on afterlives of their own across the humanities and social sciences.[51]

Within international law, however, Weber's influence has been largely overshadowed by that of Marx. Weber himself labelled his methodology a science of economics that built upon the work of Marx, yet from an anti-Hegelian perspective that rejected dialectical materialism as an unscholarly reduction of the complexity of historical fact.[52] For Weber, Marx's dialectical materialism described well the socioeconomic conditions that prevailed in Western Europe in the second half of the nineteenth century, but could not be held out as universal truth.[53] It was sufficient neither as a universal explanation of history, nor as historiographical method.[54] Weber's critique was not confined to Marx; he

---

[47] Eich and Tooze, 'The Allure of Dark Times'.
[48] Swedberg, 'Changing Picture of Max Weber's Sociology', 286.
[49] Zimmerman, 'Decolonizing Weber', 53.
[50] Fitzmaurice, 'Context in the History of International Law', 12–13.
[51] Kennedy, 'Disenchantment of Logically Formal Legal Rationality', 1031–76.
[52] Ibid., 1036–7; and Gerth and Mills (eds.), *From Max Weber*, 34.
[53] 'Weber thus tries to relativize Marx's work by placing it into a more generalized context and showing that Marx's conclusions rest upon observations drawn from a dramatized "special case", which is better seen as one case in a broad series of similar cases. This series as a whole exemplifies the comprehensive underlying trend of bureaucratization. Socialist class struggles are merely a vehicle implementing this trend.' Gerth and Mills (eds.), *From Max Weber*, 46, 50; see also 65–9.
[54] Weber, 'Objectivity in the Social Sciences', 132–3. The intention here is not to enter into debates over Marxian historiography. Anderson notes that in Marx's later notebooks, many of which are yet to be published in English, Marx engaged with the fact of cultural difference of non-Western societies subject to colonial and imperial rule, including India, Indonesia and Algeria. Anderson argues that this engagement had an effect on Marx's formulation of dialectical materialism. Kevin B. Anderson, *Marx at the Margins: On*

contested singular causal explanations altogether.[55] Beyond this distinction, however, there remained significant complementarity between Weber's concepts of rationalisation and bureaucratisation, and Marx's analysis of commodification and exchange.[56] Georg Lukacs, Maurice Merleau-Ponty and C. Wright Mills were key figures in the subsequent development over the twentieth century of a critical tradition of Weberian Marxism. By Löwy's account, this tradition of Weberian Marxism is characterised by the use of certain themes and categories from Weber 'for the benefit of an approach basically inspired by Marx'.[57]

A Weberian Marxist sensibility informs the account of post-imperial state formation offered in this book. It is therefore diametrically opposed to the Anglophone 'Weberianism' that reduced Weber's work to a universal teleology of state development.[58] As Thomas has argued, the reduction of Weber's oeuvre to a 'structuralist-functionalist' account of capitalist state development dominated the reception of Weber in US social and political theory in the 1950s, largely through the work of Talcott Parsons.[59] Such Weberianism is characterised by normative reification of Weber's account of the relationship between the 'Protestant ethic' and the character of modern capitalism in the United States on the one hand; and on the other, of his definition of the state as monopolising the legitimate use of force within a given area.[60] Neither concept is directly engaged with in the account of imperial administration in Nauru that follows.

Nationalism, Ethnicity and Non-Western Societies (Chicago: University of Chicago Press, 2016), 237–45.

[55] Max Weber, 'The "Objectivity" in the Social and Economic Sciences' in Hans Henrik Bruun and Sam Whimster (eds.), *Max Weber: Collected Methodological Writings* (London: Routledge, 2012), 100, 111; Rheinstein (ed.), *Max Weber on Law in Economy and Society*, 27–9; Kennedy, 'Disenchantment of Logically Formal Legal Rationality', 1034–76.

[56] Michael Löwy, 'Figures of Weberian Marxism' (1996) 25 *Theory and Society*, 431–46.

[57] Ibid., 432.

[58] Thomas, 'Max Weber, Talcott Parsons and the Sociology of Legal Reform', 383–424. Structuralist-functionalist Weberianism is alive and well: see Glynn Cochrane, *Max Weber's Vision for Bureaucracy* (St Lucia: Palgrave Macmillan, 2018).

[59] Thomas, 'Max Weber, Talcott Parsons and the Sociology of Legal Reform', 410.

[60] Wilhelm Hennis, *Max Weber's Central Question*, trans. Keith Tribe, 2nd ed. (Newbury: Threshold Press, 2000), 10; Gerth and Mills (eds.), *From Max Weber*, 61–3. Weber's use of Goethe to effectively denounce the effects of modern capitalism in the United States is famously damning: '(s)pecialists without spirit, sensualists without heart; this nullity imagines that it has attained a level of civilisation never before achieved'. Max Weber, *Protestant Ethic and the Spirit of Capitalism*, trans. Talcott Parsons (London: Routledge, 1992), 124.

Rather, it is Weber's insistence that bureaucratic forms of relation, once instantiated, permit only of further bureaucratisation that forms the golden thread in this book. I use the term 'administration' rather than 'bureaucracy', as in contemporary English usage the former better encapsulates Weber's reference to both public and private authority than does 'bureaucracy', which is more readily associated with public office.[61] 'Administration' is used in the sense given by Weber as the collective execution of authoritative command.[62] I use the term 'status' in a positivist sense, to refer to territorial status as recognised in contemporaneous international law.[63] I use the term 'authority' in Weber's sense of legitimised domination, rather than moral or positive legal authority.[64] I use 'form' not in a metaphysical sense; rather, borrowing from Dorsett and McVeigh's work on jurisdiction, I use it to refer to patterns of social relation that take on shape and meaning through repetition.[65] For the purposes of this project, I draw heuristic parallels between status and concept on the one hand, and form and practice on the other. As much as it revives a spirit of Weberian Marxism, then, the book illustrates Duncan Kennedy's assessment of the diffuse influence of Weber on critical legal studies as the 'reinvention, or adaptation to non-Weberian purposes, of Weberian wheels'.[66]

Due to this focus on jurisdiction and bureaucracy, this book does not privilege the received sources of international law – treaty, custom, principle, judicial decisions and received juridical writings – in the account of imperial administration in Nauru that follows. Rather, the book is constructed around two categories of source, one narrowly and the other broadly construed. The first narrowly cast category comprises the official instruments that effected changes in the international status and in the administrative form of Nauru. This category resists

---

[61] Weber himself used the terms bureaucracy and administration to similar effect. Rheinstein (ed.), *Max Weber on Law in Economy and Society*, 330-7.
[62] Rheinstein (ed.), *Max Weber on Law in Economy and Society*, 330.
[63] This differs from Orford's treatment in *International Authority and the Responsibility to Protect*, which addresses the normative foundations of international territorial administration at 205-7.
[64] Rheinstein, *Max Weber on Law in Economy and Society*, 328. As Dorsett and McVeigh observe, '(w)hile authority can be understood in many ways according to different political and jurisprudential traditions, it has broadly been concerned with the explanation of the legitimate means of affiliation and subordination'. Dorsett and McVeigh, *Jurisdiction*, 10.
[65] Dorsett and McVeigh, *Jurisdiction*, 139; Sinclair, *To Reform the World*, 12.
[66] Kennedy, 'Disenchantment of Logically Formal Legal Rationality', 1076.

disciplinary distinctions between public and private law, and includes contracts, agreements, legislative instruments, executive ordinances, treaties, annual reports and constitutions. The second, broadly construed category comprises contemporaneous sources that offer insight into how and why those official instruments were created. These include administrative correspondence, legislative papers and transcripts, commission reports, newspaper articles and scholarly works.

The examination of these sources presents certain challenges in how to construct a narrative around them. The first is the centrality of the company and private rights to the administrative history of Nauru. The bureaucratisation of administrative arrangements established around phosphate exploitation rights – from Hanseatic firm Goddefroy & Sohn, to its successor the Jaluit Gesellschaft, to the British firm the Pacific Phosphate Company, to the tripartite British Phosphate Commission comprised of the United Kingdom, Australia and New Zealand, to the post-independence statutory authority, the Nauru Phosphate Corporation – was just as significant to the history of imperial administration in Nauru as the thread of 'public' offices and institutions to which international status officially attached. The second challenge is that most of the instruments that purported to effect major changes in the international status of Nauru were brief, if not cursory. Engaging with these documents therefore called for generous contextualisation. Regulations and ordinances of the Bismarckian Reich require placement in the Reichstag and the Rechtskolonialamt (the German Colonial Office), decisions of the Pacific Phosphate Company require placement in its company offices, and so on.

1.4 The Argument: Status Shifts, Form Accretes

What emerges in this book is not a continuous chronological account of the administration of Nauru since its incorporation into the German protectorate of the Marshall Islands in 1888 but rather a detailed account of four fundamental shifts in the status of Nauru in international law, and the relationship between those shifts and subsequent changes in administrative form. The first is the declaration of protectorate status in 1888, with the incorporation of Nauru into the Schutzgebiet der Marshall Inseln, the German Marshall Islands Protectorate, and the subsequent establishment of German imperial administration on the island (Chapter 2). The second is the shift from protectorate to C Mandate status in 1920, and the assumption of British administrative control, exercised by an Australian-appointed

1.4 THE ARGUMENT: STATUS SHIFTS, FORM ACCRETES

Administrator (Chapter 3). The third is the shift from C Mandate to UN Trust Territory status in 1947, under the administration of the Australian Department of Territories (Chapter 4). The fourth is the shift from UN Trust Territory to sovereign status, with the recognition of the independence of the Republic of Nauru in 1968, and the transition to Nauruan administration (Chapter 5).

In tracing this history, the book makes two arguments. The first can be stated simply: as international status shifts, administrative form accretes. Each shift in the status of Nauru was iteratively justified according to international legal principles of protection, mandate, trust and then political independence, yet was preceded by commercial and geopolitical instabilities in the maintenance of imperial control over the island. Throughout this series of shifts in international status, the administrative form under which the island was governed underwent a process of internal bureaucratisation and external restatement according to the prevailing concepts of the period. A simple administrative outline, originally sketched in 1888 by a Hanseatic trading company in a deal with the Bismarckian Reich, was progressively bureaucratised over time. Administrative tasks and practices intensified, were restated and renamed; but the form in which they were organised held firm. This argument leads towards a sobering appraisal of the statist paradigm of decolonisation that took hold in the mid-twentieth century. At the administrative level, the final shift in the international status of Nauru from UN Trust Territory to sovereign state appears not as a break with but as a stage in the bureaucratisation of an imperial administrative form instantiated in the late nineteenth century.[67] Chapter 6, the conclusion of the book, considers the post-independence trajectory of the Republic of Nauru and its contemporary reversions towards autocratic rule in this light.

The second argument is that this relationship between international status and imperial form becomes visible through centring Nauru in an account of the transition from imperial to international administration, through to official decolonisation in the 1960s. Centring Nauru demands that attention be trained on administrative practice in the 'margins', rather than solely on conceptual debates in the metropolitan 'centres' of

---

[67] This maps onto Rasulov's assertion that 'heterodox' narratives of imperialism and international law tend to converge in observing that 'the preservation of local legal sovereignty often became a central precondition for the successful completion of the process of imperial expansion'. Akbar Rasulov, 'Imperialism' in Jean d'Aspremont and Sahib Singh (eds.), *Concepts for International Law: Contributions to Disciplinary Thought* (UK: Edward Elgar Publishing, 2019), 435.

international law. The choice to centralise a place habitually regarded as marginal or anomalous within the international order is thus both a methodological and a political one. What emerges from the book is a sense of the difference between 'the' history of international law as a mode of conceptual reasoning – the international law of negotiated agreements, treaty interpretation, judicial decisions and juridical writings – and the histories of 'international law' as practised in place, in the exercise of administrative powers, the allocation of budgets, the design of metrics and the drafting of reports, and the ad hoc forms of relation that develop in the gaps between ideal concepts and local circumstance. The heuristic argument adopted in this book – status shifts, form accretes – is one way of thinking through the relationship between concept and practice that presents a recurrent issue not only in histories of international law but also in the discipline more broadly.

1.5 Situating this Book in the Field

As Craven has observed, any contribution to the history of international law is necessarily an act of intervention in the field.[68] Treatments of the relationship between imperialism and international law have expanded into a multidisciplinary phenomenon in the decades following the end of the Cold War. Parallel conversations in the fields of international law, international history and international relations about the continuities and discontinuities between imperial and international ordering have not always engaged, or engaged well, with each other.[69] This book takes as uncontroversial the assertion that all attempts at the history of international law function as interventions in present political and legal problems, and accepts that the question of whether particular accounts are better characterised as law, history or otherwise is a matter of method.[70] It is intended as a contribution to sociolegal

---

[68] Matthew Craven, 'Theorising the Turn to History in International Law' in Anne Orford and Florian Hoffmann (eds.) *Oxford Handbook of the Theory of International Law* (Oxford: Oxford University Press, 2016), 21.

[69] Mark Hickford, 'Sovereignties Viewed Through Anomalies: *A Search for Sovereignty. Law and Geography in European Empires 1400–1900*, Lauren Benton' (2013) 15 *Journal of the History of International Law*, 103–15 at 114–15.

[70] On the debate over contextualism in the history of international law, see Anne Orford, 'International Law and the Limits of History' in Wouter Werner, Marieke de Hoon and Alexis Galan, *The Law of International Lawyers: Reading Martti Koskenniemi* (Cambridge: Cambridge University Press, 2017), 310–12; Fitzmaurice, 'Context in the History of International Law', 12–14; and Lauren Benton, 'Beyond Anachronism'.

1.5 SITUATING THIS BOOK IN THE FIELD

histories of international law that focus on institutional and administrative practice.[71] In its focus on Nauru, it does not purport to transcend the statist framing that so frequently prefigures accounts of the co-production of concepts of the national and the international from the late nineteenth into the twentieth century.[72] At the same time, in situating its account of administrative development at the intersection of imperial, corporate and inter/national planes, it owes an obvious debt to the field of global history, particularly as rendered by Jürgen Osterhammel as 'the history of continuous, but not linear intensification of interactions across vast spaces and of the crystallization of these interactions into extended networks or, sometimes, institutions which possess their own hierarchical structure'.[73]

Given its importance to the argument, the definition of 'imperialism' deployed in this book requires clarification. As Rasulov notes, the concept of imperialism frequently goes undefined, even within sub-fields of international law that take imperialism as a framing problematic.[74] Marks observes that accounts of the relationship between imperialism and international law tend to fall within three broad narrative tropes, distinguished by what 'empire' is assumed to mean.[75] Where 'empire' is equated with colonialism in the sense of direct imposition of administrative control, contemporary international law is figured as defeating imperialism in its centrality to the decolonisation projects of the later twentieth century.[76] Where 'empire' is equated with political hegemony – such as that of the post-Cold War dominance of the United States – contemporary international law is figured as defeated *by* imperialism.[77] Where 'empire' is equated with economic globalisation, international law and imperialism

---

[71] Benton, 'Beyond Anachronism', 11.
[72] Glenda Sluga and Patricia Clavin, 'Rethinking the History of Internationalism; in Sluga and Clavin (eds.) *Internationalisms: A Twentieth Century History* (Cambridge: Cambridge University Press, 2016), 3–14; and Richard Drayton and David Motadel, 'Discussion: The Futures of Global History' (2018) 13 *Journal of Global History*, 1–21 at 8–9.
[73] Jürgen Osterhammel, 'Global History in a National Context: The Case of Germany' (2009) 20 *Global History*, 40–58 at 44.
[74] Rasulov, 'Imperialism', 422; and 'Writing About Empire: Remarks on the Logic of a Discourse' (2010) 23 *Leiden Journal of International Law*, 449–71.
[75] Susan Marks, 'Three Concepts of Empire' (2003) 16 *Leiden Journal of International Law* 901. See also Susan Marks, 'Empire's Law (The Earl A. Snyder Lecture in International Law)' (2003) 10 *Indiana Journal of Global Legal Studies*, 449–66.
[76] Marks, 'Three Concepts of Empire', 902.
[77] The prominent example here is Antonio Negri and Michael Hardt, *Empire* (Cambridge, MA: Harvard University Press, 2000).

are figured as mutually constituted.[78] Rasulov elaborates on this third trope, identifying a neo- or post-Marxist tradition within critical legal studies concerned primarily with 'uncovering and explaining the role international law plays in the advancement of capitalism, economic exploitation and Western modernity across the non-Western world'.[79]

The sense of imperialism invoked in this book falls readily within this third trope and clearly originates with Marxian critiques of capital accumulation. 'Imperialism' is defined as any extraterritorial practice, whether commercial, legal, political or otherwise, initiated and maintained to extract a higher value from regions and peoples outside a given political community than is given or recognised in exchange.[80] Imperialism is therein necessarily a process of reproducing differentiation and inequality, as Pitts has noted.[81] This definition of imperialism is an umbrella concept that both includes and exceeds formal colonial relations.[82] It also allows forms of imperialism to change over time and space, allowing for difference between imperial formations to emerge, without foreclosing the possibility of structural explanations of why and how imperialism takes certain forms.

It will be known to scholars in the field that this book joins two prominent accounts of international intervention in Nauru that have emerged from the TWAIL movement: Christopher Weeramantry's *Nauru: Environmental Damage under International Trusteeship* and Antony Anghie's *Imperialism, Sovereignty and International Law*. As a third approach to the significance of Nauru in the history of international law, it is important to distinguish between them. Each of these three approaches to the story of Nauru demonstrates a distinct approach to the historiography of international law. Weeramantry's 1992 text, written prior to his appointment to the International Court of Justice, is a meticulous example of what Craven describes as 'history in international law'.[83] In the late 1980s Weeramantry was engaged by the Republic

---

[78] Marks, 'Three Concepts of Empire', 903; Rasulov, 'Writing About Empire', 461–8.
[79] Rasulov, 'Imperialism', 425. See for example B. S. Chimni, 'Capitalism, Imperialism, and International Law in the Twenty-First Century' (2012) 14 *Oregon Review of International Law*, 17–46.
[80] Rasulov, 'Imperialism' 432–5; Fitzmaurice, *Property, Sovereignty and Empire*, 5–6.
[81] Jennifer Pitts, 'Political Theory of Empire and Imperialism' (2010) 13 *Annual Review of Political Science* 211–35, 213.
[82] Rasulov, 'Imperialism', 422–4.
[83] Matthew Craven, 'Introduction: International Law and its Histories' in Matthew Craven, Malgosia Fitzmaurice and Maria Vogiatzi (eds.), *Time, History and International Law* (Leiden and Boston: Martinus Nijhoff Publishing, 2007), 7.

1.5 SITUATING THIS BOOK IN THE FIELD

of Nauru to chair a Commission of Inquiry into the Rehabilitation of Phosphate Lands, and charged with investigating whether the historical facts of imperial administration disclosed a legal case for compensation. The Commission's work formed the basis of Nauru's submissions to the International Court of Justice in the late 1980s in *Nauru v. Australia*, commonly known as the Certain Phosphate Lands Case.[84] The Commission's Report is masterfully narrativised by Weeramantry in *Nauru*.

The difference between Weeramantry's text and this one is therefore precisely a question of whether the anachronistic deployment of international legal concepts is appropriate to the purpose of the intervention.[85] Weeramantry narrativises the legal history of Nauru in order to make a legal argument for attribution of trusteeship obligations to Australia, the United Kingdom and New Zealand from 1920 onward. The intention is to frame the Nauruan demand for justice for the administrative exploitation of the island and its people as a question of positive law.[86] A similar demand for justice animates this book; but thirty years after the settlement of the Certain Phosphate Lands Case, the conclusion this book reluctantly reaches is that such justice is beyond the capacity of international law to deliver. On the interpretation of C Mandate status given in Chapters 3 and 4, it is not possible to attribute positive obligations of trusteeship to Australia (or the United Kingdom or New Zealand) until at least 1945, when trusteeship obligations were juridified in the UN Charter. It is arguably even impossible to attribute such obligations until the early 1960s, when the Trusteeship Council and General Assembly passed resolutions interpreting how those obligations applied to Nauru following the 1960 Declaration on the Granting of Independence to Colonial Peoples.[87]

Still, the demand for justice remains. The point here is not that Australia's – and the United Kingdom's and New Zealand's – responsibility to account for the exploitation of the island of Nauru and its people falls *short* of legal liability. It is rather that it far exceeds the expressive capacity of international law. It must therefore be understood as an unresolved

---

[84] Application Instituting Proceedings, *Nauru v. Australia* ('Certain Phosphate Lands Case'), International Court of Justice, General List, 19 May 1989.
[85] Orford, 'International Law and the Limits of History', 310–13.
[86] Weeramantry, *Nauru*, 307–74.
[87] Declaration on the Granting of Independence to Colonial Countries and Peoples, General Assembly Resolution 1514(XV), General Assembly Official Records, 15th session, 947th plenary meeting, UN Doc A/RES/1514(XV) (14 December 1960).

political question, not a settled legal one. As discussed in Chapter 6, the outcome of the Certain Phosphate Lands Case illustrates the point in a brutal way. In 1992 the Republic of Nauru settled for a sum far less than the value of what was taken, and far less than the predicted cost of rehabilitation. It also agreed to indemnify Australia, Britain and New Zealand from any future claims. The actual application of settlement funds was controlled by Australia over the twenty-year payment period from 1992 to 2012; and during that period, Australia relied on its indemnification to categorise settlement payments as 'development aid', rather than as compensation for wrongdoing, or wrongful retention of benefit.

The afterlife of the Certain Phosphate Lands Case – what it actually achieved, as opposed to its potential promise in the early 1990s as the first case to bring questions of breach of international trusteeship before an international court – sounds a note of caution to framing demands for decolonial justice within the framework of contemporaneous international law.[88] Such framing runs the risk of allowing imperial states like Australia yet again to reap the benefit of international law's imperial past, during periods when the law was less 'indeterminate' than actively facilitative of exploitation. It must also somehow counter the effect on court proceedings of the often daunting financial and technical inequalities between formally equal state parties that centuries of imperial relation have produced. This is not a call for the abandonment of tactical litigation in the global decolonial struggle.[89] It is rather an identification of the need for sober longitudinal assessment of the outcomes of such tactical deployments of international law in the post-independence era. States like Nauru have struggled to contend with the manifold legal and material inequalities they face in bringing submissions like *Nauru* v. *Australia* against their former imperial administrators. As discussed in Chapter 6, some twenty-seven years after the settlement of the Certain Phosphate Lands Case, the exploitation of Nauru by Australia and by a new generation of resource companies has transmuted in directions that could not have been presaged in the early 1990s, when Weeramantry's text was published.

---

[88] For a crucial formulation of the distinction between scepticism and critique in 'critical' analyses of international law, see Susan Marks, *The Riddle of All Constitutions: International Law, Democracy, and the Critique of Ideology* (Oxford: Oxford University Press, 2003), 143–44.

[89] Rob Knox, 'Strategy and Tactics' (2012) 21 *Finnish Yearbook of International* Law, 193–229; John Reynolds, 'Anti-Colonial Legalities: Paradigms, Tactics & Strategy' (2016) 18 *Palestine Yearbook of International Law*, 8–52 at 34–6.

1.5 SITUATING THIS BOOK IN THE FIELD

The second version of the Nauruan case to emerge from the TWAIL movement is given by Antony Anghie in '"The Heart of My Home"', later developed into his field-defining monograph, *Imperialism, Sovereignty and the Making of International Law*. Anghie's scholarly work on Nauru in the 1990s and 2000s followed his engagement as a researcher with the Commission of Inquiry chaired by Weeramantry.[90] From this departure point, Anghie follows the thread of the Nauruan case to unravel 'conventional histories' of the discipline that, as he charges, continue to minimise European colonialism as a 'peripheral' and 'unfortunate' past aberration in an otherwise noble teleology of progress. Stepping from sixteenth-century naturalism, to nineteenth-century positivism, to twentieth-century pragmatism, Anghie weaves a critical account of sovereignty, arguing that the concept was 'forged out of the attempt to create a legal system that could account for relations between the European and non-European worlds in the colonial confrontation', and has always applied differentially to imperial and colonial peoples.[91] Anghie's central argument is that the continuity between imperialism and international law is located in the civilising mission, itself predicated on a logic of cultural difference between 'European' and 'non-European'. That logic of cultural difference continues to condition postcolonial sovereignty.[92] As Anghie makes clear, his intention is not to provide an exhaustive history of international law but to 'suggest new lines of research and make some contribution toward the writing of alternative histories of the discipline'.[93] His text inaugurated a new era of international legal scholarship that engaged directly with the imperial legacy of international law as a question of contemporary geopolitics.

This book departs from a similar point to that of Anghie in insisting on the significance of Nauru to the history of international law, yet the path traversed from there is different. Rather than following the thread towards a critical appraisal of foundational concepts of international law, this book stays with the island, observing the way imperial interventions in Nauru from the late 1870s through to the present have been authorised, established, maintained and bureaucratised. As a result, this account traces the continuity between nineteenth-century imperialism and twentieth-century international law not through foundational

---

[90] Anghie, '"The Heart of My Home"'; Anghie, *Imperialism, Sovereignty and International Law*, 1–12.
[91] Anghie, *Imperialism, Sovereignty and International Law*, 3.
[92] Anghie, *Imperialism, Sovereignty and International Law*, 311–15.
[93] Ibid., 12. See also Orford, 'The Past as Law or History?'

concepts of international law but through grounded forms of administration. The end result is a better sense of the administrative form to which the status of sovereignty – Anghie's central problematic – was attached in 1968.

1.6 Telling an Administrative Story: Strengths and Limitations

There are both strengths and limitations in this approach. The focus on Nauru brings into relief a potentially unfamiliar configuration of global relations across the period considered, and some central themes emerge as a result of this reorientation. The first is the history and legacy of German imperialism, in the Pacific and in Africa.[94] Much work remains to be done on the significance of the formalisation and abrupt confiscation of the German imperial territories for the peoples and regions that came under German control between the 1880s and World War I.[95] The legal dimensions of German imperial intervention in Africa have been attracting increasing attention in the broader discipline.[96] Thus far, this attention has largely focused around German South West Africa. As discussed in Chapter 5, Ethiopia and Liberia's actions in the International Court of Justice across the 1950s and 1960s regarding South Africa's refusal to submit its administration of South West Africa to international oversight made the situation in the former German protectorate a focal point of anticolonial engagement with international institutions in that period. The history of South West Africa periodically re-emerges at the front lines of real conceptual and political difficulty in

---

[94] On the debate on the historiography of post-Confederation Germany, see Theodore S. Hamerow, 'Guilt, Redemption and Writing German History' (1983) 88 *The American Historical Review* 1, 53–72; Sven Oliver Muller and Cornelius Torp (eds.), *Imperial Germany Revisited: Continuing Debates and New Perspectives* (New York: Berghahn Books, 2011); and George Steinmetz, 'Decolonizing German Theory: An Introduction' (2006) 9 *Postcolonial Studies*, 3–13.

[95] Martti Koskenniemi, 'A History of International Law Histories' in Bardo Fassbender and Anne Peters (eds.), *Oxford Handbook of the History of International Law* (Oxford: Oxford University Press, 2012) at 944.

[96] Jörg Fisch, 'Law as a Means and as an End: Some Remarks on the Function of European and Non-European Law in the Process of European Expansion' in W. J. Mommsen and J. A. de Moor, *European Law and Expansion: The Encounter of European and Indigenous Law in 19th and 20th Century Africa and Asia* (Oxford and New York: Berg, 1992), 15; and Felix Hanschmann, 'The Suspension of Constitutionalism in the Heart of Darkness' in Kelly L. Grotke and Markus J. Prutsch, *Constitutionalism, Legitimacy and Power: Nineteenth Century Experiences* (Oxford: Oxford University Press, 2014), 243.

1.6 ADMINISTRATIVE FORM: STRENGTHS AND LIMITATIONS 33

international law. In 1985 the UN's Whitaker Report found the German response to the Herero uprising of 1904–8 constituted genocide. Namibia's independence was formally recognised only in 1991, and in 2004 Germany made an official apology to Namibia over the treatment of the Herero and Nama.[97]

The international legal dimensions of German imperialism in the Pacific, however, largely remain to be thoroughly examined.[98] This book makes a modest contribution to that examination. A number of historical threads are recovered, or recollected, through the focus on Nauru during the German imperial period. At the international level, focus on the fate of the German imperial territories demonstrates that the rhetoric of 'civilisation' that circulated at the Paris Peace Conference, subsequently codified into Article 22 of the Covenant of the League of Nations, was a cypher that invoked the 'barbarism' of German imperial practice just as readily as the 'barbarism' of non-European peoples. The concept of a standard of civilisation thus operated not only to inscribe a division between European and 'non-European' modes of sociopolitical organisation but also between acceptable and unacceptable modes of imperialism.[99]

The second theme that emerges in focusing on Nauru is the constitutive relationship between Australian sovereignty and its sub-imperialist posturing in the Pacific region. As told in Chapter 2, German imperialism in the Pacific was an explicit impetus for the movement towards federation of the Australian colonies from the 1880s, and as told in Chapter 3, there was close a relationship between the assumption by the British Dominions of Australia, South Africa and New Zealand of administrative control over the occupied German territories in Africa and the Pacific, and their shift towards sovereign status in international law.[100] Historians and political

---

[97] United Nations, Revised and Updated Report on the Question of the Prevention and Punishment of the Crime of Genocide prepared by Mr. B. Whitaker ('Whitaker Report'), E/CN.4/Sub.2/1985/6, 2 July 1985, para. 24. Steven Press, *Rogue Empires: Contracts and Conmen in Europe's Scramble for Africa* (Cambridge, MA: Harvard University Press, 2017).

[98] Notable exceptions include Peter Fitzpatrick, *Law and State in Papua New Guinea* (London and New York: Academic Press, 1980); and the works of Stewart Firth, including 'Colonial Administration and the Invention of the Native', in Donald Denoon with Stewart Firth, Jocelyn Linnekin, Malama Meleisea and Karen Nero (eds.), *Cambridge History of the Pacific Islanders* (Cambridge: Cambridge University Press, 2008), 253.

[99] See Ntina Tzouvala, 'Civilization' in d'Aspremont and Singh (eds.), *Concepts for International Law*, 83–104.

[100] This argument is developed in Cait Storr, '"Imperium in Imperio": Sub-Imperialism and the Formation of Australia as a Subject of International Law' (2018) 19 *Melbourne Journal of International Law*, 335–68.

scientists – from Merze Tate, to Roger Thompson, to Marilyn Lake and Henry Reynolds, to Tracey Banivanua Mar – have long made similar arguments.[101] But it is rarely acknowledged within the Australian legal mainstream that Australia's sub-imperialist policy in the Pacific was a major catalyst in Australia's mitotic path to sovereign independence, and continues to function as a primary mode of expression of that sovereignty.[102]

The historiographical point here is obviously also a political one: 'Australia' is necessarily understood as a sub-imperial as well as a colonial project. The Australian state is a colonial project built and maintained on the denial of Indigenous ownership of the continent, and in certain contexts on the denial of Indigenous existence itself.[103] Moreover, Australian policy towards the Pacific region also inherits from the avowedly white supremacist sub-imperial policies through which the Commonwealth sought to substantiate its international status in the earlier twentieth century.[104] Much of this policy work is now framed in the idiom of global governance, invoking concepts of 'leadership', 'stability' and 'development'.[105] But the continuities in Australia's regional conduct over the last century are hard to ignore, from Queensland's thwarted attempts to annex New Guinea in the 1880s, through to Australia's aggressive and unlawful conduct of maritime delimitation negotiations with newly independent Timor Leste in the Timor Sea Treaty Arbitration in the 2000s and 2010s;[106] from interwar white nationalist paranoia over

---

[101] Merze Tate, 'Australasian Monroe Doctrine' (1961) 76 *Political Science Quarterly*, 264–84; Roger C. Thompson, *Australian Imperialism in the Pacific: The Expansionist Era 1820-1920* (Melbourne: Melbourne University Press, 1980); Marilyn Lake and Henry Reynolds, *Drawing the Global Colour Line: White Men's Countries and the International Challenge of Racial Equality* (Cambridge: Cambridge University Press, 2012); and Tracey Banivanua Mar, *Decolonisation and the Pacific: Indigenous Globalisation and the Ends of Empire* (Cambridge: Cambridge University Press, 2016).

[102] Anghie presaged the need to tell this story in '"The Heart of My Home"', 505, recently returning to the theme in Antony Anghie, 'Race, Self-Determination and Australian Empire' (2019) 19 *Melbourne Journal of International Law*, 1–39.

[103] For recent debates over the concept of settler colonialism, originally articulated by Patrick Wolfe, as a framework for understanding the Australian colonial project, see Lisa Ford, 'Locating Indigenous Self-Determination in the Margins of Settler Sovereignty: An Introduction' in Lisa Ford and Tim Rowse (eds.), *Between Indigenous and Settler Governance* (USA and Canada: Routledge, 2013), 1–11 at 11; and Lorenzo Veracini, '"Settler Colonialism": Career of a Concept' (2013) 41 *Journal of Imperial and Commonwealth History*, 313–22.

[104] Storr, '"*Imperium in Imperio*"'.

[105] Commonwealth of Australia, *Foreign Policy White Paper*, November 2017, iii.

[106] *Arbitration under the Timor Sea Treaty (Timor-Leste v. Australia)* (Permanent Court of Arbitration, Case 2015-42); *Timor-Leste v. Australia (Questions Relating to the Seizure*

1.6 ADMINISTRATIVE FORM: STRENGTHS AND LIMITATIONS 35

Asian immigration to Australia via the Pacific islands in the 1920s and 1930s, to the excision of 6,000 territorial islands – and then the continent itself – from Australia's migration zone in 2013.[107] The process of stabilising the territorial boundaries of 'Australia' continues. It still exceeds the official limits of Australian sovereign territory, as the imbrications of Australian, Nauruan and Papua New Guinean sovereignty in the legal framework of Australia's offshore detention regime have most recently made clear.[108]

A third theme to emerge from the focus on Nauru concerns the thick interrelation between the formalisation of imperial administration in the global South and the geography of natural resource commodification. The fixing of place rather than concept allows geography and geology into the story of state formation offered here. It is hardly new to note the significance of phosphate to the history of Nauru. Most accounts of the island's history place phosphate at the centre of their analysis.[109] The phosphate interlude in Chapter 3 seeks to place that relationship between phosphate and state formation in Nauru in a global context. The transfer of the phosphate concession from the German-owned Jaluit Gesellschaft to the British-owned Pacific Phosphate Company in the 1900s was a pivotal moment in the trajectory of imperial control over Nauru. Here, the legal story of that transfer of private rights is contextualised within a global story of the commodification of phosphate in the later nineteenth century. The chapter traces the relationship between phosphate commodification and the development of agricultural chemistry, mass industrialisation and urbanisation in Europe and the legal distinctions between German, British and American modes of authorising extraterritorial resource extraction in the Pacific.[110]

---

and Detention of Certain Documents and Data), International Court of Justice, Summary of Judgments and Orders (2014).

[107] Anthea Vogl, 'Over the Borderline: A Critical Inquiry into the Geography of Territorial Excision and the Securitisation of the Australian Border' (2015) 38 *UNSW Law Journal*, 114–45.

[108] *Plaintiff M68/2015* v. *Commonwealth of Australia* (2016) 257 CLR 42 (Gordon J., dissent).

[109] Viviani, *Nauru*; Maslyn Williams and Barrie Macdonald, *The Phosphateers: A History of the British Phosphate Commissioners* (Melbourne: Melbourne University Press, 1985).

[110] See also Richard Grove, *Green Imperialism: Colonial Expansion, Tropical Island Edens and the Origins of Environmentalism, 1600–1860* (Cambridge: Cambridge University Press, 1996); Gregory T. Cushman, *Guano and the Opening of the Pacific World: A Global Ecological History* (Cambridge: Cambridge University Press, 2013); Katerina Martina Teaiwa, *Consuming Ocean Island: Stories of People and Phosphate from Banaba*

The global story that emerges is that the post-independence exploitation of the South to the benefit of the North occurs not only through conceptual paradigms of development and neoliberalism, through international institutions like the World Bank and the IMF, and through the international regime of investment protection, but also through the structural continuities in local administrative relations from the imperial through to the contemporary era.[111] Facilitating the outward flow of natural resources from Nauru is the raison d'etre of the state's administrative form. As Chapter 5 traces, that form was not dismantled in the adoption of a constitution and the substitution of local for imperial executives.[112] Attempts by decolonising states to interrupt such outward flows of natural resources through restructuring public and private relations at the local level have tended to reveal just how heavily conditioned the exercise of postcolonial sovereignty is.[113]

Whatever its strengths might be, there are crucial limitations in the approach adopted in this book that need acknowledgement. The first is a matter of language and translation. In its treatment of the German protectorate period, this book relies to an extent that will not satisfy historians on English translations of German legal documents and correspondence. The depth of engagement with German colonial records in Chapter 2 was made possible by the curatorial work of Wilhelm Fabricius, who acted as German ambassador to Nauru in the 1980s, and complied *Nauru 1888–1900*, a collection of records from the Colonial Section of the German Foreign Office held by the Deutsches Zentralarchiv in Potsdam, the Bundesarchiv in Koblenz and the National Library of Australia in Canberra.[114] Fabricius' work was translated and

(Bloomington: Indiana University Press, 2014); and Daniel Immerwahr, *How to Hide an Empire: A History of the Greater United States* (London: Random House, 2019).

[111] On the persistence of the North–South divide in the neoliberal development project, see Sundhya Pahuja, *Decolonising International Law: Development, Economic Growth and the Politics of Universality* (Cambridge: Cambridge University Press, 2011); Sumudu Atapattu and Carmen C. Gonzalez, 'The North–South Divide in International Environmental Law: Framing the Issues' in Shawkat Alam, Sumudu Atapattu, Carmen G. Gonzalez and Jona Razzaque (eds.), *International Environmental Law and the Global South* (Cambridge: Cambridge University Press, 2015), 1.

[112] Mohammed Bedjaoui, *Towards a New International Economic Order* (New York and London: UNESCO, 1979), 78–81.

[113] See Sundhya Pahuja and Cait Storr, 'Rethinking Iran and International Law: The Anglo-Iranian Oil Case Revisited' in James Crawford, Abdul Koroma, Said Mahmoudi and Alain Pellet (eds.) *The International Legal Order: Current Needs and Possible Responses Essays in Honour of Djamchid Momtaz* (Leiden and Boston: Brill Nijhoff, 2017), 53.

[114] Wilhelm Fabricius, *Nauru 1888–1900: An Account in German and English based on Official Records of the Colonial Section of the German Foreign Office held by the Deutsches*

1.2 Abandoned phosphate cantilever, Aiwo, Nauru, August 2018. Credit: Mike Leyral/ AFP/Getty Images.

supplemented by Dymphna Clark and Stewart Firth, and published in bilingual format by the School of Pacific Studies at the Australian National University. The existence of the bilingual text significantly augmented the scope of Chapter 2, as did related translation work of historians Stewart Firth, Dymphna Clark, Peter Sack and Dirk Spennemann. The attempt made in this book to understand the legal dimensions of German imperial administration in the Pacific owes much to the work of historians, and constitutes one small step towards advancing the conversation between this Pacific-oriented work and German language analyses of German imperial law and international history.[115] Much more remains to be done.

The second limitation is a matter of representation. This is a European story, not a Nauruan one. The Weberian account of bureaucratisation that shapes the narrative works at times to drain the book of the colour and

Zentralarchiv in Potsdam, trans. Dymphna Clark and Stewart Firth (Canberra: Research School of Pacific Studies, Australian National University, 1992).

[115] Koskenniemi briefly considers German imperial law in 'Colonial Laws: Sources, Strategies and Lessons?' (2016) 18 *Journal of the History of International Law* 248–77 at 275–6. Luigi Nuzzo offers a helpful overview of German imperial law in the African protectorates in 'Colonial Law' (16 April 2012) *European History Online*. Neither address the Pacific context.

movement of human agency – and most crucially, of Nauruan agency. Individuals appear and disappear only as they take official positions, negotiate legal agreements and act in administrative roles. As a result, the protagonists in this story are almost exclusively European men. Given the book's political intentions, this has at times made the writing process both uncomfortable and counter-intuitive. As much as it may trace the way in which law has been used to legitimise imperial exploitation in Nauru, this approach will not satisfy those calling for histories of international law that rectify the chronic marginalisation of non-European peoples' engagements with, modes of resistance to, and authorship of international laws. As Anghie notes, this is an organising objective of the TWAIL movement.[116] For him, the 'aspirations of TWAIL' reflect the concerns of independence-era Third World international lawyers: 'of viewing international law from the position of the objects of colonialism; of developing the conceptual tools that could provide an account of imperialism that corresponded with the experiences of those who were its victims; and of formulating alternative visions of justice that might contribute to thinking about global order'.[117]

This book shares the latter political objective of formulating alternative visions of justice in collective understandings of the contemporary international order. However, it does not meet the first two objectives, which amount to a politic demand that if the claims of international law to promote global justice and equality are to be more than rhetorical, the discipline must expand its histories and its conceptual vocabularies to include post/colonial perspectives. This book stands in alliance with that demand. But it makes no claim to represent Nauruan experiences of, engagements with, or modes of resistance to, the imperial interventions detailed in this book. The space remains open for accounts of that history, on Nauruan terms.[118] The intention in this book is rather to trace the

---

[116] On TWAIL, see B. S. Chimni, 'Third World Approaches to International Law: A Manifesto' (2006) 8 *International Community Law Review*, 3–27; James Thuo Gathii, 'TWAIL: A Brief History of its Origins, Its Decentralized Network, and a Tentative Bibliography' (2011) 3 *Trade, Law and Development*, 26–64; and Usha Natarajan, John Reynolds, Amar Bhatia and Sujith Xavier, 'Introduction: TWAIL – On Praxis and the Intellectual' (2016) 37 *Third World Quarterly*, 1946–56.

[117] Anghie, 'Imperialism and International Legal Theory' in Orford and Hoffmann (eds.), *Oxford Handbook of the Theory of International Law*, 165.

[118] Tracey Banivanua Mar laid masterful foundations in this respect in *Decolonisation and the Pacific: Indigenous Globalisation and the Ends of Empire* (Cambridge: Cambridge University Press, 2016). Katerina Teaiwa's *Consuming Ocean Island* constructs a brilliant account of the history of the island of Banaba, which has its own story of aggressive phosphate imperialism by the British Phosphate Commission as part of the British protectorate of the Gilbert and Ellice Islands (now Kiribati). Katerina Martina Teaiwa,

operation, in the Pacific region and beyond, of a still-evolving, multi-faceted imperial project – a project that has worked not only through categorical differentiations in international status, not only through the extraction of resources and labour via ever more complex economic and financial arrangements, but also through accretions of administrative form that are all too often presumed to be neutral or inevitable.

1.7 The Structure of the Book

Each of the chapters that follow redescribes a shift in the international status of Nauru, and the changes in administration that accompanied that shift. **Chapter 2**, 'From Trading Post to Protectorate, 1888', traces the appearance of the island on the plane of imperial administration, first as a point in the Pacific trading network of Goddefroy & Sohn, a Hanseatic firm from Hamburg, and then as a declared part of the German protectorate of the Marshall Islands, under the company administration of the Jaluit Gesellschaft. The chapter begins with a brief history of the Hansa, moving to trace the contemporaneous development of the German Pacific trading network, the Reich under Chancellor Bismarck, and the regime of imperial protectorates that proliferated across the Pacific and Africa after the Berlin Conference on the Congo in 1884. The chapter argues that the protectorate concept did not clearly explain the nature of authority asserted by the Reich over Nauru in 1888, not least because the distinctions between concepts of sovereignty, property and territory were not settled as matters of positive international law, in German imperial practice and indeed more broadly. The balance of company and state rule struck between the Reich and the Jaluit Gesellschaft in their 1888 Agreement on the administration of the Marshall Islands and Nauru responded to the pragmatic concerns of Bismarck in shoring up his political position in the Reichstag, and the demands of German corporate entrepreneurs in the Pacific, with minimal consideration of any need for clarity in the law of nations. The chapter concludes that attending to this distinction between international status and administrative form in the assertion of authority over Nauru generates its own historiographical momentum, establishing an alternative perspective from which to redescribe the shift from imperial to international ordering in the twentieth century.

Consuming Ocean Island: Stories of People and Phosphate from Banaba (Bloomington: Indiana University Press, 2014).

Chapter 3, 'From Protectorate to Colony to Mandate, 1920', redescribes the decades following the declaration of protectorate status in 1888 and the settlement of a basic division of resource rights and administrative responsibilities in Nauru between the Reich and the Jaluit Gesellschaft. Between 1888 and 1920, the formal status of Nauru was to shift twice, from German protectorate, to German colony, to British mandate. The chapter traces the accretions of administrative form that accompanied each shift. It opens with an account of the original executive ordinances issued by the Nauruan office of the Marshall Islands Protectorate, subsequently subsumed into German New Guinea in 1906, as German trade in the Pacific floundered even with the official protection the Hanseatic firms had secured in the 1880s. The chapter diverts to consider the relationship between the commodification of phosphate, the industrialisation of agricultural production and imperial competition in the Pacific, as a means of providing context to the sale in 1900 of the Jaluit Gesellschaft's phosphate exploitation rights to a British firm, the Pacific Phosphate Company. The development of the British company's Nauru operation under the joint administration of the Jaluit Gesellschaft and the Reich Colonial Office is redescribed in relation to the militarisation of the Reich under Wilhelm I, the influence of German activity in the Pacific on the federation movement in the Australian colonies and the development of self-governing Dominion status within the British empire.

Australia's military occupation of Nauru in 1914 at the request of the British Imperial government was one of the first taken by Australia in the war – an action Prime Minister W. M. Hughes subsequently argued during the Paris Peace Conference grounded Australia's claim to territorial annexation of the island.[119] Hughes failed in this gambit, and Nauru was placed under the international oversight of the new League of Nations, and declared a C Class Mandate. However, C Mandate status itself was a product of an uneasy pragmatic compromise struck at Versailles, and codified in Article 22 of the Covenant of the League, between the British Dominions of Australia and South Africa, pushing for territorial annexation of the occupied German territories of South West Africa and the Pacific, and the competing concepts of internationalisation of the occupied German and Ottoman territories that circulated during the Peace Conference.

[119] Storr, "*Imperium in Imperio*".

The chapter traces the aftermath of this shift in Nauru's international status from protectorate to colony to mandate at the local administrative level. In the 1919 Nauru Island Agreement, Britain, Australia and New Zealand struck an intra-imperial bargain, establishing a tripartite monopoly over Nauruan phosphate. The Pacific Phosphate Company's Jaluit-derived assets vested in the new British Phosphate Commission, which gained complete autonomy over phosphate operations; and administrative control, formerly exercised by the German office for Nauru, vested in an Australian Administrator, responsible for meeting mandatory obligations under the oversight of the new Permanent Mandates Commission. The chapter concludes that whilst the declaration of C Mandate status marked the official shift from imperial to international administration, the form adopted by Britain, Australia and New Zealand to administer Nauru retained the basic division of public and private authority established in 1888.

Chapter 4, 'From Mandate to Trust Territory, 1947', traces the bureaucratisation of Nauruan administration during the mandate period, pursuant to the provisions of the Mandate and the Nauru Island Agreement. Over the interwar period, the ambiguous international status of the C Mandates – which, according to Article 22 of the Covenant of the League, were to be administered 'as integral portions the territory' of the Mandatory – came to pose a juridical problem for scholars, and a diplomatic problem for the League. Nauru lay at the intersection of imperial tensions between Australia, Britain, Japan and the United States in the Pacific. For Japan and later for Germany, the situation in Nauru and in the C Mandates more broadly illustrated the hypocrisies of the new paradigm of international administration. As Australia and South Africa argued for a minimalist interpretation of their mandatory obligations, the British Phosphate Commission industriously delivered cost-price Nauruan phosphate into the agricultural sectors of the United Kingdom, Australia and New Zealand. Tensions between Australia and Japan over the Pacific C Mandates worsened after the withdrawals of Japan and Germany from the League in 1933, and the imperial frontiers that cut across the Pacific became increasingly volatile. The Australian-administered C Mandates of Nauru and New Guinea were occupied by Japan during World War II, becoming key sites in Japan's Pacific offensive, operated from Japanese military bases on Chuuk Atoll in the Japanese Pacific Islands Mandate north of the equator.

The chapter moves to redescribe the reconstitution of the League as the United Nations from 1942, with a focus on the expansion of Article 22 of the Covenant of the League into three Chapters of the Charter of the United Nations, and the reconstitution of the Permanent Mandates Commission as the UN Trusteeship Council, with significantly increased powers of review. Nauru was retaken by the Allied Powers in 1945, and the new UN Trusteeship Agreement for Nauru was finalised in 1947, with Australia reappointed as Administering Authority. The chapter concludes that the shift from mandate to trust territory status proved highly significant in providing a clearer conceptual framework in which the relationship between Australia and Nauru could be characterised as a matter of international law. At the administrative level, however, that shift required no major alterations in the administrative form through which the Australian Administrator governed the island, prompting only further bureaucratisation of the basic structure of relations established under German rule in 1888, and developed under Australian administration from 1920.

Chapter 5, 'From Trust Territory to Sovereign State, 1968', traces the shift in Nauru's international status from trust territory to sovereign state as the Republic of Nauru in 1968, and the local accretions in administrative form that accompanied that shift. The juridification of the concept of international trusteeship and the sudden removal of differentiated status for the C Mandates placed their administering powers – the United Kingdom, South Africa, Australia and New Zealand – out of step with the international post-war trend towards political self-determination. Over the trusteeship period, their attempts to maintain administrative control over the former C Mandates of South West Africa, Nauru, New Guinea and Western Samoa attracted international opprobrium, particularly from the Soviet Union and the growing body of decolonising states. The chapter considers the effects of the South West Africa Cases on the UN General Assembly's position on independence for all trust territories. The UN's subsequent embrace of the cause of Nauruan independence forced a series of protracted negotiations over the 1960s between the Australian Department of Territories and the new Nauru Local Government Council, under the leadership of Timothy Detudamo, and then Hammer DeRoburt. The issue that catalysed the negotiations was the calculation of royalty rates; but between 1965 and 1968, the Nauru Talks moved to address land and phosphate ownership, public administrative control and the environmental rehabilitation of mined-out land. By the mid-1960s, what remained to be decided during the Nauru Talks was not whether Nauru would become a sovereign state but rather the manner and extent to which control of the administrative structure on the one hand, and the BPC's phosphate rights on the other, would be transferred into Nauruan hands. The last question to be determined was who would be responsible for the rehabilitation of the island's central plateau, devastated by seven decades of aggressive phosphate mining.

The transition in international status from trust territory to sovereign statehood was an astounding achievement of the Nauruan people, under the leadership of Hammer DeRoburt. The recognition of Nauruan ownership and control of phosphate was an even greater achievement still, given the aggressive negotiation tactics of the Australian Department of Territories over the 1960s. However, the chapter argues that international recognition of Nauruan independence was in many respects profoundly ironic. It was widely presumed – including by the Trusteeship Council and the General Assembly – that the island would be mined to exhaustion, at which point it would become uninhabitable. Nauru's accession to sovereign statehood was therefore regarded not as the inauguration of a viable state, than as a principled means by which the Nauruan people would be free to determine for themselves how to respond to that uninhabitability. At the same time, the administrative structure of the new Republic of Nauru was not a displacement but a further accretion of an imperial bureaucratic form instantiated in the 1880s. In both its provisions and its silences, the 1968 Constitution rapidly drafted by Australian consultants codified an administrative structure that risked conflation of executive and legislative power, excluded the phosphate operation – the island's only source of revenue – from legislative oversight, and failed to establish financial transparency regarding the phosphate operation itself and the disposal of phosphate royalty trust funds. The administrative structure to which Nauru's sovereign status attached was built on the foundations of an improvised arrangement struck eighty years before between a Hanseatic trading company and a reluctant German empire.

Chapter 6, 'After Independence: Sovereign Status and the Republic of Nauru' is the conclusion of the book. It provides a brief account of the post-independence trajectory of the Republic, focusing on the outcomes of the Certain Phosphate Lands Case, and the impact of Australia's offshore detention regime on the rule of law in Nauru. The chapter concludes that the now notorious 'failures' of the Nauruan state identified by the Constitutional Review Committee in 2007 – 'failure of institutions'; 'lack of motivation or incentive to preserve wealth for the future, and account for its management'; 'absence of machinery for enforcing accountability and transparency'; 'failure of leaders to learn the lessons of good governance' – must be understood not as originating with the Nauruan community itself but as fundamentally continuous with imperial administrative practices of the pre-independence era.

2

From Trading Post to Protectorate, 1888

2.1 Introduction

The island of Naoerō was incorporated into the German protectorate of the Marshall Islands on the request of a trading firm from Hamburg, Godeffroy & Sohn, nominally to quell a Nauruan 'civil war' that interfered with the firm's copra trade. The island was known then in English records as 'Pleasant Island', and in German, 'Nauru'. In contrast to the sham treaty arrangements with which the protectorate period is often associated, German authority was declared over the island without any performance of agreement with the Nauruan people. Over the course of a single day in October 1888, a German gunboat moored offshore, the Nauruan chiefs were rounded up and held hostage, the population was disarmed and the German flag raised. This chapter redescribes the imperial declaration of protectorate status over Nauru in 1888, and the subsequent agreement between Godeffroy & Sohn and the Reich on an administrative form to govern the island. Commencing with an account of the commercial activity of Hanseatic trading firms in the Pacific and in Africa from the 1870s, the chapter examines the commercial, political and geographic pressures on the Bismarckian Reich that led to the declaration of 'protectorate' status over regions not already claimed by other European powers. Between 1884 and 1888, a disparate set of German corporate trading interests rapidly consolidated into a formal German empire of Schutzgebiete or protectorates. By 1888 the German empire included South West Africa, East Africa, Togoland, Cameroon, German New Guinea and the Marshall Islands in the Western Pacific. Disquiet in the Australasian colonies at the British Imperial government's laissez-faire response to the formalisation of German imperialism in the Pacific invigorated political momentum towards federation of the colonies as a means of assuming local control over external affairs powers.

The chapter then moves to revisit the reinvigoration of the protectorate form in the law of nations of the late nineteenth century. Whereas classical conceptualisations of protectorate status arose from an agreement between unequal sovereigns for 'protection' of the weaker party, in the late nineteenth century the label was increasingly used to describe a variety of imperial arrangements in which concepts of sovereignty, territory and property remained ambivalent, if not incoherent. In the Nauruan case, not only was a treaty arrangement or indeed any contemplation of Nauruan sovereignty absent; the German protectorate was explicitly intended to 'protect' not the Nauruan population, but German trading interests on the island, whilst minimising the expenditure of direct administration by the Reich. In general, the late nineteenth-century German protectorates were a unique imperial experiment – in most cases an attempt to territorialise consular jurisdiction, with delegated executive control vesting in German companies themselves, with minimal subsidisation and little to no legislative oversight. In the late 1880s and 1890s, the Institut de droit international attempted to extract some conceptual coherence from the wave of protectorates declared after the Berlin Conference on the Congo. The chapter concludes, however, that these were largely ex post facto attempts to attribute international legal design to a diverse series of ad hoc executive decisions reactive to corporate lobbying. The conceptual logic of international law was thus of minor concern in the assertion of German legal authority over Nauru. However, the pragmatic arrangement agreed upon between the Reich and the Jaluit Gesellschaft – the company created by Godeffroy & Sohn to take on the administration of the Marshall Islands Protectorate – laid the structural foundations on which the imperial and then international administration of Nauru was to develop over the twentieth century. That form worked not only to concentrate executive authority in a single corporate office, thereby confounding jurisdictional delineations between private and public authority, but also to delineate a distribution of real and mineral property rights between the company, the Reich and the Nauruan people that was to endure for eighty years.

2.2   1884: the DHPG Pays its First Dividend

Eighteen eighty-four was a momentous year in German imperial history. The year is commonly understood to mark the belated debut of the new Reich – confederated thirteen years previous in 1871 with former Minister-President of Prussia, Otto von Bismarck, appointed as

2.2 1884: THE DHPG PAYS ITS FIRST DIVIDEND

Chancellor – into the arena of late nineteenth-century high imperial competition. The list of events that amount to a beginning are indisputably significant. German intervention in Africa was formally consolidated in June 1884. In response to the repeated requests of Bremen tobacco merchant and colonial entrepreneur F. A. E. Lüderitz, the Imperial flag was hoisted in the port of Angra Pequeña, north of the Cape Colony. 'Lüderitzland' was soon renamed German South West Africa, becoming the first German protectorate.[1] A month later, in July 1884, the German protectorates of Togo and Cameroon were declared. That same year, Carl Peters incorporated the Gesellschaft für Deutsche Kolonisation or Society for German Colonisation in Berlin. In 1885 Peters' Society was renamed the Deutsch-Ostafrikanische Gesellschaft, the German East Africa Company, granted an imperial charter and delegated the authority to administer a new protectorate declared over the regions of East Africa in which Peters claimed treaties with local rulers – an expanse that eventually took in contemporary Rwanda, Burundi and areas of Tanzania.[2] On the other side of the world in the Pacific, in November 1884 a German protectorate was declared over northeastern New Guinea. That same month, the Berlin Conference on the Congo began. From November 1884 to February 1885, the 'Powers' of Germany, Britain, France, Italy, Belgium, Spain, Denmark, the Netherlands, the Ottoman Empire and the United States met in Berlin to agree upon rules of territorial acquisition in Central Africa. The culmination of the Conference in the General Act of 1885 purported to provide a legal framework for further imperial expansion in Africa, recognising at the same time the Congo Free State as the private property of Belgian King Leopold's Association internationale du Congo.[3]

However, the reason this account of imperial administration in Nauru commences in 1884 is less obvious. In 1884 a Hamburg trading firm operating in Samoa and the Marshall Islands chains in the Western Pacific paid out its first dividend of 4 per cent to holders of preference shares back in Hamburg.[4] The firm, the Deutsche Handels- und

---

[1] William Osgood Aydelotte, *Bismarck and British Colonial Policy: The Problem of South West Africa 1883–1885*, 2nd ed. (London: Russell and Russell, 1970).

[2] Woodruff D. Smith, *The German Colonial Empire* (North Carolina: University of North Carolina Press, 1978), 92–9.

[3] General Act of the Conference of Berlin concerning the Congo (entered into force 26 February 1885), reproduced in (1909) 3 *American Journal of International Law*, 7.

[4] Stewart Firth, 'German Firms in the Western Pacific Islands 1857–1914' (1973) 8 *Journal of Pacific History*, 10–28.

Plantagen-Gesellschaft der Südsee-Inseln, or German Trading and Plantation Company of the South Sea Islands (DHPG) had been established to take over the Pacific interests of Godeffroy & Sohn, the largest of a group of Hamburg trading firms that had been operating in the Pacific since the mid-nineteenth century.[5] The commercial activity of the DHPG in the Western Pacific region led directly to the inclusion of the island of Nauru in the German empire's purview. Historians of the period have observed that were it not for the established presence of the DHPG and other Hanseatic firms in the Western Pacific, the entire region would have been of little to no interest to the new Reich at all.[6] The financial success or otherwise of the Hamburg firms in the region was therefore a key condition of possibility of the establishment in 1885 of the Schutzgebiet der Marshall-Inseln, the German Protectorate of the Marshall Islands, into which Nauru was unceremoniously incorporated in 1888.

2.3 The Reluctance of the Bismarckian Reich

In *A Footnote to History: Eight Years of Trouble in Samoa*, Robert Louis Stevenson mocked the Deutsche Handels- und Plantagen-Gesellschaft der Südsee-Inseln for its ponderous title, calling it 'the Long Handle Firm'.[7] Stevenson's weak joke is not without insight. The firm's name is an intriguing historical artefact. The German Trading and Plantation Company of the South Sea Islands was not a public enterprise but a private company, hastily recapitalised in March 1878 by Hamburg banking heir Adolph von Hansemann.[8] The company was established solely for the purpose of taking over the Pacific interests of flailing Hamburg trading firm Godeffroy & Sohn.[9] Godeffroy, a merchant company of longstanding repute, had expanded west from Valparaiso in Chile to install its first Pacific agent in Apia Bay, Samoa, in 1857. Over the next three decades, the

---

[5] Stewart Firth, *New Guinea under the Germans* (Melbourne: Melbourne University Press, 1983); and A. E. Bollard, 'The Financial Adventures of J. C. Godeffroy and Son in the Pacific' (1981) 16 *Journal of Pacific History*, 3–19.

[6] See for example Florence Mann Spoehr, *White Falcon: The House of Godeffroy and its Commercial and Scientific Role in the Pacific* (California: Pacific Books, 1963), vi–vii.

[7] Robert Louis Stevenson, *A Footnote to History: Eight Years of Trouble in Samoa* (New York: Charles Scribner's Sons, 1895), 29.

[8] Firth, 'German Firms in the Western Pacific Islands', 11–13.

[9] W. O. Henderson, *The German Colonial Empire 1884–1919* (London: Frank Cass & Co., 1993), 24–5.

2.3 THE RELUCTANCE OF THE BISMARCKIAN REICH

firm proceeded to inscribe a maritime network of European trading posts across the Western Pacific.[10]

It is tempting to seize on the change in company title from 'Godeffroy & Sohn' to the 'German Trading and Plantation Company of the South Sea Islands' as representative of the consolidation of the German Confederation in 1871. Stevenson at least seems to have regarded the DHPG as a German nationalist enterprise, describing Hansemann's acquisition of the Godeffroy interests as a move to prevent those interests falling into the hands of London finance house, Baring Brothers.[11] Whatever Stevenson's opinion, the political power Hansemann sought to consolidate by taking over Godeffroy's Pacific interests in this way was not necessarily that of the new German confederation. The Disconto-Gesellschaft, the family bank Adolph von Hansemann directed after inheriting the role from his father David, was a Hamburg institution that predated German confederation. The Hansemann family were comfortable mixing banking and high politics: David Hansemann had served as the Prussian Minister for Foreign Affairs prior to confederation in 1871. Karl Marx had written of David Hansemann in 1858 that '(a)t a time when the joint-stock company was still a *rara avis* in Germany, he had the ambition of becoming a German Hudson, and proved perfectly adept in that sort of jobbery'.[12] Under the directorship of the 'German Hudson', the Disconto-Gesellschaft assisted Bismarck in financing the French indemnity after the Franco-Prussian War of 1870–1.[13] The Hansemann family bank had also moved early to finance colonial entrepreneurs, German and otherwise, in their fledging turns in Africa: it had financed Lüderitz's operations in Angra Pequeña.[14] The Hansemann family was to maintain its elite status in German finance well into the twentieth century; and in 1929, the Disconto-Gesellschaft merged with the Deutsche Bank.[15]

---

[10] Ibid., 22; and Firth, 'German Firms in the Western Pacific Islands', 11.

[11] Stevenson, *Footnote to History*, 14; Henderson, *German Colonial Empire*, 68.

[12] Karl Marx, 'The New Ministry', *The New York Tribune* (New York), 27 November 1858, reprinted in Karl Marx and Frederick Engels, *Collected Works: Volume 16, 1858–1860*, trans. Richard Dixon, Henry Mins and Salo Ryazanskaya (Chadwell Heath: Lawrence & Wishart, 2010), 102.

[13] See John Martin Kleeberg, 'The *Disconto-Gesellschaft* and German Industrialization: A Critical Examination of the Career of a German Universal Bank 1851-1914' (1988), unpublished PhD thesis, University of Oxford, 195.

[14] The South West Africa Company was part-financed by the Disconto-Gesellschaft. Richard A. Voeltz, *German Colonialism and the South West Africa Company, 1894–1914* (Ohio: Ohio University Center for International Studies, 1988), 1, 83.

[15] Both banks' annual reports for this period are available in German via the Historical Association of the Deutsche Bank at www.bankgeschichte.de/en/content/2448.html.

Yet when Adolph von Hansemann approached Chancellor Bismarck in 1880 with a plan to refinance Godeffroy interests in the Pacific that included modest state funding, the proposal was voted down by the Reichstag.[16] In 1880 public financial support of commercial activity outside sovereign territory was politically unpalatable to Bismarck. Hansemann was stung by the rejection but, determined to extend his family interests into the South Seas, proceeded to use his Hanseatic pedigree to raise the private equity required to refinance Godeffroy's Pacific interests and establish the DHPG. Hansemann later managed via personal representations to Bismarck to secure a modest shipping subsidy for the company's Pacific activity.[17] Despite Stevenson's conflation of German state and company, then, the interests of the DHPG were thus not clearly or necessarily aligned with those of the new German state.[18] It is more likely Hansemann and the DHPG were continuing to further the shared interests of the community of Hamburg investors, traders, bankers and entrepreneurs to which both the Disconto-Gesellschaft and Godeffroy & Sohn belonged: a community whose collective conduct was informed not by the new German Confederation but by five centuries of organisation under the Hansa.

2.4 Hamburg Trading Firms and the Legacy of the Hansa

The word 'Hansa' has Gothic origins, with instances of usage indicating a dual etymology: both a troop or company, and a tax on commodities.[19] As a proper noun, it refers to the medieval organisation of northern German towns which began to record itself as the *Hansa Theutonicorum* or 'Teutonic Hansa' in the thirteenth century, waxing and waning over a lifespan that officially ended with its final council in Lübeck in 1669, twenty years after the peace of Westphalia.[20] The history of the Hansa and its status and function in

---

[16] Henderson, *German Colonial Empire*, 68.
[17] Mary Henderson, *Origins of Modern German Colonialism* (New York: Howard Fertig, 1974), 115–16.
[18] As Mary Henderson notes, '(i)t was of course to be expected that the German bankers, already much interested in South Sea enterprises, would intervene and come to the rescue; but that they would do so purely on patriotic and national grounds was unlikely'. Ibid., 115.
[19] E. Gee Nash, *The Hansa: Its History and Romance* (London: Bodley Head, 1929), 1; Rolf Hammel-Kiesow, 'The Early Hansas' in Donald J. Harreld (ed.), *Companion to the Hanseatic League* (Leiden: Brill, 2015), 15–63.
[20] For the seminal history of the Hansa in English, see Phillipe Dollinger, *The German Hansa* (London: Routledge, 1999), see esp. Chapter 3 'Towards the Hansa of the Towns

2.4 HAMBURG TRADING FIRMS; LEGACY OF THE HANSA

medieval Europe is underexplored in English historical texts – a noted curiosity in itself, given the organisation's longevity and importance to the commercial development of a sweeping arc of the northern hemisphere.[21]

As a mode of medieval European political authority, the Hansa was unique. Its institutional specificity has been so eclipsed by the subsequent rise of the modern nation-state that historical accounts tend towards anachronism, either figuring the Hansa into a teleology of modern federalism, or characterising its function as merely economic.[22] In broad terms, the Hansa was an association of self-selecting medieval cities with northern German origins that expanded into Scandinavia, Belgium, central Europe, and at its furthest reaches, to England and Russia. Sailors and merchants from Lübeck, Cologne, Bremen and Hamburg had long engaged in North Sea and Baltic trade, exploiting their location around the Rhine, Weser and Elbe riverine region around the isthmus of Schleswig between the two seas.[23] Over the twelfth and thirteenth centuries, these merchants' trade consisted largely of the import and export of low-value-added products. Wine and cloth were exported to England and northern Europe in exchange for wool and salt, which were in turn traded to eastern Europe in exchange for goods including wax and furs, and occasionally luxury goods from East Asia.[24] Hanseatic business was strictly trade. The association engaged neither in the regulation of labour, nor in production of goods. Marx later figured that the Hanseatic form of merchant trading preceded capitalist modes of production, distinguished by the creation of surplus value in commodity production via exploitative labour relations.[25]

(c.1250 – c.1350)' and Chapter 14 'Renewal and Eclipse (1550–1669)'. See also Justyna Wubs-Mrozewicz, 'The Hanse in Medieval and Early Modern Europe: An Introduction' in Stuart Jenks and Justyna Wubs-Mrozewicz (eds.) *The Hanse in Medieval and Early Modern Europe* (Leiden: Brill, 2012), 1.

[21] Dollinger, *The German Hansa*, xvii–xxii; and Donald J. Harreld, 'Introduction' in Harreld (ed.), *Companion to the Hanseatic League*, 1–5.

[22] Zimmern lauded the Hansa as an 'early representative of that federal spirit ... best understood and most thoroughly carried out' in the United States. Helen Zimmern, *The Hansa Towns* (London: T. Fisher Unwin, 1891). For a recent treatment of historiographical issues, see Stuart Jenks, 'Conclusion' in Jenks and Wubs-Mrozewicz (eds.) *The Hanse*, 255–81.

[23] Carsten Jahnke, 'The Baltic Trade' in Donald J. Harreld (ed.), *Companion to the Hanseatic League*, 194–240.

[24] Dollinger, *The German Hansa*, 5–7; Johannes Schildhauer, *The Hansa: History and Culture* (Leipzig: Edition Leipzig, 1985), 42.

[25] Karl Marx, *Capital: A Critical Analysis of Capitalist Production*, ed. Frederick Engels, trans. Samuel Moore and Edward Aveling (New York and London: Appleton & Co,

2 FROM TRADING POST TO PROTECTORATE, 1888

The Hansa's authority over its member cities coexisted – seemingly without overt conflict – with both the authority of the Holy Roman Empire and the feudal hierarchy of kings and lords.[26] However, the association was not reducible to a mere mercantile or trade area, supplementary or subject to political rule from elsewhere.[27] At its peak in the fourteenth century, the Hansa was an institution regulating the internal affairs and external relations of an estimated two hundred cities across Northern Europe. Spruyt thus argues that the Hansa was not simply an economic association: it was an institutional competitor to the mode of state sovereignty that developed, in his schema at least, in Capetian France over a similar historical period.[28] The Hansa was neither a territorial nor a sovereign form of jurisdiction, at least not in the modern sense.[29] Yet it regulated the relations of cities from Dinant in contemporary Belgium to Dorpat in contemporary Estonia, with stations from London to Moscow.[30] Its authority was not regarded as mutually exclusive with that of the Holy Roman Empire, and many of its member cities continued to owe allegiance to both empire and local lords.[31]

From a legal perspective, then, Hanseatic authority was unique.[32] The essential nature of the Hansa was its radical plurality. According to Ebel, Hanseatic law consisted of dispensations that 'were in a position to create or did create a joint, uniform system for the economic activity of the Hansa, complementary to, mediating between or superior to the individual charters of Hanseatic towns'.[33] Whilst its authority is not readily reducible to modern jurisdictional categories, what is certain about the Hansa is that it created and maintained a detailed culture of regulations

---

1889), 166–74. Also Lars Maischak, *German Merchants in the Nineteenth Century Atlantic* (Cambridge: Cambridge University Press, 2013), xix.

[26] Henrik Spruyt, *The Sovereign State and its Competitors: An Analysis of Systems Change* (Princeton: Princeton University Press, 1994), 123–4.

[27] Ulf Christian Ewert and Stephan Selzer, 'Social Networks' in Harreld (ed.), *Companion to the Hanseatic League*, 162–93.

[28] See generally Spruyt, *Sovereign State and its Competitors*, 109–29.

[29] Anne Orford, 'Jurisdiction without Territory: From the Holy Roman Empire to the Responsibility to Protect' (2009) 30 *Michigan Journal of International Law*, 981–1015. On the development of the concept of territory in European thought, see Stuart Elden, *The Birth of Territory* (Chicago: Chicago University Press, 2013).

[30] Schildhauer, *The Hansa*, 10–11. On the Hansa in England, see Ian D. Colvin, *The Germans in England 1066-1598* (London: The National Review, 1915).

[31] Spruyt, *Sovereign State and its Competitors*, 123–4.

[32] Dollinger describes the Hansa as 'an anomalous institution which puzzled contemporary jurists', including the English Privy Council. Dollinger, *The German Hansa*, xvii, 88.

[33] Schildhauer, *The Hansa*, 214.

2.4 HAMBURG TRADING FIRMS; LEGACY OF THE HANSA

concerning commercial practice, communal trade protections and common modes of measure and comparative statistics.[34] From a Foucauldian perspective, this standardisation of measures was itself constitutive of Hanseatic authority.[35] The Hanseatic community sustained a continuous existence into the seventeenth century, albeit with a gradually dwindling constituency. By 1603, member cities had shrunk to only fifty.[36] Its functional demise is usually attributed to the violent interruptions to trade during the Thirty Years War from 1618.[37] By the time of the peace of Westphalia in 1648, the Hanseatic community had shrunk back to its three core cities of Lübeck, Bremen and Hamburg. The last Diet was held in Lübeck in 1669, and delegates of other towns and cities attended primarily to give formal notification of their withdrawal.[38] Its demise seems to have been met with indifference by the Westphalian states, but the Hansa was not without its mourners. In 1670, Leibnitz counselled imperial authorities to foster a Hanseatic revival to bolster German trade, recovering only slowly after the war.[39]

Despite the demise of the Hansa as a functioning collective by the mid-seventeenth century, its stronghold cities of Lübeck, Bremen and Hamburg managed to maintain almost unbroken independence well into the nineteenth century against a series of imperial and confederate advances. After the formal dissolution of the Holy Roman Empire in 1806, the three Hanseatic cities were briefly annexed into the Napoleonic Empire.[40] They regained their independence in the Congress of Vienna in 1815, and in the first German confederation or Deutscher Bund, enshrined in the German Federal Act of 8 June 1815, Hamburg, Bremen and Lübeck were recognised as free cities, along with thirty-five German states and one additional free city, Frankfurt.[41] The 1815

---

[34] Ibid., 206–9. Also Mike Burkhardt, 'Business as Usual? A Critical Investigation of the Hanseatic Pound Toll Lists' in Jenks and Wubs-Mrozewicz (eds.) *The Hanse*, 215–38.

[35] Michel Foucault, *The Order of Things: An Archaeology of the Human Sciences*, reissue ed. (London: Vintage Books, 1994), 196–200.

[36] Zimmern, *The Hansa Towns*, 354; Marie-Louise Pelus Kaplan, 'Mobility and Business Enterprise in the Hanseatic World: Trade Networks and Entrepreneurial Techniques: Sixteenth and Seventeenth Centuries' in Jenks and Wubs-Mrozewicz (eds.) *The Hanse*, 239–94.

[37] Michael North, 'The Hanseatic League in the Early Modern Period' in Harreld (ed.), *Companion to the Hanseatic League*, 101.

[38] Ibid., 117; Zimmern, *The Hansa Towns*, 368.

[39] Zimmern, *The Hansa Towns*, 369.

[40] Mark Jarrett, *The Congress of Vienna and its Legacy: War and Great Power Diplomacy after Napoleon* (London: I.B. Tauris & Co, 2013), 32.

[41] *Deutsche Bundesakte* [German Federal Act] 8 June 1815.

Deutscher Bund echoed key elements of the Hanseatic structure: it had no head of state or parliament, only a Diet which wielded no power over the sovereign rulers of each state.[42]

Over the mid-nineteenth century, partisan efforts to unite German-speaking states, provinces and cities in a stronger body politic gained political momentum, escalating into the Franco-Prussian War of 1870-1. Between 1867 and 1871, Prussia under Kaiser Wilhelm I spearheaded a smaller union of northern German provinces than had been attempted in the 1815 Deutscher Bund, excluding the Austro-Hungarian empire altogether.[43] In 1871 the Kaiser's Minister-President, Otto von Bismarck, was installed as Prime Minister and Chancellor of the new German Confederation.[44] In the new Imperial Constitution, the last three Hanseatic cities of Hamburg, Bremen and Lübeck were recognised as distinct political entities, and were each given a single representative seat in the new Bundesrat.[45] These were the only cities to be so recognised among the collection of Prussian and states and districts that comprised the new lower house of the legislature.[46] Article 34 of the Imperial Constitution provided that '(t)he Hanseatic towns of Bremen and Hamburg, with so much of their own or of the adjacent territory as may be needful for the purpose, remain as free ports outside the common customs area until they apply to be admitted therein'.[47] Hamburg and Bremen did not cede control of their economic affairs to the German federation until 1888 – four years after the DHPG paid its first dividend.

2.5 Hanseatic Firms in the Pacific

The expansion of Hamburg firms into the Western Pacific, and the political balance between private equity and state subsidy, is thus better understood not as a peripheral frontier in the rapid expansion of 'the German empire' in the late nineteenth century but as an episode in a far longer history of the shift from one form of European imperialism towards another – from the non-centralised merchant trade network

---

[42] Lynn Abrams, *Bismarck and the German Empire 1871-1918*, 2nd ed. (London and New York: Routledge, 2006), 9.
[43] Theodore S. Hamerow, *Social Foundations of German Unification 1858-1871, Volume I: Ideas and Institutions* (Princeton: Princeton University Press, 1969).
[44] Abrams, *Bismarck and the German Empire*, 26-8; and Jonathan Steinberg, *Bismarck: A Life* (Oxford: Oxford University Press, 309-11).
[45] *Die Reichsverfassung* [Imperial Constitution of 1871], arts. 1 and 6.
[46] Ibid.
[47] Ibid., art. 34.

run from the Hanseatic cities, towards the centralised state imperialism of the new Reich. Bismarck himself noted in a speech to the Reichstag that Hanseatic enterprise had prompted German imperial expansion: '(w)e were first induced, owing to the enterprise of the Hanseatic people – beginning with land purchases and leading to requests for imperial protection – to consider whether we could promise protection to the extent desired'.[48] As Giordani stated in 1916, 'the origins of German colonial expansion are undoubtedly to be sought in the *Hanse* or *Hanseatic League*',[49] an observation moderated by Smith in 1978: 'when colonial acquisition did occur after 1883, the locations of Hanseatic trading interests often provided guides to the territories to be claimed'.[50]

Hanseatic companies had established trade networks reaching far beyond the Hansa's European purview well before the new Confederation in 1871. By 1866 Hamburg firms alone maintained a web of 279 trading outposts around the world.[51] Godeffroy & Sohn entered the Pacific westward from Valparaiso in 1857; but given the global scope of its network, it could just as easily have come eastward from South East Asia. By the mid-nineteenth century, the firm had travelled from the Hanseatic ports westward around the Horn of Africa to South America, and eastward to Cochin China (now Vietnam), leaving only the Pacific to traverse latitudinally.[52] In 1857 the firm's head, Johann Cesar Godeffroy IV, instructed its agent in Valparaiso to begin making preparations to set up a factor in Samoa.[53] The new trade Godeffroy IV had set his sights upon was copra. Copra was a raw material that yielded two products of increasing value in mid-nineteenth-century trade – coconut oil and coconut meal.[54] The global copra trade boomed during European agricultural industrialisation in the later nineteenth century. Coconut oil, used primarily for cooking, is slow to rancidify, making it an ideal export-import product; and coconut meal found a market as low-cost, high-energy feed for livestock.

---

[48] Theodore S. Hamerow (ed.), *The Age of Bismarck: Documents and Interpretations* (New York: Harper & Row, 1973), 305.
[49] Paolo Giordani, *The German Colonial Empire: Its Beginning and Ending*, trans. Gustavus W. Hamilton (London: G. Bell and Sons, 1916), 1.
[50] Smith, *German Colonial Empire*, 8.
[51] Sebastian Conrad, *German Colonialism: A Short History* (Cambridge: Cambridge University Press, 2012), 25.
[52] Bollard, 'Financial Adventures of J. C. Godeffroy and Son', 3–4.
[53] Firth, 'German Firms in the Western Pacific Islands', 11–12.
[54] Ibid., 12.

The Godeffroy agent first installed at Apia Bay in Samoa was experienced firm trader August Unshelm.[55] Unshelm began to build a network, installing company agents across the smaller islands of the Western Pacific, including those with and without established European presence. Soon Godeffroy agents spread thinly but widely across the Pacific islands, including Samoa, Tonga, Wallis and Futuna, Niue, the British Gilbert and Ellice groups, the Spanish Carolines and the Marshall Islands. The firm's agents focused first on developing a trade in coconut oil, pressed by local islanders and barrelled by the company, but soon shifted to exporting copra itself in sacks, as the dried copra price was commensurate with that of oil and easier to handle.[56] The firm's Pacific agents built lines of supply by demonstrating a kiln-based drying technique to islanders, and trading arms, ammunition and alcohol for the dried copra produced.[57] Where local stores had not been established by other companies, Godeffroy set up company stores that offered store credit to islanders in exchange for future copra yields, and for securities over copra-producing land.[58] Exports were sent out in three directions: to Hamburg, to Valparaiso and to Sydney.[59]

The initial decade of Godeffroy's copra trade in the Western Pacific thus relied heavily on islanders to produce copra surplus to their own needs, as well as their willingness to trade that copra for Godeffroy-imported goods and company credit.[60] The absence of any initial attempts by Godeffroy agents to directly employ local labour, acquire land, or engage in plantation reflected the firm's Hanseatic inheritance: the Hansa had never engaged in direct employment or commodity production, engaging almost exclusively in commodity circulation.[61] Well into the later nineteenth century, the Godeffroys avoided investment in property and infrastructure 'beyond what was absolutely necessary', as it interrupted the company's liquidity, which was required to shift rapidly between commodities in response to price volatility.[62]

---

[55] Bollard, 'Financial Adventures of J. C. Godeffroy and Son', 3–4.
[56] Ibid., 5–6.
[57] Ibid., 6.
[58] Ibid., 5. In Nauru, the small German firm A. Capelle & Co had established a store prior to the arrival of Godeffroy; see Firth, 'German Firms in the Western Pacific Islands', 13. The Capelle store remains the major retailer in Nauru.
[59] Jean Ingram Brookes, *International Rivalry in the Pacific Islands 1800–1875* (Berkeley: University of California Press 1941), 290.
[60] Bollard, 'Financial Adventures of J C Godeffroy and Son', 5.
[61] Smith, *German Colonial Empire*, 38.
[62] Spoehr, *White Falcon*, 25.

Yet the Hanseatic firms' practices began to change in the Pacific over the 1860s and 1870s. Godeffroy established its first plantation in Samoa in 1865, planting both copra and cotton. The price of cotton had increased sharply following the drop in North American production over the course of the Civil War, and the formal abolition of slavery in the United States.[63] Coconut palms, which take around a decade to mature, were planted between the cotton rows. Godeffroy agents attempted to recruit Samoans as plantation labourers, yet were confounded by the Samoans' apparent 'reluctance to work'.[64] The firm quickly resorted to buying labour through the Pacific indentured labour trade, which came to be known as 'blackbirding'.[65] The indenture and slavery of islanders from eastern New Guinea to feed the Pacific labour trade persisted as late as the 1940s.[66] By 1877 Godeffroy had come to dominate import and export on Samoa and Tonga, making it the strongest German firm in the Pacific.[67] The firm's success in the region is attributed both to its decentralised mode of operations and its ingenuity in raising the end price of copra, and its comparatively easy access via Hanseatic banks including Hansemann's Disconto-Gesellschaft to the finance required to set up those operations.[68]

However, the firm's outlook began to take a turn for the worse under the management of Johann Cesar Godeffroy VI, who took a more bullish approach to the old family business than had his grandfather.[69] Godeffroy VI's shift away from old Hanseatic practices and towards direct capital investment in labour and plantation was abrupt, and poorly managed, coming too late to compete with British, French, Spanish and North American competition in the Pacific.[70] By the time the Hanseatic

---

[63] Firth, 'German Firms in the Western Pacific Islands', 14.
[64] Peter J. Hempenstall, *Pacific Islanders under German Rule: A Study in the Meaning of Colonial Resistance* (Canberra: Australian National University Press, 1978), 18.
[65] See Tracey Banivanua Mar, *Violence and Colonial Dialogue: The Australian-Pacific Indentured Labor Trade* (Honolulu: University of Hawai'i Press, 2007); and E. V. Stevens, 'Blackbirding: A Brief History of South Sea Islands Labour Traffic and the Vessels Engaged in It' (1950) 4 *Historical Society Journal*, 361–403. See also Part 5, 'Agriculture, Labour and Phosphate in the Pacific' in Chapter 3, 'From Protectorate to Mandate, 1920'.
[66] Banivanua Mar, *Violence and Colonial Dialogue*.
[67] Firth, 'German Firms in the Western Pacific Islands', 14.
[68] Bollard praises the firm's unconventionality as key to its success, whereas Firth emphasises its access to capital: Bollard, 'Financial Adventures of J. C. Godeffroy and Son', 4–5; Firth, 'German Firms in the Western Pacific Islands', 11–12.
[69] Spoehr, *White Falcon*, 3.
[70] Hempenstall, *Pacific Islanders under German Rule*, 17; see also Firth, 'German Firms in the Western Pacific Islands', 15.

firms had arrived, other empires had not only developed their own trading relations, mature plantations and infrastructure, but had also established formal colonies, protectorates and consular networks.[71] British imperialism in the region had a seventy-year head start on the Hanseatic firms. The Australasian colonies had been established from the late 1780s, followed by New Zealand in 1840 and Fiji in 1874. The French were established in Tahiti to the east of Godeffroy's foothold in Samoa, as well as in New Caledonia to the west; the Spanish, in the Philippines and the Caroline Islands to the northwest; and the North Americans, in Samoa too, as well as the Sandwich Islands (later Hawai'i) to the north.

In 1878 Godeffroy VI made two desperate moves. He sought to diversify by investing heavily in the European speculative mining market; and at the same time, he rolled all of the firm's Pacific interests into a new company, the Deutsche Handels- und Plantagen-Gesellschaft der Südsee-Inseln. His aim was a public share offer. Subscription, however, was weak, even in the firm's hometown of Hamburg.[72] Unable to secure the private equity needed to finance the firm's risky new direction, Godeffroy VI sought support from the Imperial Foreign Office in the form of a mid-term guarantee on the DHPG share price. Bismarck supported the idea enough to allow a Bill to go before the Bundesrat, but it was voted down.[73] Staring down the barrel of insolvency, Godeffroy VI accepted a loan offer from Barings London, secured against DHPG shares.[74] Only at the point of collapse did Hansemann swoop in to rescue the DHPG, fronting the five million marks required to buy Barings out of the DHPG.[75]

It took the DHPG five years from 1879 to 1884 to turn a profit and pay a dividend on its shares. The firm was publicly listed, but majority-owned by Hansemann, his Hamburg banking associates and members of the Godeffroy family.[76] That the DHPG was able to phoenix out of the ruins of Godeffroy & Sohn and survive to turn a profit, at a time when the firm's Pacific interests were already on the wane, was a notable

[71] For a survey of colonial presence in the Pacific in the earlier nineteenth century, see Brookes, *International Rivalry in the Pacific Islands*.
[72] According to Spoehr, not a single share was sold on the open market. Spoehr, *White Falcon*, 47.
[73] James Wycliffe Headlam, *Bismarck and the Foundation of the German Empire* (New York: G. P. Putnam's Sons, 1899), 427; Henderson, *Modern German Colonialism*, 113; Henderson, *German Colonial Empire*, 25.
[74] Henderson, *Modern German Colonialism*, 113–14.
[75] Henderson, *German Colonial Empire*, 24–5, 68.
[76] Ibid., 25.

achievement. But its success pointed to a factor more significant than the financial cunning of Hansemann, son of the 'German Hudson': between 1879 and 1884, German foreign policy underwent a momentous shift. Whereas political support for German corporate enterprise in the Pacific had proven difficult for Godeffroy VI to secure in 1878, the attitude of both Bismarck and the Reichstag had changed rapidly over the next few years.

2.6 The Reich, Imperial Expansion and the Berlin Conference of 1884

That it was Bismarck, famously underwhelmed by the prospect of German imperial expansion outside of Europe, who convened the Berlin West Africa Conference in November 1884 indicates at the very least the significance of the debate over the law of territorial acquisition for European realpolitik. A few months earlier, in August 1884, Bismarck had capitulated to Lüderitz's requests for official protection of his interests in Angra Pequeña on the Atlantic coast of Africa, northwest of the Cape Colony. Bismarck issued a declaration designating the areas around Angra Pequeña that Lüderitz claimed – on the basis of 'treaties' obtained from local 'chiefs' – as under the protection of the Reich.[77] Precisely what 'protection' meant, however, was unclear. Protectorate status was both a novelty in German public law and an ambiguous area in the European law of nations. In the early 1880s there was little explicit consensus or uniform practice around the legal basis, mode of establishment or rights and obligations that pertained to protectorate status. The Berlin Conference was convened primarily to settle by diplomatic means the legitimacy or otherwise of the European powers' various imperial claims in the African continent. Those claims had taken diverse forms, including direct colonial claims as well as declarations of protection.[78]

As Craven has observed, the historical and legal significance of the Berlin Conference is a matter of ongoing debate.[79] The General Act with which it concluded provided one of the only collective European

---

[77] Aydelotte, *Bismarck and British Colonial Policy*, 121; Smith, *The German Colonial Empire*, 28.
[78] See generally Stig Förster, Wolfgang J. Mommsen and Ronald Robinson (eds.), *Bismarck, Europe, and Africa: The Berlin Africa Conference 1884–1885 and the Onset of Partition* (Oxford: Oxford University Press, 1988).
[79] Matthew Craven, 'Between Law and History: The Berlin Conference of 1884–1885 and the Logic of Free Trade' (2015) 3 *London Review of International Law*, 31–59.

agreements on the legal concept of the protectorate.[80] Whilst the agenda of the Conference focused on questions of free trade in the Congo basin and freedom of navigation on the Congo and Niger Rivers, the general question of the actual legal distinction between concepts of colonial occupation and protection emerged as a central issue. During the Conference, the debate centred primarily on the formal means by which 'new occupations on the African coasts' were to be deemed 'effective'.[81] However, the rights and obligations pertaining to 'mere' declarations of protection became the comparator against which those of occupation were defined.

Similarly to the Reich, the British Imperial government was loath to extend formal colonial status to company-driven concerns in Africa. Over the 1860s and 1870s, the Imperial government demonstrated a preference for using consular jurisdiction to support British corporate enterprise outside of sovereign territory.[82] Consular jurisdiction, consolidated in the Foreign Jurisdiction Act of 1843, had proven crucial to the ascension of British economic imperialism over the nineteenth century.[83] However, the personal basis of consular jurisdiction was not sufficient to claim rights over foreign territory sufficient to exclude other European powers, a benchmark upon which Bismarck had insisted in negotiations with the British Imperial government over Southern Africa.[84] For highly leveraged European commercial enterprises in Africa and the Pacific, the legal uncertainty over the territorial efficacy of consular jurisdiction was an added commercial risk of which they increasingly complained.[85]

Unable to reach agreement, the General Act of 1885 only indirectly addressed the legal distinction between occupation and protection.[86]

---

[80] Ibid., 32-3.
[81] Ibid., 37.
[82] W. Ross Johnston, *Sovereignty and Protection: A Study of British Jurisdictional Imperialism in the Late Nineteenth Century* (Durham: Duke University Press, 1973), 167-72.
[83] Craven, 'Between Law and History', 46. Koskenniemi cites Macaulay's judgment of Indian rule in 1833: '(t)o trade with civilized men is infinitely more profitable than to govern savages'. Martti Koskenniemi, *Gentle Civilizer of Nations: The Rise and Fall of International Law 1870-1960* (Cambridge: Cambridge University Press, 2004), 111.
[84] Craven, 'Between Law and History', 46. See also Daniel Margolies, Umut Özsu, Maia Pal and Ntina Tzouvala (eds.), *The Extraterritoriality of Law: History, Theory, Politics* (London: Routledge 2018).
[85] Mark Frank Lindley, *Acquisition and Government of Backward Territory in International Law* (New York: Longmans Green, 1926), 143-4.
[86] Andrew Fitzmaurice, *Sovereignty, Property and Empire 1500-2000* (Cambridge: Cambridge University Press, 2014), 283-4.

2.1 'Die Südsee ist das Mittelmeer der Zukunft' [The South Sea is the Mediterranean of the Future], from *Kladderadatsch*, 13 July 1884. Credit: Bildarchiv Preußischer Kulturbesitz, Staatsbibliothek zu Berlin.

Article 34 provided that notification was to be given to the other Signatory Powers of any new claims of possession or protectorate on the African coasts.[87] Article 35 provided that Powers claiming occupation recognised an obligation to 'insure the establishment of authority' in occupied areas 'sufficient to protect existing rights'.[88] The Act was silent on obligations arising from protectorate claims. This negative exclusion of protectorates from obligations of 'effective occupation' agreed upon in Article 35 was the extent of agreement on the distinction between colony and protectorate. But it was enough to prompt a wave of protectorate declarations, not only across Africa but also across the Pacific and Asia.[89]

2.7 The Concept of the Protectorate

As jurists of the time were quick to assert, the concept of the protectorate had existed well before the late nineteenth century. Lindley later declared that '(t)he assumption by a comparatively powerful state of the duty of protecting a weaker state is an institution of considerable antiquity'.[90] English jurist Travers Twiss opined on the origin of treaties of protection, focusing on the agreement entered into by the Numidians with the Romans, by which the Numidians purportedly regarded themselves as having maintained their independence by placing themselves under a relation of Roman patronage.[91] In the classical law of nations, a treaty of protection was a treaty of unequal alliance.[92] However, the concept was re-enlivened in the late nineteenth century, in the conceptual space between consular and colonial jurisdiction. Consular jurisdiction protected the rights of sovereign subjects in foreign territory recognised as under the sovereignty of another state. Colonial jurisdiction purported to extend sovereignty over territory outside metropolitan jurisdiction. It was thus exclusive to claims both of local sovereignty and of annexation by other powers.

Over the 1880s and 1890s, the European powers produced a wave of treaties of protection over regions of Africa, the Pacific and parts of Asia.

---

[87] General Act of the Conference of Berlin.
[88] Ibid.
[89] Ibid.; and Craven, 'Between Law and History', 44.
[90] Lindley, *Acquisition and Government of Backward Territory*, 181.
[91] Travers Twiss, *Law of Nations Considered as Independent Political Communities – On the Rights and Duties of States in Time of Peace*, 2nd ed. (Oxford: Clarendon Press, 1884), 427.
[92] Matthew Craven, 'What Happened to Unequal Treaties? The Continuities of Informal Empire' (2005) 74 *Nordic Journal of International Law*, 335–82.

2.7 THE CONCEPT OF THE PROTECTORATE

Quite apart from the legitimacy of the treaties themselves, the legal content of relations of protection remained ambiguous.[93] The basic characteristic of the protectorate was the assumption by the 'protecting' power of the conduct of the 'protected' region's 'external sovereignty'.[94] By implication, the protected region maintained notional control over its internal affairs, but was prevented from engaging in diplomatic or trade relations with other European states.[95] Jenkyns described this division between external and internal sovereignty as a matter of sources of law. External sovereignty, meaning 'the independence of one political society in respect to all other political societies', derived from the law of nations. 'Internal sovereignty' derived from the power 'inherent in the people of any state or vested in its ruler by its municipal constitution'.[96]

Yet this simple classical conceptualisation of protectorate status – an agreement to divide internal and external sovereignty – was insufficient to describe the variety of legal relationships to which the label was applied over the late nineteenth century. The label was used to describe everything from company rule to direct colonial administration. Late nineteenth-century protectorates therein confounded two conceptual distinctions that tend to be read anachronistically back into the period. The first is the distinction between cession and conquest as legal justifications for acquisition of foreign territory. The second is the distinction between protections for corporate activity outside of sovereign territory, and the imposition of formal administrative rule. As the European imperial powers sought to divide the economic resources of Africa and the Pacific amongst themselves by 'peaceable' means after the wars of the nineteenth century, they innovated the concept of protection to justify modes of extraterritorial jurisdiction that sought to exert political and economic control over non-European regions, whilst avoiding the legal responsibility and expense of direct colonial administration.

A major area of uncertainty concerned the legal basis of declarations of protectorate status. In practice, protectorates were declared on a disparate variety of grounds. Some assertions of protectorate status conformed to the classical model in that they were justified on the basis of 'treaty' agreements with local 'chiefs', however these were obtained. In other cases, protectorate status was simply declared without any grounding in local treaty,

---

[93] Craven, 'Between Law and History', 37.
[94] Lindley, *Acquisition and Government of Backward Territory*, 181. Also Sir Henry Jenkyns, *British Rule and Jurisdiction Beyond the Seas* (Oxford: Clarendon Press, 1902), 166.
[95] Jenkyns, *British Rule and Jurisdiction*, 165.
[96] Ibid., 166.

whether unilaterally by an imperial government at the request of national traders in the region, or by agreement with other European powers.[97] This ambivalence in the legal basis of protectorate status was mirrored in a broader equivocation over what or who was actually being protected. In the later nineteenth century, British references to protectorate status tended to reflect the legal lineage of treaties of unequal alliance, treating the relation of protection as a political agreement between a stronger and weaker region, even where sovereignty of local peoples was not otherwise recognised.[98] German references to protectorate status, in contrast, tended to frame the relation of protection as one of trade protectionism between the Reich and German companies, with the local population rendered a legal irrelevance.[99]

A second area of ambivalence in protectorate law concerned the jurisdictional divisions between protector and protected. The assumption of jurisdiction over a declared region's foreign relations was generally standard. But beyond this, the extent of jurisdiction claimed by a 'protecting' power varied considerably in practice.[100] At one end of the spectrum were protectorates that simply expanded upon consular jurisdiction to the extent of assuming the 'external sovereignty' or exercise of foreign relations of the protected territory, leaving local political authorities with control of the affairs of the local population, at least to the extent that consular jurisdiction remained unenlivened.[101] An example here is the British protectorate established on the Somali coast in 1886 by treaty with the 'Elders of the Habr Toljaala', the two provisions of which extended the 'gracious favour and protection of Her Majesty the Queen-Empress' in exchange for an undertaking 'to refrain from entering into any correspondence, Agreement, or Treaty with any foreign nation or Power, except with the knowledge and sanction of Her Majesty's Government'.[102] At the other end of the spectrum were

---

[97] Charles G. Fenwick, *Wardship in International Law* (Washington, DC: Government Printers Office, 1919), 29.
[98] Johnston, *Sovereignty and Protection*, 27–8.
[99] See Alpheus Henry Snow, *The Question of Aborigines in the Law and Practice of Nations* (New York: Putnam and Sons, 1921), 90; and Friedrich Fabri, *Bedarf Deutschland der Colonien?* trans. E. C. M. Breuning and Muriel Evelyn Chamberlain, *Studies in German Thought and History*, 3rd ed. (Edwin Mellen Press, 1998) (first published 1868).
[100] Snow, *The Question of Aborigines*, 87; Fenwick, *Wardship in International Law*, 29–30.
[101] Lindley, *Acquisition and Government of Backward Territory*, 181; Jenkyns, *British Rule and Jurisdiction*, 165.
[102] Lindley, *Acquisition and Government of Backward Territory*, 183–4; Jenkyns, *British Rule and Jurisdiction*, 165.

protectorates which functioned as effective colonies, with the protecting state assuming jurisdiction both over 'external' sovereignty and internal administrative powers.[103] Examples of more expansive protectorate jurisdictions include the British protectorate of Bechuanaland in Africa, declared in March 1885; and of the Gilbert and Ellice Islands in the Pacific, declared in 1892.[104]

2.8 The 'Colonial Protectorate'

This latter extreme blurred the distinction between protectorate and colony to such an extent that the notion of the 'colonial protectorate' was invented to explain it. Colonial protectorates were established by treaty and were therefore logically reliant on the sovereign capacity of Indigenous peoples; yet in practice, they assumed almost total external and internal jurisdictional authority, whether explicitly agreed or not.[105] Later interpretations of such escalations from declarations of protectorate status towards full colonial occupation regarded the jurisdictional creep as intentional. American international lawyer Alpheus Henry Snow, for example, wrote in 1919 that the colonial protectorate had been a cynical device used by European powers to establish colonial rule. According to Snow, 'these "protectorates" were legally nothing more than colonies in which the native organization was temporarily utilized as a mean of administration until the growth of a body of colonists and the development of ways of communication made possible the direct administration of the aborigines by the colonizing State'.[106] However, it was not clear that any such foresight was necessarily or universally at work. In 1902 French economist Paul Leroy-Beaulieu surmised that the jurisdictional creep that often followed the establishment of protectorates was an often-undesired but inevitable consequence of attempting to protect commercial activity in foreign territory without assuming administrative control. Leroy-Beaulieu criticised Bismarck's

---

[103] Snow, *The Question of Aborigines*, 87: Lindley, *Acquisition and Government of Backward Territory*, 182.

[104] Lindley, *Acquisition and Government of Backward Territory*, 187-8. Doug Munro and Stewart Firth, 'Towards Colonial Protectorates: The Case of the Gilbert and Ellice Islands' (1986) 32 *Australian Journal of Politics and History*, 63-71.

[105] Ibid., 69.

[106] Snow, *The Question of Aborigines*, 87. Lindley too asserted that the colonial protectorate functioned as a step towards full colonial administration, although he is equivocal on whether the European powers were intentionally working toward that outcome. Lindley, *Acquisition and Government of Backward Territory*, 182.

favourable comparison of 'pacific' German commercial protectorates against the 'French' model of militarised colonial administration, and argued that the distinction was not really in type at all, but in time:

> when citizens of a great civilized State are dispersed in the midst of savage or barbarous populations which have no fixed governments and no exact idea of the power of the European peoples, it is inevitable that sooner or later incidents will occur which make it necessary for the colonizing State to intervene in the internal affairs of the aboriginal population in order to impose upon them a reign of law and an orderly administration ... It is therefore, to be expected, – doubtless not within the next few years but at some later time – that the German will do more or less as the French have done, and following out to its logical consequences the colonizing policy will end by administering more or less directly and completely the barbarous peoples in the midst of whom they have established their flag.[107]

2.9 The Establishment of German Protectorates

On this reading, the viability of the Hanseatic firms in the Pacific was pivotal to the formalisation of German empire in the region. In 1881 Godeffroy's Pacific network was in danger of collapse, and had been refused official support. Bismarck's early stance against colonial enterprise has been well documented.[108] His view that foreign presence was of little use to the project of German nation-building, benefiting only 'a handful of merchants and manufacturers',[109] had been established before Confederation in 1871.[110] Following the refusal of public support for Godeffroy's Pacific operations, the DHPG was able – with Hansemann's intervention – to phoenix out of the wreck of Godeffroy & Sohn long enough to survive until 1884, when Bismarck's attitude to German

---

[107] Snow, *The Question of Aborigines*, 105–6, quoting Paul Leroy-Beaulieu, *De la Colonisation chez les peuples modernes*, 5th ed. (Guillaumin et Cie, 1902).

[108] See for example Bruce Waller, *Bismarck at the Crossroads: The Reorientation of German Foreign Policy after the Congress of Berlin 1878–1880* (London: Athlone Press, 1974).

[109] In a letter to Prussian Minister of War Albrecht von Roon in 1868, Bismarck wrote that 'Germany had no navy with which to protect the colonies and it would be wrong to expect the taxpayer to foot the bill for maintaining territories which would benefit only a handful of merchants and manufacturers'. Henderson, *German Colonial Empire*, 32.

[110] As his confidant and diarist, Moritz Busch, recorded Bismarck to have said that year, 'I do not want any colonies at all. Their only use is to provide sinecures. That is all England at present gets out of her colonies, and Spain too. And as for us Germans, colonies would be exactly like the silks and sables of the Polish nobleman who had no shirt to wear under them.' Moritz Busch, *Bismarck: Some Secret Pages of His History*, vol. 1 (London: Macmillan, 1898), 552. This quote appears in Busch's entry for 9 February 1871.

2.9 THE ESTABLISHMENT OF GERMAN PROTECTORATES

imperial expansion in the Pacific warmed. Even then, the firm's position in the laissez-faire trading environment of the imperial Pacific was unsustainable without official support from the Reich to secure the trade network it had established.

Late to formal imperial expansion, the Bismarckian Reich was in a position to assess the merits of the respective colonial policies adopted by France, Britain, Spain and Holland. The Franco-Prussian War had occurred during a depression that had only deepened for Germany. After Confederation, Bismarck was primarily concerned with shoring up Germany's expanded French borders, and consolidating German diplomatic power in Europe.[111] His early distaste for public expenditure on colonial enterprise was demonstrated in initial rejections to requests for official recognition and financial assistance from German entrepreneurs. In the Pacific, requests came from Godeffroy in Samoa and Hansemann in New Guinea;[112] and in Africa, from Gustav Nachtigal in Togo and the Cameroons; Carl Peters in East Africa; and Lüderitz in Angra Pequeña.[113] The Reich's initial response to Lüderitz, who had sought declarations of protection as early as 1882, was that his interests would be afforded protection only 'in the manner and in the degree in which the empire generally allows protection to extend to the interests of its citizens living abroad'[114] – in effect, that he would be protected to no greater extent than what was provided by consular jurisdiction.

Between 1882 and 1884, however, Bismarck's attitude towards German imperial expansion outside of Europe shifted rapidly, for both international and domestic reasons. On the international front, the Imperial government seems to have reconsidered ongoing diplomatic debates over the rules of acquisition and occupation of foreign territory not as a minor theatre in European realpolitik, but as a means of consolidating the diplomatic strength of the new Reich.[115] On the domestic front, the prospect of German imperial expansion had attracted vocal public champions, led by Carl Peters' Gesellschaft für Deutsche Kolonisation, and Friedrich Fabri's Deutsche Kolonialverein, or German

---

[111] A. J. P. Taylor, *Germany's First Bid for Colonies 1884–1885* (London: Macmillan, 1938), 17–18.

[112] Smith, *German Colonial Empire*, 28.

[113] Giordani, *German Colonial Empire*, 18; Taylor, *Germany's First Bid for Colonies*, 32; Aydelotte, *Bismarck and British Colonial Policy*, 27.

[114] Aydelotte, *Bismarck and British Colonial Policy*, 29, quoting from the German White Book on Angra Pequeña.

[115] Taylor, *Germany's First Bid for Colonies*, 59.

Colonial Society.[116] The colonial societies were instrumental in reframing German imperial expansion as in the interests not only of the 'handful of merchants and manufacturers' that Bismarck had dismissed a decade previous, but also of the working classes displaced by the industrialisation of agriculture and the long depression that followed the Franco-Prussian War.[117] The growing popularity of the colonial movement as a German nationalist vehicle offered Bismarck an opportunity to reconsolidate his position in domestic politics, which was flagging amid tension with the Reichstag. By 1885 Bismarck had changed his tune, going so far as to state that 'public opinion in Germany so strongly emphasizes colonial policy that the position of the German government essentially depends on its success'.[118]

Correspondence in December 1883 between Bismarck and the German ambassador in London, Count Georg Herbert zu Münster, illustrated both Bismarck's changing attitudes to the formalisation of German empire and the experimental nature of the project. In deciding how to respond to Lüderitz's repeated requests that the Reich take steps to protect his interests in Angra Pequeña from annexation by Britain via an expansion northward of the Cape Colony, Bismarck mused to Münster, 'for that we must either take possession, or recognise Lüderitz as sovereign'.[119] The latter alternative of personal sovereignty was of course what was in fact decided upon at the Berlin Conference in recognition of the claims of King Leopold II over the Congo basin. Leopold's Association internationale du Congo was recognised as sovereign on the basis of over 450 treaties obtained by Henry Morton Stanley with local chiefs. The Congo Free State was officially recognised in May 1885.[120]

Only a year earlier, however, the Reich's prevarication over Lüderitz' requests was forced to an unexpected conclusion by the self-governing Cape Colony's declaration of its intention to annex the entire region of South West Africa, a declaration that Germany refused to recognise.[121]

---

[116] Conrad, *German Colonialism*, 23–7.
[117] Felix Hanschmann, 'The Suspension of Constitutionalism in the Heart of Darkness' in Kelly L. Grotke and Markus J. Prutsch (eds.), *Constitutionalism, Legitimacy and Power: Nineteenth Century Experiences* (Oxford: Oxford University Press, 2014), 243, 246; Hamerow, *Social Foundations of German Unification*, 40–1.
[118] Smith, *German Colonial Empire*, 30. Also Taylor, *Germany's First Bid for Colonies*, 4–5.
[119] Aydelotte, *Bismarck and British Colonial Policy*, 54.
[120] Lindley, *Acquisition and Government of Backward Territory*, 112–13; Craven, 'Between Law and History', 41–2.
[121] Aydelotte, *Bismarck and British Colonial Policy*, 54.

2.9 THE ESTABLISHMENT OF GERMAN PROTECTORATES

On 4 June 1884 the Reich communicated to the British government that it would indeed be extending formal protectorate status over 'Lüderitzland' – a declaration that in turn seems to have surprised the British government, whom the German ambassador Münster had assured even a few days before of Germany's lack of interest in any such move.[122] The resulting diplomatic incident over Angra Pequeña stemmed in part from Bismarck's equivocal use of the term 'protectorate' at different times over the preceding year in his communications with British Secretary of State Lord Granville.[123]

By 26 June 1884 Bismarck had settled on a line to present to the Reichstag on this new stance. In this speech, Bismarck was at pains to distinguish between a colony and a protectorate, and to make his preference for the latter clear:

> I repeat that I am opposed to colonies – I will say rather to the colonial system, as most of the States have carried it on during the last century ... against colonies which have as their basis a piece of land, then the seeking to draw immigrants thither, to establish there officials and to erect fortified places ... Entirely different is the question, first, as to whether it is judicious, and second, as to whether it is the duty of the German Empire, as respects those of its citizens who have entered such undertakings in reliance on the protection (*schutz*) of the Empire, so that those structures that have grown out of the superabundance of the whole German body, in foreign lands, may be granted our trusteeship and protection.[124]

Bismarck's 1884 framing of the protectorate concept, with its echoes of Locke's labour-based justification of property rights,[125] gestures towards the competing influences on the development of the German concept of Schutzgebiet. On one hand were economic considerations regarding who should be expected to bear the cost of imperial administration established to protect corporate enterprise. On the other were political considerations of how to respond to the problem of mass German emigration provoked by prolonged economic depression and the industrialisation of agriculture. Bismarck's financial limitations were clear: the new federal government was constitutionally unable to levy direct taxes.[126] It was

---

[122] Ibid., 73–8.
[123] Ibid., 59.
[124] Giordani, *German Colonial Empire*, 18.
[125] John Locke, *Two Treatises of Government*, ed. Peter Laslett, 17th ed. (Cambridge: Cambridge University Press, 2005), 101. Henry Jones, 'Property, Territory, and Colonialism: An International Legal History of Enclosure' (2019) 39 *Legal Studies*, 187–203.
[126] *Die Reichsverfassung* [Constitution of the German Confederation, 1871].

thus inherently limited in the funds it could commit to colonial enterprise without the approval of the Reichstag, which by the early 1880s was not politically inclined to support the Chancellor.[127] The limitation of executive responsibility for cost was thus central to the German adoption of the protectorate model, as Bismarck emphasised:

> (o)ur intention is not first to create provinces to be administered, but so take under our protection colonial enterprises and to aid them during their development ... In so doing, where such creations are unsuccessful, the Empire will not lose much and the expense will not have been considerable.[128]

In Bismarck's cheaper model, the only aid to be provided to protectorates would be official recognition by the Reich of a given company's trading rights within the claimed region, backed up by the threat of enforcement via German warship.[129] German companies successful in obtaining declarations of protection would be expected to fund and perform any necessary administrative functions over the claimed area themselves – including the protection of already acquired private rights of German and other European citizens and the costs of maintaining an executive official in situ.[130]

The political question of how to manage the growing population of rural unemployed had quickly become urgent for the new Reich.[131] The discourse of emigrationist colonialism took shape over the 1870s, promoted by colonial societies that advocated the reservation of areas of Africa and the Pacific for the German working classes to re-establish the 'traditional' German rural lifestyle that had been decimated by the industrialisation of agriculture in Europe.[132] Fabri's 1879 pamphlet *Bedarf Deutschland der Kolonien?* ('Does Germany Need Colonies?') laced colonial advocacy with populist chauvinism, declaring that 'only a mother country which is able to produce a continuous supply of superfluous labour is qualified to found agrarian colonies; and that therefore it is

---

[127] Smith, *German Colonial Empire*, 43.
[128] Letter from Bismarck to the Reichstag, 26 June 1884, quoted in Giordani, *German Colonial Empire*, 19.
[129] Smith, *German Colonial Empire*, 43.
[130] Wilhelm Fabricius, *Nauru 1888–1900: An Account in German and English based on Official Records of the Colonial Section of the German Foreign Office held by the Deutsches Zentralarchiv in Potsdam*, trans. Dymphna Clark and Stewart Firth (Canberra: Research School of Pacific Studies, Australian National University, 1992), 166.
[131] Aydelotte, *Bismarck and British Colonial Policy*, 21.
[132] Smith, *German Colonial Empire*, 11–12; Conrad, *German Colonialism*, 27–8.

today only for the Germanic race to engage in this more modern form of colonial creation'.[133] Yet despite its political traction as a multivalent policy response to economic recession and the perceived threat of socialist collectivisation, the rhetoric of emigrationist colonialism translated only weakly into practice. With the exception of South West Africa, German emigration to the protectorates was minor.[134] Nevertheless, the populist rhetoric of emigrationist colonialism contributed significantly to the Reichstag's eventual approval of the extension of protectorate status to trading interests that had two or three years earlier been refused.[135]

The Reich's abrupt turnaround in imperial policy in 1884 translated quickly into the formalisation of empire in the Western Pacific. After the Reichstag voted down Hansemann's proposal for a public bailout of Godeffroy & Sohn's Pacific interests in 1880, head of the Foreign Office, Count von Limburg-Stirum, had advised Hansemann that the Reich would offer no more than 'protection, naval and consular, to property in land acquired by private adventurers'.[136] Yet, like Lüderitz in Angra Pequeña and Carl Peters in East Africa, Hansemann persisted in his requests for further protection. But he shifted tactics, making more modest entreaties to the German Foreign Office for protection of his own family investments in northeastern New Guinea. By August 1884 the official position on the Western Pacific had been reversed. The shift was indicated in a memorandum sent by Secretary of State Count Hatzfeld to the German Ambassador to London, Count Münster, who a few months earlier had been at the centre of the diplomatic dispute over Angra Pequeña: '(o)ur experience in other respects makes it desirable that all

---

[133] Fabri, *Bedarf Deutschland der Kolonien?*, 85. Conrad, *German Colonialism*, 27–8. Hanschmann notes that this nationalist rhetoric in favour of colonialism was neatly consonant with the anti-socialist conservatism of the German ruling class, which regarded the economic displacement of the agricultural class as a 'breeding ground of the social democratic agitation'. Hanschmann, 'Suspension of Constitutionalism', 247.

[134] By the mid-1890s, over 70 per cent of land within the Protectorate of German South West Africa had been claimed by the Reich and offered to German farmers, who numbered around 12,000 by World War I. Conrad, *German Colonialism*, 39–40; and Horst Dreschsler, 'South West Africa 1885–1907' in Helmuth Stoecker (ed.) *German Imperialism in Africa: From the Beginnings until the Second World War*, trans. Bernd Zöllner (London: C. Hurst and Company, 1986), 39–61.

[135] Smith, *German Colonial Empire*, 22.

[136] Count von Limburg-Sturm on a Conversation with Herr von Hansemann on 15 February 1881, in Parliament of Victoria, German Interests in the South Sea: Abstracts of White Books Presented to the Reichstag, December 1884 and February 1885, Parliamentary Paper No. 36 (Melbourne: John Ferres, Government Printer, 1885), 25.

territories in which German commerce preponderates, or which have become the goal of costly expeditions, the legitimacy of which no one can question, should be placed under the direct protection of the Empire'.[137]

2.10 Concern in the Australasian Colonies over German Imperial Expansion

The increasing activity of the Hanseatic firms in the Western Pacific was a matter of public indignation in the Australasian colonies. By the 1880s New South Wales, Victoria, South Australia, Queensland and Tasmania had been granted self-government with respect to internal affairs, yet increasingly found their collective attitudes to external affairs at odds with the British Imperial government. The colonies regarded Hanseatic commercial activity in the Western Pacific, and particularly in New Guinea to the north of Queensland, as a subterfuge for German imperial aspirations in the region, and thus as a direct threat to the colonies' presumed regional supremacy.[138] The colony of Queensland had in 1882 entreated the British Colonial Secretary, Lord Derby, to recognise its attempt to annex to its territory the entire eastern half of the island of New Guinea, the Dutch empire having long claimed the western half.[139] Lord Derby refused the request, responding that the added expense was unnecessary, given Germany's express lack of interest in acquiring territory in the region. In Lord Derby's opinion there was 'no reason for supposing that the German Government contemplates any scheme of colonisation'.[140]

The colonies were outraged at the Imperial government's refusal to recognise Queensland's annexation of eastern New Guinea. The colonial governments quickly resolved to meet, to settle on a collective response. The Australasian Convention on the Annexation of Adjacent Islands and the Federation of Australasia was held in Sydney in November and December 1883.[141] All colonies expressly supported Queensland's position and expressed unrest at the Imperial government's perceived lack of interest in shoring up the regional supremacy of the Australasian

---

[137] Memorandum sent by German Secretary of State Count Hatzfeld to German Ambassador to London Count Münster, Berlin, 2 August 1884. Ibid., 40.
[138] J. L. Whittaker, N. G. Nash, J. F. Hookey and R. L. Lacey (eds.), *Documents and Readings in New Guinea History: Pre-History to 1899* (Milton: Jacaranda Press, 1975), 479.
[139] Ibid., 475–7.
[140] Ibid., 478.
[141] Parliament of Victoria, Australasian Convention on the Annexation of Adjacent Islands and the Federation of Australasia, Parliamentary Paper No. 48 (Melbourne: John Ferres, Government Printer, 1883).

colonies.[142] Queensland Premier Thomas McIlwraith's memorandum of July 1883 to the other colonial governments drew unambiguous connection between the perceived German threat and the need to federate:

> there can be no doubt that the [British] refusal to annex New Guinea, together with the possible acquisition by foreign Powers of some of the Pacific Islands contiguous to Australia, does raise very serious questions intimately connected with the future interests of the Australasian Colonies ... The circumstances of the present seem to point to a necessity for combination among the Australian Colonies – a combination for both legislative and executive purposes. Australian interests are involved in securing the peaceful and progressive supremacy of Australian influences in the adjoining seas. In order to effect this, it is necessary that there should not only be sentiments held in common, but that a form of government should be provided capable of giving expression to these sentiments. The federation of the Australian colonies may thus be forwarded.[143]

The Reich was aware of Australian colonial unrest at German commercial activity in the Western Pacific – and of the resulting tension between colonial and Imperial governments within the British empire. As late as January 1884, Moritz Busch, Bismarck's press adviser and favoured appointee in the German Foreign Office, explicitly denied any imperial aspirations in the region on the part of the Chancellor, expressing his frustration to Münster over coverage of German commercial activity in Australian newspapers: 'on the one hand, the existence of German commercial interests is wilfully denied, and on the other non-existent projects of German annexation are asserted to exist, in order to further the desires of Australia to annex the independent islands of the South Sea'.[144]

As Busch was disavowing any official annexation plans, however, Hansemann was campaigning for protection of his interests in New Guinea. In the end it was Busch who proved mistaken. Following negotiations between the German and British Foreign Offices, it was decided in August 1884 – two months after the declaration of protectorate status over German South West Africa – that the Reich would extend protection over the northeast of New Guinea only, where Hansemann's interests were concentrated. The southeast of New Guinea would be left not to the

---

[142] Parliament of New Zealand, Intercolonial Convention 1883: Report of the Proceedings of the Intercolonial Convention held in Sydney, in November and December 1883, Parliamentary Paper A–3 (Wellington: George Didsbury, Government Printer, 1883).
[143] Parliament of Victoria, Australasian Convention, 6.
[144] Parliament of Victoria, German Interests in the South Sea, 33.

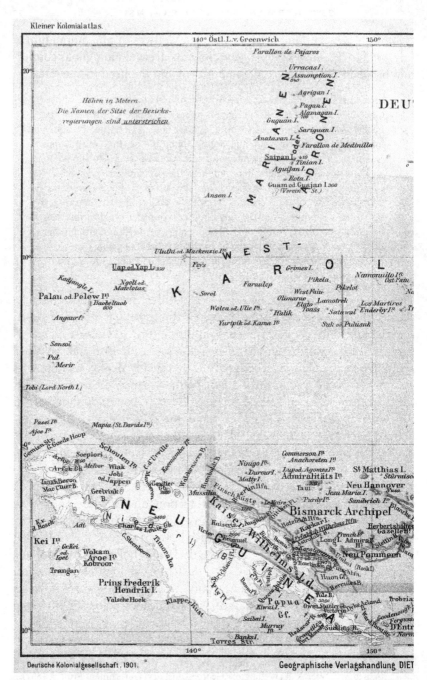

2.2 German map of the Marshall Islands, est. 1884. Credit: Universitätsbibliothek Johann Christian Senckenberg Frankfurt am Main.

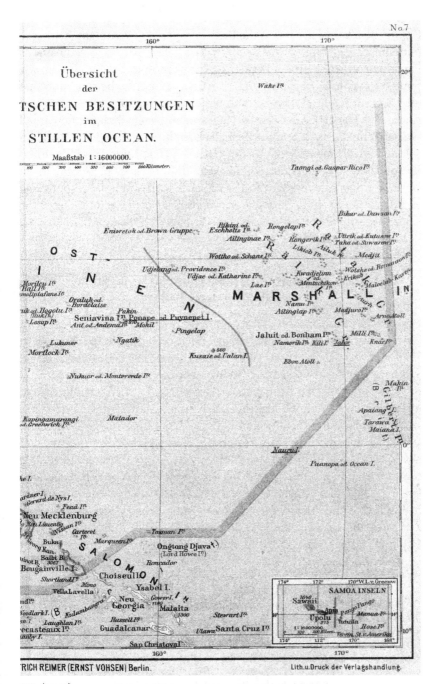

2.2 (cont.)

Colony of Queensland but to the British Imperial government. Bismarck notified Hansemann of the decision in a telegram: '(t)he acquisitions made by you will be placed under the protection of the Empire, on the same conditions as in south-western Africa, subject to the condition that they are not made in territories to which other nations have legitimate claims'.[145] The areas claimed by Hansemann were subsequently named 'Kaiser Wilhelmsland' and the 'Bismarck Archipelago'.[146] The Australian colonial governments were, again, outraged. The Imperial government was accused of duplicitousness at best, and at worst, of complicity in German imperial expansion in the region.[147] The Imperial response, in turn, was the hasty declaration of a new British protectorate over the southwestern part of New Guinea in October 1884, a month before the Berlin Conference.[148]

2.11 German and British Consular Jurisdiction in the Western Pacific

Prior to the consolidation of the protectorate regime, a patchy regime of German consular jurisdiction had extended over the Western Pacific. In 1879 – over twenty years after Godeffroy established a foothold in Samoa – the Reich passed the Gesetz über die Konsulargerichtsbarkeit or 'Law on Consular Jurisdiction', which established extraterritorial jurisdiction over 'subjects of the Reich' and 'other protected persons', where exercisable by 'tradition or treaty'.[149] By 1884 both the DHPG and another Hanseatic firm from Hamburg, Hernsheim & Kompagnie, had headquartered their Pacific operations on the island of Jaluit in the Ralick chain of islands, around halfway between New Guinea and the Sandwich Islands. The Ralicks, together with the Radack chain, had become known in English as the 'Marshall Islands' around a century earlier, following a visit of the British barque *Scarborough* in 1788, under the helm of Captain Thomas Marshall.[150] Captain Marshall and the *Scarborough* had

---

[145] Ibid., 42.
[146] Firth, New Guinea under the Germans, 21–2.
[147] Whitaker et al. (eds.), *Documents and Readings in New Guinea History*, 474–6.
[148] See Charles Lyne, *New Guinea: An Account of the Establishment of the British Protectorate over the Southern Shores of New Guinea* (London: Sampson Low, 1885); Johnston, Sovereignty and Protection, 141.
[149] Gesetz über die Konsulargerichtsbarkeit [Law on Consular Jurisdiction] (Germany) 7 April 1900, DRB 1900, 213.
[150] Francis X. Hezel, *Strangers in Their Own Land: A Century of Colonial Rule in the Caroline and Marshall Islands* (Honolulu: University of Hawai'i Press, 1995).

carried English convicts to Botany Bay earlier that year as part of the 'First Fleet' of convict ships, and were on their way to Canton.[151] By the 1880s the Marshall Islands had become a major source of copra for the European market and a key trade port in the Western Pacific. Together, the two Hanseatic firms from Hamburg, Godeffroy and Hernsheim, controlled around two thirds of the copra trade moving through Jaluit.[152] Hernsheim had been established in the Marshalls from the mid-1870s, and had also lobbied the Reich for official protection of its commercial interests in the region from the late 1870s.[153] The Hernsheims had been successful only in prompting the creation of the new Imperial consulate of Jaluit in 1880. Rather than sending a Foreign Office official, Franz Hernsheim himself was appointed consular agent of an expansive region that took in the better part of the Western Pacific, including Hansemann's interests in New Guinea.[154] From 1880 to 1885, the geographic boundaries of the consular jurisdiction of Jaluit were indeterminate, following Hanseatic commercial enterprise from New Guinea in the west, to the Caroline Islands in the north and to the Gilbert and Ellice Islands in the east.[155]

By contrast, British consular jurisdiction in the Western Pacific was more clearly defined, building on the established legislative basis of the Foreign Jurisdiction Act of 1843.[156] The geographical limits of the Western Pacific jurisdiction, and procedures for enforcement of consular law, were detailed in the Western Pacific Orders in Council, issued in 1877.[157] The expression of British consular jurisdiction in the region was typical of the period. The Order in Council provided that 'the jurisdiction of the High Commissioner extends over all British subjects, but over British subjects exclusively'.[158] In the absence of a treaty with another sovereign power, British imperial jurists understood there to be no basis on which to assert jurisdiction over foreign

---

[151] Charles Bateson, *The Convict Ships 1787-1868*, 2nd ed. (Glasgow: Brown, Son and Ferguson, 1969), 82.
[152] Hezel, *Strangers in Their Own Land*, 46.
[153] Ibid., 47.
[154] Eduard Hernsheim, *South Sea Merchant*, trans. and ed. Peter Sack and Dymphna Clark (Boroko: Institute of Papua New Guinea Studies, 1983).
[155] Parliament of Victoria, German Interests in the South Sea, 15.
[156] Johnston, *Sovereignty and Protection*, 36-7.
[157] Parliament of Victoria, Western Pacific Orders in Council: Report of a Royal Commission appointed by the Imperial Government to Inquire into the Working of the Western Pacific Orders in Council and the Nature of the Measures Requisite to Secure the Attainment of the Objects for which those Orders in Council Were Issued, Parliamentary Paper No. 42 (Melbourne: John Ferres, Government Printer, 1884).
[158] Ibid., 4.

subjects, in accordance with the principle of *extra territorium ius dicenti impune non paretur*.[159] In contrast to the Reich, Britain's principal concern in administering its consular jurisdiction in the Western Pacific was not the protection of trade but the punishment of British subjects caught blackbirding, or trading in slaves, a market that had developed in the Pacific to service commercial plantations.[160] But consular jurisdiction meant that the British High Commissioner of the Western Pacific could punish British subjects for slavery offences, but not non-British subjects for the same crime, or islanders who retaliated with violence. The inconsistent prosecution of slavery offences was yet another source of disquiet in the Australasian colonies, where it was widely held that prosecution of British subjects only for offences connected to the blackbirding trade was unfair.[161]

As such, it was not only Britain's French and German competitors in Africa and the Pacific that became increasingly irritated by the British empire's reliance on the frugality of consular jurisdiction to manage its informal empire. It was also British imperial subjects themselves. The Imperial government's repeated refusals to expand the basis of British jurisdiction in the Western Pacific fed the Australasian colonial governments' drive to determine a basis on which they could officially annex the region on their own behalf.[162] Despite the comparative clarity of British consular jurisdiction in this period, then, the practical and political difficulties of maintaining this position in the context of European imperial competition increased pressure on the Imperial government to devise a basis of jurisdiction over foreign subjects outside of colonial territory.[163] The British jurisprudential debate in this period over whether Pacific Islanders and Africans possessed sovereignty pursuant to which a treaty could be established was therefore prompted as much by political pressure to devise a basis on which to render consular jurisdiction territorial, as by conceptual or moral questions over the equality or otherwise of non-European peoples.[164]

Within the German empire, however, the question of the grounds for asserting jurisdictional authority over foreign subjects was outside the scope of official debate. With the shift in policy in 1884 and

---

[159] Johnston, *Sovereignty and Protection*, 13.
[160] Ibid., 119.
[161] Parliament of Victoria, Western Pacific Orders in Council, 4–5.
[162] Ibid., 13–14.
[163] Johnston, *Sovereignty and Protection*, 119–20.
[164] Ibid., 29.

the declaration of the protectorates of South West Africa, the Cameroons, Togoland and New Guinea, Bismarck's initial intention seemed simply to emulate the British model. Whereas the area of the Protectorate of South West Africa was delimited on the basis of Lüderitz' treaties with local rulers, as became the general practice for company protectorates in Africa, in the case of New Guinea it is not clear that cession of Indigenous sovereignty as such was ever contemplated. The Schutzbrief or 'Letter of Protection' granted to Hansemann in respect of his New Guinea interests is ambiguous on the international legal basis of the declaration. The instrument itself makes plain that sovereignty was understood to be both divisible and delegable:

> Having in August 1884 promised our protection to a society of German subjects and citizens who have since then adopted the name of 'New Guinea Company' in a colonial scheme initiated by them and directed to island groups in the Western Pacific not yet under the protection of another power ... we therefore grant to the New Guinea Company this Letter of Protection, and confirm herewith that we have assumed the sovereignty over the territories in question ... We likewise grant to said Company (subject to the obligation of its introducing and maintaining the political institutions agreed to, as well as of defraying the expenses of a sufficient administration of justice) rights of sovereignty corresponding thereto ... Our Government also reserves to itself the regulation of the administration of justice, as well as the management of the relations between the protected territories and foreign governments.[165]

In the absence of any consideration of Indigenous sovereignty, it was Hansemann's Neuguinea Kompagnie, established to take on administration of the protectorate, which was cast in the position of 'protected' party. In the Schutzbrief, the Reich purports to assume the external sovereignty of the territory, leaving the internal sovereignty to the Kompagnie. There was no reckoning with the jurisprudential question of local sovereignty which had so preoccupied the British imperial jurists in their work on consular jurisdiction in the Western Pacific. Hansemann himself was appointed both 'Commercial Councillor' and judicial officer of the new protectorate.[166] A colleague subsequently remarked of Hansemann that he 'governed New Guinea in the morning hours before

---

[165] 'Charter of the German New Guinea Company', *The Argus* (Melbourne) 24 July 1885, 10.
[166] Ibid., 10. The Annual Reports of the New Guinea Company are available in translation in Dymphna Clark and Peter Sack (eds.), *German New Guinea: The Annual Reports* (Canberra: Australian National University Press, 1979).

he came into the bank'.[167] After the New Guinea declaration followed East Africa: on 27 February 1885, the Protectorate of German East Africa was declared, and the Deutsch-Ostafrikanische Gesellschaft or German East Africa Company was formed out of Carl Peters' Gesellschaft für Deutsche Kolonisation to take on its administration.[168]

2.12 The Establishment of the German Protectorate of the Marshall Islands

A few months later in August 1885 the German consulate of the Marshall Islands established in Jaluit, with Franz Hernsheim as consular agent, was upgraded to protectorate status. The established presence of more than one German firm in the area affected the model of the Marshall Islands Protectorate. Neither Hernsheim, nor the DHPG predominated in such a way that they could be exclusively ordained with official administrative responsibilities, as had occurred in South West Africa, New Guinea and East Africa. An unusual treaty process was devised to establish a jurisdictional basis for the new Marshall Islands Protectorate. In contrast with New Guinea, where a Schutzbrief had been issued directly to Hansemann without contemplation of Indigenous sovereignty, but in keeping with the African protectorates, a treaty mechanism was deployed. In contrast to the African cases, however, the treaties were collected months after the protectorate was declared in August 1885, not before; and they were entered into by the Reich itself, not by the companies that were to take on administrative control. In October 1885 the German Foreign Office charged Captain Rötger of the *Nautilus*, a German corvette, with visiting the Marshall Islands, pro forma treaty documents in hand, to obtain the signatures of Marshallese chiefs.[169] Marshall Islands Consul Franz Hernsheim was to accompany Captain Rötger on this treaty harvesting mission. They began in Jaluit on 15 October 1885, and proceeded on a tour of the Radack and Ralick islands where German settlements had been established. By the end of the tour, Rötger and Hernsheim had gathered the signatures or marks of eighteen *iroij* or Marshallese chiefs.[170]

---

[167] Firth, 'German Firms in the Western Pacific Islands', 23.
[168] Henderson, *German Colonial Empire*, 57. Henderson notes that Peters' requests were denied in November 1884, only to be granted two months later.
[169] *Brisbane Courier*, 'The Annexation of the Marshall Islands by Germany', *The Brisbane Courier*, 17 February 1886, 3. Also Hezel, *Strangers in Their Own Land*, 45.
[170] *Treaty of Friendship between the Marshallese Chiefs and the German Empire*, signed 1 November 1885, trans. Dirk Spennemann, available at www.marshall.csu.edu.au

2.12 THE GERMAN PROTECTORATE

The *iroij* approached to sign treaty documents were simply those known to Hernsheim through the copra trade, the most prominent being Kabua of Jaluit, the *iroij* with whom European traders preferred to deal.[171] The treaty harvesting tour undertaken by Rötger and Hernsheim seems to have appeared a sham undertaking even at the time. A member of the *Nautilus* crew was reported to have written of the agreement with Kabua:

> (t)he treaty was written both in German and in the Marshall Islands language, which for this purpose had to be Romanised, as the islanders have no written language of their own. The document was signed by King Kabua and four other principal chiefs, all of whom, with the exception of one, managed to affix their names to the paper in English letters, though their handwritings were but sorry specimens of calligraphy ... This having been done, preparations were made to hoist the German flag on the islands.[172]

What the *iroij* understood the treaty document presented to them by Rötger and Hernsheim to signify was, unsurprisingly, not recorded. Postdated to 1 November 1885 after the *Nautilus* returned to Jaluit, the Treaty between the Marshallese Chiefs and the Reich invokes the concept of protection in multiple and contradictory ways.[173] The treaty is drafted to mimic the logic of the classical protectorate. The agreement is described as prompted by the chiefs' request for the protection of Kaiser Wilhelm I – a request purportedly motivated by the chiefs' desire both to maintain independence from colonisation by other European powers and to protect German trade on their islands.[174] In the text, the Kaiser offers his protection to the chiefs, and the chiefs undertake to protect 'all German subjects and protected persons' in their lands.[175] The chiefs are then prohibited from providing land or entering into agreements with any other foreign powers without the permission of the

---

/Marshalls/html/history/Treaty1885.html. Also *Brisbane Courier*, 'Annexation of the Marshall Islands by Germany', 3.

[171] Ibid., 47.
[172] *Brisbane Courier*, 'Annexation of the Marshall Islands', 3.
[173] *Treaty between the Marshallese Chiefs and the German Empire*.
[174] Clause 1 of the treaty provides that 'King Kabua, as well as the chiefs Lagajimi, Nelu, Loiak and Launa, guided by the desire to protect the legal trade, which is predominantly in German hands, and to provide the German traders with full security, request the protection of His Majesty, the German Emperor, so that they may be enabled to maintain the independence of the area. His Majesty, the German Emperor affords His Protection subject to all legal rights of third parties'. Ibid.
[175] Ibid., cll. 1 and 3.

Kaiser; and from 'passing any legislation' that would affect German companies without the permission of the Reich.[176]

2.13 The Legal Structure of the German Protectorate Regime

Over the subsequent year of 1886, a legal framework for the German protectorate regime was rapidly settled. Whereas only two years previous, Bismarck had refused to extend anything beyond consular assistance to German commercial interests outside of Europe, the Reich now had the protectorates of South West Africa, Togo, Cameroon, German East Africa, New Guinea, and the Marshall Islands to manage, according to a largely undefined and untested model of extraterritorial administration. The Imperial Constitution of 1871 did not contemplate colonial expansion.[177] In the absence of any constitutional direction for the protectorate regime, in April 1886 the Reichstag passed the Gesetz, betreffend die Rechtsverhältnisse der deutschen Schutzgebiete, or Law Governing the Legal Status of the German Protectorates ('Protectorate Law').[178] The Protectorate Law became the domestic legal foundation of the German protectorate regime. In Section 1, the Law provided that the power to make laws for the protectorates was executive, exercisable by the Kaiser on behalf of the Reich. This circumvented the potential for direct oversight of the regime by the Reichstag.[179] Reflecting the operation of British Orders in Council as the primary means by which extraterritorial governance was effected, the Protectorate Law then vested in the Kaiser or his delegate the power to issue regulations or ordinances (*Verordnungen*) for each protectorate.[180] In this respect, however, the Protectorate Law departed from the British model in that it effectively

---

[176] 'King Kabua, as well as the chiefs Lagajimi, Nelu, Loiak and Launa, will not provide any part of their land to any foreign power without permission by His Majesty, the German Emperor, nor will they enter into treaties with foreign powers without prior permission by His Majesty, the German Emperor'. Ibid., cll. 2 and 4.

[177] *Die Reichsverfassung*. Also Wolfram Hartmann, 'Making South West Africa German? Attempting Imperial, Juridical, Colonial, Conjugal and Moral Order' (2007) 2 *Journal of Namibian Studies*, 51–84 at 53–4.

[178] Gesetz, betreffend die Rechtsverhältnisse der deutschen Schutzgebiete [Law Governing the Legal Status of the German Protectorates] (Germany) 17 April 1886, RGBl 1886, 75.

[179] Gesetz, betreffend die Rechtsverhältnisse der deutschen Schutzgebiete, s. 1.

[180] Gesetz, betreffend die Rechtsverhältnisse der deutschen Schutzgebiete, s. 4. On the function of Orders in Council in the British colonial regime, see Johnston, *Sovereignty and Protection*, 36–7.

suspended the principles of constitutional rule for any special laws adopted for the protectorates. Executive and legislative power were centralised within a single office and there was no provision for legislative review.[181]

In Section 2 of the Protectorate Law, the provisions of the Gesetz über die Konsulargerichtsbarkeit, the Law on Consular Jurisdiction, were stipulated to apply in protectorates in respect of all matters of private law, criminal law and procedural law. Within protectorates, however, such laws were enforceable not by the consular agent but by the official placed in charge of the protectorate by the Chancellor.[182] In this way, consular law – and not German domestic law – was adopted as the foundation of substantive law in the German protectorates, where no specific ordinances had been issued. As Nuzzo points out, this shift was paradigmatic: it purported to convert consular jurisdiction from personal to territorial.[183] Whereas the Law on Consular Jurisdiction described a personal jurisdiction for subjects of the Reich and other Europeans, limited in its territorial application to those countries in which German consular jurisdiction was exercisable by 'tradition or treaty', the protectorate jurisdiction was claimed in a single legislative section to be territorial, to be imposed simply via declaration by the Kaiser of a given region as a protectorate.[184]

However, in the crucial matter of the extension of protectorate jurisdiction over non-Europeans within declared territory, the Protectorate Law was largely silent. The power vested in the Kaiser or his delegate to issue decrees included the power to subject additional categories of persons to protectorate jurisdiction than those explicitly subject by virtue of the application of the Law on Consular Jurisdiction to 'subjects of the Reich' and 'other protected persons'.[185] But other than this general – and

---

[181] Hanschmann, 'Suspension of Constitutionalism', 250–1.
[182] Gesetz, betreffend die Rechtsverhältnisse der deutschen Schutzgebiete, s. 2; Gesetz über die Konsulargerichtsbarkeit [Law on Consular Jurisdiction] (Germany) 7 April 1900, DRB 1900, 213.
[183] Luigi Nuzzo, 'Colonial Law' *European History Online*, 16 April 2012, available at www.iegego.eu/en/threads/europe-and-the-world/european-overseas-rule/luigi-nuzzo-colonial-law, 10.
[184] Gesetz über die Konsulargerichtsbarkeit, s. 1.
[185] Gesetz, betreffend die Rechtsverhältnisse der deutschen Schutzgebiete, s. 4(1); Gesetz über die Konsulargerichtsbarkeit, DRB 1900, 213. S. 1. Also Jakob Zollmann, 'German Colonial Law and Comparative Law 1884–1919' in Thomas Duve (ed.) *Entanglements in Legal History: Conceptual Approaches* (Frankfurt: Max Planck Institute for European Legal History, 2014), 261.

technically unlimited – provision, the Protectorate Law left unspoken the matter of jurisdiction over Indigenous peoples. The Protectorate Law did not expressly refer at all to Indigenous populations (Eingeborene or 'Natives'), beyond stipulating that the waiver of the right to legal representation did not apply to Natives named as defendants or accused in cases before the protectorate court.[186] As Hanschmann notes, this silence effectively created a dual legal order in the protectorates.[187] On one hand was the regime of existing consular law applicable to Europeans and subject to such legislative and judicial review as provided for in the Constitution. On the other was a *tabula rasa* regime of protectorate law by executive decree, exempt from review entirely, by which Indigenous peoples within the protectorates were to be governed.

The Imperial *Verordnung* or Ordinance establishing the Marshall Islands Protectorate was issued in September 1886.[188] The Ordinance decreed that consular law applied in the Marshall Islands to all residing within the new Protectorate, including Natives, but only to the degree expressly stipulated by the Chancellor.[189] Most importantly, the Ordinance then delegated to the Chancellor the power to determine firstly, who was Native for the purposes of the Ordinance; and secondly, whether Natives thus defined were to be governed under consular law, or under the executive ordinances issued by the Kaiser's delegate in the Marshall Islands Protectorate.[190]

2.14 The Agreement between the Jaluit Gesellschaft and the Reich

The Marshall Islands Protectorate thus established in the law of nations by 'treaty' with the *iroij*, and in German law by imperial decree, the DHPG and Hernsheim & Kompagnie agreed to amalgamate their interests in the Marshalls into one company, to be formally delegated administrative control of the new protectorate. In December 1887 the Jaluit Gesellschaft was incorporated in Hamburg, merging the two largest Hanseatic firms in the Pacific. In January 1888 the new Gesellschaft

---

[186] Gesetz, betreffend die Rechtsverhältnisse der deutschen Schutzgebiete, s. 4(4).
[187] Hanschmann, 'Suspension of Constitutionalism', 252–3. Also Nuzzo, 'Colonial Law', 34.
[188] Verordnung, betreffend die Rechtsverhältnisse in dem Schutzgebiete der Marschall-, Brown- und Providence-Inseln [Law Governing Legal Relations in the Marshall, Brown and Providence Islands Protectorates] (Germany) 17 September 1886, RGBI, 1886, 291.
[189] Ibid., s. 1.
[190] Ibid., s. 2.

2.14 THE REICHS AGREEMENT

formally completed an Agreement with the Reich on the administration of the Marshall Islands Protectorate.[191] The Agreement provided *inter alia* as follows:

> Whereas the Marshall Islands ... have been placed under the protection of His Majesty the Kaiser; and whereas, on 21 December 1887, the Jaluit-Gesellschaft was incorporated in Hamburg on the basis of the Articles of Association appended under A, and this Company has undertaken to meet the cost of the administration of the Protectorate, subject to His Majesty's assent the following agreement has been concluded between the Foreign Office and the Jaluit-Gesellschaft;
>
> 1. The Jaluit-Gesellschaft is granted the following exclusive rights and privileges within the domain of the aforesaid Protectorate:
>   a. the right to take possession of ownerless land,
>   b. the right to engage in fishing for pearlshell, insofar as this is not carried on by the natives in accordance with tradition,
>   c. the right to mine guano deposits, without prejudice to the duly acquired rights of third parties.
> 2. The administration of the Protectorate will be conducted by an Imperial Commissioner assisted by a Secretary, to be appointed.
> 3. The Imperial Commissioner will appoint the requisite officials for the local administration of the Protectorate as proposed by the agents of the Company in Jaluit, subject to the assent of the German Chancellor.
> 4. A budget for the administration of the Protectorate will be drawn up annually, to be agreed upon between the Foreign Office and the Jaluit-Gesellschaft.
> 5. The Jaluit-Gesellschaft undertakes to meet the costs arising from the administration.
> 6. Licence fees and head-taxes as specified in the budget are to be collected annually in the Protectorate.
> 7. Laws and Ordinances affecting the administration of the Protectorate are to be introduced only after a hearing before the Jaluit-Gesellschaft.
> 8. In the promulgation of local administrative regulations, the Imperial Commissioner will, as far as possible, act in agreement with the agents of the Jaluit-Gesellschaft.
>
> ...
>
> 10. Voluntary liquidation of the Company may take place only after previous notice of severance of this agreement.
> 12. Pleasant (Navoda) Island will be subject to the terms of this agreement as soon as the same is placed under the protection of the Reich.
>
> ...

---

[191] Fabricius, *Nauru*, 201–4.

Berlin, on the twenty-first day of January, eighteen hundred and eighty eight.

> The *Jaluit Gesellschaft*
> for the Board of Directors:
> A. Weber Hernsheim
>
> The Secretary of State
> The German Foreign Office
> Count von Bismarck'

The 1887 Agreement between company and empire establishes an administrative structure that defies contemporary distinctions between public and private authority. The company was to nominate all administrative officials for the new Protectorate, subject to Bismarck's executive approval. The company was to fund the cost of the Protectorate's administration, with an annual budget to be agreed between company and Foreign Office. Laws and ordinances for the Protectorate were to be determined in consultation with the company, and the Imperial Commissioner was to act 'as far as possible' in agreement with it. This administrative blueprint is sketched around the initial clause of the Agreement, which deals with possession of land, fishing and mining rights.

The property and guano clauses of the Agreement, brief as they are, warrant careful consideration. Establishing certainty of property rights over land and resources was a central concern of German commercial interests in the consolidation of the international protectorate regime in the Pacific. Requests for official guarantee that land acquired prior to the extension of formal protection would be treated as property were made by Lüderitz in Angra Pequeña, by Hansemann in Papua New Guinea and by Godeffroy in the Marshall Islands.[192] But there remained considerable uncertainty more generally as to whether, in the absence of formal sovereign territorial acquisition, land and resources claimed in areas outside European sovereign territory could be recognised as attracting protections of property within metropolitan law. It is possible to read requests by private individuals and companies for official protection of commercial interests outside of Europe during this period as precisely

---

[192] See for example Letter from Messrs. Godeffroy and Eberhard Schmid, Directors of the German Commercial and Plantation Company at Hamburg to Prince Bismarck, Hamburg, 30 January 1884, in Parliament of Victoria, German Interests in the South Sea, 35.

requests that such interests would be recognised as proprietary in municipal law.

The debate at the international level in the 1880s over legitimate means of territorial acquisition thus dealt squarely with the status of European property claims in Africa and the Pacific. The jurisprudential solution of *territorium nullius* proposed as the rationalisation of the protectorate regime by German jurist Ferdinand de Martitz, discussed further below, was grounded in the logic of property. Indigenous peoples were capable of owning land in the Lockean sense of possession gained via occupation and cultivation, but not of evincing sovereignty over it comparable to the sovereignty of civilised European nations.[193] However Martitz' conceptual wrangling with *territorium nullius* as a jurisprudential justification for protectorates left unanswered the question of who owned 'ownerless land' within a protectorate. Absent sovereignty over territory, Indigenous peoples could not be recognised as owning more land than they directly occupied; yet for the European empires, the point of claiming a protectorate rather than a colony was precisely to *avoid* the legal obligations and administrative costs of effective occupation that came with formal territorial acquisition.

As discussed, the German Protectorate Law provided that consular law would apply in respect of private law matters; thus it was already settled that pre-existing European claims to private property would be upheld within the Marshall Islands Protectorate. However, the question of which between the Reich and the Gesellschaft had a better claim to those areas of the Protectorate not already recognised as subject to private possession was not clear. The reference to 'ownerless land' contemplated in the Jaluit Agreement thus seems to have settled the question in favour of the company. In contemporary terms, the Marshall Islands Protectorate was not, at least on its establishment, German territory. It was inchoate corporate territory.

But even this assessment of the status of 'ownerless land' within the Protectorate as inchoate corporate territory does not fully reflect the imbrication of private and public in the Jaluit Agreement. A crucial exception is carved out by the guano clause. The Jaluit Gesellschaft is granted only the right to *mine* guano or phosphate deposits – not property in the deposits themselves. On a practical

---

[193] Fitzmaurice, *Sovereignty, Property and Empire*, 282–6; Lindley, *Acquisition and Government of Backward Territory*, 173–4.

level, at the time the clause was seemingly moot. In keeping with their Hanseatic inheritance, neither the DHPG nor Hernsheim had been involved in mining operations in the Pacific. Nor had any phosphate deposits been discovered on the Ralick and Radack chains when the Protectorate was declared. Given its delegated authority to write its own commercial regulations, the merged Jaluit Gesellschaft had little incentive to alter its trading practices to begin mining in the new Marshall Islands Protectorate.[194]

The reference to mining in the Agreement was therefore entirely speculative; but it was not without decent cause. European commercial interest in 'guano islands' had been strong since at least the mid-nineteenth century.[195] By the 1880s phosphate mining was a booming industry in the Pacific, and a subject of major imperial competition.[196] American entrepreneurs had been guano prospecting in the Pacific islands for decades. In 1856 the United States had passed the Guano Islands Act, which purported to claim all islands not already occupied upon which guano was discovered by a US citizen as 'appertaining to' the United States.[197] The United States had proceeded to claim – as 'appurtenances' – sixty-six islands across the Caribbean and the Pacific.[198] Claims included the Line Islands, the Phoenix Islands, Baker Island and Jarvis Island, all to the southeast of the Marshalls.[199] The United States Guano Company had commenced mining on the Phoenix Islands with the use of Indigenous labour in 1858.

The guano provision in the Jaluit Agreement thus seems to have been the means by which the company and the Reich determined how prospective profits from the exploitation by third parties of any phosphate

---

[194] Firth, 'German Firms in the Western Pacific Islands', 24–5.
[195] Gregory T. Cushman, *Guano and the Opening of the Pacific World: A Global Ecological History* (Cambridge: Cambridge University Press, 2013), 26–9.
[196] Ibid., 16–17.
[197] The Act's first section provided as follows: '(w)henever any citizen of the United States discovers a deposit of guano on any island, rock, or key, not within the lawful jurisdiction of any other government, and not occupied by the citizens of any other government, and takes peaceable possession thereof, and occupies the same, such island, rock, or key may, at the discretion of the President, be considered as appertaining to the United States.' Guano Islands Act of 1856, 48 United States Code § 1411.
[198] Cushman, *Guano and the Opening of the Pacific World*, 82. At least eight islands and atolls claimed under the Guano Islands Act remain 'United States Minor Outlying Islands'. For a recent history, see Daniel Immerwahr, *How to Hide an Empire: A History of the Greater United States* (London: Random House, 2019).
[199] See Part 5, 'Agriculture, Labour and Phosphate in the Pacific' in Chapter 3, 'From Protectorate to Mandate, 1920'.

deposits found within the Marshall Islands Protectorate would be allocated. When read together with the property clause, the guano clause seems to provide the Gesellschaft only with a transferable licence to mine phosphate, implying that the Reich itself claimed property in mineral deposits within the entire Protectorate, and therefore any royalty rights. This interpretation is in keeping with metropolitan German mineral law of the time, and the arrangements made in the other German protectorates of South West Africa and German East Africa with respect to mineral rights.[200] Read together, then, the property and guano clauses appear incoherent according to contemporary understandings of sovereignty, territory and property. The Reich did not make a sovereign territorial claim over the Protectorate as German territory; yet it nevertheless purported to claim sovereign rights in all mineral resources within the Protectorate, whether privately owned or not, as a basis for profit sharing in any future mining.

2.15 The Incorporation of Nauru into the Marshall Islands Protectorate

The Jaluit Agreement singled out only one island for special mention: 'Pleasant (Navoda) Island'. Following the declaration of the Marshall Islands Protectorate, the Jaluit consulate established seven years before was unceremoniously abolished in January 1887. This left German traders operating outside the newly established New Guinea and Marshall Islands Protectorates with only the consulate in Apia, Samoa for official support. For DHPG and Hernsheim agents posted on Pleasant Island, a single coral atoll hundreds of kilometres south of the Marshalls, this arrangement was as good as no protection at all. The German traders on Pleasant Island wrote letters of complaint to the Imperial Consul in Apia, who in turn wrote to Bismarck. The story they told was melodramatic: the natives of Pleasant Island had for a decade been in a state of 'civil war', armed with the guns and ammunition used as trade for copra.[201] The Consul in Apia was too far away to be of timely assistance in case of

---

[200] On German South West Africa and German East Africa, see Lindley, *Acquisition and Government of Backward Territory*, 352. See also Part 7, 'The right passed from the Gesellschaft to the Pacific Phosphate Company' in Chapter 3, 'From Protectorate to Mandate, 1920'.

[201] Letter from Imperial Commissioner for the Marshall Islands Protectorate Wilhelm Knappe to Prince Herbert von Bismarck, 6 May 1887, reproduced in Fabricius, *Nauru*, 181.

emergency. A Hernsheim trader, Hansen, was in 'mortal danger', 'in consequence of having killed a native – allegedly in self-defence'.[202] In direct correspondence with the Reich, the DHPG went a step further and requested that Pleasant Island be included within the new Marshall Islands Protectorate. The firm did not just profess to 'regard the incorporation of Pleasant Island in the Protectorate of the Marshall Islands as highly desirable'. It also took the 'liberty of stressing that peace and order would be established on Pleasant Island with much greater ease and despatch if the flag-raising ceremony could be accompanied by a major show of force'.[203]

The island known to Europeans then as Pleasant Island had been named in 1798 by British captain John Fearn of the merchant ship *Hunter*.[204] It had been mapped as a source of food and water since at least the 1830s by European whalers working the Line Islands in the central Pacific. Lacking a harbour which could be easily approached, and over 300 kilometres from its nearest neighbour, Ocean Island in the Gilberts, first-hand European reports of the islanders and the landscape of Pleasant Island remained scant well into the 1870s.[205] Written records consisted of a scattering of reports of approach in ships' logs, and details in the Australian and New Zealand press filtered through dramatised accounts of runaway whalers and escaped convicts.[206] In the mid-1870s, a Godeffroy agent arrived on the island, sent by Unshelm in Apia. The Godeffroy agent was joined over the next decade by Hernsheim agents; and then by British agents of two New Zealand trading companies, Tiernan Venture and Henderson & McFarlane. By 1887 as the German Imperial Consul in Apia reported back to Bismarck, there were 'ten white residents' on the island, all trading in copra: two Germans, four British, two Norwegians, one Dutch and one American.[207] Between dramatised extremes of pleasantry and violence, early corporate records gave little indication of the islanders themselves.

In correspondence with the Imperial Consul in Apia in 1884, Cesar Godeffroy VI – working now for the DHPG, after having nearly sunk the

---

[202] Ibid., 178.
[203] Letter from the *Deutsche Handels- und Plantagen-Gesellschaft der Südsee-Inseln zu Hamburg* to Minister von Kusserow, 1 October 1887. Ibid., 184–5.
[204] Nancy Viviani, *Nauru: Phosphate and Political Progress* (Canberra: Australian National University Press, 1970), 9–11.
[205] Ibid., 9–11; Fabricius, *Nauru*, 160–1.
[206] Viviani, *Nauru*, 10–13.
[207] Fabricius, *Nauru*, 181.

old family firm – reported that the Eingeborene or Natives on Pleasant Island numbered somewhere between 1,000 and 3,000, and had been warring since 1878.[208] According to Godeffroy, conditions had become intolerably dangerous for traders on the island. One trader's house had been ransacked; another had been shot. On Godeffroy's reckoning, it would not be sufficient to have an imperial warship just visit the island, or simply to pass Ordinances in the Protectorates prohibiting Germans and other Europeans from perpetuating the trade in arms and alcohol on the islands. The Natives of Pleasant Island, Godeffroy averred, would need to be physically disarmed.[209] One official resident on the small island would be sufficient, Godeffroy wrote; and the new Jaluit Gesellschaft would fund all costs of administration. All that was needed was the assent of the Reich.[210]

With no more than a brief note in the files of the Foreign Office, on 21 October 1887 Bismarck agreed to the request.[211] Kaiser Wilhelm signed an imperial assent to the incorporation of Pleasant Island within the Marshall Islands Protectorate a few days later on 24 October 1887.[212] The Imperial Proclamation of the Reich's latest South Seas island that followed a few months later on 16 April 1888 was insignificant in the national news of the time: the Kaiser himself had died a month earlier, and his successor, his grandson Wilhelm II, was to be crowned that June.[213] In contrast to the treaty harvesting tour that followed the declaration of the Marshall Islands Protectorate, once the new Protectorate had been officially declared to include Pleasant Island, little thought was given to obtaining the signatures of Native chiefs. Attention turned not to pens but guns. There was no contemplation of treaty arrangements, only strategising on how best to disarm the Natives. The island had no harbour or anchorage for a warship, and after decades of corporate agents trading guns and ammunition for copra, the island was flooded with firearms.[214] On the day of the Imperial Proclamation in April 1888, issued during the imperial interregnum in Germany, an

---

[208] Letter from Imperial Consul in Apia Dr Steubel to Prince Herbert von Bismarck, 2 September, 1884. Ibid., 178–9.
[209] Letter from the *Deutsche Handels- und Plantagen-Gesellschaft* to Minister von Kusserow, 1 October 1887. Ibid., 184–5.
[210] Ibid., 184–5; also Memorandum, German Foreign Office, 20 October 1887, at 187.
[211] Ibid., 188.
[212] Imperial Assent, 24 October 1887. Ibid., 188–9.
[213] *Bekanntmachung* [Proclamation], 16 April 1888. Ibid., 196.
[214] Ibid., 190–5.

Ordinance was issued under the Protectorate Law, preventing the importation of any further firearms, ammunition or explosives into Pleasant Island.[215] The German gunboat *SMS Eber* was then ordered by the Reich to anchor at the island, disarm the Natives, and hoist the Imperial flag. More detailed instructions, it appears, were not given.[216] Left to determine a plan of attack, the newly appointed Imperial Commissioner to the Marshall Islands, Franz Sonnenschein, and the Commander of the *Eber*, Sub-Lieutenant Emsmann, decided on ambush. The *Eber* landing party would 'march around and across the island'. The Native chiefs would be 'persuaded amicably to join in'. They would be led to a German trading station close to the gunboat's mooring. The Native chiefs would then be 'kept in custody as hostages'; and the Natives would be 'informed that they have to hand in all firearms and ammunition within the next 24 hours, failing which the chiefs will then be taken away into captivity'.[217]

On 1 October 1888, the *Eber* moored off the southwest of Pleasant Island, and a party of thirty-six German soldiers proceeded to enact the hostage plan. On Commissioner Sonnenschein's account, later given in a detailed report to the Foreign Office, the Native chiefs were taken prisoner overnight in a German copra house as planned. By the morning of 2 October, the islanders had gathered there 'in a great crowd'. The Imperial flag was hoisted, and the Imperial Proclamation of 16 April 1888 read out. The islanders were then ordered to hand in their firearms and ammunition, in exchange for the release of their chiefs.[218] By the next day, Sonnenschein reported, '1 revolver, 109 pistols and 655 rifles' had been handed in.[219] The Protectorate declared and Natives disarmed, the chiefs were released and the *Eber* departed that same afternoon. In his report, Sonnenschein substituted the English name of Pleasant Island for 'Nauru', a Germanic spelling of Naoerō or Nawodo, the phonetic Indigenous name for the island.[220]

---

[215] Verordnung betreffend das Verbot der Einfuhr von Feuerwaffen, Schießbedarf und Sprengstoffen in Pleasant Island, 16 April 1888. Ibid., 197.

[216] Ibid., 208.

[217] Resolution of the Imperial Commissioner and the Acting Commander of the Gunboat *SMS Eber*, 1 October 1888. Ibid., 214–15.

[218] Report of Imperial Commissioner of the Marshall Islands to Prince Herbert von Bismarck, 31 October 1888. Ibid., 208–13. Also *The Week*, 'Germans in the Pacific', *The Week* (Brisbane) 29 December 1888, 13.

[219] Fabricius, *Nauru*, 211.

[220] Report of Imperial Commissioner of the Marshall Islands to Prince Herbert von Bismarck, 31 October 1888. Ibid., 208–13.

2.16 Nauru's Incorporation into the Marshall Islands Protectorate as a Matter of Law

As discussed, the late nineteenth-century protectorate had become increasingly unmoored from the logic of the classical model. But from the perspective of German imperial expansion in the Pacific, jurisprudential elaborations of the new wave of protectorates – and specifically those proffered by the new Institut de droit international – seem little more than ex post facto attempts to attribute conceptual coherence to a series of ad hoc executive decisions, reactive to corporate demands for legal certainty around investments outside sovereign territory. The actual legal framework of Nauru's incorporation into the Marshall Islands Protectorate therefore bears restatement, as the term 'protectorate' itself gives little insight. The German protectorate regime was grounded in German public law of the Imperial Constitution of 1871, and was not officially expressed as deriving from any international rule.[221] Whilst it is possible that the Berlin Conference was understood in Germany as having either confirmed or established a general principle permitting the establishment of protectorates in the absence of treaty, it is not clear from the records considered that a foundation in the law of nations for imperial expansion was considered by the Reich, at least between the years 1884 to 1888, to be necessary at all. Predictably enough, Bismarck's preoccupations were political and financial.

A legal framework for the German protectorate regime developed quickly, and was concerned more with insulating executive control over the regime from legislative oversight than with coherence in international law. In legal terms, the imposition of protectorate status on Nauru was as follows. Section 1 of the Protectorate Law purported to vest the Schutzgewalt – the power of the Reich to make laws for protectorates – in the Kaiser. According to section 3, the power so vested was exercisable via imperial decree. In September 1886 an Imperial Ordinance establishing the Marshall Islands Protectorate was issued by Kaiser Wilhelm I. Pursuant to the same section, Nauru was formally

---

[221] Hanschmann, 'Suspension of Constitutionalism', 248–9. Koskenniemi makes a related observation: 'While German lawyers started to write about colonialism only after Bismarck's famous volte face in 1884, their treatment of it drew more upon the tradition of national public law than upon international law: the focus of German interest lay in how the German *Schützgebiete* should be seen from the perspective of the imperial constitution.' Koskenniemi, *Gentle Civilizer*, 109.

proclaimed part of the Marshalls Islands Protectorate on 16 April 1888 by Sonnenschein, the Commissioner of the Marshall Islands, as the Kaiser's delegate.[222] In German Imperial law, this was the legal foundation for the Reich's assertion of authority over Nauru: a piece of legislation passed by the Reichstag; an Ordinance issued by the Kaiser; and a Proclamation issued by the Kaiser's delegate in the Marshall Islands, Commissioner Franz Sonnenschein.

In terms of international law, the legal foundation of protectorates in the absence of treaty was not settled in 1888, and indeed never clearly was.[223] From a political perspective, the purpose of the late nineteenth-century protectorate model was to avoid formal territorial acquisition of the area in question, so as to limit administrative obligations. As such, recognised modes of territorial acquisition – namely conquest, cession, or occupation in case of *res nullius* – could not be invoked, at least not without modification, as legal justification for the establishment of protectorates. Articles 34 and 35 of the General Act of the Berlin Conference settled that if the European imperial powers wished to acquire territory by occupation, they were legally obliged to effectively administer annexed territory to a degree sufficient to protect private rights and trade therein (although it should be noted that the Institut regarded this obligation, subsequently restated as the principle of effective occupation, as already settled in practice prior to the Conference, and indeed potentially limited by the Berlin treaty's confinement to the African coasts).[224]

The uneasy silence left in the Act over the legal obligations that attended protectorate status prompted a wave of protectorate declarations across Africa, the Pacific and parts of Asia. Compared to the onerous requirements of effective occupation, protectorate status seemingly offered a cheaper, largely outsourced mode of protecting corporate proprietary and trade claims outside of sovereign territory. But significant conceptual uncertainties remained as to how protectorates – as opposed to colonies – could be lawfully established, and how local populations were to be reckoned with in law. Subsequent to the Berlin Conference, in September 1885 the Institut de droit international commissioned Ferdinand de Martitz to chair a committee into the law of

---

[222] Imperial Proclamation extending the German Protectorate to include Pleasant Island, 16 April 1888, reproduced in Fabricius, *Nauru*, 196.
[223] Thanks to Matthew Craven for his time and generosity across a number of discussions on this topic.
[224] Koskenniemi, *Gentle Civilizer*, 149.

2.16 THE LEGAL FRAMEWORK OF NAURU'S INCORPORATION 95

occupation.[225] Martitz introduced his reformulation of *territorium nullius*, denoting 'any region not actually under the sovereignty or protectorate of a member of the community of the law of nations, whether inhabited or not'.[226] On his account, lands considered *territorium nullius* were thus open to occupation by European states. Effective occupation would ground a claim either of sovereignty or of protectorate over the relevant area.[227] In the case of a protectorate over *territorium nullius*, Martitz analogised from the classical formulation: there should generally be an agreement with Indigenous authority, which would retain political and administrative authority over local affairs, with the European state assuming authority vis-à-vis other European states.[228]

That protectorates could be declared in the absence of a treaty, or geographically expanded across regions in which no treaties had been obtained, came to be justified by the jurists of empire on the basis of Indigenous peoples' purported lack of capacity to exercise sovereignty. Martitz proposed to the Institut that the protectorate without treaty could be justified where Indigenous peoples were capable of holding rights of private property, grounded in physical occupation – but not rights of sovereignty, grounded in political organisation.[229] For Martitz, where Indigenous peoples were deemed capable of occupation in the sense required to ground recognition of property rights, but not in the sense required to ground recognition of sovereign rights, protectorates without treaty were justifiable.[230]

Martitz' formulation of *territorium nullius*, however, was not adopted by the Institut.[231] French diplomat Edouard Engelhardt took exception on two grounds to the uncertainty in Martitz' use of the concept of 'membership of the community of the law of nations' as the test for determining which political entities possessed sovereignty to an extent

---

[225] Andrew Fitzmaurice, 'Discovery, Conquest and Occupation of Territory' in Bardo Fassbender and Anne Peters (eds.) *The Oxford Handbook of the History of International Law* (Oxford: Oxford University Press, 2015), 840, 857.

[226] Ferdinand de Martitz, 'Occupation des territoires – Rapport et projet de résolutions présentés à l'Institut de droit international' ['Occupation of Territories – Report and Draft Resolutions submitted to the Institute of International Law'] (1888) 9 *Annuaire de l'Institut de droit international* 243, 247.

[227] Ibid., 247–8.

[228] Ibid., 249.

[229] Fitzmaurice, *Sovereignty, Property and Empire*, 284–6.

[230] Lindley, *Acquisition and Government of Backward Territory*, 173–4.

[231] Institut de droit international, 'Sixième commission – Examen de la théorie de la conférence de Berlin sur l'occupation des territoires' (1889) 10 *Annuaire de l'Institut de droit international*, 173.

sufficient to render the land they inhabited as other than *territorium nullius*. Firstly, Engelhardt cited the cases of Morocco, Abyssinia and Zanzibar to illustrate the difficulty of determining which political entities fell within the 'community of nations', and which did not. Secondly, he noted that it was possible to hold that even in the case of land inhabited by 'savages' outside the 'community of nations', it would be 'exorbitant' to consider such land *territorium nullius* for the purposes of occupation.[232] The issue remained unresolved. Although it was left open that inhabited lands could potentially be subject to protectorate without treaty, ultimately no agreement was reached within the Institut as to the legal definition of those Indigenous peoples whose lands were legitimately subject to declarations of protectorate status by European states without a treaty agreement.[233]

The German assertion of authority over Nauru therefore neither clearly complied with, nor contravened contemporaneous international law. The finer points of conceptual debate in the law of nations, and in particular the debate within the Institut over *territorium nullius*, were of limited relevance in the Reich's rapid establishment of a legal framework for its protectorate regime. If the law of nations was considered at all, the emphasis was on rules of engagement between the imperial powers, not between imperial powers and the peoples and regions they claimed.[234] Taken forcibly and without treaty, the incorporation of Nauru into the protectorate of the Marshall Islands was characterisable as an act – however small – of war. Given its self-proclaimed success, that act could therefore have been recognisable in the European law of nations as conquest, sufficient to ground the acquisition of Nauru as German territory. But the pragmatic purpose of the ambush was precisely *not* to assume sovereignty in the sense that would generate the administrative obligations of effective occupation but to assert the Reich's exclusive authority to regulate European interests on the island as private rights in property and trade.[235]

In this assertion of the existence of property in the absence of sovereignty, the logic of legal authority asserted over Nauru was something of

---

[232] Ibid., 177–8. Also Fitzmaurice, 'Discovery, Conquest and Occupation', 857.
[233] Koskenniemi, *Gentle Civilizer*, 150–1.
[234] Ibid., 109.
[235] Weeramantry discusses the question of whether sovereignty over Nauru was validly acquired in the European law of nations. See Christopher Weeramantry, *Nauru: Environmental Damage under International Trusteeship* (Oxford: Oxford University Press, 1992), 8.

an uncanny mirror: both Europeans and Nauruans were recognised as holding private rights in property and resources, but neither was recognised as holding rights of sovereignty. In Sonnenschein's report back to Bismarck proclaiming the success of the *Eber*'s hostage mission, he included specific acknowledgment of Nauruan property in land under the heading 'Land Ownership', noting that '(t)he white residents own little land as the natives, who need the land for their own livelihood, are reluctant to part with it'.[236] This statement suggests that Indigenous property interests were understood to survive the invasion. The implication is that Nauruan property rights may have been understood as deriving either from Indigenous legal authority capable of creating proprietary rights recognisable in European law, but incapable of qualification as sovereignty; or from a principle of occupation in the law of nations. The former view – that via the fact of physical occupation, Indigenous peoples possessed property recognisable in private law, but not sovereignty recognisable in international law – was subsequently expressed by German jurist Robert Adam and by British jurist John Westlake.[237] The latter view – that Indigenous occupation created property rights recognisable in international law via the principle of occupation derived from Roman civil law, but not sovereignty – was open to take. Indeed, both alternatives worked within the sketchy logic of *territorium nullius* proposed by Martitz.

2.17 International Status and Imperial Form: Administration in Nauru

However, to attempt to perfect retrospectively the jurisprudential reasoning behind the incorporation of Nauru into the German protectorate of the Marshall Islands is to miss the point. It is possible to describe the actions taken by the Reich with respect to Nauru in 1888 as founded on an understanding of Nauruan land as *territorium nullius*, in order to fit the creation of the Nauruan protectorate within a conceptual taxonomy sensible to the international law of territorial acquisition. As a matter of history, however, that law was yet to be settled. It is more accurate to describe those actions as ad hoc administrative responses to a series of commercial demands that had become significant within the context of

---

[236] Report of Imperial Commissioner of the Marshall Islands to Prince Herbert von Bismarck, 31 October 1888, reproduced in Fabricius, *Nauru*, 224.
[237] Koskenniemi, *Gentle Civilizer*, 127–8.

European realpolitik and German domestic politics. If the actions taken by the German empire were characterised at the time within a jurisprudential framework at all, they were characterised within German constitutional law and the private law of property. The efforts of the Institut to settle those actions within a coherent jurisprudence of sovereignty, property and territory followed the event. On this view, the incoherence of the international law of protectorates resulted from the relatively quick failure of the protectorate model as a viable solution to that policy problem.

When viewed from Nauru, then, if the law of nations played a role in the imposition of protectorate status on the island, it was hardly as a coherent European project, but as an ex post facto rationalisation of a series of executive decisions reactive to corporate lobbying in a volatile domestic and diplomatic environment. Koskenniemi has stated of the Institut that '(i)t was their failure to spell out the meaning of sovereignty in social and political terms, as applied in non-European territory, that in retrospect made international lawyers seems such hopeless apologists of empire'.[238] However this assessment implies that there was 'a' meaning of sovereignty to be spelled out. When viewed from the Western Pacific, what was attempted in the protectorate model was a reconciliation of contradictory corporate and state aims: to protect European claims to private property outside the domain of European sovereignty whilst avoiding formal territorial acquisition. The attempt to achieve this via the territorialisation of consular jurisdiction was, in the end, doomed to fail.

2.18 Conclusion

The classical concept of the protectorate does not clearly explain the nature of authority asserted by the Reich over Nauru in 1888, not least because the distinctions between concepts of sovereignty, property and territory were not settled as matters of positive international law. The authority asserted over Nauru was less a reflection of contemporaneous international law, than a pragmatic arrangement of administrative authority and corporate financial responsibility struck between the Reich and the Jaluit Gesellschaft. The narrative of the Hanseatic inheritance of Godeffroy, Hansemann, Hernsheim and Lüderitz thus serves as a counterweight to narratives of international legal history that anachronistically read concepts of sovereignty, territory and property back into

---

[238] Ibid., 169.

2.18 CONCLUSION

the history of nineteenth-century imperial expansion. The balance of state and company rule struck between the Reich and the Jaluit Gesellschaft in the 1888 Jaluit Agreement on the administration of the Marshall Islands reflected a complex political moment in which the respective powers of company, empire and state were being reconfigured. Only tangentially could the Reich's assertion of authority over Nauru be understood as informed by the intellectual project that was coming to know itself in Europe as international law.

Attention to this distinction between international status and administrative form in the assertion of authority over Nauru generates its own historiographical momentum. As argued in the following chapters, the basic form of company administration established in the 1888 Agreement – with its concentration of executive power, its conflation of corporate and public authority and its implied distribution of land and phosphate rights between the Reich, the company and the Nauruan people – was bureaucratised over the following decades, as the international status of Nauru shifted from protectorate to colony, and then to mandate. The exclusive right to mine phosphate created in the 1888 Agreement was transferred by the Jaluit Gesellschaft to the British-owned Pacific Phosphate Company. In turn, the consolidation of the Pacific Phosphate Company's mining operation on Nauru was a key condition of possibility of the occupation of the island by Australian troops on behalf of the British empire in 1914. Australia's occupation of Nauru, and insistence on ownership of Nauruan phosphate, in turn prefaced not only the designation of Nauru as a C Mandate in the new League of Nations mandate system, but as will be argued in the followed chapter, the creation of the C Mandate itself. Focus on imperial administrative form as a phenomenon distinct from, yet related to, international status establishes an alternative perspective from which to redescribe the attempt to establish a new international order in the aftermath of World War I.

3

From Protectorate to Colony to Mandate, 1920

3.1 Introduction

In the decades following the declaration of protectorate status in 1888 and the settlement between the Reich and the Jaluit Gesellschaft of a basic division of resource rights and administrative responsibilities in Nauru, the status of Nauru was to shift twice, from German protectorate to German colony to British mandate. This chapter traces the accretions of administrative form that accompanied each shift, and argues that the basic structure of private and public relations instantiated by the 1888 Jaluit Agreement was later incorporated into the tripartite Nauru Island Agreement struck between Britain, Australia and New Zealand in 1919, for joint administration of the island as a C Mandate of the new League of Nations. The international status of Nauru was determined by the Mandate conferred in 1920 by the Allied Powers on the British empire, yet it was the Nauru Island Agreement, settled intra-imperially during Peace Conference negotiations in 1919 prior to official conferral of the Mandate, that determined how Nauru would be administered. Under the Nauru Island Agreement, public authority previously exercised by the Nauru District Office of the German Marshall Islands Protectorate, and later German New Guinea, was vested in the new Australian-appointed office of Administrator, and private rights originally vested in the Jaluit Gesellschaft were transferred to a new tripartite Board of Commissioners, which in time became known as the British Phosphate Commission.

The shift from protectorate to colony to C Mandate status reflected a broader – and far more familiar – set of paradigm shifts over the turn of the century, at intra-imperial, inter-imperial and international levels. C Mandate status was itself a product of an uneasy pragmatic compromise struck between the British Dominions' push for territorial annexation of the occupied German territories and the various concepts of internationalisation that circulated at Versailles. The bureaucratic separation of claimed authority over Nauru into the new Office of Administrator and the new tripartite Board of Commissioners marked a set of tensions within the British empire over control of the Dominions' external affairs powers. Yet the accretions in administrative form that responded to these structural changes did not uproot but rather grew around the basic structure of public and private authority instantiated in the 1888 Agreement.

The chapter begins with an account of the ad hoc development from 1888 of the jurisdiction of Nauru as a District Office of the German protectorate of the Marshall Islands, under the administration of the Jaluit Gesellschaft. The arrangement proved less than successful for the Gesellschaft, as did similar arrangements of company rule across the German protectorates. Within a decade, the company was seeking to back out of the arrangement. In the early 1900s, the Reich assumed direct colonial administration of German New Guinea, subsuming the Marshall Islands Protectorate within it. The chapter moves to redescribe the sale of the Gesellschaft's phosphate exploitation rights to a British firm, the Pacific Islands Company. The global phosphate market expanded rapidly during the industrialisation of agricultural production over the nineteenth century, and corporate claims over phosphate islands staked out many of the frontiers of imperial competition in the Pacific. The Pacific Islands Company's mining operation in Nauru under German administration developed during a period of rising anti-German sentiment in newly federated Australia. Australian anxiety over a formal German presence in the Western Pacific emphasised the tension between 'White Australia's racially grounded presumption to sub-imperial dominance in the Pacific region, and the limitations on the Commonwealth's control over its external affairs. The British Imperial government insisted into the 1920s that its retention of control over the self-governing Dominions' external affairs powers was crucial to the coherence of the empire.

The chapter then moves on to consider the relationship between the occupation of the German Pacific and South West Africa by Australia and South Africa on behalf of the British empire in 1914, the negotiations over the fate of the occupied German and Ottoman territories at the Paris Peace Conference, and the compromise struck between advocates of internationalisation and territorial annexation in the creation of a classed mandate system, codified in Article 22 of the Covenant of the League of Nations. The chapter concludes that whilst the creation of

C Mandate status as ascribed to Nauru marked the official shift from imperial to international administration, the administrative structure adopted by Britain, Australia and New Zealand to administer Nauru as a phosphate operation marked an accretion of the administrative form established under German rule.

3.2 Administration of Nauru as Part of the Marshall Islands Protectorate

As covered in Chapter 2, the imposition of protectorate status on Nauru occurred via a series of instruments of German law. The 1886 Protectorate Law purported to vest the power of the Reich to make laws for protectorates in the Kaiser. The power so vested was exercisable via imperial decree and, in September 1886, the Imperial Ordinance establishing the Marshall Islands Protectorate was issued by Kaiser Wilhelm I. Pursuant to the same section, Nauru was decreed a German protectorate on 16 April 1888 and incorporated into the administration of the Marshall Islands Protectorate by the Commissioner of the Marshall Islands as the Kaiser's delegate.[1] The 1888 Agreement between the Reich and the Jaluit Gesellschaft divided administrative responsibilities and substantive rights between empire and company. The Protectorate Law provided that German consular law applied with respect to private law, criminal law and related procedure and any other matters covered by consular law.[2] The Reich's Consular Law itself provided for personal jurisdiction over German and other European subjects in regions to which it applied, and defaulted to German municipal law unless specifically provided.[3] Beyond this basic jurisdictional scaffolding, the content of the law that applied in Nauru remained to be determined.

In effect, then, the default position within the territory of the German protectorates was that German municipal law applied to relations between Europeans, but jurisdiction over Indigenous peoples was not

---

[1] *Bekanntmachung* [Proclamation], 16 April 1888, in Wilhelm Fabricius, *Nauru 1888–1900: An Account in German and English Based on Official Records of the Colonial Section of the German Foreign Office Held by the Deutsches Zentralarchiv in Potsdam*, trans. Dymphna Clark and Stewart Firth (Canberra: Research School of Pacific Studies, Australian National University, 1992), 196.

[2] *Gesetz, betreffend die Rechtsverhältnisse der deutschen Schutzgebiete* [Law Governing the Legal Status of the German Protectorates], 17 April 1886, RGBl, 1886, 75 ('Protectorate Law'), s. 2.

[3] *Gesetz über die Konsulargerichtsbarkeit* [Law on Consular Jurisdiction], 10 July 1879, RGBl, 1879, 197 ss. 2, 3.

expressly contemplated.[4] The attempt to territorialise consular jurisdiction effectively created a juridical vacuum with respect to the legal status of Indigenous peoples within regions over which German protectorates were declared. However, the Protectorate Law provided that the executive power to make laws in the protectorates was exercised by the Kaiser on behalf of the Reich.[5] In practice, this power was delegated to the Imperial Commissioners on the creation of each protectorate. Once this delegation occurred, the Imperial Commissioners were effectively regarded under German law as having unlimited executive power in the protectorates where the Protectorate Law and the Consular Law were silent; and with respect to Indigenous peoples, the Laws were almost entirely so.[6] Around the basic jurisdictional scaffolding established between 1886 and 1888, the Imperial Commissioners governed by executive decree.[7] Given Bismarck's attempt to limit the scope of the Reich's administrative responsibilities in the protectorates, the irony of this structure is clear. As a legal form, the German protectorate was originally intended to minimise formal administrative intervention outside the bounds of sovereign territory whilst protecting corporate interests, but in the absence of consideration of the legal status of Indigenous peoples the protectorates effectively subjected Indigenous peoples – the majority in every case, given minimal German emigration – to absolute executive rule.

The Kaiser's power to make laws for the Marshall Islands Protectorate was delegated to the new office of Kaiserlicher Kommissar or Imperial Commissioner in September 1886.[8] Following the Agreement between

[4] Snow, Alpheus Henry, *The Question of Aborigines in the Law and Practice of Nations* (New York: Putnam and Sons, 1921), 97. Luigi Nuzzo, 'Colonial Law', *European History Online*, 16 April 2012, available at www.ieg-ego.eu/en/threads/europe-and-the-world/eur opean-overseas-rule/luigi-nuzzo-colonial-law, 10.
[5] Protectorate Law, ss. 1, 4.
[6] 'As respects the juridical situation of the aborigines and of all other colored people assimilated to them, the right of the Emperor to make ordinances by the delegation of the statute above mentioned [the Protectorate Law] is theoretically unlimited.' Snow, *Question of Aborigines*, 99–100.
[7] Felix Hanschmann, 'The Suspension of Constitutionalism in the Heart of Darkness' in Kelly L. Grotke and Markus J. Prutsch (eds.), *Constitutionalism, Legitimacy and Power: Nineteenth Century Experiences* (Oxford: Oxford University Press, 2014), 252.
[8] *Verordnung, betreffend die Rechtsverhältnisse in dem Schutzgebiete der Marschall-, Brown- und Providence-Inseln* [Law Governing Legal Relations in the Marshall, Brown and Providence Islands Protectorates], 17 September 1886, RGBl, 1886, 291. Ordinances for the Marshall Islands Protectorate published in Otto von Kolisch, *Die Kolonialgesetzgebung des deutschen Reichs mit dem Gesetze über die Konsulergerichtsbarkeit* (Hanover: Helwing, 1896), Chapter XII.

the Reich and the Jaluit Gesellschaft, in which the company agreed to cover all costs of extending the protectorate over Nauru,[9] a new Nauru District Office was proclaimed by the Imperial Commissioner in April 1888. From that date – six months prior to the gunboat occupation of Nauru in October 1888 – ordinances issued by the Imperial Commissioner for the Marshall Islands Protectorate were understood to apply in Nauru, ineffective only for want of enforcement rather than lack of foundation. The preoccupation with establishing effective control as opposed to legitimacy of rule is evident in the fact that the first ordinances specific to Nauru were the Ordinance relating to the Prohibition of the Importation of Firearms, Ammunition and Explosives into Pleasant Island, issued the same day as the Proclamation declaring the incorporation of Nauru into the Marshall Islands Protectorate, and the Ordinance relating to the Declaration of Jaluit as the Port of Entry for Pleasant Island, issued the following day.[10]

From April 1888, then, the structure of German law applicable in Nauru was as follows: German consular law applied to European traders in matters of private and criminal law and procedure, and in all else ordinances specific to the Marshall Islands or Nauru applied.[11] The Jaluit Gesellschaft's original concern to monopolise trade in the islands and pacify the Nauruan people is reflected in the initial ordinances, which required non-German vessels to report first to the Imperial Commissioner in Jaluit, and prevented the sale of arms, ammunition and alcohol to Natives.[12] These were followed by ordinances establishing

---

[9] 'Agreement between the Jaluit Gesellschaft and the Reich', 21 January 1888. Fabricius, *Nauru*, 202–4.

[10] *Verordnung betreffend das Verbot der Einfuhr von Feuerwaffen, Schießbedarf und Sprengstoffen in Pleasant Island* [Prohibition of the Importation of Firearms, Ammunition and Explosives into Pleasant Island], 16 April 1888; and *Verordnung betreffend die Eklärung des Hafens von Jaluit zum Eingangshafen für Pleasant Island* [Ordinance relating to the Declaration of Jaluit as the Port of Entry for Pleasant Island], 17 April 1888. Ibid., 198–9.

[11] Dirk H. R. Spennemann, 'A Hand List of Imperial German Legislation Regarding the Marshall Islands (1886–1914)' (2007) 3 *Studies in German Colonial Heritage*, 1–13. On the ad hoc development of law in the German protectorates, see Snow, *Question of Aborigines*, 97; and Hanschmann, 'Suspension of Constitutionalism', 249.

[12] For example, *Verordnung, betreffend die Verpflichtung nichtdeutscher Schiffe zur Meldung bei dem Vertreter der kaiserlichen Regierung in Jaluit* [Ordinance regarding the Obligation of Non-German vessels to Notify the Representative of the Imperial Government at Jaluit], 2 June 1886; and *Verordnung, betreffend den Verkauf von Waffen, Munition, Sprengstoffen und berauschenden Getränken und Eingeborene der Marshall Inseln oder andere auf denselben sich aufhaltende Farbige* [Ordinance regarding the Sale of Weapons, Munitions, Explosives and Intoxicating Beverages to the Indigenous Peoples of the

local judicial authorities and delineating a hierarchy for appeals, and ordinances regulating the raising of personal and business taxes.[13] The content of ordinances thus moved on quickly to deal with the enforcement of credit arrangements and property disputes between European traders and Natives.[14]

Criminal jurisdiction over Indigenous peoples took a few years to be positively established. In July 1889 Imperial Commissioner Friedrich Biermann reported that although German law was effectively in operation, the situation required formal clarification, and that in the interim, some gesture towards the customary authority of Nauruan chiefs had been deemed symbolically necessary:

> (i)n Nauru, as also here in the Marshall Islands, the people believe that the German government official automatically has the right in given circumstances to punish anyone, whether native or foreigner, chief or commoner, and that he has in fact to settle all disputes. As however the Commissioner has not thus far been formally vested with criminal jurisdiction over natives, hitherto such cases have always been tried and sentenced passed by calling in chiefs as judges. On these occasions the chiefs are in fact only puppets, who concur automatically in every proposal put forward by the white official.[15]

Indicative of the broader German unconcern regarding the basis of jurisdiction over Indigenous peoples in the new protectorates, clarification at the legislative level was not forthcoming. In February 1890 Biermann himself filled the vacuum by simply issuing an executive ordinance declaring general jurisdiction over Natives in the protectorate of the Marshall Islands.[16]

Marshall Islands or Other Coloured Persons Present Thereon], 3 June 1886, trans. Spennemann, 'Imperial German Legislation', 4.

[13] *Verordnung, betreffend die Erhebung von persönlichen Steuern* [Regulation, regarding the Levy of Personal Taxes] and *Verordnung, betreffend die Erhebung von persönlichen Steuern* [Regulation, regarding the Levy of Business Taxes in Jaluit], both passed on 28 June 1888. Ibid.

[14] *Verordnung, betreffend das Kreditgeben an Eingeborene und die Anmeldung alter Schulden derselben in den Marshall Inseln* [Ordinance regarding the Giving of Credit to Natives and the Registration of Old Debts in the Marshall Islands], 25 January 1887; and *Verordnung, betreffend Verträge mit Eingeborenen über unbewegliche Sachen* [Regulation regarding Contracts with Natives regarding Immovable Properties], 28 June 1888. Ibid.

[15] Letter from Imperial Commissioner Biermann to His Highness Prince Bismarck dated 29 July 1889. Fabricius, *Nauru*, 240, 241.

[16] *Verordnung, betreffend die Gerichtsbarkeit über die Eingeborenen im Schutzgebiete der Marshall-Inseln* [Ordinance regarding the Jurisdiction over the Indigenous Peoples in the Protectorate of the Marshall Islands], issued 26 February 1890, trans. Spennemann, 'Imperial German Legislation', 6.

As discussed in Chapter 2, Indigenous peoples in the Marshall Islands and in Nauru were treated by German officials as possessing real and personal property rights recognisable in German law.[17] Records indicate that the new Nauruan District Office considered itself obligated not only to respect, but also to enforce those proprietary rights where disputes arose. The Agreement between the Gesellschaft and the Reich purported to grant the company the right to 'take possession of all ownerless land', understood to exclude land owned by both traders and Nauruans.[18] Following the establishment of the Nauruan District Office, in September 1889 Imperial Commissioner Biermann entered into a contract for the sale and purchase of land and buildings to house the new Office.[19] This contract between the Imperial government and 'Häuptling Jim', or Chief Jim, purported to pass ownership in an area of land and buildings, 'together with all the coconut palms growing thereon'.[20] The express reference to palms was included in recognition of local Nauruan property practices, which the German administration understood to separate absolute ownership of land from absolute ownership of trees growing on that land. According to a report written by Nauru District Officer Fritz Jung in 1897, ownership in land and trees could pass separately, and owners of trees could grant usufructuary rights to third parties, which land owners would be required to recognise.[21] Acting Secretary to the Imperial Commissioner Arno Senfft reported on his inspection of the Nauru District Office in September 1895 that land

---

[17] See also Christopher Weeramantry, *Nauru: Environmental Damage under International Trusteeship* (Oxford: Oxford University Press), 186–7.

[18] *Vereinbarung zwischen dem Auswärtigen Amt und der Jaluit-Gesellschaft* [Agreement between the Jaluit Gesellschaft and the Reich], cl. 1(a). Fabricius, *Nauru*, 202.

[19] *Vereinbarung zwischen der Kaiserliche Regierung und dem Häuptling Jim von Nauru* [Contract between the Imperial German Government and Chief Jim of Nauru], 29 September 1889. Ibid., 250. Häuptling Jim was the name given by the German traders to the father of Aweijeda or Aweida/Oweida, one of the chiefs taken hostage by the crew of the *SMS Eber*, who came to be known by the Germans as King Aweida.

[20] Ibid.

[21] 'Property in land is of primary importance. Almost every native on Nauru owns land or palms, with the exception of the slaves. Every patch of ground and every palm, the reef surrounding the island and even the sea washing the coastline has its owner ... Land is seldom sold, but different portions of land are frequently exchanged. It is worthy of mention that in many places the land itself and the palms growing thereon are owned by two different proprietors.' District Officer Fritz Jung, 'Aufzeichnungen über die Rechtsanschauungen der Eingeborenen von Nauru' [Notes on the Legal Concepts of the Natives of Nauru] (1897) 10 *Mittheilungen aus den deutschen Schutzgebieten*, 64; cf. Peter H. McSporran, 'Land Ownership and Control in Nauru' (1995) 2 *Murdoch University Electronic Journal of Law* 1, 2.

3.3 THE COLLAPSE OF THE COMPANY PROTECTORATES

3.1 Nauruan community with German naval officers, 1896. Credit: ullstein bild/ullstein bild via Getty Images.

disputes constituted the bulk of the Office's work, and were resolved by Jung according to Nauruan customary law. According to Senftt, the Office was in 'exemplary order', and District Officer Jung enjoyed the 'due respect' of the Nauruan people.[22]

3.3 The Collapse of the German Protectorates and the Assertion of Direct Rule

As the Nauru District Office of the Marshall Islands Protectorate developed its own law and procedure to govern the Nauruan people, the Jaluit Gesellschaft incorporated by Goddefroy and Hernsheim was required to meet the costs of administration under the terms of its 1888 Agreement with the Reich.[23] As discussed in Chapter 2, in 1886 the firms had entreated

---

[22] *Briefe von Sekretär a.i. der Kaiserlichen Landeshauptmannschaft an den Kaiserlichen Landeshauptmann Herrn Dr. Irmer* [Letter from Temporary Secretary to the Administrator Arno Senftt to Imperial Administrator Georg Irmer], 27 September 1895. Fabricius, *Nauru*, 258–60.

[23] 'Agreement between the Jaluit Gesellschaft and the Reich', 21 January 1888. Ibid., 202–4, cl. 4.

the Reich to extend official protection of their commercial interests in Nauru; but barely eight years after the *SMS Eber*'s hostage operation and the raising of the German flag, the Gesellschaft was trying to back out of the deal. In January 1896 the Gesellschaft sent a letter directly from Hamburg to the Foreign Office in Berlin – bypassing both the Nauru District Officer and the Imperial Commissioner of the Marshall Islands – seeking to exercise its right under the Agreement to terminate the Nauru arrangement.[24] Its primary complaint was that the trading tax payable to the Reich was fixed at an excessively high annual rate, and did not reflect changes in copra yield.[25] In addition to the trading tax, a head tax had been imposed on the Nauruans in the form of an annual copra quota. One third of the price obtained from taxed copra was returned to chiefs as incentive to facilitate its collection.[26] Where this combined tax revenue failed to meet the costs of administration – the highest of which were salary costs for the District Officer and secretary, including pension contributions – the company accountants in Hamburg recorded a loss against its Agreement with the Reich.[27] In justifying its request, the Gesellschaft emphasised the commercial rationale for the establishment of the District Office:

> (w)hen Nauru was incorporated in the Protectorate of the Marshall Islands, the main concern was to put an end to the totally lawless situation on this island, to disarm the natives, who were at the time in possession of a large number of firearms ... The desired reforms have now been implemented for a number of years; the situation on Nauru as regards personal safety and security of property no longer falls short of that on the other islands ... The returns from Nauru are relatively low ... In these circumstances we take the liberty of proposing that, on expiry of the present contract with Herr Jung, the District Office on Nauru be abolished.'[28]

However, when consulted by the Foreign Office on the Gesellschaft's proposal to abolish the Nauru District Office, the new Imperial Commissioner of the Marshall Islands Georg Irmer roundly rejected the company's claims.[29] Responding directly to the Chancellor, Commissioner Irmer retorted that 'the only concrete argument in favour

---

[24] Letter from Jaluit Gesellschaft to the Political Section of the Foreign Office in Berlin dated 10 January 1896. Ibid., 275–6.
[25] Ibid., 248–9.
[26] Ibid.
[27] Ibid., 272.
[28] Ibid.
[29] *Bericht No. 49 Kaiserliche Landeshauptsmann für das Schutzgebiet der Marshall–Inseln* ['Report No. 49 of the Imperial Administrator of the Protectorate of the Marshall Islands'], 15 June 1896. Ibid., 275–8.

3.3 THE COLLAPSE OF THE COMPANY PROTECTORATES 109

of abolishing the position in Nauru is the bad trading position of the *Jaluit-Gesellschaft*.[30] According to Irmer, peace on Nauru was maintained only by the presence of the District Officer; and the Gesellschaft was either underreporting its returns on the copra trade, or directly responsible for its decline.[31]

The Gesellschaft's rapid disenchantment with its administrative responsibilities reflected comparable developments across the German empire. Each of the protectorates developed their own culture of executive rule, as the Protectorate Law delegated executive rule directly from the Kaiser to the Imperial Commissioners – many of whom then delegated that power on to District Officers.[32] Yet on the whole they failed to fulfil the policy objectives they had been created to meet: the companies whose interests they had been created to protect failed as commercial ventures, and the protectorates required the ever-escalating administrative and financial involvement of the Reich, directly contradicting Bismarck's 1884 assurances to the Reichstag. German East Africa was the first of the company protectorates to falter. In 1885 Peters' Gesellschaft für Deutsche Kolonisation had been granted the patronage of Kaiser Wilhelm I in an agreement that came the closest to an imperial charter of all the commercial interests supported by the Reich in the late nineteenth century, creating the Deutsch-Ostafrikanische Gesellschaft to take on the administration of the protectorate.[33] Yet by 1889 the Deutsch-Ostafrikanische Gesellschaft had effectively failed in its attempt to administer the region west of Zanzibar over which Carl Peters had so brashly claimed control.[34] The company proved unable to finance the

---

[30] Ibid.
[31] Ibid.
[32] Sebastian Conrad, *German Colonialism: A Short History* (Cambridge: Cambridge University Press, 2012), 72.
[33] The imperial declaration explicitly referred to company sovereignty: '[A]s the said Dr. Carl Peters in November and December of last year concluded treaties with the rulers of Usagara, Mguru, Useguba, and Ukami, by which these territories were taken over by the Society for German Colonization with the right of sovereignty, and has petitioned me to place these territories under our authority; so do we confirm that we have taken over this authority and we have placed these territories ... under our imperial protection.' *Kaiserlicher Schutzbrief für Carl Peters' Gesellschaft für deutsche Kolonisation* [Imperial Letter of Protection for Carl Peters' Society for German Colonization], in Johannes Hohlfeld (ed.) *Deutsche Reichsgeschichte in Dokumenten 1849–1926*, vol. 1 (Berlin: Deutsche Verlagsgesellschaft für Politik und Geschichte, 1927), 186–7.
[34] Helmuth Stoecker, 'German East Africa 1885–1906' in Helmuth Stoecker (ed.) *German Imperialism in Africa: From the Beginnings until the Second World War*, trans. Bernd Zöllner (London: C. Hurst and Company, 1986), 93–9; Constant Kpao Saré, 'Abuses of German Colonial History: The Character of Carl Peters as a Weapon for *Völkisch* and

administration of the territory it sought to rule, and its aggressive conduct in pursuit of a trading monopoly from the mountains to the coast of Zanzibar was met with vigorous local resistance.[35] Bismarck responded to Peters' requests for military support to shore up the company's position with characteristic ambivalence towards increased colonial commitment: as late as September 1888 he declared he 'would rather give up the whole East African endeavour than agree to imperial military undertakings in the interior'.[36] Yet a few months later, in January 1889, the embattled Chancellor issued orders for military intervention with the Reichstag's support, and the protectorate of German East Africa was placed under the direct administration of the Reich.[37] In German South West Africa too, the Deutsche Kolonial Gesellschaft für Südwest-Afrika created by Bremen tobacco merchant F. A. E. Lüderitz to administer the protectorate was failing financially by mid-1889, unable to compete with Cecil Rhodes' consolidation of his corporate empire in Southern Africa.[38]

Bismarck himself was forced to resign from his double post as Chancellor and Prussian Foreign Minister in March 1890 by the new Kaiser, Wilhelm II.[39] Bismarck's retirement followed protracted parliamentary discord over the Chancellor's anti-socialist agenda, and his failure to maintain a stable coalition of parties in the Reichstag.[40] On

National Socialist Discourses: Anglophobia, Anti-Semitism, Aryanism' in Michael Perraudin and Jürgen Zimmerer with Katy Heady (eds.), *German Colonialism and National Identity* (London: Routledge, 2011), 161.

[35] On the Abushiri uprising, see Stoecker, 'German East Africa 1885–1906', 93–9; and Arthur J Knoll and Hermann J Hiery (eds.), *The German Colonial Experience: Select Documents on German Rule in Africa, China and the Pacific 1884–1914* (Maryland: University Press of America, 2010), 67.

[36] *Statement of Chancellor Bismarck*, 18 September 1888. Ibid., 67.

[37] Stoecker, 'German East Africa 1885–1906', 99.

[38] Horst Dreschsler, 'South West Africa 1885–1907' in Stoecker (ed.) *German Imperialism in Africa*, 41–43. On Cecil Rhodes and the British South Africa Company, see John S. Galbraith, *Crown and Charter: The Early Years of the British South Africa Company* (London: University of California Press, 1977) and Robert I. Rotberg, *The Founder: Cecil Rhodes and the Pursuit of Power* (Oxford: Oxford University Press, 1988).

[39] On competing historiographies of the Wilhelmian Reich, see for example Michael Perraudin and Jürgen Zimmerer, 'Introduction: German Colonialism and National Identity' in Perraudin and Zimmerer with Heady, *German Colonialism and National Identity*, 1–8; John C. G. Röhl, 'Goodbye to All That (Again)? The Fischer Thesis, the New Revisionism and the Meaning of the First World War' (2015) 91 *International Affairs*, 153–66; and Lynn Abrams, *Bismarck and the German Empire 1871–1918*, 2nd ed. (London and New York: Routledge, 2006).

[40] *Bismarck: A Political History*, 2nd ed. (London and New York: Routledge, 2014) esp. 245–8.

Bismarck's ousting from office, the young Wilhelm II appointed Leo von Caprivi, former Commanding General of the Army Corps, as Chancellor, and embarked on what has subsequently become known as the 'New Course' in German foreign policy.[41] Under Wilhelm II, the new regime departed from the essentially reactionary realpolitik of Wilhelm I and Chancellor Bismarck, and accommodated the Kaiser's increasingly autocratic, unpredictable expansionism.[42]

Kaiser Wilhelm II's New Course in German governance was reflected in the centralisation of colonial policy. In October 1890 Caprivi created the Kolonialabteilung or Colonial Department, which sat within the Foreign Office. The Colonial Department took over the appointment of officials in the protectorates from the Imperial Commissioners.[43] The shift towards direct colonial administration was motivated at least in part by an attempt to quell political discord within Germany via a unifying nationalist discourse of imperial strength.[44] In March 1891 the Reich passed a law providing military support to Peters' failing administration in German East Africa and the new Imperial Commissioner for the protectorate, Hermann Wissmann, was authorised to recruit local mercenaries to quash local resistance, under the command of German officers.[45] In March 1893 the same occurred for Lüderitz' Deutsche Kolonial Gesellschaft für Südwest-Afrika: Caprivi declared the protectorate to be a German colony and increased military support.[46] In 1896 the Reichstag passed a law aggregating the administration of the colonial armed forces or Schutztruppen of German East Africa, South West Africa and Cameroon, and formalising the conscription of Indigenous Africans into the forces.[47] In 1907 the Colonial Department was separated

---

[41] John C. G. Röhl, *Wilhelm II: The Kaiser's Personal Monarchy, 1888–1900* (Cambridge: Cambridge University Press, 2004), 320–33.

[42] On *Weltpolitik*, see ibid., 343–4; also E. Malcolm Carroll, *Germany and the Great Powers 1866–1914: A Study in Public Opinion and Foreign Policy* (London: Archon Books, 1966), 475–8. For competing accounts of Wilhelmian imperialism, see Hans-Ulrich Wehler, *The German Empire 1871–1918* trans. Kym Traynor (Leamington Spa: Berg Publishers, 1985); and Eric Hobsbawm, *The Age of Empire: 1875–1914* (London: Weidenfeld and Nicolson, 1987).

[43] L. H. Gann and Peter Duignan, *The Rulers of German Africa 1884–1914* (Stanford: Stanford University Press, 1977), 46, 67; also Snow, *Question of Aborigines*, 101–2.

[44] Wehler, *The German Empire*, 174–9.

[45] *Gesetz, betreffend die Kaiserliche Schutztruppe für Deutsch-Ostafrika* [Law concerning the Imperial Colonial Force for German East Africa], 22 March 1891. Gann and Duignan, *Rulers of German Africa*, 65; Stoecker, 'German East Africa 1885–1906', 99.

[46] Dreschsler, 'South West Africa 1885–1907', 43.

[47] *Gesetz wegen Abänderung des Gesetzes, betreffend die Kaiserliche Schutztruppe für Deutsch-Ostafrika und des Gesetzes, betreffend die Kaiserlichen Schutztruppen für Südwestafrika und für Kamerun* [Law amending the Laws on the Imperial Colonial

from the Foreign Office and became its own Office, the Reichskolonialamt.[48] Over the course of twenty years, Bismarck's reluctant extension of official protection to disparate German commercial interests in Africa and the Pacific had developed into a ministry of government with its own armed force. Within Germany, support for the escalation was not unanimous: the Social Democratic Party opposed the centralisation of colonial policy and the militarisation of German presence in Africa, arguing that it furthered the interests of the ruling elite at the expense of the German majority.[49]

The German Pacific protectorates faltered too. In 1898 Hansemann's Neuguinea Kompagnie was rescued from bankruptcy by an agreement with the Reich, which paid out the ailing company and assumed direct administration of the region.[50] That same year, the ad hoc regime of tripartite rule of Samoa by German, British and United States empires came to an end. The 'tridominium' arrangement had been brokered by Bismarck in the Berlin Samoan Conference of 1889 on the basis of equality of their respective commercial interests in the Samoan islands.[51] But sharing the administration of Samoa irritated the Reich of Wilhelm II, which held out Samoa as the idyllic exemplar of German empire in domestic politics. Adolf Marschall – Herbert von Bismarck's replacement as Foreign Secretary in the new regime – wrote of the 'Samoan question' that 'the reputation of the New Course depends upon it'.[52] The tridominium was severed in the Samoan Tripartite Convention of 1899, negotiated in the context of civil war in the Samoan islands. The three powers agreed that Germany would exercise exclusive control of the western Samoan islands; the United States, the eastern Samoan islands; and Britain, the Solomon Islands to the west, as

Forces for German East Africa, South West Africa and Cameroon] 17 July 1896, RGBl 1986, 53.

[48] *Allerhöchster Erlaß, betreffend die Errichtung des Reichs-Kolonialamts* [Decree on the Establishment of the Reich Colonial Office] 17 May 1907, RGBl 1907, 239.

[49] *Stenographische Berichte über die Verhandlungen des Reichstags* [Stenographic Reports on the Proceedings of the Reichstag), 7th legislative period, 4th session 1888–1889, vol. 1 (January 1889), 627–31.

[50] Stewart Firth, 'German Firms in the Western Pacific Islands, 1857–1918' (1973) 8 *Journal of Pacific History*, 10–28 at 21; Conrad, *German Colonialism*, 54.

[51] See generally Paul M. Kennedy, 'Germany and the Samoan Tridominium, 1889–1898: A Study in Frustrated Imperialism' in John A Moses and Paul M. Kennedy (eds.), *Germany in the Pacific and the Far East, 1870–1914* (St Lucia: University of Queensland Press, 1977), 89–114. Also Great Britain Foreign and Commonwealth Office, *British and Foreign State Papers* vol. 91 (1898–1899), 1272–3.

[52] Kennedy, 'Germany and the Samoan Tridominium', 101.

3.3 THE COLLAPSE OF THE COMPANY PROTECTORATES 113

compensation for giving up its Samoan claim altogether.[53] In this way, the Reich came to exercise direct colonial rule over the islands where Hanseatic firm Godeffroy & Sohn had established their first Pacific trading post in 1857.

The Jaluit Gesellschaft's request that the Nauru District Office be abolished was thus part of a broader trend: the German experiment in company protectorates was unravelling. On the advice of Imperial Commissioner Irmer, the Foreign Office refused the Gesellschaft's request to abandon its Nauruan post, as the Wilhelmian Reich consolidated its New Course in foreign and colonial policy. Whilst the term Schutzgebiet continued to be used to refer to German imperial territories in Africa and the Pacific, the substance of the arrangements to which the term referred altered greatly over the 1890s and 1900s, from a mode of protecting German commercial interests without assuming direct administrative control, to direct administrative control supported by military force. Ten years after the Gesellschaft's failed attempt to exit its arrangement with the Reich, the Marshall Islands Protectorate was incorporated into German New Guinea in April 1906.[54] Executive authority over the Nauru District Office shifted from the Marshall Islands Imperial Commissioner at Jaluit to the Governor of New Guinea, Albert Hahl, who by 1907 answered directly to the head of the Colonial Office, Secretary of State for Colonial Affairs, banker Bernhard Dernburg.[55]

By 1907, then, the status of Nauru had shifted from protectorate to colony. The 1888 Agreement between the Jaluit Gesellschaft and the Reich came to an end with respect to all terms except one: the Gesellschaft's exclusive right to exploit phosphate deposits was renewed as a separate mining Concession, with a term of ninety-four years and rights of assignment.[56] The Nauru District Office now reported to the

---

[53] Ibid., 109–10; also W. M. Roger Louis, *Great Britain and Germany's Lost Colonies 1914–1919* (Oxford: Clarendon Press, 1967), 27.

[54] *Verordnung betreffend die anderweitige Regelung der Verwaltung und der Rechtsverhältnisse im Schutzgebiet der Marshall-, Brown und Providence Inseln* [Ordinance regarding the Changed Execution of the Administration and the Jurisdiction in the Protectorate of the Marshall, Brown- and Providence-Islands], 17 January 1906, RGBl 1906, 138.

[55] Peter G. Sack and Dymphna Clark (eds.), *Albert Hahl: Governor in New Guinea* trans. Peter G. Sack and Dymphna Clark (Canberra: Australian National University Press, 1980), esp. 56.

[56] Agreement between His Most Gracious Majesty King George V and Others and The Pacific Phosphate Company, Westminster, 25 June 1920, First Schedule, 'Concession'.

Governor of New Guinea rather than the Marshall Islands Imperial Commissioner, and powers of appointment passed to the Colonial Office in Berlin. Yet as the Schutzgebiete became colonies in all but name, the legal frameworks established under the Protectorate Law remained in place. Colonial officers continued to exercise an executive authority unfettered by legislative and judicial review.[57]

3.4 The Federation of Australia and Taxonomies of British Imperial Form

The Reich's adoption of the New Course over the 1890s and the transition from the protectorate to the colonial form were keenly followed in the Australian colonies to the southeast of the German Pacific protectorates. The British Imperial government's laissez-faire acquiescence to the activities of German firms in the Pacific in the 1870s and 1880s was a crucial catalyst for the federation conventions that commenced in the early 1880s.[58] The 1886 Demarcation Agreement between Britain and Germany, in which the two imperial governments purported to divide the western Pacific into British and German spheres of influence by plotting a line through the eastern half of the island of New Guinea and out into the Western Pacific, had aggravated the Australian colonies' irritation with the Imperial government's lack of obligation to consult the colonial governments on matters which they considered directly to affect their regional interests.[59] As the German empire shifted in form towards direct colonial administration, the legal structure of the British empire and the comparative status of its constituent parts came under increasing scrutiny from within. In 1887 the first Colonial Conference met in

---

[57] Hanschmann thus describes the unfolding of the German protectorate and its collapse into direct colonial rule as a spatially expressed divergence from the constitutional principles that were coming to define 'modern' Europe: '(t)he further the distance from the political centre and its chain of delegation, the more autocratic the colonial system became and the less "European" legal principles were brought into effect. Legislative, executive, and judicial powers were concentrated and personalized and so set free from normative commitments.' Hanschmann, 'Suspension of Constitutionalism', 254.

[58] Parliament of Victoria, Australasian Convention on the Annexation of Adjacent Islands and the Federation of Australasia, Parliamentary Paper No. 48 (Melbourne: John Ferres, Government Printer, 1883).

[59] Declaration between the Governments of Great Britain and the German Empire relating to the Demarcation of the British and German Spheres of Influence in the Western Pacific, Berlin, 6 April 1886. On unrest in the Australian colonies, see J. L. Whittaker, N. G. Nash, J. F. Hookey and R. L. Lacey (eds.), *Documents and Readings in New Guinea History: Pre-History to 1899* (Milton: Jacaranda Press, 1975), 475.

London, commencing a series of meetings that continued for over twenty years without resolving the basic question which had prompted it: namely, the international status of the colonies.[60]

By the late nineteenth century the British empire had evolved into an entity of extraordinary internal diversity.[61] Following the Berlin Conference on the Congo in 1884, the British empire too revived the classical protectorate model, for reasons similar to those offered by Bismarck on the floor of the Reichstag in 1884: it offered a means of protecting British commercial interests by keeping out other imperial powers from a given region, without attracting the rights and obligations of territorial sovereignty in international law. However, the German and British iterations of the protectorate were to diverge over the 1890s and 1900s, in both theory and practice. As the German Imperial government shifted towards direct colonial administration in substance if not in name, German jurists concerned themselves with the status of the Schutzgebiete in German constitutional law, with only minor attention paid to the legitimacy of the protectorate in the law of nations. In contrast, as British protectorates proliferated, British jurists engaged in earnest with the theoretical coherence of the practice across British law and the law of nations.[62]

Of key concern in the British jurisprudential debate over protectorate status was whether a protectorate could be established via unilateral domestic action, legislative or otherwise, or whether it required an act of territorial acquisition effective in the law of nations.[63] Parliamentary counsel Henry Jenkyns, who prepared the Foreign Jurisdiction Bill of 1888, advocated an understanding of the protectorate as a division of the sovereignty of the weaker entity.[64] Where the weaker entity was not recognised as sovereign in international law, the protecting state could effectively assume the external sovereignty of the region via domestic

---

[60] H. Duncan Hall, *The British Commonwealth of Nations: A Study of its Past and Future Developments* (London: Methuen & Co Ltd, 1920), 94–121.

[61] Sarah E. Stockwell (ed.),*The British Empire: Themes and Perspectives* (Wiley-Blackwell, 2008).

[62] See W. Ross Johnston, *Sovereignty and Protection: A Study of British Jurisdictional Imperialism in the Late Nineteenth Century* (Durham: Duke University Press, 1973), 216–23.

[63] Ibid., 216–23; and Matthew Craven, 'Between Law and History: The Berlin Conference of 1884–1885 and the Logic of Free Trade' (2015) 3 *London Review of International Law*, 31–59.

[64] Henry Jenkyns, *British Rule and Jurisdiction Beyond the Seas* (Oxford: Clarendon Press, 1902), 165–7; and Johnston, *Sovereignty and Protection*, 214–17.

legislation asserting the assumption of jurisdiction, as the Reich had in fact done.[65] But Jenkyn's view was not uncontested. Junior counsel to the Treasury, Robert Wright, countered Jenkyns' formulation on the basis of Austin's principle of the indivisibility of sovereignty.[66] Holding sovereignty to be territorial, Wright argued that assumption of sovereign powers over a foreign region could not occur via domestic legislation, and required an act of territorial acquisition effective in the law of nations. Weighing up the debate, Lord Chancellor Halsbury took a pragmatic approach, concluding that the protectorate was an established international convention that simply did not require explication in terms of sovereignty, as to do so would limit the flexibility of the form in practice:

> (p)rotectorate furnishes a convenient middle state between annexation and mere alliance so long as it is allowed to remain mere convention, but if you assert a principle which practically annihilates any distinction between the rights and obligations of a protecting power and those of complete sovereignty, then the function of protectorate is at an end.[67]

The consolidation of the Foreign Jurisdiction Acts in 1890 reflected Halsbury's pragmatism, remaining silent on the conception of sovereignty at play in assertions of protectorate status.[68]

The tension between legal principle and historical convention in British imperial policy was only to sharpen over the following decades. Whereas the German empire had consolidated rapidly with a universal adoption of the protectorate, the British protectorate was but one of a multiplicity of designations given to imperial administrative arrangements that from the sixteenth century had evolved across place and time, in the Americas, in Eurasia, in the Caribbean, Africa and the Pacific. These included 'Crown colony', 'self-governing colony', 'dependency', 'dominion' and 'condominium'.[69] As with the protectorate, these designations lacked consistent legal definition in the late nineteenth and early twentieth centuries. This mutability of terminology reflected the iterative nature of British imperialism; Welsh lawyer and historian Charles Prestwood Lucas wrote in 1891, '(t)he British empire has grown of itself;

---

[65] Jenkyns, *British Rule and Jurisdiction*, 174–5.
[66] Johnston gives an account of this exchange. Johnston, *Sovereignty and Protection*, 217–20.
[67] Memorandum of Lord Chancellor Halsbury of 28 March 1890, FO 97/562. Ibid., 222.
[68] Johnston, *Sovereignty and Protection*, 222–3.
[69] Jenkyns, *British Rule and Jurisdiction*, 1–8; for an historical survey of terminology used in the long transition from 'British empire' to 'British Commonwealth', see Sir Kenneth Roberts-Wray, *Commonwealth and Colonial Law* (London: Stevens & Sons, 1966), 1–73.

it has owed little or nothing to the foresight of soldiers or statesmen; it is the result of circumstances, or private adventure, and of national character; it is not the result of any constructive power on the part of the government'.[70]

Yet attempts retrospectively to rationalise as a matter of legal principle the diversity of administrative arrangements that constituted the British empire were underway by the late nineteenth century. The Interpretation Act of 1889 offered a basic taxonomy in a section titled 'Geographical and Colonial Definitions in Future Acts', which defined all 'British possessions' as 'dominions', of which the 'colony' was a subset including all except British India, which the Act singled out as unique.[71] British jurists extrapolated on the theme. For Lucas, the preferred term was not the territorially inflected 'dominion' given in the Interpretation Act but the personally inflected 'dependency', where a 'dependency' was defined as 'part of an independent political community which is immediately subject to a subordinate government'.[72] On his account, the key distinction was between dependencies governed by the British but populated by a native majority, and dependencies both governed and populated by the British, which he regarded as 'colonies in the true sense of the word'.[73] In Lucas' schema, self-government properly belonged with true 'colonies', in all matters except 'the regulation of foreign relations' and the 'disposal of the public lands'.[74] William Anson cut the cloth differently. For him, the key categorical differences were between the 'Crown colonies', in which English people had settled; India, which the English ruled; and the 'miscellaneous possessions, dependencies and protectorates' that comprised the remainder of the empire.[75] For Charles James Tarring, the categorical distinction was between colonies formed by settlement of 'unoccupied or barbarous country', and colonies formed by conquest or cession.[76] In Tarring's schema, the common law established that in occupied colonies, English law and sovereignty was carried with English

---

[70] Ibid., lxiii.
[71] Interpretation Act 1889 (UK) 52 & 53 Vict, ch. 63, s. 18.
[72] Charles Prestwood Lucas (ed.) *George Cornewall Lewis: An Essay on the Government of the Dependencies* (Oxford: Clarendon Press, 1891), xlii. This definition of dependency was given by Lewis in 1841.
[73] Ibid., xix.
[74] Ibid., xxxi. See also British Settlements Act 1887 (UK) 50 & 51 Vict. ch. 54.
[75] Sir William Reynell Anson, *The Law and Custom of the Constitution*, vol. 2 (Oxford: Clarendon Press, 1886), 274, 288, 269.
[76] Charles James Tarring, *Chapters on the Law Relating to the Colonies*, 3rd ed. (London: Stevens and Haynes, 1906), 3.

subjects, 'and therefore such countries are to be governed by the laws of England'.[77] In the case of conquered or ceded countries, on the other hand, native law remained on foot 'until altered by the conqueror', except in the case of laws 'contrary to the fundamental principles of the British constitution', which ceased at the moment of conquest.[78]

Attempts to divine a coherent imperial constitution intensified as demands for increased levels of self-rule emerged from the subjects of empire. With respect to the Australasian, Southern African and Canadian colonies, those demands developed not so much as demands for independence from empire, as for greater autonomy within it. Yet debates over the extent of autonomy that should be devolved to Lucas' 'colonies in the true sense of the word' proved to require definition of the juridical nature of empire itself. Self-government over internal affairs had been devolved progressively by subject matter to the Australasian, Southern African and Canadian colonies from the mid-nineteenth century. By the 1890s jurisdiction over immigration and emigration, internal commerce and trade, and taxation and expenditure were all recognised as properly residing with colonial government, not with the Imperial government in London.[79] Yet the matter of power over the colonies' external affairs remained contentious. The Imperial government regarded control over foreign policy as basic to imperial authority – including both the power to enter into treaties of commerce and trade and power to enter into defence treaties. In 1899 the Imperial government conceded the former, granting the self-governing colonies autonomy with respect to regional commercial treaties; yet insisted again on retaining the latter.[80] Even as the colonies federated – as the Dominion of Canada in 1867, the Commonwealth of Australia in 1901, and the Union of South Africa in 1910 – treaties entered into by the Imperial government continued to bind them all with respect to all other areas of foreign policy.[81]

As a result, the newly federated Australian Commonwealth continued to be bound by the 1886 Demarcation Agreement between the British and German empires, which recognised Germany's claim to the northeast of New Guinea. The shift in German foreign policy under Kaiser

---

[77] Ibid., 3.
[78] Ibid., 16–20.
[79] W. W. Willoughby and C. G. Fenwick, *Types of Restricted Sovereignty and of Colonial Autonomy* (Washington, DC: Government Printers Office, 1919), 16–17.
[80] Philip J. Noel-Baker, *Present Juridical Status of the Dominions in International Law* (New York: Longmans Green, 1929), 43–4.
[81] Ibid., 44–7.

Wilhelm II was a theme of public debate in Australia.[82] The Reich had taken over the administration of German New Guinea from Hansemann's Neuguinea Kompagnie in 1898; and in 1902, the Commonwealth government took over the administration of British New Guinea from the Queensland colonial government, later renaming the region the Australian Territory of Papua.[83] From 1902, then, the Reich and the Australian Commonwealth shared a land border running between Papua and German New Guinea; but the British Imperial government was not legally required to consult with Australia on matters of imperial defence.

At the 1907 Colonial Conference in London, Australia and the other self-governing colonies sought direct representation on the Committee of Imperial Defence established after the Boer War in 1902.[84] The Imperial government agreed that the Committee would consult with the self-governing Dominions on matters of local defence; but the new Committee of Imperial Defence would be 'purely a consultative body, having no executive powers or administrative functions'.[85] In the opinion of jurist Lassa Oppenheim, maintained up until the War, the status of the self-governing Dominions was clear: the inability of the 'Colonial States' of the British empire to conduct their own affairs with respect to defence meant that from the perspective of international law, they had 'no international position whatever'.[86]

3.5 Agriculture, Phosphate, Labour and Race in the Pacific

The militarisation of the German empire, and internal tensions in the British, provided the geopolitical backdrop to the commercial concerns of European trading firms in the Pacific. The Hanseatic model of

---

[82] See C. E. W. Bean (ed.), 'German Colonization in the Pacific: The Outbreak of War' in *Official History of Australia in the War 1914–1918*, 1941 ed., vol. X (Canberra: Australian War Memorial, 1941), 2.

[83] Papua Act 1905 (Cth); Thomas Dunbabin, *The Making of Australasia: A Brief History of the Origin and Development of the British Dominions in the South Pacific* (London: A. & C. Black Ltd, 1922), 217.

[84] Commonwealth of Australia, 'Memorandum as to the Functions of the Committee of Imperial Defence', *Papers Laid before the Colonial Conference, 1907* (London: His Majesty's Stationery Office, 1907), 15–16.

[85] Ibid., 15. Noel-Baker, *Present Juridical Status of the Dominions*, 41–3, 47.

[86] Lassa Oppenheim, *International Law: A Treatise*, 2nd ed. (New York: Longman Greens and Co, 1905), 102.

commodity circulation constituted a minor part of Pacific trade, overshadowed by British, French and American investments in plantation, mining and primary production – all dependent on human labour. In the new Australian Commonwealth, the issue of imperial competition in the Pacific was inextricable from issues of agricultural production, labour and race. It is widely known that one of the first legislative moves of the Commonwealth was to pass the Immigration Restriction Act 1901, which officially inaugurated the 'White Australia' policy.[87] It is less widely known that the Commonwealth's preceding move was to pass the Pacific Island Labourers Act 1901.[88] This purported to end the use of Pacific islanders as labour on agricultural plantations in Australia, not because of the widespread use of forced indenture, but because of the perceived threat to white Australian labourers.[89] The Labourers Act did not seek to prohibit but rather regulate the use of indentured islander labour in the Commonwealth, providing for the forced removal of labourers already in Australia, and prohibiting the importation of Pacific labourers without a licence.[90] The practice of using indentured labour had become widespread in the second half of the nineteenth century among French and British trading firms in the Pacific.[91]

From the 1850s European firms in the Pacific had developed a forced labour industry using violent indenturing and slavery practices that became known euphemistically as blackbirding.[92] It was estimated at the time of Australian federation that around 10,000 Western Pacific islanders from New Guinea, the Solomon Islands, Fiji and Vanuatu were

---

[87] Immigration Restriction Act 1901 (Cth). On the White Australia policy, see Jane Carey and Claire McLisky (eds.), *Creating White Australia* (Sydney: University of Sydney Press, 2009); and Ghassan Hage, *White Nation: Fantasies of White Supremacy in a Multicultural Society* (NSW: Pluto Press, 1998).

[88] Pacific Island Labourers Act 1901 (Cth).

[89] Peter Corris, '"White Australia" in Action: The Repatriation of Pacific Islanders from Queensland' (1972) 15 *Historical Studies*, 237–50.

[90] Pacific Island Labourers Act, ss. 4, 8.

[91] Tracey Banivanua Mar, *Violence and Colonial Dialogue: The Australian-Pacific Indentured Labour Trade* (Honolulu: University of Hawai'i Press, 2007); K. R. Howe, 'Tourists, Sailors and Labourers: A History of Early Labour Recruiting in Southern Melanesia'; (1978) 13 *Journal of Pacific History*, 22–35; and Sally Engle Merry and Donald Brenneis, 'Introduction' in Sally Engle Merry and Donald Brenneis (eds.), *Law and Empire in the Pacific: Fiji and Hawai'i* (New Mexico: School of American Research Press, 2003).

[92] Karin Speedy, 'The Sutton Case: The First Franco-Australian Foray into Blackbirding' (2015) 50 *Journal of Pacific History*, 344–64; and Peter Corris, '"Blackbirding" in New Guinea Waters, 1883–84: An Episode in the Queensland Labour Trade' (1968) 3 *Journal of Pacific History*, 85–105.

3.5 AGRICULTURE, LABOUR AND RACE IN THE PACIFIC

present in the colony of Queensland, which had unsuccessfully tried to annex the eastern half of New Guinea in the early 1880s; according to Banivanua Mar, this figure was closer to 60,000.[93] Although the British Imperial government claimed superiority over other European empires for having officially abolished slavery in the 1830s, much imperial commerce remained dependent on indenturing practices at least until the turn of the century.[94] The Imperial government's approach to labour 'shortages' in Fiji was indicative: Sir Arthur Gordon, the Governor of Fiji, requested that the Pacific colony be provided with indentured labourers from India as an alternative to perpetuating the blackbirding trade.[95] A family friend of British Prime Minister Gladstone, Gordon had previously been posted as Governor of Trinidad and of Mauritius, where plantations were reliant on Indian indentured labour.[96] Whilst the Imperial government imported Indian labour to meet the demands of industrialising British commerce in the Pacific territories, within the Commonwealth, blackbirding persisted into the twentieth century, primarily on sugar plantations in Queensland.[97] Whereas in the early nineteenth century, the Australian colonies depended economically on the pastoral industry, and from the 1840s, on gold and coal mining, by federation in 1901 the sugar, wheat and dairy industries were emerging as the stalwarts of the colonial economy, dependent on regulated, racialised labour migration.[98]

This shift towards industrial agriculture in the Australian colonial economy was facilitated not only by federal regulation of indentured labour, but also by the global commodification of phosphate in the later nineteenth century. The top-dressing of soil with phosphate improves the root growth of young plants, increasing nitrogen fixation and nutrient

---

[93] Dunbabin, *Making of Australasia*, 211. Banivanua Mar, *Violence and Colonial Dialogue*, 1.
[94] Banivanua Mar, *Violence and Colonial Dialogue*, 175-86.
[95] For a revisionist appraisal of Gordon's legacy in Fiji as an early instance of British imperial 'development', see I. M. Cumpston, 'Sir Arthur Gordon and the Introduction of Indians into the Pacific: The West Indian System in Fiji' (1956) 25 *Pacific Historical Review*, 369-88. See also John D. Kelly, 'Gordon Was No Amateur: Imperial Legal Strategies in the Colonization of Fiji' in Merry and Brenneis (eds.), *Law and Empire in the Pacific*, 62-4.
[96] Brij V. Lal, *Girmitiyas: The Origins of the Fiji Indians* (Canberra: Journal of Pacific History, 1983).
[97] Dunbabin, *Making of Australasia*, 211; Banivanua Mar, *Violence and Colonial Dialogue*.
[98] Dunbabin, *Making of Australasia*, 177; Robert D. Watt, *Romance of the Australian Land Industries* (Sydney: Angus and Robertson, 1955), 126-70. For a contemporary analysis of the relationship between labour migration and international administration in the Pacific, see Sara Dehm, 'Ordering Human Mobility: International Law, Development, Administration' (2018), PhD thesis, University of Melbourne, 171 et seq.

absorption.[99] Pre-industrial agricultural traditions commonly used organic waste – including manure, bones and ash – to replace phosphoric acid in soil depleted through continual cropping, or to increase the arability of low yield land. The renowned Prussian naturalist Alexander von Humboldt had observed in 1803 that the Quechua peoples living at high altitudes in contemporary Peru and Bolivia traded fossilised *huanu* or bird droppings with communities living on the Peruvian coastal islands.[100] By the 1830s, a global trade in 'guano' – a conquista-era Spanish adaptation of the Quechua word – was developing. In 1840 the Peruvian Republic passed a resolution granting the President of the Peruvian Chamber of Commerce, Don Francisco Quiros, exclusive rights to export Peruvian guano, with property in guano remaining with the Republic.[101] Quiros' main customers were British firms trading in the Pacific.[102] As Peruvian guano reached the domestic market, British agricultural chemists soon reported that it contained higher concentrations of phosphate and nitrogen than any other form of organic fertiliser in use.[103] By the 1860s Peruvian guano was the most significant South American import into Britain.[104] The term 'guano' thus became synonymous with the commodification of phosphate in the mid-nineteenth century. Yet Peruvian supply was fragile and finite, and already waning by the early 1860s.[105] Insatiable demand for Peruvian guano in Britain and the United States pushed global prices skyward, and the Pacific trading firms began to hunt for new supply.

In the United States, members of Congress were repeatedly petitioned by American firms to introduce administrative measures to break the Peruvian monopoly on the Pacific phosphate trade.[106] In 1856 the US Congress passed the Guano Islands Act, which purported to protect any guano claim made by a US citizen over any otherwise unclaimed island.[107]

---

[99] See Petra Marschner (ed.), *Marschner's Mineral Nutrition of Higher Plants*, 3rd ed. (UK: Elsevier Ltd, 2012), 158–65.

[100] W. M. Mathew, *The House of Gibbs and the Peruvian Guano Monopoly* (London: Royal Historical Society, 1981), 22. Jimmy M. Skaggs, *The Great Guano Rush: Entrepreneurs and American Overseas Expansion* (New York: St. Martin's Press, 1994), 4.

[101] Mathew, *House of Gibbs*, 23.

[102] Ibid., 24. Albert F. Ellis, *Ocean Island and Nauru: Their Story* (Sydney: Angus and Robertson, 1935), 279.

[103] Mathew, *House of Gibbs*, 27.

[104] Ibid., 2, 94.

[105] Ibid., 167.

[106] Skaggs, *Great Guano Rush*, 51.

[107] Guano Islands Act 1856 48 USC 1411. See Christina Duffy Burnett, 'The Edges of Empire and the Limits of Sovereignty: American Guano Islands' (2005) 57 *American Quarterly*,

Mimicking the European protectorate laws, the Guano Islands Act performed a kind of pragmatic alchemy, attempting to protect US guano claims outside of sovereign territory without attracting the obligations of effective occupation:

> Whenever any citizen of the United States discovers a deposit of guano on any island, rock, or key, not within the lawful jurisdiction of any other government, and not occupied by the citizens of any other government, and takes peaceable possession thereof, and occupies the same, such island, rock, or key may, at the discretion of the President, be considered as appertaining to the United States.[108]

The language of 'appurtenance' was intentionally ambiguous, leaving unclear the international status of islands claimed under the Act. The US State Department itself acknowledged that the purpose of the novel terminology was to 'lend itself readily to circumstances and the wishes of those using it'.[109] The pragmatism of the Act was underscored by the fact that 'after the guano shall have been removed', the United States was not bound to retain possession of any island claimed under it.[110] Within a decade, fifty-nine islands, rocks and keys in the Pacific and the Caribbean had been claimed by US entrepreneurs and companies under the Guano Islands Act.[111]

The Act's association of guano with islands reflected the fact that the global phosphate trade had begun with commodification of Peruvian *huanu*, rather than scientific understanding of the origins of phosphate itself. Within the emerging field of agricultural chemistry, scientific research into phosphate was funded initially by companies seeking to meet growing demand, and later by states seeking to regulate the composition of guano on the market.[112] Agricultural chemists were hired by companies, including Gibbs & Sons in Britain and the American Guano Company in the United States, to locate and test deposits and maximise the value of phosphate rock as an agricultural fertiliser.[113] In the 1840s

---

779–803; and Daniel Immerwahr, *How to Hide an Empire: A History of the Greater United States* (London: Random House, 2019).

[108] Guano Islands Act, s. 1.
[109] Skaggs, *Great Guano Rush*, 57.
[110] Guano Islands Act, s. 4.
[111] Skaggs, *Great Guano Rush*, 71.
[112] Justus Liebig, Chemistry in its Application to Agriculture and Physiology (Cambridge: John Owen, 1842). See also Gregory T. Cushman, *Guano and the Opening of the Pacific World: A Global Ecological History* (Cambridge: Cambridge University Press, 2013), 51–3.
[113] Skaggs, *Great Guano Rush*, 142–3.

Irish chemist James Murray patented the creation of 'superphosphate', mixing ground phosphate rock with sulphuric acid to produce high concentration phosphoric acid.[114] The commodification of superphosphate enabled the scaling up of agricultural production to industrial levels.

Commercial demand drove corporate entrepreneurs to identify larger and deeper continental and seabed deposits of phosphate. Large inland deposits were identified in Algeria and Tunisia in the 1870s, and in Florida and South Carolina in the 1880s. Under the Guano Islands Act, more than seventy islands in the Pacific and Caribbean had been recognised as 'appertaining to the United States' by the turn of the century – even though the legal significance of 'appurtenance' still remained unclear, forty years after the passage of the Act.[115] Agricultural chemists abandoned the colloquial term 'guano', with its popular association with birds and islands; but the association of high concentration phosphate with bird manure was fixed early in the industry's development.[116] That association persists even now, after the ubiquitisation of the concept of the phosphorus cycle in later twentieth century geology. The geological accumulation of tricalcium phosphate in geologic matter is currently understood as a phase in a biogeochemical cycle that includes atmospheric precipitation, concentration in micro- and macro-organisms, accumulation in the ocean floor and hydrothermal volcanic activity.[117]

World phosphate production increased from an estimated 505,000 tons in 1875 to 3,150,000 tons in 1900, and then to 8,800,000 tons in 1925.[118] The commodification of phosphate rock from the mid-nineteenth century was thus a crucial yet often overlooked aspect of the industrial revolution. In ecological terms, Cushman has argued that '(h)uman intervention in the cycling of nitrogen and phosphorous represents one of the central manifestations of human domination of the earth's ecosystems'.[119] In terms of international political economy, ready access to superphosphate brought a certainty to agricultural

---

[114] United States Agricultural Research Service, *Superphosphate: Its History, Chemistry and Manufacture* (Washington, DC: Government Printers Office, 1964), 19–26.
[115] Duffy Burnett, 'Edges of Empire', 787.
[116] George Scott Robertson, *Basic Slags and Rock Phosphates* (Cambridge: Cambridge University Press, 1922); Cushman, *Guano and the Opening of the Pacific World*, 117.
[117] On the phosphorus cycle, see P. C. M. Boers, Th E. Cappenberg and W. Raaphorst (eds.), *Proceedings of the Third International Workshop on Phosphorus in Sediments* (Netherlands: Springer Netherlands, 1993).
[118] Ellis, *Ocean Island and Nauru*, appendix B.
[119] Cushman, *Guano and the Opening of the Pacific World*, 13.

production that favoured market speculation and economic growth. The commodification of phosphate was central to the industrialisation of agricultural production, which in turn provided a response to Malthusian arguments of an arithmetical relationship between population and agricultural yield.[120] The economic effects of phosphate were particularly significant in the Australian colonies, where the ancient continental soil is naturally low in phosphatic content. The increasing availability of commercial phosphate from the mid-nineteenth century not only increased yield of existing crops, but also enabled otherwise unarable land to be farmed, and increased yield of grasses used as fodder for cattle on pastoral land.[121] The development of the sugar, wheat, dairy, cattle and sheep industries in Australia – industries the new Commonwealth already regarded as central to Australian identity – was thus dependent on the industrialisation of two modes of regional exploitation: the exploitation of islander labour, and the exploitation of Pacific phosphate.[122]

3.6 The Pacific Islands Company and its Agreement with the Jaluit Gesellschaft

As the global phosphate price soared over the 1860s and 1870s, competition between the British and American empires over phosphate claims in the Pacific intensified. In 1874 English entrepreneur John T. Arundel, former employee of London shipping company Houlder Brothers and associate of the London Missionary Society, established John T. Arundel and Company. Arundel's plan was to establish himself in the Pacific phosphate trade.[123] With Houlder Brothers, Arundel had visited the Peruvian Chincha Islands in 1860, scouting opportunities for Houlder to add guano lines to its Pacific shipping operations, which included emigrant transport from England to Australia and New Zealand.[124] The early business of John T. Arundel and Company was parasitic on the rush of American entrepreneurial activity incentivised by the Guano Islands

---

[120] See for example George K. Rickards, *Population and Capital: A Course of Lectures Delivered Before the University of Oxford* (London: Longman, Brown, Green and Longmans, 1854).

[121] Ellis, *Ocean Island and Nauru*, 288.

[122] Ibid., 288–90.

[123] Skaggs, *Great Guano Rush*, 135.

[124] Cushman, *Guano and the Opening of the Pacific World*, 94. Maslyn Williams and Barrie Macdonald, *The Phosphateers: A History of the British Phosphate Commissioners* (Melbourne: Melbourne University Press, 1985), 6.

Act. Arundel's business model was simple. He approached American entrepreneurs who had claimed islands under the US Act but did not have the capital to exploit their claims, leaving them at risk of forfeit under the Act; noting the risk of forfeiture, Arundel would offer to lease the exploration and exploitation rights, and dig on their behalf.[125] Arundel supplemented his company's fledgling operations by planting copra plantations near phosphate diggings, eventually leveraging his early profits to buy exclusive rights to islands claimed by US companies under the Guano Islands Act outright. By 1897 Arundel had done well enough to negotiate the merger of his company with Auckland firm Henderson & McFarlane, one of Goddefroy & Sohn's early Pacific competitors.[126] Henderson & McFarlane continued to operate trading posts in the British protectorate of the Gilbert and Ellice Islands, and in the German protectorate of the Marshall Islands.[127] The merged company was renamed the Pacific Islands Company; and Sir Arthur Gordon himself – later retitled Baron Stanmore by his friend Gladstone – was appointed by Arundel as chair.[128] On the merger, the Pacific Islands Company became the largest British-held commercial interest in the Pacific.[129]

One of the interests acquired by Arundel in the 1897 merger was Henderson & McFarlane's trading post on Nauru. As the Jaluit Gesellschaft's interest in the Nauru District Office became increasingly grudging, fewer Gesellschaft ships visited the island, the company store's supplies dwindled, and the Office's attempt to engage with Nauruan property rights became increasingly fraught.[130] Imperial Commissioner Senfft reported back to the Colonial Office that the Nauruans were becoming insubordinate to the Gesellschaft administration. He complained that land disputes were 'both tedious and difficult to deal with. The parties are usually women who are difficult to induce to accept a compromise.'[131] As the Jaluit Gesellschaft increasingly left its administrative duties derelict, the Nauruans, Senfft reported, began to take any

[125] Skaggs, *Great Guano Rush*, 135.
[126] 'Pacific Islands Company', *The Week* (Brisbane), 28 May 1897.
[127] Fabricius, *Nauru*, 278–9.
[128] Williams and Macdonald, *The Phosphateers*, 8.
[129] Ibid., 9. Firth, 'German Firms in the Western Pacific Islands', 18.
[130] *Briefe von Kommando S M S Bussard an den kommandierenden Admiral* [Letter from Commander Alandt of the *SMS Bussard* to the Admiral in Command], Berlin, 1 January 1898. Fabricius, *Nauru*, 281–2.
[131] *Briefe von Kaiserliche Landeshauptmann für das Schutzgebiet der Marshall-Inseln an das Auswärtige Amt, Kolonial Abteilung, Berlin* [Letter from the Imperial Administrator of

3.6 THE PACIFIC ISLANDS COMPANY & THE GESELLSCHAFT

copra left surplus to the German head tax to Henderson & McFarlane agents to trade for better-stocked supplies.[132] By the time of the Pacific Islands Company merger, Henderson & McFarlane's copra exports from Nauru were more than double those of the Jaluit Gesellschaft.[133] The German company's objectives in incorporating Nauru into the Marshall Islands Protectorate – namely pacifying the Nauruan population and facilitating its copra trade – had within a decade either failed to materialise, as the Gesellschaft complained, or had been squandered, as Imperial Commissioner Senfft insisted.[134] As the Gesellschaft lost interest in Nauru and sought to extricate itself from its Agreement with the Reich, neither company nor Colonial Office took much notice of the new Pacific Islands Company's assumption of the greatest share of the Nauruan copra trade, or of the Company's regional interest in phosphate.

The story of the 'discovery' of Nauruan phosphate has lodged itself, much as the Pacific Islands Company intended, in the European mythology on the island as a tale of British ingenuity.[135] The story dislocates Nauruan phosphate from the island and from the Nauruan people, and relocates it in imperial time and place, to be acted upon by a white colonial protagonist: July 1899; the Sydney office of the Pacific Islands Company; the company's Australian employee, Albert Ellis. Albert's father George Ellis, an agricultural chemist, had been appointed by Arundel as a director of the Pacific Islands Company, and George's three sons were all subsequently employed by the company.[136] According to Albert, in July 1899 he noted similarities between the 'office doorstop', a lump of rock picked up on Nauru in 1896 by a former agent of Henderson and McFarlane, and 'rock guano' dug on nearby Baker Island by Arundel and Company.[137] Baker Island had been claimed under the US Guano Islands Act by the American Guano Company in 1857. Arundel bought out the American company's rights in 1886. Ellis tested a sample of the doorstop and by his own

---

the Marshall Islands Senfft to the Colonial Section of the Foreign Office], 17 March 1898. Ibid., 283.
[132] Ibid., 285.
[133] Ibid.
[134] 'Report No. 49 of the Imperial Administrator of the Protectorate of the Marshall Islands', 15 June 1896. Ibid., 275–9.
[135] See for example Paul L. Montgomery, 'Tiny Nauru, a Colony No Longer, Sues Australia for Neglect', *New York Times* (New York), 5 June 1989; Tony Thomas, 'The Naughty Nation of Nauru', *Quadrant* (Melbourne), 1 January 2013.
[136] Williams and Macdonald, *The Phosphateers*, 10.
[137] Ellis, *Ocean Island and Nauru*, 52–3.

account, was proven right: 'it was phosphate rock of the highest quality, and from the structure of the material one could tell that it was a very old and probably extensive deposit'.[138] The Sydney office immediately wrote to Arundel in London. With a dramatic sense of the commercial-in-confidence, the letter referred to Nauru as 'Frezzant Island', lest the letter be intercepted by the PIC's competitors in the Pacific phosphate trade:

> The whole island I firmly believe to be one huge mass of Rock Guano. How this is to be worked, I cannot suggest, as you are aware the island is under German jurisdiction and under German laws, the Gescell Scharft have sole right to work the deposits.[139]

The Company's board came up with a novel strategy: to avoid alerting the Gesellschaft or the German Foreign Office to the value of the Nauruan find, it would offer to buy all of the ailing Gesellschaft's phosphate rights across the Pacific islands.[140]

The Gesellschaft, already looking to reorient its Pacific interests, needed little convincing. In 1900 the Agreement between the Jaluit Gesellschaft and the Pacific Islands Company was approved by the German Colonial Office.[141] The contract provided that the Gesellschaft's rights to exploit guano deposits in the Marshall Islands Protectorate would be licensed to the Pacific Islands Company; and in exchange, the PIC would sign over all its trading interests and copra plantations within the Protectorate, with an immediate payment of 500,000 marks.[142] A new company was to be created by the PIC to hold the Protectorate-wide mining right; and the Gesellschaft would be gifted 10 per cent of the new company's shares, as well as receiving an annual royalty of half a mark on each ton of phosphate mined above 50,000 tons.[143] Arundel's Pacific Islands Company was wound up; and with additional capital from Prussian fertiliser company Die Union Fabrik Chemische Produkte, in 1902 the new Pacific Phosphate Company was incorporated and registered in Britain.[144] Together, the Gesellschaft and Die Union Fabrik held about one-third of the new Company's share capital.[145]

---

[138] Ibid., 53.
[139] Williams and Macdonald, *The Phosphateers*, 10.
[140] Ibid., 13.
[141] Weeramantry, *Nauru*, 53.
[142] Williams and Macdonald, *The Phosphateers*, 52.
[143] Stewart Firth, 'German Labour Policy in Nauru and Angaur 1906–1914' (1978) 13 *Journal of Pacific History*, 36–52 at 38.
[144] Weeramantry, *Nauru*, 53.
[145] Firth, 'German Labour Policy in Nauru and Angaur', 25.

As the Pacific Islands Company settled its deal with the Gesellschaft, Arundel was negotiating with the British Colonial Office for a phosphate concession for the island of Banaba, known in English as Ocean Island, 300 kilometres to the east of Nauru. A PIC employee had in Henderson & McFarlane days visited Banaba, and on the 'discovery' of Nauruan phosphate reported that he knew of another nearby island with a single raised atoll formation.[146] Although near to the British protectorate of the Gilbert and Ellice Islands, Banaba had not yet been claimed by Britain, the United States or the Reich.[147] With the support of the Commissioner of the Gilbert and Ellice Islands, Telfer Campbell, the British Colonial Office agreed to Arundel's request that the island be annexed into the British Protectorate before knowledge of the unclaimed island's value reached the PIC's competitors.[148]

The British Colonial Office granted a concession to mine Banaba's phosphate to the new Pacific Phosphate Company – subject to the securing of an agreement with Banaban people.[149] In early 1900 Albert Ellis was sent on a Company ship, the *Archer*, to Banaba.[150] Ellis later reported that he secured the 'signature' of Temate – referred to in the agreement as the 'King of Ocean Island' – on 3 May 1900. The agreement purported to pass the 'sole right to raise and ship all the alluvial and rock phosphate on Ocean Island' for a period of 999 years, in exchange for a yearly payment to 'the said natives' of fifty pounds, and the maintenance of a company store on the island at which this income could be spent.[151] In September 1901 Ocean Island was officially incorporated into the British Protectorate of the Gilbert and Ellice Islands.[152]

3.7 The Right Passed from the Gesellschaft to the Pacific Phosphate Company

When formed in 1902 the Pacific Phosphate Company had purportedly acquired phosphate mining rights for two neighbouring islands via two very different legal routes, under two imperial jurisdictions: Nauru,

---

[146] Williams and Macdonald, *The Phosphateers*, 14.
[147] Ibid., 15.
[148] Ibid., 26.
[149] Ibid., 18.
[150] Ellis, *Ocean Island and Nauru*, 55–8.
[151] The text of the Agreement is reproduced in Williams and Macdonald, *The Phosphateers*, 31–2.
[152] Doug Munro and Stewart Firth, 'Towards Colonial Protectorates: The Case of the Gilbert and Ellice Islands' (1986) 32 *Australian Journal of Politics and History*, 63–71.

within the German Protectorate of the Marshall Islands, and Banaba or Ocean Island, within the British Protectorate of the Gilbert and Ellice Islands. The Company acquired exclusive rights to Nauruan phosphate in an Agreement with the Jaluit Gesellschaft that purported to pass on a concessionary right originating with the Reich. The Company acquired exclusive rights to Banaban phosphate in a direct Agreement between itself and the Banaban 'king', Temate, who by implication held proprietary rights recognisable in English law. Both Nauruan and Banaban populations were understood by the German and British empires, respectively to hold proprietary rights in land; and both mining rights originated in a concessionary system that purported to respect existing proprietary rights. The difference in the chain of title of mining rights in Nauru and Banaba was due not only to different German and British approaches to the basis of protectorate declarations in international law, but also to different treatments of phosphate in German and British mining law in 1900. Under British law, phosphate was already a designated mineral; and therefore phosphate mining in the protectorates was regulated by the logic of the concession, in that the state held the power to assign mining rights.

Under German mining law in 1900, however, phosphate was not yet a designated mineral. As such, the basis of the Reich's claim to phosphate royalties in its protectorates, as claimed in its 1888 Agreement with the Gesellschaft, remained unclear. The jurisdictional basis of the Reich's claim might never have attracted attention; but less than ten years after the Gesellschaft had tried and failed to shed its administrative responsibilities in Nauru, the guano concession created by that Agreement had suddenly become the most profitable German corporate right in the Western Pacific.[153] After its 1901 Agreement with Arundel, the Gesellschaft and the Colonial Office worked together to build a coherent jurisdictional framework around the claimed right to Nauruan phosphate. In 1905 the Gesellschaft secured a renewal of its 1888 guano concession for Nauru from the Reich for a period of ninety-four years from 1 April 1906 – the date on which the administration of Nauru and the Marshall Islands Protectorate was to pass out of Gesellschaft hands and over to the colonial administration of German New Guinea.[154] In February 1906 phosphate was designated under

---

[153] Firth, 'German Labour Policy in Nauru and Angaur', 38.
[154] Agreement between His Most Gracious Majesty King George V and Others and The Pacific Phosphate Company, Westminster, 25 June 1920, First Schedule, 17.

German mining law as a 'free' mineral, in which ownership vested in the state; and a Mining Regulation was issued with respect to the 'African and South Sea Protectorates', explicitly importing German mining law into the protectorates and thereby claiming state title in phosphate.[155] In 1907 a supplement to the Gesellschaft's 1905 concession retrospectively applied the Mining Regulation to the concession agreement – thereby purporting to regularise the 1888 passage of title from Reich to company.[156] By 1907, then, the legal interests in Nauruan phosphate were as follows: the German and British financed, British-registered Pacific Phosphate Company held an exclusive right in German law to mine phosphate on Nauru, under licence from a German company, within the colony of German New Guinea. Property in Nauruan phosphate purportedly vested in the Reich, whilst property in the land from which phosphate was to be mined was recognised as remaining with Nauruan landowners, under Nauruan law.

3.8 The Commencement of Phosphate Operations on Nauru

Between 1902 and 1906 the Pacific Phosphate Company developed the commercial, administrative and industrial infrastructure required to extract and export phosphate from Nauru. Staff houses, labourers' dormitories and jetties were built on the coast at Yangor, near the contemporary Nauruan district of Aiwo.[157] Roads and cableways were built from the island's central plateau, running down to the company at Yangor.[158] Phosphate exports commenced in 1907. In accordance with German and British protectorate law, the Company leased its land from Nauruan landowners for nominal rent.[159] From 1907 in accordance with German mining law as applied to the concession, the Company also paid a royalty to Nauruan landowners.[160] The royalty was calculated at five pfennigs a ton of phosphate removed from an owner's land; but the royalty was paid by the Pacific Phosphate Company not to landowners,

---

[155] Weeramantry, *Nauru*, 184.
[156] *Nachtrag zur Guano-Konzession der Jaluit Gesellschaft für die Marshall Inseln erteilt vom Reichskanzler am 21 November 1905* [Supplement to the Guano Concession of the Jaluit Gesellschaft for the Marshall Islands Granted by the Imperial Chancellor on 21 November 1905] trans. Spennemann, 'Imperial German Legislation'. Also Weeramantry, *Nauru*, 188.
[157] Ellis, *Ocean Island and Nauru*, 128.
[158] Ibid.; see also map inside back cover.
[159] Weeramantry, *Nauru*, 192.
[160] Ibid., 391.

but directly to the German colonial administration, to be distributed to Nauruan landowners via the 'chiefs'.[161] Paul Hambruch, a German anthropologist from the Ethnological Museum in Hamburg, estimated in 1909 in his compendious illustrated study of Nauru that five pfennigs held a value of around half a box of matches.[162] As soon as the Nauruan people were officially paid nominal rent and halfpenny royalties – in practice quarantined by the German administration – the Governor of German New Guinea, Albert Hahl, declared that the existing Nauruan head tax, which under the Gesellschaft had been collected in copra, would henceforth be payable German marks. According to Hahl, the payment of rent and royalties meant that 'the natives were now able to earn a good income in connection with the phosphate works', and were therefore able to pay their tax in money.[163]

The Pacific Phosphate Company soon found that its mining operations on Nauru required intensive human labour. Extraction and export of Nauruan phosphate was logistically difficult: phosphorus had to be dug out from around the hard limestone pillars that comprised the island's central elevation. The coral reef surrounding the coast prevented safe landing, and phosphate had to be unloaded from the cable bins onto surfboats, then rowed out to cargo ships waiting off the reef.[164] Sourcing labour for the remote island posed a problem. The Nauruans themselves resisted attempts to be put to work in the phosphate operations on their land.[165] In 1906 the German Colonial Office approved the Pacific Phosphate Company's request to import labourers from the German Protectorate of Kiaochow in the region of contemporary Jiaozhou in mainland China, a bay concession the Reich leased from the Chinese imperial administration.[166] Around five hundred labourers were shipped

---

[161] Bean, *Official History of Australia in the War*, vol. X, ch. 9, 141. Nancy Viviani, *Nauru: Phosphate and Political Progress* (Canberra: Australian National University Press, 1970), 35.

[162] Weeramantry, *Nauru*, 391, taken from Paul Hambruch, *Nauru: Ergebnisse der Südsee-Expedition, 1908–1910* ['Nauru: Results of the South Sea Expedition, 1908–1910'] (Hamburg: L Friedrichsen, 1914).

[163] Sack and Clark (eds.), *Albert Hahl*, 37.

[164] Firth, 'German Labour Policy in Nauru and Angaur', 42.

[165] For a seminal analysis of the discourse of the 'lazy native' and its relation to colonial capitalism, see Syed Hussein Alatas, *The Myth of the Lazy Native* (London: Frank Cass, 1977).

[166] Firth, 'German Labour Policy in Nauru and Angaur 1906–1914', 39. On Kiaochow/Qingdao, see George Steinmetz, *The Devil's Handwriting: Precolonial Ethnography and the German Colonial State in Qingdao, Samoa, and Southwest Africa* (Chicago: University of Chicago Press, 2007); and Conrad, *German Colonialism*, 58–62.

from the Kiaochow Protectorate, and around another five hundred from the Marshalls and the Carolines.[167]

Labour recruitment was outsourced by the Pacific Phosphate Company to regional sub-contractors. In a standard recruitment process, men were induced into individual contracts for a fixed period of three years' labour, on the basis of pay and conditions detailed in a second document.[168] On arrival in Nauru, recruits were told by the Company that the second document was not legally binding, and they were dumped on the remote island without independent means of return. Strikes and uprisings by deceived recruits were met with the joint force of the Company and the German colonial administration. By 1910 around 250 labourers from Kiaochow had died on Nauru from dysentery, or from protein deficiency due to punitive rations provided by the Company in response to strikes.[169] Mortality rates among recruits from

3.2 Pacific Phosphate Company officers with Chinese labourers, est. 1906–1908. Credit: Image courtesy of the National Archives of Australia. NAA: R32, VOLUME 118/41.

---

[167] Bean, *Official History of Australia in the War*, vol. X. ch. 9, 141. Firth, 'German Labour Policy in Nauru and Angaur', 40, 42.
[168] Firth, 'German Labour Policy in Nauru and Angaur', 40.
[169] Ibid., 41.

the Chuuk Islands in the Marshalls and from the Carolines were similarly high.[170] The violence of the Pacific Phosphate Company's indentured labour operations on Nauru produced high returns: between 1906 and the outbreak of war in 1914, the Pacific Phosphate Company shipped 781,000 tons of phosphate from Nauru.[171] Nauruan phosphate was fed into the agricultural markets in Australia and New Zealand, and in Germany and Japan.[172]

3.9 Nauru, War and Australian 'Sub-Empire' in the Pacific

On the back of indentured labour and under German administration, the Pacific Phosphate Company's operations on Nauru thrived in the first decade of the twentieth century, paying large dividends to its British and German investors. As commercial relations delivered returns, however, diplomatic relations between the German and British empires soured.[173] Following the Anglo-Russian Entente of 1907, hostility between the triple alliance of the Reich, the Austro-Hungarian empire and Italy on the one hand, and the British, French and Russian empires on the other escalated sharply. In the Pacific, the European empires maintained their existing commercial relations right up until August 1914.[174] There were no colonial troops in the German Pacific, unlike in the African protectorates, where Kaiser Wilhelm II's shift towards direct, militarised colonial rule resulted in the creation of the Schutztruppe. Despite the Reich's expanding naval force, no German warships were permanently stationed in the Pacific and the German Colonial Office maintained minimal police forces in New Guinea and Samoa. By August 1914 no official instructions had been received by the German colonial administration in the Pacific on how to respond in the event of war. The German Pacific – to which Foreign Secretary Adolf Marschall had hyperbolically pinned the fate of the New Course fifteen years before – had effectively been deserted.[175]

---

[170] Ibid., 42.
[171] British Foreign Office, 'Economic Conditions: German Melanesia' in *German Possessions in the Pacific*, Handbooks prepared under the Direction of the Historical Section of the Foreign Office, no. 145, June 1919, 70.
[172] Ibid.
[173] Erich Brandenburg, *From Bismarck to the World War: A History of German Foreign Policy 1870–1914*, trans. Annie Elizabeth Adams (Oxford: Oxford University Press, 1927).
[174] Ibid., 514–17; Hermann Hiery, *The Neglected War: The German South Pacific and the Influence of World War I* (Honolulu: University of Hawai'i Press, 1995), 11–12.
[175] Brandenburg, *From Bismarck to the World War*, 517; Hiery, *The Neglected War*, 20–1.

3.9 NAURU, WAR AND AUSTRALIAN 'SUB-EMPIRE' 135

In contrast, Australia and New Zealand had by 1911 already adopted formal plans for military occupation of the German Pacific colonies, should war be declared between Britain and Germany.[176] As the European empires clashed over territorial claims in northern Africa and eastern Europe, the political discourse of sub-imperialism that had emerged in the 1880s once again gained momentum in Australia. Explicitly reviving the notion of a 'Monroe Doctrine for the Pacific', which had circulated in the colonies since the 1870s, the Commonwealth government increasingly postured as the 'sub-imperial' power in the Pacific.[177] Australian sub-imperialism drew on both anti-German and anti-Japanese sentiment, which grew in White Australia as Meiji Japan was increasingly recognised by Europe and the United States as a Great Power in the first decades of the twentieth century.[178]

Yet Australia's racially grounded self-posturing as the ascendant power in the Pacific was undermined by the Commonwealth's inability to enter autonomously into treaties on the use of force. Australia was not consulted on the Franco-British Entente of 1904 or the Anglo-Japanese Alliance of 1907, despite French and increasing Japanese activity in the Western Pacific.[179] At the Imperial Conference in 1907, the Dominions again raised the issue. It was accepted that on British declaration of war, they would be automatically regarded in international law as belligerents; yet Canadian Prime Minister Sir Wilfred Laurier openly questioned the extent of the Dominion's legal obligations to give military assistance.[180] Four years later, at the 1911 Imperial Conference in London, the conceptual tension between the Dominions' putative self-government and

---

[176] Hiery, *The Neglected War*, 19.
[177] On the 'Monroe Doctrine for the Pacific', see Roger C. Thompson, *Australian Imperialism in the Pacific: The Expansionist Era 1820–1920* (Melbourne: Melbourne University Press, 1980), 45; Merze Tate, 'The Australasian Monroe Doctrine' (1961) 76 *Political Science Quarterly*, 264–84; and Cait Storr, '"Imperium in Imperio": Sub-Imperialism and the Formation of Australia as a Subject of International Law' (2018) 19 *Melbourne Journal of International Law*, 335–68.
[178] For a historical account of the relationship between the Meiji Constitution of 1889 and the international status of Japan, see Taksuji Takeuchi, *War and Diplomacy in the Japanese Empire* (Doubleday, Doran and Company, 1935).For contemporary analyses, see Tash Minohara, Evan Dawley and Tze-ki Hon (eds.), *The Decade of the Great War: Japan and the Wider World in the 1910s* (Leiden and Boston: Brill, 2014); and Mohammad Shahabuddin, 'The "Standard of Civilisation" in International Law: Intellectual Perspectives from Pre-War Japan' (2019) 32 *Leiden Journal of International Law*, 13–32.
[179] Noel-Baker, *Present Juridical Status of the Dominions*, 47–8.
[180] Ibid., 48–9.

their obligations to comply with Imperial foreign policy ran high.[181] Australian Prime Minister Andrew Fisher, a vigorous proponent of a Monroe Doctrine for the Pacific, openly demanded prior consultation on entry into treaties understood by the parties to bind the British empire. Fisher drew an explicit connection between the issue of control over external affairs and the integrity of the empire, describing the limitations on the Dominions' external sovereignty with respect to non-commercial treaty obligations as 'a weak link in the chain of our common interests'.[182]

The tension between Australia's posturing as a sub-imperial power in the Pacific and its legal obligations with respect to British foreign policy was barely concealed in diplomatic communications and statements between Australia and the Imperial government on the outbreak of war in Europe. On 6 August 1914, two days after Britain's declaration of war on Germany, the Secretary of State for the Colonies, Viscount Lewis Harcourt, sent a carefully worded telegram to the Governor-General of Australia, Ronald Ferguson:

> If your Ministers desire and feel themselves able to seize German wireless stations at Yap in the Marshall Islands, Nauru or Pleasant Island, and New Guinea, we should feel that this was a great and urgent Imperial service. You will, however, realise that any territory now occupied must be at the disposal of the Imperial Government for purposes of an ultimate settlement at conclusion of the war. Other Dominions are acting in a similar way on the same understanding.[183]

The British declaration of war and subsequent request for Australian occupation of German interests in the Pacific occurred during a federal election campaign in Australia. The 1914 election was a contest between the Commonwealth Liberal party under incumbent Prime Minister Joseph Cook, and the Labor party under Andrew Fisher, an established Pacific imperialist.[184] In the context of the election campaign, *The Age*

---

[181] *Minutes of Proceedings of the Imperial Conference 1911* (London: His Majesty's Stationery Office, 1911), 97–116.

[182] Prime Minister Andrew Fisher in *Proceedings of the Imperial Conference 1911*, 98.

[183] Telegram from the German Secretary of State to the Governor-General of Australia sent 7.30p.m. 6 August 1914, reproduced in Great Britain Colonial Office, *Correspondence respecting Military Operations against German Possessions in the Pacific* (London: His Majesty's Stationery Office, 1915), No. 1. On the international legal status of the Dominions prior to the war, see Lassa Oppenheim, *International Law: A Treatise*, 2nd ed., vol. I (London: Longmans, Green and Co, 1912), s. 65, 109–10.

[184] Thompson, *Australian Imperialism in the Pacific*, 204.

3.9 NAURU, WAR AND AUSTRALIAN 'SUB-EMPIRE'

newspaper in Melbourne on 12 August framed the British request as an opportunity to realise Australia's sub-imperialist ambitions in the Pacific:

> We have long since realised that we have a Pacific Ocean destiny, and for some years past we have been striving to attain Imperial recognition for our right to enforce a definite Pacific Ocean policy. By virtue of the European war an unexpected path has been opened to the furtherance of our ambition ... The whole business should not take more than a month. We should then have laid the foundations of a solid Australian sub-empire in the Pacific Ocean, and we should own five groups of islands.[185]

In the midst of such expansionist clamouring, a further telegram from Viscount Harcourt reiterated that Australian occupation of German interests in the Pacific should not be understood as a pretext for unilateral attempts at Australian territorial expansion:

> In connection with the expedition against German possessions in the Pacific, British flag should be hoisted in all territories occupied successfully by His Majesty's Forces and suitable arrangements made for temporary administration: but no proclamation formally annexing any such territory should however be made without previous communication with His Majesty's government.[186]

As the war was received in Australia as a renewed opportunity to annex the German Pacific territories, denied by the Imperial government in the 1880s, the German Pacific administration itself was without official instructions from the Colonial Office on how to proceed in the event of war. The Nauru District Office responded to the British declaration of war by deporting the forty British employees of the Pacific Phosphate Company to Banaba in the British Gilbert and Ellice Protectorate.[187] On 9 September 1914 – four days after a federal election that returned the Monroeist Andrew Fisher as prime minister – the Australian naval cruiser *HMAS Melbourne* arrived in Nauru. That same day, the *Melbourne* reported via telegram that it had 'put the wireless station out of action' as requested, then left without leaving troops to occupy the

---

[185] 'Melbourne, Wednesday, 12th August 1914', *The Age* (Melbourne), 12 August 1914, 8.
[186] Telegram from the German Secretary of State to the Governor-General of Australia, in Great Britain Colonial Office, *Correspondence respecting Military Operations against German Possessions*, No. 3.
[187] Harold B. Pope, *Nauru and Ocean Island: Their Phosphate Deposits and Workings* (Melbourne: Albert J. Mullett, Government Printer, 1920), 25; Williams and Macdonald, *The Phosphateers*, 107.

remote island.[188] On 14 September the Acting Governor of German New Guinea, Eduard Haber, without official instructions or standing troops, surrendered Herbertshöhe and Rabaul to the troops of Australian cruiser, the HMAS Sydney.[189] Unable to receive news of the official surrender of German New Guinea, the Nauru District Office was left in limbo for a month. In mid-October, the Governor-General of Australia, the British High Commissioner for the Western Pacific and the Pacific Phosphate Company whose officers had been deported to Banaba, agreed on a plan for the occupation of Nauru: the Australian military would assume administrative control, and the Company would resume phosphate operations, and provision the island for the duration of the occupation.[190] On 6 November 1914 sixty-six Australian troops arrived on the Pacific Phosphate Company steamer and hoisted the British flag.[191] Reporting the success of the occupation in a telegram to the British Secretary of State of the Colonies, Australian Governor-General Ferguson signed off with a pointed question: 'May Nauru now be considered open to trade?'[192]

From the outset of Australian occupation, tension between the Pacific Phosphate Company and the Commonwealth over substantive control of the administration of Nauru was evident. Immediately after the occupation, the Company declared and delivered up its shares owned by the Jaluit Gesellschaft and Die Union Fabrik Chemische Produkte to the Public Trustee in London, for auction to British buyers.[193] Once comprised predominantly of British capital, the Pacific Phosphate Company regarded Australian military administration of Nauru as a temporary wartime measure; the expectation was that administration of the

---

[188] Telegram from the Commonwealth Naval Board of Administration to Admiralty received 9 September 1914, reproduced in Great Britain Colonial Office, *Correspondence respecting Military Operations against German Possessions in the Pacific*, No. 4. Bean, *Official History of Australia in the War*, vol. X, ch. 9, 145.
[189] Bean, *Official History of Australia in the War*, vol. X, ch. 5, 51–2.
[190] Telegram from the High Commissioner of the Western Pacific to the Secretary of State received 4.50a.m. 14 October 1914, in Great Britain Colonial Office, *Correspondence respecting Military Operations against German Possessions*, No. 8.
[191] Pope, *Nauru and Ocean Island*, 25.
[192] Telegram from the Governor-General of Australia to the German Secretary of State received 4.44p.m. 19 November 1914, reproduced in Great Britain Colonial Office, *Correspondence respecting Military Operations against German Possessions in the Pacific, presented to both Houses of Parliament by Command of His Majesty* (London: His Majesty's Stationery Office, 1915), No. 14.
[193] Pope, *Nauru and Ocean Island*, 20.

profitable island would be taken over by the High Commissioner for the Western Pacific.[194] Yet Australian aspirations to claim the German Pacific for itself only intensified after October 1915, when William Morris Hughes replaced Andrew Fisher as prime minister of Australia. The prospect of British control of Nauru after the war was roundly critiqued in the Australian media, and the Pacific Phosphate Company was disparaged as 'a few big European capitalists' who had 'allowed themselves to be puppets in the hands of German plotters against the interests of Australia'.[195]

From mid-1917, the idea that Australia should be granted possession of Nauru in recompense for war losses gained significant traction in the media. The likely worth of Nauruan phosphate became a matter of common speculation.[196] Hobart's *Daily Post* put the point bluntly:

> Australia's share of the cost of the war will be at least £200,000,000 sterling. The question is how to recoup ourselves for this enormous expenditure, equal to the indemnity paid by the French to the Germans in 1870. Nauru Island was mainly German property ... German properties, interests and territories captured in the Pacific Islands by the valor of Australians and New Zealanders could be used as a national investment for the purpose of paying back the cost of the war to Australia and New Zealand.[197]

The *Sunday Times* in Sydney took a more sophisticated approach, noting that the real economic benefit of formal possession of Nauru was not in the export value of phosphate, but in increased agricultural production: 'the value to the Commonwealth is not to be estimated in figures of phosphate. It must be calculated in figures of wheat'.[198]

The tension over Dominion annexation of the German colonies was finally debated at the Imperial Conference of 1917 in London, ever more closely bound up with growing demands for control over external affairs. The 1917 Conference headed by the new British prime minister, Lloyd George, proceeded without Australian representation, as Hughes remained in Australia to campaign in a notorious federal election fought on the issue of conscription.[199] But the case for Dominion annexation had strong

---

[194] Bean, *Official History of Australia in the War*, vol. X, ch. 9, 146.
[195] 'The Riches of Nauru', *Daily Post* (Liverpool), 19 May 1917, 9.
[196] Ibid; and 'Nauru Island – Great Wealth in Phosphatic Rock', *The Sunday Times* (London), 20 May 1917.
[197] 'The Riches of Nauru', *Daily Post* (Liverpool), 19 May 1917.
[198] 'Nauru Island – Great Wealth in Phosphatic Rock', *The Sunday Times* (London), 20 May 1917.
[199] L. F. Fitzhardinge, *William Morris Hughes: A Political Biography* (Sydney: Angus and Robertson, 1964), vol. I, 45.

representation: Lieutenant-General Jan Smuts, the South African Minister for Defence, and William Massey, the prime minister of New Zealand, put the case for Dominion sub-imperialist expansion in their own regions. Unable to reach agreement, the Conference adopted a Resolution on the 'Constitution of the Empire', which provided that 'the readjustment of the constitutional relations of the component parts of the Empire is too important and intricate a subject to be dealt with during the War'.[200] On the insistence of Smuts and Massey, the Resolution further provided that any such 'readjustment' 'should be based on a full recognition of the Dominions as autonomous nations of an Imperial Commonwealth', and should 'recognise the right of the Dominions and of India to an adequate voice in foreign policy and foreign relations'.[201] In the Imperial War Cabinet of 1917, established by Lloyd George as a means of giving the Dominions a forum on British foreign strategy, Smuts and Massey explicitly pushed for territorial annexation of the occupied German colonies by the Dominions after the war, proposing that South West Africa be handed over to South Africa, and the Pacific colonies to New Zealand and Australia.[202] Whereas Australia and New Zealand's justified their claims in the logic of imperial realpolitik, arguing that annexation was necessary for regional security, Smuts adopted an ideological framing for annexation that better anticipated the internationalist zeitgeist. On Smuts' account, German imperial administration had in practice proved 'barbaric', in comparison to the benevolent and civilised British empire.[203] In the interests of native populations, therefore, the occupied German colonies in South West Africa and the Pacific could not be handed back to Germany after the war, and the principled alternative was that they be annexed by the adjacent Dominions.

3.10 Internationalisation, the Mandatory Principle and the Peace Treaty

Smuts had read the moment well. Australia and New Zealand's blunt insistence on post-war annexation conflicted directly with the rising tide of calls for internationalisation of the occupied German and Ottoman territories. Within the British labour movement, internationalisation had

---

[200] Resolution IX, 'Constitution of the Empire' in *Imperial War Conference 1917: Extracts from Minutes of Proceedings Laid Before the Conference* (London: His Majesty's Stationery Office, 1917), 5.
[201] Ibid.
[202] Louis, *Great Britain and Germany's Lost Colonies*, 82–5.
[203] Ibid., 85–6.

3.10 INTERNATIONALISATION & MANDATORY PRINCIPLE

been advocated as an alternative to annexation from as early as 1915, primarily by prominent public intellectuals associated with the Fabian Society including H. G. Wells and Leonard Woolf, and socialist associations including the Inter-Allied Conference of Labour and Socialist Organisations.[204] Advocates of internationalised administration of the occupied territories converged in asserting that European imperial competition had been the primary cause of the war, and that any attempts at post-war territorial aggrandisement should be rejected.[205] In a significant blow to the Dominions' aspirations, President Woodrow Wilson aligned rhetorically with the internationalist movement on the United States' entry into the war in April 1917 after three years of avowed neutrality, declaring the States' interest in 'vindicat(ing) the principles of peace and justice in the world as against selfish and autocratic power'.[206]

Yet despite the growing rhetorical popularity of internationalisation of the occupied territories as a principled alternative to imperial realpolitik, details on how internationalised administration would actually work in practice remained vague. Various proposals for internationalised administration circulated. Conservative proposals for internationalisation focused on economic principles of 'open door' trade and imagined the occupied territories as internationally administered areas of free commerce, with the General Act of the Berlin Conference providing a structural blueprint.[207] Even British Conservative politicians including Lord Robert Cecil advocated this commercially oriented brand of internationalisation, arguing that an international structure to guarantee economic liberalisation in the former German and Ottoman territories was the only means by which international political stability could be re-established.[208] Progressive proposals for internationalised administration grounded in political concepts of national self-determination rather

---

[204] See for example J. A. Hobson, *Towards International Government* (George Allen & Unwin, 1915); L. S. Woolf, *International Government: Two Reports by L. S. Woolf Prepared for the Fabian Research Department* (Brentano's, 1916); E. D. Morel, *Africa and the Peace of Europe* (London: National Labour Press, 1917).

[205] See for example H. G. Wells, *In the Fourth Year: Anticipations of a World Peace* (London: Macmillan Company, 1918), 62.

[206] President Woodrow Wilson, Speech delivered to the Congress of the United States, Washington, DC, 2 April 1917.

[207] Examples include E. D. Morel, *Africa and the Peace of Europe* (London: National Labour Press, 1917); and the proposal put forward (and later abandoned) by the British Labour Party in its 'Memorandum of War Aims' published on 28 December 1917.

[208] Robert Cecil, 'Memorandum on Proposals for Diminishing the Occasion of Future Wars', reproduced in Robert Cecil, *A Great Experiment: An Autobiography of Viscount Cecil* (London: Jonathan Cape, 1941), 353–6.

142   3 FROM PROTECTORATE TO COLONY TO MANDATE, 1920

than economic concepts of free trade emerged from the left of British politics, including from economist John Hobson and journalist Henry Noel Brailsford.[209]

On 5 January 1918 in a speech to the British Trades Union Congress later labelled his 'War Aims' speech, Lloyd George adopted the rhetoric of self-determination in any internationalised peace settlement, defining 'self-determination' as 'government by the consent of the governed'.[210] Without ruling out annexation, Lloyd George declared that 'government with the consent of the governed must be the basis of any territorial settlement in this war'.[211] Wilson did not go so far as to adopt even this weak version of self-determination. Three days later, in his 'Fourteen Points' address to a joint session of Congress on 8 January 1918, Wilson instead advocated for an internationalisation that reconciled imperial claims to annexation with 'the interests of the populations concerned'.[212] Wilson's fifth point called for:

> A free, open-minded, and absolutely impartial adjustment of all colonial claims, based upon a strict observance of the principle that in determining all such questions of sovereignty the interests of the populations concerned must have equal weight with the equitable claims of the government whose title is to be determined.[213]

With both Lloyd George and Wilson broadly adopting internationalist rhetoric but sidestepping pragmatic questions of administrative control of the occupied territories after the war, it was the sub-imperialist Smuts whose plan for internationalisation gained the most traction in the lead up to the Versailles negotiations. In his influential 1918 manifesto on the subject, titled *A League of Nations: A Practical Suggestion*, Smuts purported to adopt the principle of internationalisation of the occupied territories; yet in the detail of his proposal, the Dominions' claims to territorial annexation in the Pacific and Africa remained intact.[214] Both

---

[209] John Atkinson Hobson, *Towards International Government* (G Allen and Unwin, 1915); and Henry Noel Brailsford, *A League of Nations* (Headley Bros, 1917).

[210] Prime Minister Lloyd George, speech delivered to Trades Union Congress, Caxton Hall, London, 5 January 1918.

[211] Ibid.

[212] Woodrow Wilson, 'Address to Congress outlining the Program of the World's Peace, giving the Fourteen Points Necessary to its Consummation', 8 January 1918, reproduced in John Randolph Bolling and others, *Chronology of Woodrow Wilson* (New York: Frederick A Stokes Company, 1927), 251–8.

[213] Ibid., 256.

[214] J. C. Smuts, *A League of Nations: A Practical Suggestion* (Hodder and Stoughton, 1918), 26.

principles of open-door trade and national 'self-determination' as consent of the governed would inform the new international regime. In contrast to Lloyd George and Wilson, Smuts described precisely how the occupied German and Ottoman territories should be administered after the war. In Smuts' view, it was simply a pragmatic truth that any new international body or League of Nations would not have the necessary experience to take on direct administrative control of the occupied territories, as had been advocated by Brailsford and other internationalists.[215] Whilst territorial annexation by adjacent states was perhaps not ideal, Smuts submitted that it was only existing states – and not the new League – that would have the experience and capacity to successfully manage the task of extraterritorial administration:

> (t)he only successful administration of undeveloped or subject peoples has been carried on by States with long experience for the purpose and staffs whose training and singleness of mind fit them for so difficult and special a task. If serious mistakes are to be prevented and the League is to avoid discrediting itself before public opinion, it will have to begin its novel administrative task by making use of the administrative organisation of individual States for the purpose.[216]

Smuts is often credited as the originator of the mandatory principle.[217] Yet from the outset, he advocated mandatory administration for all occupied territories except German South West Africa and the German Pacific – precisely those territories claimed as their sub-imperial right by the Dominions. In response to Lloyd George on self-determination as 'government by the consent of the governed', Smuts again contorted the justification for Dominion annexation of the occupied German territories without any such consent. Not only would it be improper to return the territories to the comparatively 'barbaric' German administration, but it was also impossible to gain such consent, as the 'barbarian' peoples of the German territories were unable to comprehend their own interests:

---

[215] Ibid., 19.
[216] Ibid.
[217] Mark Mazower, 'Jan Smuts and Imperial Internationalism' in *No Enchanted Palace: The End of Empire and the Ideological Origins of the United Nations* (Princeton University Press, 2009), 28–65. Christopher Gevers argues that the concept of the mandate was proposed earlier by W. E. Du Bois. See Christopher Gevers, 'An Intellectual History of Pan-Africanism and International Law', PhD thesis, in progress, University of Melbourne.

> the German colonies in the Pacific and Africa are inhabited by barbarians, who not only cannot possibly govern themselves, but to whom it would be impracticable to apply any ideas of political self-determination in the European sense ... The disposal of these Colonies should be decided on the principles which President Wilson has laid down in the fifth of his celebrated Fourteen Points.[218]

As discussed above, Wilson's fifth point left open the possibility of territorial annexation, and did not mention consent. All that was required was an 'impartial adjustment of colonial claims' that balanced the interests of the local population against the 'equitable title' of the occupying government.[219]

In contrast to Smuts' deft manipulations of the political moment, Australian Prime Minister Hughes did not bother himself with diplomatic niceties in the debate over the occupied territories. Instead, Hughes continued to apply the old logic of imperial realpolitik. Against the mounting consensus around internationalisation as external administration in the interests of the local population and maintaining open-door trade, Hughes continued to insist that it had been 'decided definitely' in the British Imperial War Cabinet in July 1918 that German New Guinea, Samoa and South West Africa 'must be ceded to the Dominions'.[220] Pushed to consider the matter in terms of internationalist principle, Hughes maintained that even if a mandatory system was to be adopted in which individual powers would administer occupied colonies under some form of international oversight, it should not be applicable to the German Pacific territories. Not only did the 'primitive stage of civilisation' of the natives of New Guinea and Nauru make the principle of self-determination inapplicable, as Smuts had argued, but the mandatory proposal was also 'incompatible' with the 'great policy of a White Australia', which demanded freedom from the intervention of other imperial powers in the Pacific.[221]

Despite the growing prominence of Smuts and Hughes in the debate over the fate of the German colonies, the Dominion governments were

---

[218] Smuts, *A League of Nations*, 15; Louis, *Great Britain and Germany's Lost Colonies*, 81–5.
[219] Smuts' reasoning resonated with jurist James Lorimer's racial division of 'humanity' into 'civilised', 'barbarous' and 'savage'. See James Lorimer, *Institutes of the Law of Nations* (Edinburgh: William Blackwood and Sons, 1883), vol. I, 101–3.
[220] The Right Hon W. M. Hughes, *The Splendid Adventure: A Review of Empire Relations Within and Without the Commonwealth of Britannic Nations* (Ernest Benn Limited, 1929), 83; and L. F. Fitzhardinge, 'Hughes, Borden and Dominion Representation at the Paris Peace Conference' (1968) 49 *Canadian Historical Review*, 160.
[221] Hughes, *The Splendid Adventure*, 100.

3.10 INTERNATIONALISATION & MANDATORY PRINCIPLE 145

not consulted by the Imperial government on the terms of the armistice agreed between the Allies and the defeated Reich on 11 November 1918, the Reich on the basis of Wilson's Fourteen Points.[222] In the Imperial War Cabinet convened immediately after the armistice, Hughes demanded that the Dominion governments be directly represented at the planned Peace Conference, so that they could 'state their aspirations plainly'.[223] Faced with the demands of Hughes, and similar calls from Smuts, Massey and Canadian Prime Minister Robert Borden for self-representation in Conference proceedings, the Imperial War Cabinet was forced to concede that the Dominions would be permitted to 'be present' at all sessions of the Peace Conference on the same footing as the 'smaller Allied states' like Belgium, Romania and Serbia.[224]

The inclusion of the Dominion delegations in official Conference proceedings was understood to mark a fundamental shift in Dominion status not only within the British empire, but also in international law.[225] However, the nature of that shift was not yet clear. The third edition of Oppenheim's *International Law*, published in 1920, a year after the German jurist's death, asserted that the international status of the Dominions had undergone a 'fundamental change' after the Great War.[226] The Dominions' self-representation at Versailles had given them 'a position in International Law'; although it 'defie[d] exact definition', it was 'none the less real for being hard to reconcile with precedent'.[227] Sir Philip Noel-Baker, Assistant to Lord Robert Cecil, agreed, later concluding that 'the admission of their separate delegations to the Peace Conference was the decisive step in the development of the international status of the Dominions'.[228]

Over the six months of the Paris Peace Conference from 18 January 1919 to the signing of the Treaty of Versailles on

---

[222] Williams and Macdonald, *The Phosphateers*, 126; and Alma Luckau, *The German Delegation at the Peace Conference* (New York: Columbia University Press, 1941), 140–3.

[223] Hughes, *The Splendid Adventure*, 93–5; on the position of Canadian Prime Minister Borden, see Fitzhardinge, 'Hughes, Borden and Dominion Representation', 160–9.

[224] Hughes, *The Splendid Adventure*, 102; and Arthur Berriedale Keith, *The Sovereignty of the British Dominions* (London: Macmillan and Co. Limited, 1929), 315–17.

[225] Assistant to Lord Robert Cecil, Philip Noel-Baker, wrote in 1929 that 'the admission of their separate delegations to the Peace Conference was the decisive step in the development of the international status of the Dominions'. Noel-Baker, *Present Juridical Status of the Dominions*, 56.

[226] Lassa Oppenheim, *International Law: A Treatise*, ed. Ronald F. Roxburgh, 3rd ed. (New York and London: Longmans, Green and Co, 1920), 169–70.

[227] Ibid., 170.

[228] Noel-Baker, *Present Juridical Status of the Dominions*, 56.

28 June 1919, the delegations of thirty-two nations negotiated the terms of the peace agreements, the future of the occupied territories and the terms and functions on which a League of Nations would be instituted.[229] As the mandatory principle gathered strength as the principle on which internationalisation of the occupied territories would take place, Smuts, Hughes and Massey continued to maintain that whilst the principle properly applied to occupied territories in the Middle East and North Africa, it could not apply to the German colonies of South West Africa, New Guinea or Samoa. Eventually in open conflict with Wilson, Hughes reiterated the unacceptability to Australia of German New Guinea and Nauru passing to any other imperial power.[230]

Part I of the Treaty of Versailles comprised the draft Covenant of the League of Nations, and Article 22 articulated the position reached by the Conference on the future of the occupied colonies. In heavily negotiated language, Article 22 attempted to reconcile three contradictory imperatives: first, internationalisation on the basis of weak national self-determination, defined as 'government with the consent of the governed'; secondly, internationalisation on the basis of open-door trade; and thirdly, the exception of South West Africa and the German Pacific from the operation of either self-determination or open door trade.[231] The Article defined the mandatory principle as providing that the 'well-being and development' of peoples formerly under German or Ottoman rule and 'unable to stand by themselves under the strenuous conditions of the modern world' formed 'a sacred trust of civilisation'; and that the 'best method of giving practical effect to this principle' was 'that the tutelage of such peoples should be entrusted to

---

[229] For contemporaneous accounts of the Conference, see, from the US perspective: Edward Mandell House and Charles Seymour (eds.), *What Really Happened at Paris: The Story of the Peace Conference by American Delegates* (London: Hodder and Stoughton, 1920); and Charles Homer Haskins, 'Tasks and Methods of the Conference', *Some Problems of the Peace Conference* (Cambridge: Harvard University Press, 1920), 3–34. From the British perspective, see David Lloyd George, *The Truth about the Peace Treaties*, vol. I (London: Victor Gollanz Ltd, 1938); and John Maynard Keynes, 'Chapter III: The Conference' in *The Economic Consequences of the Peace* (New York: Harcourt, Brace and Howe Inc, 1920), 27–55.

[230] Hughes, *The Splendid Adventure*, 100; Lloyd George, *The Truth about the Peace Treaties*, 515–22, 542.

[231] For a contemporaneous account of the settlement of Article 22, see H. W. V. Temperley, 'The Mandatory System' in *History of the Peace Conference of Paris*, vol. VI (Oxford: Oxford University Press, 1924), 500–23; and Pedersen, *The Guardians*, 27–35.

advanced nations' and 'exercised by them as Mandatories on behalf of the League'.[232]

The success of Hughes' and Smuts' campaigns with respect to South West Africa and the German Pacific is evident in the section half of Article 22. The article went on to provide for differential application of the principle, stating that 'the character of the mandate must differ according to the stage of the development of the people, the geographical situation of the territory, its economic conditions, and other similar circumstances'. Distinguishing first 'certain communities formerly belonging to the Turkish Empire' as having 'reached a stage of development where their existence as independent nations can be provisionally recognized, subject to the rendering of administrative advice and assistance by a Mandatory', then 'other peoples, especially those of central Africa' as being 'at such a stage that the Mandatory must be responsible for the administration of the territory', Article 22 ends with an awkward capitulation to Smuts and Hughes:

> There are territories, such as South-West Africa and certain of the South Pacific Islands, which, owing to the sparseness of their population, or their small size, or their remoteness from the centres of civilisation, or their geographical contiguity to the territory of the Mandatory, and other circumstances, can be best administered under the laws of the Mandatory as integral portions of its territory, subject to the safeguards above mentioned in the interests of the Indigenous population.[233]

The precise form in which South West Africa and 'certain of the South Pacific Islands' were to be 'administered under the laws of the Mandatory as integral portions of its territory, subject to the safeguards above mentioned' was left to the new League to be determined.

The three categories of mandate distinguished in Article 22 subsequently became known as the A, B and C Class Mandates. The C Class would include only the former German colonies of South West Africa, German New Guinea, and German Samoa. Under the terms of Article 22, an 'open door' to other members of the League with respect to trade and commerce would not be required in the C Mandates. Precisely how C Mandate status differed from territorial annexation, however, remained unclear. In 1920 the lack of clarity in the legal obligations

---

[232] Treaty of Peace between the Allied and Associated Powers and Germany ('Treaty of Versailles'), opened for signature 28 June 1919, 2 USTS 43 (entered into force 10 January 1920), Pt. I, Art. 22.

[233] Ibid. On the influence of Smuts in the drafting of Article 22, see Aaron Margalith, *The International Mandates* (Baltimore: Johns Hopkins Press, 1930), 25–6.

owed by mandatory administrations with respect to C Mandates prompted the new League to commission Belgian statesman and international lawyer Paul Hymans to advise on the legal obligations falling under Article 22 to Mandatories and to the new Permanent Mandates Commission.[234] Hymans reasoned that with respect to the B and C Mandates, the Mandatory Power appointed by the Allied Powers and granted a mandate by the League would 'enjoy' 'a full exercise of sovereignty, in so far as such exercise is consistent with the carrying out of the obligations' imposed by Article 22; and that with respect to the C Class, 'the scope of those obligations is narrower', 'thus allowing the Mandatory Power more nearly to assimilate the Mandated territory to its own'. The difference between a C Mandate and territorial annexation was real; but it was slight, and remained unclear.

3.11 The Nauru Island Agreement of 1919

With Nauru under Australian military occupation and Hughes' annexationist intentions evident from his ascent to the prime ministership in October 1915, during the war the board of the now British-controlled Pacific Phosphate Company – including Foreign Secretary Lord Balfour and Sir Arthur Gordon, by then Baron Stanmore – moved to leverage its influence with the British ruling class to campaign for Nauru to be placed under British administration.[235] In 1918 Balfour wrote on behalf of the Company to Lord Milner, Secretary of State for the Colonies, declaring that its shareholders were entitled to 'some voice in determining the future jurisdiction' of Company property on Nauru, and to propose that Nauru be included in the British Gilbert and Ellice Islands Protectorate with Ocean Island, thereby bringing Nauru under the 'direct administrative control of the Imperial Government' via the Commissioner for the Western Pacific.[236] Milner appears to have personally supported this proposal, later writing confidentially to Lloyd George that 'British agriculture is vitally interested in Nauru'.[237]

In February 1919 with the Peace Conference underway, Lord Milner called a separate meeting with Dominion delegates and proposed a carve-

---

[234] Paul Hymans, 'Obligations Falling Upon the League of Nations under the Terms of Article 22 of the Covenant (Mandates)' (1920) *League of Nations Official Journal*, 334–41 at 337.
[235] Williams and Macdonald, *The Phosphateers*, 124–5.
[236] Ibid., 125.
[237] Weeramantry, *Nauru*, 50.

3.11 THE NAURU ISLAND AGREEMENT OF 1919   149

up of the German Pacific. Milner proposed that the German Pacific territories north of the equator – including the Marshall Islands and the Caroline Islands – be offered to Japan, in recognition of the 1907 Anglo-Japanese Alliance; and that those south of the equator be divided between the British empire, with German Samoa to New Zealand, Nauru to Britain under the Commission for the Western Pacific and the rest of German New Guinea, to Australia.[238] Hughes agreed to the arrangement with Japan, having long marked the equator as the de facto delineation of Australian sub-empire.[239] But he pushed back against Milner's proposal for Nauru. Distrustful of the Pacific Phosphate Company's close connection with the Imperial government, Hughes insisted that Nauru be included in the Australian allocation. In March 1919 he reiterated his position in writing to the British and Dominion delegates, arguing that permanent annexation of occupied Nauru was Australia's due for losses sustained during the war.[240] Massey disputed Hughes' claim to exclusive title to Nauru, arguing that New Zealand had both similar need for phosphate and a comparable claim to control of the German Pacific on the basis of regional security and sub-imperial status.[241] Milner's diaries record over twenty meetings about Nauru during the Conference: nine with Hughes; six with Massey; and eight with Sir Alwyn Dickinson, the Director of the Pacific Phosphate Company, with Lord Balfour present at three in his capacity as chair.[242]

The compromise reached between Britain, Australia and New Zealand over Nauru severed the island from the rest of German New Guinea and demonstrated equal concern with administrative control and the disposition of phosphate rights.[243] As detailed above, prior to Australian military occupation the legal framework around Nauruan phosphate had been constructed as follows: under its agreement with the Gesellschaft, the Pacific Phosphate Company held the exclusive right to exploit Nauruan phosphate; proprietary rights in phosphate were held by the Reich; and proprietary rights in land resided with Nauruan landowners under Nauruan law, leased to the Company. The Nauru Island

---

[238] Williams and Macdonald, *The Phosphateers*, 126.
[239] Fitzhardinge, 'Hughes, Borden and Dominion Representation', 164.
[240] Williams and Macdonald, *The Phosphateers*, 127; Weeramantry, *Nauru*, 43.
[241] 'Triangular Battle between Milner, Hughes and Massey', *The Sun* (Sydney), 17 March 1919.
[242] Williams and Macdonald, *The Phosphateers*, 129.
[243] Nauru Island Agreement Act 1919 (Cth). The Agreement is included as the Schedule to the Act.

Agreement was signed by George, Hughes and Massey in Paris on 2 July 1919, less than a week after the signing of the Treaty of Versailles. The Agreement purported to derive its authority to deal with Nauru from the Treaty of Versailles, describing its source of authority as 'a Mandate ... conferred by the Allied and Associated Powers upon the British Empire' to operate from the coming into force of the 'Peace Treaty with Germany'. Whilst the Agreement was novel in its tripartite compromise that reflected the changing status of the Dominions within the empire, the administrative structure it contemplated was continuous with that of the protectorate era.

The Nauru Island Agreement, however, effected one crucial accretion of administrative form. In the 1888 Agreement, the Reich had vested both administrative powers and phosphate rights directly in the Jaluit Gesellschaft, which had maintained those administrative powers through to 1906 when administrative control passed over to the colonial administration of German New Guinea, and had licensed the phosphate rights to the Pacific Phosphate Company in 1901. The tripartite 1919 Nauru Island Agreement effected the transfer of both administrative powers and phosphate rights; but it created two new bodies to exercise them. Article 1 vested administrative powers previously exercised by the Nauru District Officer in a new office of Administrator, with power to 'make ordinances for the peace, order, and good government of the Island, subject to the terms of this Agreement' and to 'provide for the education of children on the Island, to establish and maintain the necessary police force, and to establish and appoint courts and magistrates with civil and criminal jurisdiction'. The Administrator was initially to be appointed by the Australian government for the first five years, and 'thereafter ... appointed in such manner as the three Governments decide'.

Phosphate rights, however – first created under German law in the Gesellschaft, subsequently licensed to the Pacific Phosphate Company – were vested in a new Board of Commissioners. Article 3 provided that the new Board would comprise three members, one appointed by each government; and Article 6 provided that 'title to the phosphate deposits on the Island of Nauru and to all land, buildings, plant, and equipment on the island used in connexion with the working of the deposits, shall be vested in the Commissioners'. Article 9 provided that '(t)he deposits shall be worked and sold under the direction, management, and control of the Commissioners', and that it was the 'duty of the Commissioners to dispose of the phosphates for the purpose of the agricultural requirements of the United Kingdom, Australia and New Zealand'. The Board of

3.12 THE AGREEMENT AND ITS RELATION TO ARTICLE 22   151

Commissioners would later become known as the British Phosphate Commission.

The defining characteristic of the tripartite Commission was its dominant relationship to the new Administration. The 1919 Agreement effectively rendered the Administration financially dependent on the Commission, at the same time prohibiting it from exercising any powers of oversight over Commission operations. Article 2 of the 1919 Agreement replicated the revenue arrangement set up by the 1888 Agreement, which had made the Jaluit Gesellschaft responsible for meeting the costs of the Nauru District Office: it provided that '(a)ll the expenses of the administration (including the remuneration of the Administrator and of the Commissioners), so far as they are not met by other revenue, shall be defrayed out of the proceeds of the sales of the phosphates'. At the same time, Article 14 providing that there was to be 'no interference by any of the three Governments with the direction, management, or control of the business of working, shipping, or selling the phosphates' – thereby effectively excluding the Commission's phosphate operations from the oversight of the Australian-appointed Administrator. Article 15 formalised the heart of the tripartite bargain, stipulating how Nauruan phosphate was to be divided up: 42 per cent to the United Kingdom, 42 per cent to Australia and 16 per cent to New Zealand, at cost. Article 17 added a condition to the shared monopoly, providing that 'such allotment shall be for home consumption for agricultural purposes in the country of allotment, and not for export'.

3.12 Incorporation of the Nauru Island Agreement and its Relationship to Article 22

The Nauru Island Agreement was the subject of debate in all three countries over the following year, as Article 15 required legislative ratification. In Australia, the Nauru Island Agreement and the text of the Peace Treaty were tabled in the Commonwealth House of Representatives on the same day, 18 September 1919.[244] In his second reading speech on 24 September 1919, Hughes framed the Nauru Island Agreement as a commercial one, in which the administrative arrangements were secondary to the commercial objective of securing phosphate for Australian agricultural use. He described the mandate principle agreed on in Paris as

---

[244] Commonwealth, *Parliamentary Debates*, House of Representatives, Thursday 18 September 1919.

the basis for administration of the occupied German and Ottoman territories not as a shift towards internationalisation of authority, but rather as 'the tenure under which the sovereignty of the island is held at present'.[245] In the parliamentary debate that ensued, the contradictions between the new international principles of mandate rule and open-door trade in the Covenant and the tripartite commercial monopoly enshrined in the Nauru Island Agreement were not raised. Rather, the Australian Members of Parliament occupied themselves with the numbers, querying the calculations of the quantity and value of Nauruan phosphate which would determine under Article 7 how much the Pacific Phosphate Company was to be compensated.[246] The Nauru Island Agreement Bill was passed in October 1919.

A few months later, in January 1920, the Council of the League of Nations held its first meeting in Paris.[247] As stated by the first Council chairman, French Senate President Leon Bourgeois, the first of the two tasks given to the League was 'the practical execution of the Treaties of Peace'.[248] The second Bourgeois termed the 'task of the future', which he described as securing 'the definite foundation of international justice' and the 'protection of races not yet able to stand by themselves, whose welfare and development, in the words of Article 22, "form a sacred trust of civilisation"'. The allocation of the mandates was not, however, decided on by the Council. The Treaty vested the power to allocate the new mandates in the Allied Powers, and formal allocation did not occur until May 1920 – some ten months after the execution of the tripartite Nauru Island Agreement, and eight months after its ratification by the Australian Parliament.[249]

Lloyd George, more sensitive to the performance of international diplomacy than Hughes, waited until after the formal allocation of the Mandate for Nauru by the Allied Powers to introduce the Nauru Island Agreement into the House of Commons.[250] The Bill was tabled for second reading on 16 June 1920. In the debate that ensued, the coalition government and the opposition disagreed on the nature of the Agreement and its compliance

---

[245] Commonwealth, *Parliamentary Debates*, House of Representatives, 24 September 1919.
[246] Ibid.
[247] Council of the League of Nations, '*Proces-Verbal* of the First Meeting of the Council of the League of Nations' (February 1920) *League of Nations Official Journal*, 1–27 at 17.
[248] Ibid., 19.
[249] See H. Duncan Hall, *Mandates, Dependencies and Trusteeship* (London: Stevens & Sons Limited, 1948), 31–2.
[250] Commonwealth, *Parliamentary Debates*, House of Representatives, 16 June 1920, vol. 130, 1299–1351 (Nauru Island Agreement Bill second reading).

3.12 THE AGREEMENT AND ITS RELATION TO ARTICLE 22

with the new Covenant of the League. With the government, Charles Palmer argued that the Agreement contemplated the purchase of British corporate interests under private law, and therefore fell outside the purview of the new League altogether.[251] The opposition argued that the Agreement was an international administrative agreement that fell squarely within the purview of Article 22 of the Covenant. On that basis, William Ormsby-Gore, the British representative to the Permanent Mandates Commission of the League and an avowed internationalist, vigorously opposed passage of the Bill on numerous grounds.[252] First, he disputed that authority to dispose of the island derived from the Treaty of Versailles, arguing that the British empire had no authority over Nauru until formally delegated mandatory obligations by the new League. Secondly, Ormsby-Gore argued that if the 'British Empire' did indeed derive mandatory authority from the Treaty and not the League, he took issue with the assumption made in the Agreement that the 'British Empire' could be read down to include only Britain, Australia and New Zealand; in his terms, '(i)f the mandate is conferred upon the whole British Empire you cannot without gross violation of our whole Imperial arrangement confine the mandate to two self-governing Dominions and the Mother Country, and shut out the others'.

Thirdly, Ormsby-Gore argued that the Agreement contravened the two major principles agreed upon at the Peace Conference. In effectively creating a 'Government monopoly' over Nauruan phosphate, it directly contradicted both the principle of open door trade in the occupied territories, and the mandatory principle of administrative trusteeship on behalf of the League. Ormsby-Gore was supported by Lord Robert Cecil, who argued that the Nauru Island Agreement directly contravened the spirit of Article 22, and that there was no authority to dispose of Nauru until the League granted a formal mandate. Despite the lengthy submissions of Ormsby-Gore and Cecil, the Bill was passed without amendment by the House of Commons that same day, by a resounding majority of 218 votes to 57.[253] In New Zealand, the Agreement was ratified unconditionally by parliamentary resolution.[254]

---

[251] Ibid., 1335–7.
[252] On Ormsby-Gore's opposition to the Nauru Island Agreement, see Pedersen, *The Guardians*, 74–6.
[253] Campbell L. Upthegrove, *Empire by Mandate: A History of the Relations of Great Britain with the Permanent Mandates Commission of the League of Nations* (New York: Bookman Press, 1954), 84.
[254] *Public Acts of New Zealand 1908–1931* (Wellington: Butterworth, 1933), vol. 2, 657.

154   3 FROM PROTECTORATE TO COLONY TO MANDATE, 1920

3.13   The Transfer Agreement with the Pacific Phosphate Company

Once the Nauru Island Agreement had been ratified by all three signatories, it remained for the Commission to formally acquire the rights of the Pacific Phosphate Company. The Company, established by Arundel to run both the Nauruan and the Banaban phosphate operations – one under German administration, one under British – was unhappy with the tripartite plan for acquisition of Nauru only. Balfour argued on the Company's behalf that its Banaban concern would not be able to compete with the new tripartite monopoly over Nauruan phosphate, and that the new Commission – on which the Administration of Nauru was dependent – should therefore buy out both concerns.[255] On 25 June 1920 the Company and the Imperial government signed an agreement of purchase and sale of both the Nauruan and Ocean Island phosphate rights.[256] The rights transferred from the Company to the new tripartite Commission were stipulated to include 'all the right title and interests of the Company in the guano phosphate deposits in and upon the said Islands and in the lands buildings, plant and equipment on the said Islands', for consideration of £3,500,000.[257] The Transfer Agreement was heralded in Australia not as the purchase of a licence, but of property; and not just of property in Nauruan phosphate, but of property in Nauru itself. When the Appropriations Bill for Australia's proportion of the purchase price was tabled by Hughes in the House of Representatives, the Transfer Agreement was discussed not as the purchase of the Pacific Phosphate Company's Nauruan operation, but as 'the purchase of Nauru Island'.[258]

3.14   The Mandate for Nauru and the Tension between International and Sub-Imperial Status

With the execution of the Nauru Island Agreement and the Transfer Agreement, the administrative authority over the island vested in the new office of Administrator, and all rights pertaining to the phosphate operation vested in the new British Phosphate Commission. On their face, both Agreements constituted British intra-imperial rather than international

---

[255] Williams and Macdonald, *The Phosphateers*, 130–1.
[256] Agreement between His Most Gracious Majesty King George V and Others and The Pacific Phosphate Company, Westminster, 25 June 1920.
[257] Ibid., cll. 1–9, 5–12.
[258] Commonwealth, *Parliamentary Debates*, House of Representatives, 29 July 1920.

accords. But the international status of the self-governing Dominions was rapidly shifting, and the post-war instabilities in the constitution of the British empire were evident in the formal allocation of the mandates. On 29 November 1920, the Council of the League passed the Constitution of the Permanent Mandates Commission, which provided that the majority of the PMC was to comprise nationals of non-Mandatory powers, and one representative of the International Labour Organisation.[259] The PMC was not vested with the power to formally allocate mandates – already in fact decided by the Allied Powers, and officially delegated to the Council of the League. Rather, it was delegated the power to 'receive and examine' the reports that Mandatory Powers would be required to render to the Council each year, and to 'advise' the Council on 'all matters relating to the Mandates'.

On 17 December 1920 the Council formally settled the mandatory allocation for 'South West Africa and certain of the South Pacific Islands', labelled together as the C Mandates. The 'Mandate for German South-West Africa' was conferred upon 'His Britannic Majesty to be exercised on his behalf by the Government of the Union of South Africa'. The 'Mandate for German Samoa' was conferred upon 'His Britannic Majesty to be exercised on his behalf by the Government of the Dominion of New Zealand'.[260] Reflecting the line drawn across the Pacific along the equator between Japan and Britain at Paris, German New Guinea was dealt with in the 'Mandate for German Possessions in the Pacific Ocean Situated South of the Equator, Other than German Samoa and Nauru', conferred upon 'His Britannic Majesty to be exercised on his behalf of the Government of the Commonwealth of Australia'.[261] The Marshall Islands, north of the equator – formerly the German Marshall Islands Protectorate, brought within German New Guinea in 1906 following the Jaluit Gesellschaft's abandonment of its protectorate responsibilities – were once again administratively separated from New Guinea and Nauru, and allocated to Japan, along with the Caroline Islands and the Mariana Islands, becoming the 'Mandate for the Former German Possessions in the Pacific Ocean Lying North of the Equator', conferred upon 'His Majesty the Emperor of Japan'.[262]

---

[259] Council of the League of Nations, 'Constitution of the Permanent Mandates Commission' (Nov.–Dec. 1920) 1 *League of Nations Official Journal*, 87–8.
[260] Council of the League of Nations, 'The Mandates Question' (Jan.–Feb. 1921) 2 *League of Nations Official Journal*, 89–90, 91–92.
[261] Ibid., 85–6.
[262] Ibid., 87–8.

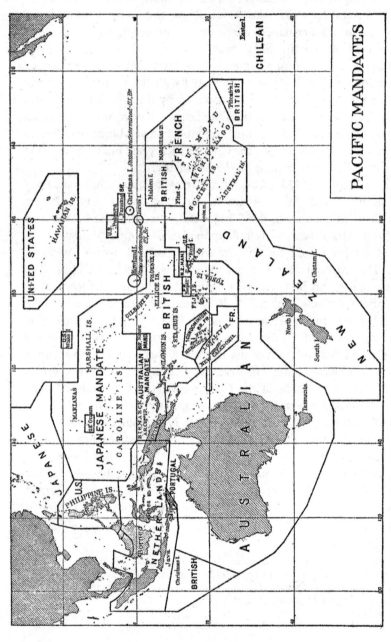

3.3 'Pacific Mandates', map published in George Blakeslee, 'Mandates of the Pacific' (1922) *Foreign Affairs* 1, 102. Republished with permission of *Foreign Affairs*, conveyed through Copyright Clearance Center Inc.

3.14 THE MANDATE FOR NAURU

The island of Nauru was dealt with separately from the Marshall Islands and New Guinea by the Council of the League, as pre-empted in the Nauru Island Agreement. In contrast to the other C Mandates conferred on the British empire, which all included in their title a recognition of Dominion status fought for so doggedly by Hughes and Smuts, the 'Mandate for Nauru' was conferred upon 'His Britannic Majesty' alone.[263] A mere seven articles long, the Mandate provided that the Mandatory would have 'full power of administration and legislation over the territory ... as an integral portion of his territory'; and would 'promote to the utmost the material and moral well-being and the social progress of the inhabitants'.[264] The Mandatory was required to report annually to the Council of the League, providing 'full information with regard to the territory', and indicating 'measures taken to carry out the obligations assumed'. There was no mention of the Nauru Island Agreement in the Mandate conferred on the British Crown.

As such, the tripartite arrangement agreed upon by Britain, Australia and New Zealand seventeen months earlier to administer the pre-empted mandate was never officially approved by the new League. Whilst Hughes had succeeded in gaining administrative control of the northeast of New Guinea in addition to the southeast already under Australian administration, his attempt at outright annexation of Nauru to Australian territory had failed.[265] At the international level, administrative control of Nauru passed to the entire British empire, not to Australia; and whilst the international status of the Dominions remained unclear, the tripartite Nauru Island Agreement was an intra-imperial and not international instrument. Yet whilst the Australian and South African governments failed in their goal of outright territorial annexation of the occupied German territories, in the process of trying to assert themselves as the sub-imperial powers in their respective regions, they had achieved two significant international outcomes: the recognition of the Dominions as subjects of international law, and the creation of the C Mandate.

---

[263] Mandate for Nauru, Council of the League of Nations, 17 December 1920 (London: His Majesty's Stationery Office, 1921), art. 1. Council of the League of Nations, 'The Mandates Question', 93–4.

[264] Mandate for Nauru, art. 2.

[265] Hughes subsequently maintained that the failure was not his, but his Cabinet's. See Commonwealth of Australia, *Parliamentary Debates*, House of Representatives, 2 July 1920 (Prime Minister Hughes, Procedural Text).

3.15 Conclusion

The shift in the international status of Nauru from protectorate to colony to mandate between 1888 and 1920 overlay three far more complex processes of legal formation: the accretion of a particular configuration of company and administrative rule fixed under the German protectorate regime; the disintegration of the British empire along longstanding lines of tension between the Imperial government and the self-governing Dominions over control over external affairs powers; and the geopolitical compromise between territorial annexation and internationalisation of occupied territory struck at the Paris Peace Conference, and codified in Article 22 of the Covenant of the League. Whereas at the commencement of the protectorate era, German concern with Nauru was entirely commercial, between 1888 and 1920 a legal framework for the administration of Nauru gradually sedimented into place, ordinance by ordinance. As with the other German protectorates, Nauru was administered under what was effectively unfettered executive rule, severed from the development of German constitutional jurisprudence. As the model of company protectorate that Bismarck had attempted proved unworkable and the Reich under Wilhelm II embarked upon its New Course of expansionism and militarisation, Nauru's status formally shifted from protectorate to colony. In other parts of the German empire, this shift was accompanied by military force.

Fourteen years later, and after four years of war, Nauru's status was to shift again, this time from German colony to C Mandate. The contrast between the protectorate and the C Mandate as models of external administration was stark. On the one hand, the protectorate and C Mandate were similar in that both struck a pragmatically ambiguous pose between administrative control and territorial annexation.[266] On the other, the Bismarckian Reich had in the 1880s considered the protectorate attractive precisely because it did *not* attract the obligations of effective occupation that declaring sovereignty would have done, whilst at the same time providing some legal protection to Hanseatic trading interests. Twenty years later, Australia – along with its fellow Dominions of South Africa and New Zealand – considered the C Mandate form attractive because it was the closest to territorial annexation that could be

---

[266] Anghie makes a similar point in '"The Heart of My Home": Colonialism, Environmental Damage, and the *Nauru* Case' (1993) 34 *Harvard Journal of International Law*, 445, 494–5.

negotiated in the crush of competing internationalisms that jostled for position in the rooms of Versailles.

Between 1888 and 1920 the basic administrative form set down in the Agreement between the Gesellschaft and the Reich took root and began to branch. Just as the District Officer had unfettered executive power, so too did the new Administrator, without any clear mechanism for legislative oversight. Just as the Gesellschaft had legal responsibility for funding the island's administration, the new British Phosphate Commission was now responsible for meeting all costs of the new mandatory Administration. At the same time, the Commission's finances were exempted from administrative oversight; and, as had been the case in 1888, the power of the Administrator to issue new laws and ordinances was restricted by a requirement that the Commission be consulted, and commercial operations not affected.

Focus on the chain of legal agreements that affected these shifts in international status and administrative form make one thing clear: the Nauruan people themselves were treated as a peripheral concern in the British imperial move to claim the island of Nauru from the German empire. The Hanseatic firms' story incorporates the Nauruan people first only as traders in copra, then as unruly natives to be disarmed. Under German protectorate rule, the Nauruan people take shape as Eingeborene, recognised only via a limited capacity to hold property rights in land and trees – but not sovereignty, nor rights in the now-valuable phosphate that comprised the island's central plateau; and as disputes over the interaction of these limited rights with those of the European traders mounted, that shape is slowly given detail, as German attempts to 'apply' 'Nauruan' property rights resulted in the reactive expansion of total executive jurisdiction over the Nauruan people.

As European trading interests in Nauru shifted from Hanseatic commodity circulation to industrial production, the Pacific Phosphate Company's story, for its part, incorporates the Nauruan people initially as a labour problem. The refusal of the Nauruan people to render themselves as an amenable labour force to the new phosphate operation occurred during the industrialisation of indentured labour across the Pacific region. As the European empires jostled within and between themselves at the turn of the century, European firms and imperial administrations in the Pacific experimented with 'solutions' to that labour problem, which ranged from deception and duress to slavery in all but name. The blackbirding trade forced islanders from New Guinea around the Pacific, and down into the cane fields of Australia; Governor

Sir Arthur Gordon, applying his colonial expertise acquired in Mauritius and Trinidad, orchestrated the shipping of people from India to Fiji; and shady sub-contractors shipped people from China, the Marshall Islands and the Caroline Islands to Nauru. With the shift from imperial into international paradigms of geopolitical ordering in 1919, the now-emblematic principles of 'native welfare and development' and the 'sacred trust of civilisation' espoused in Article 22 of the Covenant of the League became problems to be answered by mandatory administrations. Chapter 4 traces the shift from mandate to trust territory status, and the accretion of the Nauruan Administration over the period to 1947. As the concepts of international administration and mandatory oversight developed in the new League of Nations regime, mandatory administrations and international jurists concerned themselves with justifying as matters of principle the legal and economic subjugation of the Nauruan people, a subjugation which only forty years before had simply been presumed in the commercial competition between European empires.

4

From Mandate to Trust Territory, 1947

4.1 Introduction

From 1921 Nauru was categorised as a C Mandate of the British empire. But the actual exercise of administrative power over the island was determined by the 1919 Nauru Island Agreement. The Agreement installed an Australian-appointed Administrator and rendered the office financially dependent on the new British Phosphate Commission, which had no obligations of financial transparency to the Administrator, and therefore to the Permanent Mandates Commission to which the Administrator reported. This chapter commences with an account of the accretion of the structure of administration in Nauru during the mandate period, in accordance with the provisions of the Mandate and the Nauru Island Agreement. The ambiguous international status of the C Mandates – to be administered 'as integral portions of the territory' of the Mandatory, under the terms of Article 22 of the Covenant of the League – came to pose a juridical problem for scholars, and a diplomatic problem for the League. As South Africa and Australia argued for a strict interpretation of their mandatory obligations, the British Phosphate Commission industriously exploited its tripartite monopoly over Nauruan phosphate, delivering cost-price phosphate into the agricultural sectors of the United Kingdom, Australia and New Zealand. The impact of Nauruan phosphate on the development of Australian agriculture is traced in the context of international debates on global population growth and food security, prompted by the Great Depression of the late 1920s and early 1930s. In Australia, these debates played out on an explicitly racial basis. Soaring global food prices were seen as precursor to an impending tide of 'Asiatic' immigration that justified the Commonwealth's White Australia policy. The racial framing of Australia's self-positioning in the Pacific exacerbated the tensions with Japan that had surfaced during the Paris Peace Conference. These

4 FROM MANDATE TO TRUST TERRITORY, 1947

tensions worsened as Australia insisted diplomatically on the exemption of its Pacific C Mandates from otherwise general mandatory obligations of open-door trade.

Nauru lay at the intersection of imperial competition in the Pacific between Australia, Japan, the United States and Germany. For both Japan and Germany, the C Mandates illustrated the hypocrisies of the new internationalist paradigm. Tensions between Australia and Japan worsened after the withdrawals of Japan and Germany from the League in 1933, and the imperial frontiers that cut across the Pacific became increasingly volatile. The Australian C Mandates of Nauru and New Guinea were occupied by Japan during World War II as key sites in the Japanese offensive in the Pacific, operated from Japanese military bases on Chuuk Atoll in the Japanese C Mandate. In 1941 Nauru was occupied by Japanese troops, the majority of the Nauruan population shipped to Chuuk and officials from Nan'yō Kōhatsu Kabushiki Kaisha, the Japanese South Seas Development Company, took over phosphate operations on the island.[1] As the exiled Nauruan people faced starvation on Chuuk, the reconstitution of the League as a new United Nations was already under negotiation. In the Charter of the United Nations adopted at the 1945 San Francisco Conference, the concept of mandatory status inaugurated in Article 22 of the Covenant of the League developed into the concept of trust territory status, codified in two full chapters in the Charter of the United Nations. Chapter XII expanded the obligations owed by administering powers with respect to all 'trust territories', removing the distinctions between A, B and C Mandates. Chapter XIII expanded the composition and powers of the new Trusteeship Council that replaced the Permanent Mandates Commission. Chapter XI, meanwhile, declared general principles of international administration pertaining to all 'non-self-governing territories', troubling the pragmatic distinction between the Allied Powers' colonial administration of their own territories, and the mandatory administration of confiscated German and Ottoman territories.

The status of Nauru officially shifted from C Mandate to Trust Territory in 1947, with the approval of the Trusteeship Agreement for Nauru in 1947 by the new Trusteeship Council. The successor body to the Permanent Mandates Council, the Trusteeship Council comprised an

---

[1] Yuki Tanaka, 'Japanese Atrocities on Nauru During the Pacific War: The Murder of Australians, The Massacre of Lepers and the Ethnocide of Nauruans' (2010) 45 *The Asia-Pacific Journal*, 1–19.

expanded membership including newly independent states and increased powers of review. The shift from mandate to trust territory status proved highly significant in providing a clearer conceptual framework in which the nature of the relationship between Australia and Nauru could be characterised as a matter of international law. It also provided an international platform from which the Nauruan people and their supporters could push for political independence, and a legal vocabulary in which the case for reckoning with the compounding environmental and economic damage that imperial intervention was wreaking on Nauru could begin to be expressed. At the administrative level, however, the shift from mandate to trust territory status in 1947 prompted further accretions in the basic structure of relations established under German rule in 1888, and developed under Australian administration from 1920.

4.2 Administration of Nauru as a C Mandate of the League of Nations

As detailed in Chapter 3, the Pacific Phosphate Company's operations in Nauru had continued without interruption from Australian military occupation in 1914 right through the Paris Peace Conference negotiations on internationalisation of the occupied territories, and the tripartite side deal struck in the 1919 Nauru Island Agreement between the British Imperial government, Australia and New Zealand. The transition from Australian military occupation to Australian mandatory administration was smooth. Under the Transfer Agreement that had assigned the Pacific Phosphate Company's rights to the new Board of Commissioners, the operation was transferred as a going concern. All employees of the Company were employed by the new Commission; and the first three Commissioners were themselves all Company executives.[2] Sir Alwyn Dickinson, a member of the Company's Board of Directors, became the Commissioner for the United Kingdom; Harold Pope, the Company's accountant, became the Commissioner for Australia; and Albert Ellis, Company employee and later Director, who claimed to have discovered Nauruan phosphate from the office door stop, became the Commissioner for New Zealand.[3] Harold Pope reported in 1921 that phosphate exports

---

[2] Agreement between His Most Gracious Majesty King George V and Others and the Pacific Phosphate Company, Westminster, 25 June 1920, cl. 10.

[3] Maslyn Williams and Barrie Macdonald, *The Phosphateers: A History of the British Phosphate Commissioners and the Christmas Island Phosphate Commission* (Melbourne: Melbourne University Press, 1985), 94 et seq.

were the highest they had ever been, and continued to grow. Pope's rhetoric laid bare both the Commission's sense of its own importance, and its plan for the total exhaustion of Nauruan phosphate: '(t)he Australian farmer, therefore, has no need to be anxious about his supplies of superphosphate. Whatever may happen in less fortunate countries, his supplies are assured for the next four or five generations at any rate'.[4]

As the PPC became the new BPC, the first Administrator appointed by the Australian Government was English-born war veteran Brigadier Thomas Griffiths, who took office in June 1921.[5] Under Australian Administration, the Commission's phosphate production took priority over all else. The Nauru Island Agreement provided that the Australian Administrator's powers to 'issue ordinances for the peace, order, and good government of the island' were limited only by the power of the British Phosphate Commission to conduct phosphate operations without interference.[6] In the first year of mandatory administration, Griffiths issued a series of ordinances that clarified the transition from German protectorate to British mandatory rule. The Laws Repeal and Adopting Ordinance of 1922 provided that all laws 'of the German Empire and of the German State' would cease to apply in Nauru – to be replaced by the laws of the State of Queensland.[7] However, continuity of all private rights was assured: rights and obligations created under German law would be recognised, until either satisfied or discharged. Any lands formerly owned by the German state would vest in the Administrator. The Judiciary Ordinance of 1922 established a Central Court of record and a District Court of petty sessions.[8] Whilst the Judiciary Ordinance purported to vest 'judicial power' in the new courts, it also stipulated that the courts would consist of the Administrator and his appointees. Even as the administrative structure of Nauru expanded from an executive office to include a separate court, the Administrator was vested with the same totality of executive and judicial power, subject to the powers of the

---

[4] Harold B. Pope, *Nauru and Ocean Island: Their Phosphate Deposits and Workings – Progress Under Government Ownership* (Melbourne: Government Printer, 1921), 22–3.

[5] Parliament of the Commonwealth of Australia, Report on the Administration of Nauru During the Year 1922, Prepared by the Administrator for Submission to the League of Nations (Melbourne: Albert J. Mullett, Government Printer, 1923), 5.

[6] Nauru Island Agreement Act 1919 (Cth), arts. 1 and 13.

[7] Laws Repeal and Adopting Ordinance (No. 8 of 1922), appended to Parliament of the Commonwealth of Australia, Report on the Administration of Nauru During the Year 1922, 22–3.

[8] Judiciary Ordinance (No. 9 of 1922), appended to Parliament of the Commonwealth of Australia, Report on the Administration of Nauru During the Year 1922, 24.

4.2 ADMINISTRATION OF NAURU AS A C MANDATE

phosphate operation, as the Nauru District Officer had been under German rule.

Other ordinances passed in the early years of Australian administration responded to obligations imposed on mandatories by Article 22 of the Covenant, soon formalised by the Permanent Mandates Commission in its annual questionnaire to the Administrator. Due at least in part to the ambiguity in C Mandates and the limited powers of the PMC, the incorporation of international obligations at the local level required little more than reframing of established practice. In crucial respects, however, the incorporation of mandatory obligations provoked an augmentation of executive power over the Nauruan people. This was particularly marked with respect to property. As discussed in Chapters 2 and 3, from the outset of German imperial intervention, the Nauruan people were recognised as holding property rights in land and resources. In 1921 the Australian Administrator issued the Nauru Lands Ordinance, which prohibited Nauruan landowners from selling, leasing or contracting with respect to their land.[9] Similar measures were adopted in many mandates, purportedly to prevent exploitation of 'natives' by 'unscrupulous' commercial operators. However, having created a general prohibition on free dealing in property, the Lands Ordinance then created an exception for Nauruan leases to the BPC. Leases to the BPC were the only dealing in real property that could be entered into and were rendered subject to the approval of the Administrator, and at regulated rates set by the Administration.[10]

According to the Lands Ordinance, the Administrator's approval purported to protect the 'well-being and development' of native peoples as secured in Article 22. The new international vocabulary was used to introduce total executive control over the exercise of Nauruan property rights, such as they had been recognised and conceived by trading agents, then the Nauru District Officer under German administration. In exchange for this restriction on the exercise of rights that had – even if only technically – been freely exercisable under German rule, the Lands Ordinance increased the going rate of royalties to Nauruan landowners, raising the rate from the German halfpenny to threepence per ton of phosphate.[11] However, here too the Ordinance extended executive

---

[9] Nauru Lands Ordinance (No. 12 of 1921), appended to the Report of the Administration of Nauru covering the period from date of Confirmation of the Mandate, 17 December 1920, to 31 December 1921.
[10] Ibid.
[11] Ibid.; also A. H. Charteris, 'The Mandate over Nauru Island' (1923–1924) 4 *British Yearbook of International Law* 137–52, 151.

control, this time over the Nauruan peoples' exercise of this limited financial return. For each threepence owed per ton, the Ordinance provided that only twopence was to be paid directly to the landowner. The remaining one penny was to be paid by the BPC to the Administrator, to be held on trust for the Nauruan population.[12] The fund into which the BPC was to pay the quarantined third of royalty payments subsequently became known as the Nauru Landowners Phosphate Royalty Trust. The Landowners Phosphate Royalty Trust was to be held out by the Australian Administrator as evidence of its satisfaction of mandatory obligations for years to come.

On an international level, the inauguration of the mandate system in the occupied German and Ottoman territories and the assumption of international oversight by the League of Nations effectively resolved the question of jurisdiction over the 'native' populations of protectorates that had so vexed British jurists in the late nineteenth century. Whereas German authority over Nauruan peoples had never been clearly articulated in terms of the law of nations, British authority over the Nauruan people was explicitly derived from the Allied Powers, pursuant to the German surrender of imperial territory in the Treaty of Versailles. Under the Mandate for Nauru – issued by the Allied Powers, not the new League – the Administrator was vested with the 'full power of administration and legislation over the territory'.

In the first raft of executive orders in mandatory Nauru, the Administrator issued the Native Status Ordinance of 1921, which defined 'native' regionally as 'any aboriginal of any island in the Pacific Ocean, or of any of the East Indian Islands or of Malaysia'.[13] The Native Administration Ordinance of 1922 stipulated that the Administrator had the power to make 'any regulation affecting the affairs of natives', including marriage, property rights, criminal and civil offences.[14] Indicating a pragmatic conflation of 'native' and 'labourer', the Administration Ordinance applied not only to 'natives' as defined in the Status Ordinance, but also included 'aboriginal native(s) of China, or of any island of the Pacific Ocean', explicitly bringing the indentured labour force under executive control.

---

[12] Nauru Lands Ordinance 1921; and Charteris, 'The Mandate over Nauru Island', 151.
[13] Nauru Status Ordinance (No. 12 of 1921), appended to Parliament of the Commonwealth of Australia, Report on the Administration of Nauru during the Year 1922.
[14] Native Administration Ordinance (No. 17 of 1922), appended to Parliament of the Commonwealth of Australia, Report on the Administration of Nauru during the Year 1922.

Whereas the transition from Australian military to civilian administrative control was smooth, never interfering with extraction and export of phosphate, the transition to official League oversight of the new British Mandate for Nauru was far less so. Under the Nauru Island Agreement, the Administrator was funded entirely from the profits of the BPC, which existed purely for the purpose of exploiting Nauru's phosphate deposits; and for all the Administrator's executive power, the office had no authority whatsoever over phosphate operations, and no official visibility regarding BPC accounts. But the British Imperial government never officially communicated either the tripartite Nauru Island Agreement of 1919, or the delegation of mandatory responsibility to the Australian Commonwealth government, to the League. The Permanent Mandates Commission discussed the discrepancy when it first turned its attention to Nauru in 1922.[15] Belgian diplomat Pierre Orts noted that the Nauru Mandate had been conferred by the Allied Powers on the British empire only, not Australia; and queried why the tripartite arrangement that delegated administrative control to the Commonwealth government had not been formally communicated. The PMC noted from the outset that the Nauru arrangement conflicted with both the political self-determination and open-door trade components of the mandatory principle. First, the interests of the Nauruan people were at risk of subordination to the interests of the tripartite governments in exploiting phosphate; and second, the monopolisation of phosphate was not 'in true harmony' with the exercise of an international mandate.[16]

In discussion of Australia's 1922 Report on Nauru, the PMC commented further on the peculiarity of the new regime in Nauru: the Australian Administrator was responsible for meeting mandatory obligations, but the tripartite BPC was in effective control.[17] According to the PMC chairman, the Italian marquis Alberto Theodoli, there was thus 'a confusion between the system of exploitation and the administration of the territory', and a 'State monopoly existed'.[18] Australian High Commissioner Sir Joseph Cook, the Accredited Representative of the three governments at the League, brushed off the PMC's concerns, obliquely insisting that any potential conflicts in the arrangement

---

[15] League of Nations Permanent Mandates Commission, 'Minutes of the Second Session held in Geneva August 1st–11th, 1922', 46.
[16] Permanent Mandates Commission, 'Minutes of the Second Session', 55.
[17] League of Nations Permanent Mandates Commission, 'Minutes of the Third Session held in Geneva July 20th–August 10th, 1923', 51–2.
[18] Ibid., 51.

between Administrator and BPC 'did not really arise'.[19] Cook maintained that the arrangement had to be understood as a continuation of the pre-war status quo: the British Phosphate Commission represented 'merely the substitution of a publicly owned monopoly for a privately owned one', the Pacific Phosphate Company.[20] Cook emphasised the corporate analogy to defend the arrangement, submitting that the BPC did not actually escape administrative oversight, as its legal position was 'strictly analogous to that of the directorate of a company'; in all matters except the phosphate operation, the Commissioners 'were subject to the control of the Administrator'.

Cook also brushed off the PMC's concern that the interests of the Nauruan people had been subordinated to the interests of phosphate wealth extraction. He submitted that there was no risk of conflict between the mandatory obligation to promote Nauruan 'well-being and development' and the phosphate operation, arguing that the Nauruan people themselves made no use of the island's central plateau from which phosphate was removed: 'the population is confined to narrow coastal strips, which are more or less fertile. The phosphate deposits themselves, situated within these strips, occupy an area that is neither populated nor food-producing'.[21] Prime Minister Billy Hughes, reporting Cook's submissions to the PMC in Parliament, reiterated Cook's argument that the interests of the Nauruan people and the BPC's interest in mining of phosphate did not conflict in practice. On Hughes' account, '(t)he working of the phosphate deposits is in no way prejudicial to the interests of the natives who, on the contrary, have never been so well off as they are under the present Administration'.[22] These early Australian rebuttals of PMC concerns that the tripartite deal contradicted the mandate principle were to be repeated as dogma by Administrators for decades to come. Australia continued to insist throughout the mandate period that the scope of BPC authority contravened no mandatory obligations; and that the Nauruan people's 'well-being and development' was not subordinated to the tripartite governments' interests of extracting phosphate

---

[19] 'General Observations of the Permanent Mandates Commission concerning the Reports relating to the Administration of the Island of Nauru, under the Mandate of His Britannic Majesty, August 1922'. Christopher Weeramantry, *Nauru: Environmental Damage under International Trusteeship* (Oxford: Oxford University Press), 380–1.
[20] Ibid.
[21] Ibid.
[22] Commonwealth of Australia, House of Representatives Official Hansard, 'Ministerial Statement made by the Prime Minister with Reference to the Administration of Nauru', Parliamentary Papers No. 36, 8 September 1922.

4.1 Phosphate workings near Number 2 Unit, British Phosphate Commission, April 1923. Image courtesy of the National Archives of Australia. NAA: R32, NAURU 5/502.

wealth, because the Nauruans had 'no use' for the island's central plateau, and now received royalties from the BPC at a rate set by the Administrator pursuant to the new Lands Ordinance.

Whilst the PMC could do little more than report its concerns to the Council of the League, Australia's rhetoric did not go unscrutinised internationally. The C Mandate concept itself, that uneasy pragmatic compromise that had been struck during the Peace Conference between advocates of Wilsonian internationalisation and the annexationist Dominions, attracted significant juridical attention in the interwar years. Reviewing the Nauru arrangement, A. H. Charteris, then Chair of International Law at the University of Sydney, offered a strict interpretive approach of mandatory obligations, arguing that neither Article 22, nor the mandate agreements themselves created positive obligations on mandatories with respect to free trade.[23] As such, he argued, the monopolisation of Nauruan phosphate contravened no mandatory obligations. All that was required of

[23] Charteris, 'The Mandate over Nauru Island', 150–1.

the Administrator was the promotion of the 'well-being and development' of the Nauruan people; and under the new Lands Ordinance, Nauruans received a higher royalty than had been the case under the German regime, indicating that their 'well-being and development' was indeed being prioritised over profit.[24] Charteris then went further to opine more broadly on the C Mandates in international law, positing that they represented a new form of conditioned annexation. In providing that C Mandates were 'best administered under the laws of the Mandatory as integral portions of its territory, subject to the safeguards above mentioned', Article 22 allowed 'incorporation subject to conditions', strictly construed.[25]

Charteris' legal opinion, popular with the Australian government, was not shared internationally. In Thomas Baty's estimation, the drafting of Article 22 was catastrophically poor. As he lamented, 'nothing less like a legal instrument than this section can be imagined. It reads like a University Extension lecture.'[26] He countered Charteris' view, arguing that the C Mandate could not be considered 'incorporation' into the territory of the mandatory power, as in no case did a C Mandate involve the extension of rights of nationality to Indigenous populations, nor the subsumption of the fiscal affairs of the mandated territory into the economy of the mandatory power.[27] Baty went on to reject the analogy drawn by some commentators between the C Mandate and a private law trust. For Baty, whatever the rhetoric of 'sacred trust', the C Mandate relationship could not be characterised as one in which powers of sovereignty were assumed by the mandatory as trustee on behalf of the Indigenous population as beneficiary, as there was no positive obligation placed on the mandatory power not to profit from their role. He reluctantly concluded that the administrative power conferred on both B and C mandatories was so extensive as to amount to substantive annexation. For Baty, what was at issue was the law of territory; and it was 'the fact and the processes of administration, not its ultimate ends or its pecuniary profits, that are important in identifying a territory with a State'.[28]

---

[24] Charteris was not only legally but also seemingly ideologically in support of the Australian government's position on Nauru: 'The remuneration is small, perhaps, in the eyes of a civilised man in view of the immense value of the product in the Commonwealth, but it is not small to a child of nature who lives on cocoa-nuts and fish and sunshine.' Ibid., 151.
[25] Ibid., 149.
[26] Thomas Baty, 'Protectorates and Mandates' (1922) 2 *British Yearbook of International Law*, 109–21, 119.
[27] Ibid., 118.
[28] Ibid., 119.

4.2 ADMINISTRATION OF NAURU AS A C MANDATE 171

The conflict between the mandatory principle and resource exploitation in the Nauru case was thus less an anomaly than a demonstration of the defining ambivalence of the C Mandate. During the 1920s scholarly analysis of the mandate system came to focus on the question of where the sovereignty of the mandated territory resided.[29] Reviewing the 'law and practice' of the South African Mandate of South West Africa and the New Zealand mandate of Western Samoa, American political scientist Luther Harris Evans argued, *contra* Charteris, that the C Mandates were not territorial annexations in which sovereignty vested in the mandatory power. But he so found for a remarkably telling reason. On Evans' view, the 'semi-autocratic' concentration of administrative power in a single office 'would be considered to be too undemocratic to be tolerated within the confines of the territory' of each mandatory power.[30] Instead, Evans argued, the C Mandates were *sui generis* entities in international law, in which sovereignty resided with neither the mandatory power nor the Indigenous population, but 'in the mandatory power and the Council [of the League] acting together'.[31]

Similarly to Evans, political scientist Elizabeth van Maanen-Helmer reasoned that the C Mandates were differentiated from territorial annexation by the existence of the League itself – or more specifically, by the existence of the Permanent Mandates Commission.[32] As limited as the PMC was to issuing questions and receiving reports, the fact of PMC oversight of matters of 'native well-being and development' marked the line between the new mandate regime and 'old-fashioned' annexation.[33] This interpretation of the C Mandate as a *sui generis* form of international

---

[29] H. V. Evatt, *The British Dominions as Mandatories* (Melbourne: Melbourne University Press, 1934), 5–11; Susan Pedersen, *The Guardians: The League of Nations and the Crisis of Empire* (Oxford: Oxford University Press, 2015), 204–5.

[30] Luther Harris Evans, 'Are "C" Mandates Veiled Annexations?' (1927) 7 *Southwestern Political and Social Science Quarterly*, 381–400, 389 et seq. Evans aligned with Quincy Wright, who surmised 'a close approach to truth in ascribing sovereignty of mandated territories to the mandatory acting with the consent of the Council of the League'. Quincy Wright, 'Sovereignty of the Mandates' (1923) 17 *American Journal of International Law*, 691–703, 698.

[31] Evans, 'Are "C" Mandates Veiled Annexations?', 389 et seq. Evans aligned with the position of compatriot Quincy Wright, who surmised 'a close approach to truth in ascribing sovereignty of mandated territories to the mandatory acting with the consent of the Council of the League'. Quincy Wright, 'Sovereignty of the Mandates' (1923) 17 *American Journal of International Law*, 691, 698.

[32] Elizabeth van Maanen-Helmer, *The Mandates System in Relation to Africa and the Pacific Islands* (London: P. S. King and Son Ltd, 1929), 202 et seq.

[33] Ibid., 203.

administration providing for joint sovereignty held between the mandatory power and the Council was not adopted by the Council itself. When the matter was raised, the Council opted against taking a position on the juridical question of sovereignty over the C Mandates, instead directing the PMC to request submissions from the mandatory powers themselves as to their interpretations of their legal relationship with the mandated territories.[34] Charged with reporting on the matter to the Council, the Netherlands representative on the PMC Frans Beerlaerts von Blokland concluded without further elaboration that the C Mandate relationship was 'clearly a new one in international law'.[35]

By the 1930s, administration of the Mandate of Nauru had settled into the rhythm of the phosphate operation. In 1930 the BPC completed construction of an industrial cantilever that overhung the reef fringe of the Aiwo district to the island's southwest. The new crown in the BPC's plant allowed phosphate to be carted from the central plateau down along the cableways that ran through Aiwo and out across the reef, directly into the holds of cargo ships anchored in the ocean.[36] Northeast of the cantilever on the forested rises of Aiwo was the 'European Settlement', where Administration and Commission officials resided in houses, some with swimming pools. By ordinance of the Administrator, no 'natives' were permitted to enter the European Settlement between sunset and sunrise.[37] Adjacent to the cantilever directly on the coast was the BPC labourers' accommodation camp. The Administrator reported to the PMC that the 'Chinese coolies' – on three-year contracts, and numbering between 700 and 1,100 at any one time – were now 'healthy and contented'.[38] The financial structure the

---

[34] 'As regards territories under C mandate, the Commission desired further information concerning the views of the Government of the Union of South Africa on the question of its legal relationship to the mandated territory of South-West Africa. This question was raised previously in the report of the Commission on its Tenth Session, and in March last the Council decided that it should not express any opinion on the difficult point as to where sovereignty over a mandated territory resides.' Permanent Mandates Commission, 'Report of the Permanent Mandates Commission on the Work of its Eleventh Session' (October 1927), 8 *League of Nations Official Journal*, 1118–21 at 1119–20.

[35] Ibid.

[36] Parliament of the Commonwealth of Australia, Report to the Council of the League of Nations on the Administration of the Island of Nauru during the Year 1931 (Canberra: Commonwealth Government Printer, 1932).

[37] Movement of Natives Ordinance (No. 12 of 1921), appended to Report of the Administration of Nauru covering the period from date of Confirmation of the Mandate, 17th December 1920, to 31st December 1921.

[38] Parliament of the Commonwealth of Australia, Report to the Council of the League of Nations on the Administration of the Island of Nauru during the Year 1931.

4.2 ADMINISTRATION OF NAURU AS A C MANDATE

Administration, whilst now more elaborate than the simple arrangement struck between the Reich and the Gesellschaft, retained the same basic form. Nauruan phosphate paid not only for the entire BPC operation, but also for the administration of the Mandate as well. Every year, the Administrator claimed the cost of administration directly from the BPC via an Appropriations Ordinance. This included provision for wages and other costs of maintaining the police station and prison, wireless station, post office, medical services and all other public works.[39] In its own financial records, the BPC deducted appropriations from its accounts as a liability.[40]

It was in the annual ritual of reporting to the PMC that tensions arose. The PMC questionnaires required the Administrator to account for the satisfaction of mandatory obligations, including the obligation to advance the 'social, moral and material welfare of the natives'.[41] In his Annual Reports, Administrator Griffiths pointed the PMC towards two new initiatives. First was the creation of a Nauruan 'Council of Chiefs', formalising an ad hoc practice of consultation developed by Nauru District Officer Fritz Jung in the early years of the protectorate, after the original detention of the chiefs in 1888. Second was the provision of compulsory primary education for Nauruan children. In his 1924 Report to the PMC, Griffiths wrote that Nauru had 'since time immemorial' been divided into fourteen districts, each under a 'Chief', from whose number a 'Head Chief' was drawn.[42] He continued that as the policy of the Administration was to 'encourage the preservation of native customs and rights where it can reasonably do so', the Council of Chiefs had been formally recognised, and 'charged with the maintenance of order in their districts', including the power to deal with 'minor offences' as stipulated by the Administrator in the Native Regulations.[43] In 1924 Griffiths reported that Timothy Detudamo of Uaboe had been elected as Head Chief; and a monthly meeting would be held with the Chiefs during which they would be 'afforded an opportunity' to bring matters to the notice of the Administration.[44]

---

[39] See for example Appropriations Ordinance (1 of 1931), Parliament of the Commonwealth of Australia, Report to the Council of the League of Nations on the Administration of the Island of Nauru during the Year 1931, Appendix A.
[40] Ibid., Appendix B.
[41] Permanent Mandates Commission, 'Minutes of the Second Session', Annex 3, 'C Mandates', 83-4.
[42] Parliament of the Commonwealth of Australia, Report to the Council of the League of Nations on the Administration of the Island of Nauru during the Year 1924 (Victoria: H. J. Green, Government Printer), 13-14.
[43] Ibid.
[44] Ibid., 14.

The Administration's Reports to the PMC came to focus heavily on the provision of education as satisfying mandatory obligations. The Compulsory Education Ordinance of 1921 provided that all Nauruan children between eight and sixteen would be required to attend one of the two mission schools, both subsidised with funds taken from the Landowner's Royalty Trust by the Administration.[45] In the early 1930s Griffiths' replacement as Administrator, W. A. Newman, introduced a new education initiative that proved critical in the decades to come. In addition to the existing program of compulsory primary education, Newman introduced selective secondary education for Nauruan boys. As there was no secondary school on the island, a small cohort of male students – mostly between the ages of eighteen and twenty – were sent to the Australian regional city of Geelong, west of Melbourne, for further education in 'technical subjects'.[46] All costs of the Geelong program were appropriated by ordinance from the Royalty Trust. In his 1931 Report to the PMC, Newman made a rhetorical move that had been largely absent from official Australian discourse regarding Nauru: reporting on the introduction of the Geelong program, he declared that '(e)ncouragement and sympathetic assistance have been given with a view to enabling, in due course, the native inhabitants of the Territory to administer their own affairs'.[47]

Privately, however, both Administrator Newman and the Phosphate Commissioners worried that secondary education even of a handful of male students could lead to Nauruan demands for more substantive self-government than the Council of Chiefs allowed. The second British Commissioner, Thomas Lodge, appointed to the BPC from the refugee section of the League of Nations in Geneva, expressed concern that British interest in Nauruan phosphate could be 'seriously affected' if such 'ill-considered policy on native questions' were to continue.[48] Lodge drew from his League experience to warn that secondary education of the Nauruan people could only result in 'native unrest'.[49] Administrator

---

[45] See 'Measures Taken to Carry Out the Obligations Assumed under Articles 2, 3, 4 and 5 of the Mandate' in Parliament of the Commonwealth of Australia, Report of the Administration of Nauru covering the period from date of Confirmation of the Mandate, 17th December 1920, to 31st December 1921, 6.

[46] *The Argus*, 'Nauru Boys' Progress', *The Argus* (Melbourne), 22 December 1938. See also Don Chambers, *'Boss' Hurst of Geelong and Nauru* (South Melbourne: Hyland House, 1994), 114 et seq.

[47] Parliament of the Commonwealth of Australia, Report to the Council of the League of Nations on the Administration of the Island of Nauru during the Year 1931.

[48] Williams and Macdonald, *The Phosphateers*, 252–3.

[49] Ibid.

Newman himself soon expressed the same doubt, worrying that even selective secondary education of the Nauruan people would 'inevitably lead to unsettlement and difficulties such as would appear to be the case in at least one of the dominions of the Empire'.[50] Within a few short years, Newman's Geelong program came to be regarded as a serious mistake. Newman was replaced in 1933 by a retired naval officer, Commander Rupert Garsia. In the 1937 Report to the PMC, Garsia reported that the Geelong program had been wound back.[51] The explicit reason given to the PMC for this policy reversal was the limited long-term prospects of the Nauruan people:

> education must take into account the changing social and economic conditions and circumstances of life of the communities concerned. This implies a need for periodical revision of the education programme. Such a revision has been initiated in Nauru in 1937, the idea being to have an education system which will be genuinely related ... to the developmental needs and changing conditions of the island as interpreted by the Administration; in other words, an education suitably adapted to the Nauruan environment.[52]

4.3 Phosphate, Agriculture, Population and Race in the Australian Interwar Period

On the BPC's own estimate, approximately 1.25 million tons of phosphate was extracted from Nauru under mandate rule from 1920 to 1940.[53] During the mandatory period, Australian agriculture came to depend heavily on the continuous supply of cost-price phosphate from the BPC, sourced from its two operations in Nauru and in Banaba in the British Gilbert and Ellice Islands protectorate.[54] As Australian Commissioner with the BPC, Harold Pope proved a dogged propagandist for the Nauru arrangement. Deploying Article 22's new trope of civilisational development, Pope equated the 'progress' of the phosphate industry with the 'progress' of the Nauruan people.[55] New Zealand Commissioner Albert Ellis was similarly zealous on

---

[50] Weeramantry, *Nauru*, 113.
[51] Parliament of the Commonwealth of Australia, Report to the Council of the League of Nations on the Administration of the Island of Nauru during the Year 1937 (Canberra: L. F. Johnson, Commonwealth Government Printer, 1938), 33–4.
[52] Ibid., 33.
[53] Albert Ellis, *Mid-Pacific Outposts* (Auckland: Brown and Stewart Limited, 1946), 8.
[54] See S. M. Wadham and G. L. Wood, *Land Utilization in Australia* (Melbourne: Melbourne University Press, 1939), 59, 164, 199; and Robert D. Watt, *The Romance of the Australian Land Industries* (Sydney: Angus and Robertson, 1955), 133–9.
[55] Pope, *Nauru and Ocean Island*, 23, 38.

the virtues of Nauruan phosphate, not only for New Zealand's agricultural development, but also as a salve for the global problem of population growth:

> there is practically no crop which does not respond to phosphoric acid, and indeed it can be said, without the annual top-dressing of water soluble phosphatic fertilizer, agriculture as it exists to-day could not be conducted ... there can be no doubt as to the use of phosphate and the growing importance it will have in helping to provide food for the world's increasing population.[56]

Guaranteed access to superphosphate at cost fed into the boom in the Australian sugar, wheat, cattle and sheep industries, which by the early 1930s were all firmly fixed nationalist emblems for the new Commonwealth.[57] As Australia's primary production rose, routine use of phosphate had immense implications for colonial patterns of land distribution and exploitation away from the coasts, intensifying the violent dispossession of Aboriginal peoples.[58] The intensive farming of sugar, wheat, cattle and sheep became possible in regions the colonial governments had in the nineteenth century regarded as worthy only for pastoral grazing and mining. The Commonwealth government marketed emigration to booming rural communities to returned soldiers and prospective British immigrants.[59] The implications of sustained phosphate use were ecological as well as industrial. Forced raising of crops further depleted the continent's ancient soils of mineral content, aggravating erosion. Introduced plant species raised as stock fodder, including rye grass and clover, quickly became endemic weeds throughout the temperate regions of the continent.[60]

The boom in Australian primary production in the interwar years took on particular geopolitical significance as global food prices

---

[56] Albert F. Ellis, *Ocean Island and Nauru: Their Story* (Sydney: Angus and Robertson Limited, 1935), 290–3.

[57] See for example *The Cumberland Argus*, 'On the Sheep's Back', *The Cumberland Argus* (Parramatta), 3 May 1934; and *The West Australian*, 'Australian Agriculture: None Better in the World', *The West Australian* (Perth), 10 November 1934. This account of Australian national identity was already by the 1930s pitted against the nationalism of the 'city wage-earning unionist'. *The Mackay Daily Mercury*, 'Backbone of the Nation: Farmers' Difficulties', *The Mackay Daily Mercury* (Mackay) 28 September 1935.

[58] Aileen Moreton-Robinson, *The White Possessive: Property, Power and Indigenous Sovereignty* (Minneapolis: University of Minnesota, 2015).

[59] Commonwealth Scientific and Industrial Research Office, *The Australian Environment*, 3rd ed. (Melbourne: Melbourne University Press, 1960), 52–3.

[60] Ellis, *Ocean Island and Nauru*, 288–90; Gregory T. Cushman, *Guano and the Opening of the Pacific World* (Cambridge: Cambridge University Press, 2013), 129–30.

4.3 AGRICULTURE AND RACE: THE INTERWAR PERIOD

increased sharply during the global deflationary recession that followed World War I.[61] Rising food prices contributed to the revival in the interwar period of Malthusian arguments of the relation between population growth and agricultural production, and prompted increasing interest in international technocratic governance as a means of regulating food production and distribution.[62] In Australian public discourse, both Europe and Asia were regularly invoked as posing geopolitical problems of 'overpopulation' relative to food production. The comparative 'underpopulation' of Australia was held out as a security risk that required active policy response. Australian treatments of the world 'population problem' routinely drew explicit connection between Australia's agricultural capacity and the White Australia policy. Sydney lawyer and social scientist Henry Lane Wilkinson, for example, argued that in order to avert the 'risk' of mass immigration from Asia, the Commonwealth should actively solicit British immigration, whilst increasing agricultural export to Japan, China and India.[63] Agricultural export to Asia was, Wilkinson argued, a 'logical extension' of the White Australia policy. At the same time, the problem of 'depopulation' of the Pacific Islands was widely held out as a basis for extending Australian control of the Pacific region to prevent 'Asiatic' immigration to Australia via the islands.[64]

Japan's Pacific Islands Mandate to the north became a focal point of Australia's racialised anxiety over the security risks posed by global overpopulation. During the drafting of Article 22, the Japanese delegation headed by Makino Nobuaki had protested the absence of economic equality obligations in the C Mandates, observing correctly that Hughes' arguments against the application of the open-door principle in the occupied German Pacific territories were not only commercial, but racial. Unable to secure outright territorial annexation of New Guinea and Nauru, Hughes had insisted on rights of commercial exclusion in the territories, as security

---

[61] Cushman, *Guano and the Opening of the Pacific World*, 205–42; and Alison Bashford, *Global Population: History, Geopolitics, and Life on Earth* (New York: Columbia University Press, 2014).

[62] See for example Alexander Morris Carr-Saunders, *The Population Problem: A Study in Human Evolution* (Oxford: Clarendon Press, 1922); Edward East, *Mankind at the Crossroads* (New York: Scribners, 1923); and Warren S. Thompson, *Danger Spots in World Population* (New York: Alfred A Knopf, 1930).

[63] Henry Lane Wilkinson, *The World's Population Problems and A White Australia* (London: P. S. King and Son Ltd, 1930), 317.

[64] Stephen H. Roberts, *Population Problems of the Pacific* (London: George Routledge and Sons, Ltd, 1927).

against Asian immigration.[65] In the interwar period, the tension between the two mandatory powers was only to get worse: Japan and Australia shared maritime borders where the C Mandates of New Guinea, Nauru and the Islands North of the Equator met, but across which commercial activity could no longer freely pass.

As rising food prices intensified international debate over food production and population distribution, assuring phosphate supply became a national imperative. By the 1920s global phosphate production which had in the later nineteenth century pushed westward into the Pacific from the guano islands of Peru was booming. The Pacific Islands remained a key source of supply, fed not only from the BPC's operations in Nauru and Banaba, but also from Angaur in the Japanese Pacific Islands Mandate; Makatea in the French protectorate of Etablissements des français en Océanie (now French Polynesia); and Howland, Baker and the Phoenix Islands, claimed in the nineteenth century as 'appurtenances' to the United States under the Guano Islands Act.[66] But the global market was now fed also from terrestrial deposits in the southern states of the United States; in the French and Spanish protectorates of Morocco; and in the French protectorate of Tunisia. By the 1930s imperial monopolisation of phosphate resources in the mandates and protectorates had become a question of international concern. In 1938 the Permanent Court of International Justice handed down its decision in the *Phosphates in Morocco Case*, brought by Italy on behalf of an Italian company in protest at French monopolisation of the phosphate industry in the French protectorate of Morocco.[67] Italy argued that the establishment of a French phosphate monopoly was inconsistent with France's obligation in international law to maintain an 'open door' for European commerce in the protectorate.[68]

Whilst the PCIJ decided on France's preliminary objection that the Court had no jurisdiction to hear the matter, the strength of the Italian

---

[65] 'Japan feels strongly in this matter ... She sees herself excluded on an attenuated legal quibble from these very islands, in a way which Germany never attempted. It really is not a good demonstration of the benefits of the era of mutual helpfulness which she supposed to have been inaugurated by the Covenant of the League of Nations'. Baty, 'Protectorates and Mandates', 121. See also George H. Blakeslee, 'The Mandates of the Pacific' (September 1922) *Foreign Affairs*, 98–115 at 101; and van Maanen-Helmer, *Mandates System*, 34.

[66] See for example A. N. Gray, 'Phosphate Rock: The World's Output', *Perth Western Mail*, 11 August 1932. Also Ellis, *Ocean Island and Nauru*, Appendix C, 300–1.

[67] *Phosphates in Morocco (Italy v. France) (Judgment)* [1938], Permanent Court of International Justice, ser A/B74, 4.

[68] Ibid., 7.

case accentuated the contradictions in C Mandate status regarding the monopolisation of natural resources in mandated territories. The peculiarity of the C Mandate was further emphasised by the fact that the League routinely held out the 'economic equality' of States Members with respect to trade in the A and B mandates as one of its major successes.[69] In 1929 – ten years after Nobuaki had argued the point in Paris – van Maanen-Helmer identified that the absence of obligations of economic equality in the C Mandates was a crucial weakness in the mandate system, if not in the League itself. It directly undermined the principle of free trade in the confiscated territories that had supposedly animated the Versailles settlement; and on van Maanen-Helmer's reckoning, 'the reason that the principle of equality of treatment was not included in the C Mandates was the desire of the Australians for the exclusion of Asiatic immigration'.[70] Van Maanen-Helmer's account understated the contributions of the other British Dominions – and of General Smuts in particular – in forcing the C Mandate compromise. But it recognised the fundamental relationship between white supremacism and regional sub-imperialism that continued to animate the Commonwealth in its external affairs, and the serious effects the C Mandate compromise had on the legitimacy of the League.[71]

4.4 The Co-Existence of Mandates and Protectorates: the Interwar International

The increasingly volatile geopolitics of the interwar period were framed by the ungainly, staggering transitions from imperial to international administration. As the mandate system applied only to the former German and Ottoman territories, internationalised mandates sat alongside the imperial protectorates, dependencies and colonies of the Allied Powers. In 1935 the League's list of 'States, Colonies, Protectorates, Overseas Territories and Territories under Suzerainty or Mandate' included 69 states and at least 118 'territories'.[72] This heterogeneity of administrative form produced odd juxtapositions in which one imperial

---

[69] Secretariat of the League of Nations, *The Aims, Methods and Activity of the League of Nations* (Geneva: League of Nations Office de Publicité, 1935), 114.
[70] Van Maanen-Helmer, *Mandates System*, 237.
[71] See Part 10, 'Internationalisation, the mandatory principle and the Peace Treaty' in Chapter 3, 'From Protectorate to Colony to Mandate, 1920'.
[72] H. Duncan Hall, *Mandates, Dependencies and Trusteeship* (London: Stevens & Sons Limited, 1948), 44; League of Nations Secretariat, *Aims, Methods and Activity of the League*, 220.

power administered two adjacent territories under different administrative structures, one subject to League oversight, the other not.[73] In the Pacific, the British protectorate of the Gilbert and Ellice Islands existed adjacent to the British Mandate of Nauru; and the Australian Territory of Papua existed adjacent to the Australian Mandate of New Guinea. In Africa, German Togo and German Cameroon had each been divided between the British and French empires. The B Mandate of British Togo existed adjacent to the British protectorate of the Gold Coast; and the B Mandate of French Togo existed adjacent to the French colony of Dahomey, in the federation of French West Africa.[74] The B Mandate of British Cameroon existed adjacent to the British protectorate of Nigeria. German East Africa, meanwhile, had been divided between Belgium and Britain. The Belgian B Mandate of Ruanda-Urundi existed adjacent to the colony of Belgian Congo; and the British B Mandate of Tanganyika existed adjacent to the protectorate of British East Africa, later British Kenya.

At the international level, this cacophony of status and form became a juridical puzzle. International jurists struggled to settle a coherent juridical taxonomy that provided principled reasons for the inconsistencies between international and imperial status. Within the British empire itself, the co-existence of A, B and C Mandates, Dominions, protectorates and colonies proved a fertile jurisprudential problem. Exegeses on the advent of international administration jostled for attention with exegeses on the changing imperial constitution. Following the Dominions' involvement in the Paris negotiations, they were widely recognised as having acquired some measure of international status.[75] The Imperial Conferences that had begun in the 1880s continued to provide a platform for the Dominions to assert their claims for greater autonomy with respect to foreign affairs.[76] At the Imperial Conference of 1923, the Imperial government finally conceded that the practice of consultation with Dominion governments on matters of defence begun in the late nineteenth century had advanced to the status of a right to

---

[73] Evans, 'Are "C" Mandates Veiled Annexations?', 389.
[74] Ralph Bunche wrote his PhD dissertation on the contrasting administrative systems of French Togoland and Dahomey, submitted to Harvard University in 1934. Susan Pedersen, *The Guardians: The League of Nations and the Crisis of Empire* (Oxford: Oxford University Press, 2015), 323.
[75] See Part 10, 'Internationalisation, the mandatory principle and the Peace Treaty' in Chapter 3, 'From Protectorate to Colony to Mandate, 1920'.
[76] Arthur Berriedale Keith, 'Notes on Imperial Constitutional Law' (1924) 6 *Journal of Comparative Legislation and International Law*, 193–209. See also Robert MacGregor Dawson (ed.), *The Development of Dominion Status 1900–1936* (Oxford: Oxford University Press, 1937).

4.4 THE CO-EXISTENCE OF MANDATES & PROTECTORATES 181

be informed in advance of any prospective treaty negotiations with foreign states.[77] It was further agreed that the Dominions would not be bound by any new treaties without executive signature and legislative ratification.[78] At the Imperial Conference of 1926, this shift in the status of the Dominions towards full external sovereignty was confirmed by a new definition: the Dominions were declared 'autonomous Communities within the British Empire, equal in status, in no way subordinate one to another in any aspect of their domestic or external affairs, though united by a common allegiance to the Crown, and freely associated as members of the British Commonwealth of Nations'.[79] At the same time, the declared principle of equal status was acknowledged as not entirely reflected in practice; the Imperial government still exercised a catalogue of ad hoc executive, legislative and judicial powers over the Dominions.[80] The slow discursive shift from 'empire' to 'Commonwealth' was accompanied by a surge in reappraisals of imperial history.[81]

As the international status of the Dominions took on clearer legal definition, however, the status of the other British imperial territories remained opaque. At the 1926 Imperial Conference, this opacity was defensively declared a strength rather than a weakness of the empire as a whole. But the issue was not so easily defused. Sir Cecil Hurst, British lawyer and judge on the Permanent Court of International Justice, attempted to qualify the nature of the British empire, describing it as a political rather than a juridical entity.[82] Hurst offered a pragmatic explanation: whereas the relationship between the Dominions and the Imperial government was a proper subject

---

[77] For an extended treatment of the development of international status of the Dominions, see P. J. Noel-Baker, *The Present Juridical Status of the British Dominions in International Law* (New York: Longmans, Green and Co., 1929).

[78] Ibid.

[79] The Summary of Proceedings of the 1926 Conference is reproduced in Keith, 'The Imperial Conference 1926'. See also Arthur Berriedale Keith, *The Sovereignty of the British Dominions* (London: Macmillan and Co Limited, 1929).

[80] The Summary of Proceedings goes on to state that '(e)xisting administrative, legislative, and judicial forms are admittedly not wholly in accord with the position described'. Keith, 'The Imperial Conference 1926'.

[81] See for example H. Duncan Hall, *The British Commonwealth of Nations: A Study of its Past and Future Development* (London: Methuen & Co. Ltd, 1920); Manfred Nathan, Empire Government: An Outline of the System Prevailing in the British Commonwealth of Nations (Cambridge, MA: Harvard University Press, 1930); Shankat Anant Desai, *Constitutional Law of England, Colonies, Dominions, and India* (Byculla: Tatva-Vivechaka, 1932); and Royal Institute of International Affairs, *The British Empire: A Report on its Structure and Problems* (Oxford: Oxford University Press, 1937).

[82] Cecil B. Hurst, 'British Empire as a Political Unit under International Law' in Harris Foundation, *Great Britain and the Dominions* (Chicago: Chicago University Press, 1928), 3–32.

of constitutional jurisprudence, the relationships between the 'non-self-governing units of the Empire' and the 'self-governing units' – here now including both Britain and the newly empowered Dominions – was not constitutional but a question of international politics. Ten years later, the Royal Institute of International Affairs, in its 1937 report on the 'structure and problems' of the British empire, offered another attempt at conceptual coherence that dispensed with Hurst's attempt at insulating imperial constitutionalism from international politics. The Royal Institute replaced Hurst's bifurcation of the empire with a linear universal: the internal heterogeneity of the empire, it concluded, reflected differential stages of 'constitutional development'.[83]

4.5 The 'Colonial Question' and the Failing Legitimacy of the League of Nations

The tensions between mandatory and colonial administrative practice were but one theme in a growing list of critiques of the League itself. Both the territorial settlement reached at Paris and its implementation through the Covenant of the League were increasingly charged with hypocrisy by Japan, Germany and Italy.[84] The 'dissatisfied Powers' pointed to the material benefit that mandatory powers continued to extract from their imperial territories as a clear contradiction of internationalist principle.[85] At the same time, the institutionalisation of strong anti-imperialist movements, including the post-revolutionary Union of Soviet Socialist Republics (USSR), the Indian National Congress and the Pan-African Congress, steadily undermined pragmatic justifications for imperial administration in non-mandated territories. Against the proliferation of anti-imperialisms, British internationalists concocted various proposals to resolve the 'colonial question'. The Royal Institute of International Affairs proposed the internationalisation of all imperial territories through the allowance of free trade and submission to League oversight.[86] Historian Arnold Toynbee proposed a readjustment of the 1919 territorial settlement in favour of Germany, Italy and Japan, a concept that came to be known over the interwar period as 'colonial appeasement'.[87]

---

[83] Ibid., 135.
[84] Royal Institute of International Affairs, *The British Empire*, 251–3.
[85] Pedersen, *The Guardians*, 298.
[86] Royal Institute of International Affairs, *The British Empire*, 265–8.
[87] Arnold Toynbee, 'Peaceful Change or War? The Next Stage in the International Crisis' (1936) 15 *International Affairs*, 26–56; and Pedersen, *The Guardians*, 326–9.

4.5 THE 'COLONIAL QUESTION' AND THE LEAGUE

The League was terminally undermined by the withdrawals of Germany, Japan and Italy from 1933. Germany had joined the League in 1926 during the Weimar period, with the support of German liberal internationalists including Foreign Minister Gustav Stresemann and jurist Hans Wehberg.[88] However, many German jurists shared Carl Schmitt's assessment that the advent of the League signalled not the rise of internationalism but the ascendance to global hegemony of the United States.[89] In October 1933, nine months after Adolf Hitler was appointed to the office of Chancellor by President von Hindenburg, Germany abruptly withdrew from the League without giving the requisite two years' notice.[90] From the mid-1920s, the confiscation of the German and Ottoman territories had become a rallying theme in Weimar Germany. Dr Heinrich Schnee, former Deputy Governor of German New Guinea, the last Governor of German East Africa and post-war member of the Reichstag, railed publicly against the 'lie of German colonial guilt'.[91] Schnee was intent on negating the idea – promulgated originally by Smuts – of the comparative 'barbarism' of German imperialism as justification for confiscation of its imperial territories. On Schnee's reckoning, the notion that the 'welfare of the natives' motivated the confiscations was brazenly false: the real objective of the mandate system was territorial annexation, barely dressed up with weak obligations of self-reporting to a powerless PMC.[92] To support his argument, he invoked US Secretary of State Robert Lansing, who in his 1921 memoirs had opined that 'if the advocates of the system intended to avoid through its operation the appearance of taking enemy territory as the spoils of war, it was a subterfuge that deceived no-one'.[93] Schnee was focused on denouncing British attempts at annexation by stealth of his former territorial remit of the Mandate of Tanganyika (now Tanzania) into the

---

[88] For a recent account of Germany's involvement in the League, and particularly in the PMC, Sean Andrew Wemper, 'From Unfit Imperialists to Fellow Civilizers: German Colonial Officials as Imperial Experts in the League of Nations, 1919–1933' (2016) 34 *German History*, 21–48.

[89] See G. L. Ulmen, 'Introduction' in Carl Schmitt, *The Nomos of the Earth in the International Law of the Jus Publicum Europaeum* (USA: Telos Press Publishing, 2006), 16–19.

[90] League of Nations, 'Notification by the German Government of its Intention to Withdraw from the League of Nations' (January 1934) *League of Nations Official Journal*, 16.

[91] Dr Heinrich Schnee, *German Colonization Past and Future: The Truth about the German Colonies* (London: George Allen and Unwin Ltd, 1925).

[92] Ibid., 153–4. Also G. L. Steer, *Judgment on German Africa* (London: Hodder and Stoughton Ltd, 1939), 24–35.

[93] Heinrich Schnee, 'The Mandate System in Germany's Lost Colonies' (April 1930) 32 *Current History*, 76–80, 76.

neighbouring British East African colonies (now Uganda and Kenya). However, he also pointed to the Dominions' maladministration of the C Mandates, indicting in particular Australia's violent responses to Indigenous resistance in New Guinea, and New Zealand's failure to stem the devastating epidemic of Spanish influenza in occupied Western Samoa during the war, which had killed around a fifth of the population.[94]

Schnee's strident critique of the imperial objectives of the mandate system found ironic support in the arguments put forward by its proponents. Van Maanen-Helmer concluded that the mandate regime was preferable to the old system of 'economic imperialism' – not because it prioritised native 'well-being and development' but because 'it would no longer be necessary for a Power to conquer a territory and secure political control over it in order to benefit by its material resources'.[95] The Secretariat of the League itself argued that the objective of the mandate system was to enable the extraction of material resources of a territory to the 'advantage of both colony and home country':

> formerly, a good colonial administration was deemed to be that which procured the greatest economic advantages for the home country without sacrificing the future. The standard of good colonial administration is now that, while facilitating trade between the colony and the home country to the advantage of both, the administration should take the greatest care of the native population'.[96]

Japan's engagement with League activity was overshadowed from the outset by the thwarting of its attempts at Paris to include a racial equality provision in the Covenant, and to include the C Mandates within the scope of open-door trade obligations.[97] The diplomatic tension came to a head following Japan's escalation of the militarised Manchukuo regime in mainland Manchuria.[98] As Japan was both a member of the Council of the League and a Mandatory Power, the unanimity rule that governed

---

[94] Ibid., 79.
[95] Van Maanen-Helmer, *Mandates System*, 202.
[96] League of Nations Secretariat, *Aims, Methods and Activity of the League*, 115. This position echoed the concept of the 'dual mandate' espoused by former Governor General of Nigeria and British member of the PMC, Frederick Lugard. See Frederick Lugard, *The Dual Mandate in British Tropical Africa* (Edinburgh and London: William Blackwood and Sons, 1922), 606–20.
[97] Naoko Shimazu, *Japan, Race and Equality: The Racial Equality Proposal of 1919* (London and New York: Routledge, 1998). See also Thomas W. Burkman, *Japan and the League of Nations: Empire and World Order 1914–1938* (Honolulu: University of Hawai'i Press, 2008).
[98] League of Nations, 'Fifth Meeting (Private, then Public)' (December 1932) *League of Nations Official Journal*, 1870 et seq.

4.5 THE 'COLONIAL QUESTION' AND THE LEAGUE

Council decision making created an impasse on the 'Manchurian question'. The impasse was resolved only by Japan's announcement in 1933 of its intention to withdraw from the League altogether.[99] Japan's exit from the League threw into stark relief the weakness of League control over the C Mandates.[100] Following its effective withdrawal, Japan maintained administrative control over the Pacific Islands Mandate but refused international inspection, amidst widespread rumours of the construction of airfields – and later, full military bases – in mandated territory, at Chuuk Atoll, Saipan, Palau, Yap and Ponape.[101] The Mandate lay between two island territories the United States had claimed in the late nineteenth century: the Hawai'ian Islands to the east, and the island of Guam to the west.[102] With Japan's departure from the League, diplomatic tension between the two 'new' international Powers over regional dominance in the Northern Pacific veered towards military aggression.[103] To the south of Japan's Pacific Islands Mandate lay the Australian controlled C Mandate of New Guinea.[104]

From the mid-1930s, geopolitical frictions were rapidly escalating. In October 1935 Italy invaded Abyssinia, itself a Member of the League following its admission in 1923.[105] Italy justified its breach of the prohibition of aggression between League Members by refusing to accept

---

[99] League of Nations, 'Notification by the Japanese Government of its Intention to Withdraw from the League of Nations' (May 1933) *League of Nations Official Journal*, 657–8. See also Ian Nish, *Japan's Struggle with Internationalism: Japan, China and the League of Nations, 1931–1933* (London and New York: Kegan Paul International, 1933).

[100] Shao-Hwa Tan, 'The Legal Status of the Japanese Mandate for the Ex-German Islands and the Question of Japan's Withdrawal from the League' (1933) 6 *China Law Review*, 296–317; also Pedersen, *The Guardians*, 289–90.

[101] Mark R. Peattie, *Nan'yō: The Rise and Fall of the Japanese in Micronesia, 1885–1945* (Honolulu: University of Hawai'i Press, 1988), ch. 8; and Pedersen, *The Guardians*, 289–90.

[102] On Hawai'i, see Noelani Arista, *The Kingdom and the Republic: Sovereign Hawai'i and the Early United States* (Pennsylvania: University of Pennsylvania Press, 2018). On Guam, see Anne Perez Hattori, 'Textbook Tells: Gender, Race, and Decolonizing Guam History Textbooks in the 21st Century' (2018) 14 *AlterNative: An International Journal of Indigenous Peoples*, 173–84.

[103] Huntington Gilchrist, 'The Japanese Islands: Annexation or Trusteeship?' (1944) 22 *Foreign Affairs*, 635–42; and Peattie, *Nan'yō*, ch. 8.

[104] Pedersen, *The Guardians*, 290.

[105] League of Nations, 'Report of the Council under Article 15, Paragraph 4 of the Covenant submitted by the Committee of the Council on October 5th and adopted by the Council on October 7th, 1935' (November 1935) *League of Nations Official Journal*, 1605 et seq. See also Rose Parfitt, 'Empire des Nègres Blancs: The Hybridity of International Personality and the Abyssinia Crisis of 1935-6' (2011) 24 *Leiden Journal of International Law*, 849–72.

Abyssinia's equality.[106] Coming after the Manchurian crisis, the Italian invasion of Abyssinia placed significant pressure on the League to defend the distinction between its mandate system and the Japanese and Italian attempts at territorial annexation – a pressure sharpened by the presence of the Italian Marquis Theodoli on the PMC.[107] The League prevaricated. Rather than enforcing Article 15 of the Covenant – which stipulated that an act of war against one Member would be deemed an act of war against all – the Council adopted a recommendation that Abyssinia be placed under the mandatory administration of the League itself. The League's proposal was vehemently rejected by both Italy and Abyssinia.[108]

The legitimacy of the entire mandate system was undermined by critical contradictions in the British A Mandate for Palestine.[109] The Mandate incorporated the language of the 1917 Balfour Declaration in providing that Britain was responsible for 'placing the country under such political, administrative and economic conditions as will secure the establishment of the Jewish national home', 'facilitat(ing) Jewish immigration', and encouraging 'close settlement of Jews on the land'.[110] At the same time, the Mandate included an obligation to ensure 'that the rights and position of other sections of the population are not prejudiced', a provision repeatedly invoked by Arab nationalists in petitions to the PMC protesting dispossession of land under British rule.[111] The seizure of power in Germany by the Nazis accelerated the immigration of European Jews to Palestine, where British policy facilitated the sale of land to Jewish people.[112] Amidst escalating protest in Palestine at mandatory administration, League principles of internationalisation and self-government were invoked in support of both Jewish and Arab causes.[113] The PMC adopted an essentially pro-Zionist position, interpreting the explicit obligation placed on Britain in the

---

[106] League of Nations, 'Report of the Council under Article 15'.
[107] Pedersen, *The Guardians*, 297.
[108] League of Nations, 'Report of the Council under Article 15'.
[109] Pedersen, *The Guardians*, 361.
[110] Council of the League of Nations, British Mandate for Palestine, signed and entered into force on 24 July 1922 (August 1922) *League of Nations Official Journal*, 1007, arts. 2, 6.
[111] Ibid.
[112] Neil Macaulay, *Mandates: Reasons, Results, Remedies* (London: Methuen and Co. Ltd, 1937), 160–9; Pedersen, *The Guardians*, 366–8.
[113] See Louis J. Gribetz, *The Case for the Jews: An Interpretation of their Rights under the Balfour Declaration and the Mandate for Palestine* (New York: Block Publishing Company, 1930); and League of Nations, 'Report from the Executive Committee of the Arab Palestine Congress' (June 1921) *League of Nations Official Journal*, 331–40.

Mandate instrument to facilitate Jewish immigration as taking precedent over the more ambiguous references in Article 22 to self-government, well-being and development, on which Arab nationalists relied.[114] The PMC's interpretation of Britain's mandatory obligations provoked intensified protests against British imperial rule in other majority Arab territories, including in the protectorate of Egypt, and in the A Mandates of Syria and Iraq.[115] By 1936 Arab Palestine was in open revolt against British rule.[116] The British Imperial government responded with military intervention within mandated territory, explicitly prohibited by Article 22.[117] From 1936 the PMC and Britain – by then the strongest remaining proponent of the mandate system amongst the Allied Powers – were in open disagreement.[118]

4.6 The Return to War and the Japanese Occupation of Nauru

Between Germany's invasion of Poland in September 1939 and Japan's attack on Pearl Harbour in Hawai'i in December 1941, the configuration of imperial administration in the Pacific largely remained in its pre-war status quo. Mining on Nauru continued unabated until December 1940, when two German raiders made an attempt at seizing the island.[119] The German offensive succeeding in sinking three of four BPC vessels moored off the coast, and then in bombarding the phosphate cantilever, the largest piece of infrastructure on the island, and setting alight the BPC's oil tanks, used to run the electricity plant.[120] In mid-1941 the Australian Administrator of Nauru sent what was to prove its final Annual Report to the PMC. The PMC, however, was never to meet again.[121] By early 1942 Nauru Administrator Lieutenant Chalmers had evacuated all Europeans from the island except for a skeleton staff of five,

---

[114] Pedersen, *The Guardians*, 359–66.
[115] Usha Natarajan, 'Creating and Recreating Iraq: Legacies of the Mandate System in Contemporary Understandings of Third World Sovereignty' (2011) 24 *Leiden Journal of International Law*, 799–822.
[116] Royal Institute of International Affairs, 'British Policy in Palestine, 1937–8 (1938) 15(23) *Bulletin of International News*, 3–7. Zeina B. Ghandour, *A Discourse on Domination in Mandate Palestine: Imperialism, Property and Insurgency* (London: Routledge, 2009).
[117] Pedersen, *The Guardians*, 385–93.
[118] Ibid., 373–84.
[119] *The Australian Worker*, 'Raider Shells Nauru Island', *The Australian Worker* (Sydney), 1 January 1941, 8.
[120] Ellis, *Mid-Pacific Outposts*, 11–15.
[121] Pedersen, *The Guardians*, 395.

and all BPC assets that could be dismantled were either buried on the island, or shipped to Melbourne.[122] Around 390 Chinese labourers were also evacuated to Australia, leaving around 190 Chinese and 150 Gilbertese BPC recruits on the island without support.[123] The abrupt halt in export of Nauruan phosphate to Australia subjected primary producers to world market prices for the first time in twenty years. The question of phosphate supply prompted lengthy debates in federal Parliament over whether the government should subsidise the difference, to scaffold the agricultural boom that Nauruan phosphate had fuelled.[124]

Japan's attack on Pearl Harbour in December 1941 was followed by a rapid succession of assaults across the Pacific, all mounted from the Japanese Pacific Islands Mandate.[125] Guam was attacked in January 1942, followed by Rabaul in the Australian Mandate of New Guinea. Australia withdrew south from the Mandate of New Guinea into the Australian territory of Papua, leaving the former German New Guinea effectively under Japanese control from April 1942. A few months later, in June 1942, Japanese troops attacked the BPC islands of Nauru and Banaba. On 23 August 1942 Nauru was officially surrendered by Australia to Japan.[126] Over 300 Japanese troops were initially stationed in Nauru in 1942. By 1944 that number had increased to over 2,600.[127] In addition to military troops, over seventy officials of the Japanese South Seas Development Company were installed to run the phosphate plant, and over 1,000 Japanese construction workers were shipped to Nauru to construct an airfield.[128]

The Nauruan people themselves numbered over 2,000 in 1941. As the Australian Parliament debated agricultural subsidies to bolster the agricultural industry, food shortages arose quickly on Nauru, with Japanese supply lines from the Pacific Islands Mandate repeatedly attacked by Allied forces. Famine loomed on the island, for the 2,000 Nauruans

---

[122] *Courier Mail*, 'Evacuation of Nauru and Ocean I.', *Courier Mail* (Brisbane), 10 March 1942, 3.
[123] Ellis, *Mid-Pacific Outposts*, 140; Williams and Macdonald, *The Phosphateers*, 315.
[124] See for example Parliament of the Commonwealth of Australia, *Parliamentary Debates*, House of Representatives, 25 June 1941 (MP Thomas Marwick, WA, second reading speech of Supply Bill No. 1 (1941–1942)); and *The Land Sydney*, 'Farmers Urge Local Search for Phosphate', *The Land Sydney*, 13 March 1942, 1.
[125] Stewart Firth, 'The War in the Pacific' in Donald Denoon, with Stewart Firth, Jocelyn Linnekin and Karen Nero (eds.), *Cambridge History of the Pacific Islanders* (Cambridge: Cambridge University Press, 2008), 294–5.
[126] Ellis, *Mid-Pacific Outposts*, 24–5.
[127] Tanaka, 'Japanese Atrocities on Nauru during the Pacific War'.
[128] Ibid., 2–3.

4.6 WAR AND THE JAPANESE OCCUPATION OF NAURU   189

themselves, for the Chinese and Gilbertese labour recruits and for the occupying Japanese population of nearly 3,000.[129] The Japanese army's response to the food shortage was blunt: the majority of Nauruan men and some Nauruan women were forcibly shipped to Chuuk Atoll, the site of Japan's military base in the Pacific Islands Mandate.[130] Between 1942 and 1943, 1,200 Nauruans were moved from Nauru to Chuuk. Food shortages soon arose on Chuuk Atoll too.[131] The malnourished Nauruan exiles were forced to work, many contracting dysentery, tuberculosis and yaws.[132] Over 460 Nauruans – nearly a quarter of the Nauruan people – died at Chuuk, most of starvation. The survivors were returned to Nauru after Japan's surrender on 31 January 1945.[133] The date took on vital symbolic significance for the Nauruan people, marking not only homecoming, but survival.

From January 1944 the United States had been reversing Japan's offensive in the Pacific.[134] Over the following year, the US Army forced Japanese troops back out of pre-war Allied territories, with the aim of occupying the Japanese Pacific Islands Mandate between Hawai'i and Guam.[135] In February 1944 the US Army bombarded the Japanese military base at Chuuk, destroying Japan's stronghold in the Northern Pacific.[136] Nauru, too, was bombed by US planes for a year before it was retaken.[137] After the bombing of Chuuk, the Australian media and the Parliament focused on Nauruan recapture and the resumption of phosphate extraction.[138] The US Army, however prioritised the occupation of Chuuk and rest of the Pacific Islands Mandate, leaving Nauru itself under Japanese control. Following the end of the war in Europe in May 1945, the Australian

---

[129] Ellis, *Mid-Pacific Outposts*, 29.
[130] On the internment of Nauruans, see Nancy Viviani, *Nauru: Phosphate and Political Progress* (Canberra: Australian National University Press, 1970), 82–7.
[131] Tanaka, 'Japanese Atrocities on Nauru during the Pacific War', 11–13.
[132] Ibid., 13.
[133] Williams and Macdonald, *The Phosphateers*, 342.
[134] On the Japanese-United States conflict, see Saburo Ienaga, *Japan's Last War: World War II and the Japanese, 1931–1945*, trans. Frank Baldwin (London: Blackwell, 1979).
[135] Firth, 'War in the Pacific', 296; Williams and Macdonald, *The Phosphateers*, 329–30.
[136] Firth, 'War in the Pacific', 299.
[137] *Tweed Daily*, 'Large Fires at Nauru', *Tweed Daily* (Tweed Heads), 14 December 1943, 3.
[138] 'Having regard to the changed position in the South Pacific, and the great need of Australia to-day for phosphatic fertilizers, will the Minister for Commerce and Agriculture state what steps the Government has taken to ensure that supplies of phosphatic rock will be obtainable from Nauru as soon as that island is occupied by the Allies?' Parliament of the Commonwealth of Australia, *Parliamentary Papers*, House of Representatives, 20 July 1944 (Question from Member for Flinders).

Commonwealth and the BPC entreated the British High Commissioner to prioritise the resumption of phosphate extraction on Nauru.[139] In early September 1945 the United States officially handed military control of the Pacific south of the equator to Britain, maintaining its military occupation of the Pacific Islands Mandate.[140] The Australian government moved quickly to retake Nauru. On 13 September 1945 a small Australian convoy

4.2 North American B-25 Mitchell bomber above Nauru during Japanese occupation. Credit: Seventh Air Force Photo/The LIFE Picture Collection via Getty Images.

---

[139] In May 1945 Labour Minister Ben Chifley, speaking on behalf of Prime Minister John Curtin two months prior to Curtin's death in July 1945, addressed the matter of recommencing the BPC's phosphate operation in the Commonwealth House of Representatives: '(t)he Government has taken an active interest in this matter, because of the great importance to Australia of the phosphate deposits of Ocean Island and Nauru Island. The Prime Minister communicated some time ago with the Prime Minister of Great Britain. He had previously discussed the matter with the British Government, during his visit to that country. My recollection is that the British Government had taken the matter up with the authorities concerned.' Parliament of the Commonwealth of Australia, *Parliamentary Debates*, House of Representatives, 10 May 1945 (John Curtin). Also Williams and Macdonald, *The Phosphateers*, 337–9.

[140] Williams and Macdonald, *The Phosphateers*, 339.

led by Brigadier Stevenson arrived on Nauru, and the island was formally surrendered by the Japanese officers remaining on the island. Amongst the Australian convoy was Albert Ellis, the BPC's New Zealand Commissioner, loyal former employee of the Pacific Phosphate Company.[141]

4.7 The Formation of the United Nations and the Trusteeship Council

Four months prior to the Japanese attack on Pearl Harbour in 1941, the renovation of the mandate system of international administration had already begun. The Atlantic Charter was settled by British Prime Minister Winston Churchill and US President Franklin D. Roosevelt in August 1941.[142] Comprising eight principles, the Charter first rejected territorial annexation through the use of force, declaring that neither Britain nor the United States would seek 'aggrandizement, territorial or other' from the war. It then went on to restate and reformulate the two competing concepts that had animated proposals for internationalisation of occupied German and Ottoman territories over twenty years before: self-determination on the one hand, and open-door trade on the other. The second and third principle of the Charter rejected any 'territorial changes that do not accord with the freely expressed wishes of the peoples concerned' and declared a 'right of all peoples to choose the form of government under which they will live', echoing Lloyd George's 1918 formulation of self-determination as 'government by the consent of the governed'.[143] The fourth principle affirmed a general concept of 'open door' or free trade, committing to 'endeavor, with due respect for their existing obligations, to further the enjoyment by all States, great or small, victor or vanquished, of access, on equal terms, to the trade and to the raw materials of the world which are needed for their economic prosperity'. The fifth declared a 'desire to bring about the fullest collaboration between all nations in the economic field with the object of securing, for all, improved labor standards, economic advancement and social security'.

On January 1942 as Japan occupied Guam and Rabaul, the Atlantic Charter drafted by Churchill and Roosevelt was endorsed by twenty-six countries, including the British Dominions, in the 'Declaration by United

---

[141] Ellis, *Mid-Pacific Outposts*, 53–7.
[142] Atlantic Charter, opened for signature 14 August 1941, ATS 1942(4).
[143] David Lloyd George, 'Speech delivered to Trades Union Congress', Caxton Hall, London, 5 January 1918.

Nations'.[144] In October 1943 as 1,200 Nauruans were interned by Japan on Chuuk Atoll, British and US negotiations with the USSR and the Republic of China ended with the Moscow Declarations, which sketched out the basis of alliance against Italy and Germany, and the re-establishment of international organisation.[145] The Joint Four-Nation Declaration affirmed the 'necessity of establishing at the earliest practicable date a general international organization, based on the principle of the sovereign equality of all peace-loving states, and open to membership by all such states, large and small, for the maintenance of international peace and security'. As the United States occupied Chuuk Atoll in May 1944, the Commonwealth Prime Ministers Conference – the successor to the Imperial Conferences commenced in the late-nineteenth century – was held in London, and the United Kingdom secured the support of the Dominion governments for the Moscow Declarations.[146]

In July 1944 delegates of forty-four nations met at Bretton Woods in New Hampshire to settle a general framework for post-war international financial and monetary organisation, establishing the International Bank for Reconstruction and Development, and the International Monetary Fund.[147] Three months later, Churchill, Roosevelt and Stalin met at Dumbarton Oaks Manor in Washington DC to agree on the constitution of the new replacement for the League.[148] With an avowed focus on 'international peace and security' and 'economic and social cooperation', the Dumbarton Oaks communiqués sketched out the basic composition and process for a General Assembly, Security Council, International Court of Justice and Secretariat; but they omitted any official treatment of mandated or imperial territory.[149] In February 1945 at Yalta in the Crimea, with Japan still in occupation of Nauru, Churchill, Roosevelt and Stalin met to agree on the terms of Germany's defeat, and resolved to hold the inaugural Conference of the

---

[144] Declaration by United Nations (Subscribing to the Principles of the Atlantic Charter), opened for signature 1 January 1942, ATS 1942(4).
[145] Moscow Conference Declarations, 19–30 October 1943.
[146] The Argus, 'A Great Conference', The Argus (Melbourne), 13 May 1944.
[147] United Nations Monetary and Financial Conference, 1–22 July 1944, reproduced in Royal Institute for International Affairs, *United Nations Documents 1941–1945* (London and New York: Broadwater Press, 1946) 28–91.
[148] Dumbarton Oaks Conference on World Organization, 21 August–7 October, 1944, reproduced in Royal Institute for International Affairs, *United Nations Documents 1941–1945* (London and New York: Broadwater Press, 1946) 92–104.
[149] See Sundhya Pahuja, *Decolonising International Law: Development, Economic Growth and the Politics of Universality* (Cambridge: Cambridge University Press, 2011), 49–54.

United Nations General Assembly.[150] It was agreed at Yalta that opening the 'colonial question' to the new General Assembly should be avoided. Instead, the Allied Powers would be invited to put forward individual proposals on a system to replace the mandates, and an ad hoc committee would decide between them.[151]

In April 1945 three months after the homecoming of the Nauruan survivors, the United Nations General Assembly met in San Francisco for its inaugural Conference, to settle a Charter to replace the Covenant of the League.[152] As planned at Yalta, however, the 'colonial question' was not included for debate in the General Assembly. A technical committee was formed to decide between the five proposals for an international system of 'trusteeship' to replace the mandates put forward by the United States, the United Kingdom, China, France and Australia.[153] Whereas all five drafts declared that the aspiration of a new trusteeship system would be the 'self-government' of subject peoples, the definition of self-government remained contentious. China's was the only proposal explicitly to embrace independence, describing the objective of trusteeship as 'independence or self-government'.[154] As contentious as the definition of self-government was the question of whether a new trusteeship regime would apply to former mandates only, or to both mandates and imperial territories the Allied empires had retained after World War I. Churchill, alarmed that a new trusteeship system would be deemed to apply to the entirety of the British empire and not just the British mandates, anticipated the risk. The British proposal did not mention independence or define self-government, calling rather for 'self-government in forms appropriate to the varying circumstances of each territory'.[155]

---

[150] Report of the Crimea Conference, 11 February 1945, reproduced in Royal Institute for International Affairs, *United Nations Documents 1941–1945* (London and New York: Broadwater Press, 1946), 142–8.

[151] Charmian Edwards Toussaint, *The Trusteeship System of the United Nations* (London: Stevens & Sons Limited, 1956), 18–19.

[152] Australia Delegation to the United Nations Conference on International Organization, United Nations Conference on International Organization, held at San Francisco, USA, from 25th April to 26th June, 1945: Report by the Australian Delegates (Canberra: Commonwealth Government Printer, 1945).

[153] Yassin El-Ayouty, *The United Nations and Decolonization: The Role of Afro-Asia* (The Hague: Martinus Nijhoff, 1971), 17–22.

[154] Chowdhuri attributed the introduction of the language of independence to the Indian delegation at San Francisco. R. N. Chowdhuri, *International Mandates and Trusteeship Systems: A Comparative Study* (The Hague: Martinus Nijhoff, 1955), 234.

[155] Toussaint, *Trusteeship System*, 21; Pahuja, *Decolonising International Law*, 50.

The ad hoc committee appointed to decide between the five proposals consisted of the Mandatory Powers, minus Japan – namely the United Kingdom, France, Belgium, Australia and New Zealand – plus the United States, the Soviet Union and China. The committee, later renamed the Trusteeship Council, opted to maintain the categorical distinction between former mandates and other imperial territories. Mandates were recast as 'trust territories'; and imperial territories were recast as 'non-self-governing territories'.[156] An expanded set of general administrative principles would apply to both categories, and an additional set of specific obligations would apply to the administration of trust territories.[157] These additional trusteeship obligations would apply to the former mandates, and to additional territories confiscated from Germany, Japan and Italy – including the Pacific Islands Mandate, occupied by the United States. The transition from mandate to trusteeship status would in each instance require a renovated agreement between the new UN and the administering power.[158] This mechanism of individual negotiation of trusteeship terms obviated the need for a hierarchical classification of internationalised territories. The awkward distinction between the A, B and C mandates settled upon as a compromise with the sub-imperial Dominions twenty-six years earlier was officially dissolved.

However, another awkward categorical distinction was to emerge from diplomatic tensions over the trusteeship system. The question of military fortification of trust territories emerged as a major point of tension between the United States and the Soviet Union in the ad hoc committee. The United States insisted that its military occupation of the former Japanese Pacific Islands Mandate be maintained.[159] The Soviet Union refused, arguing that military fortification of territories under international administration was tantamount to breaching the prohibition on territorial aggrandisement that had been agreed between Stalin, Roosevelt and Churchill in the Atlantic Charter.[160] The US rebuttal was that the Dumbarton Oaks imperative of 'international peace and security' supported its case for military fortification of trust territories. To break the deadlock, the US, French and Chinese delegations proposed a pragmatic solution. Two types of trust territory could be created: one

---

[156] Hall, *Mandates, Dependencies and Trusteeship*, 277 et seq.
[157] Ibid., 285; and Toussaint, *Trusteeship System*, 39;
[158] Chowdhuri, *International Mandates and Trusteeship Systems*, 76–82.
[159] Ibid., 41–2.
[160] Gilchrist, 'The Japanese Islands', 642.

4.7 THE UNITED NATIONS AND THE TRUSTEESHIP COUNCIL

'strategic' and one 'non-strategic'.[161] Military fortification would be permitted in 'strategic' trust territories. The Soviet Union agreed, on condition that oversight of strategic trusts would be exercised by the Trusteeship Council reporting directly to the Security Council – in which it had a power of veto – and not to the General Assembly, as would be the case for 'non-strategic' trust territories.[162]

The trusteeship negotiations at San Francisco resulted in a remarkable elaboration of the basic structure of international administration. The 'university extension lecture' of Article 22 of the Covenant of the League was expanded into three full chapters for inclusion in the new Charter of the United Nations. Chapter XI, titled 'Declaration Regarding Non-Self-Governing Territories', codified the general principles of administration that would apply both to former mandates and imperial territories.[163] Article 73 stipulated general principles for the administration of territories 'whose peoples have not yet attained a full measure of self-government'. Echoing the language of Article 22 of the Covenant, administering authorities were exhorted to 'recognize the principle that the interests of the inhabitants of these territories are paramount', and to 'accept as a sacred trust the obligation to promote to the utmost, within the system of international peace and security established by the present Charter, the well-being of the inhabitants of these territories'. Churchill's strategy of attenuating obligations to promote self-government within the British empire by including reference to local 'circumstance', however, paid off. Article 73 obliged UN States Members 'to develop self-government, to take due account of the political aspirations of the peoples, and to assist them in the progressive development of their free political institutions, according to the particular circumstances of each territory and its peoples and their varying stages of advancement'.

Chapter XII set out the terms of the new 'International Trusteeship System'. The chapter struggled to reconcile the five proposals, and their

---

[161] Toussaint, *Trusteeship System*, 25–6.

[162] William Rappard, Swiss professor of law and PMC heavyweight, noted in 1946 that the US invention of the 'strategic trust' paralleled the C Class Mandate in operating as a political compromise between 'disinterested humanitarianism and acquisitive nationalism': 'as the Mandates System, so the Trusteeship was also born of a compromise between disinterested humanitarianism and acquisitive nationalism. But whereas in 1919 the two conflicting urges animated two rival sets of states, today it would seem as if they were fighting for the soul of the same nation'. William Rappard, 'The Mandates and the International Trusteeship Systems' (1946) 61 *Political Science Quarterly*, 408–19 at 413.

[163] Charter of the United Nations, Chapters XI and XII.

competing objectives of self-government, free trade, and military security. Echoing the language of the Moscow Declarations, the first objective of the trusteeship system was listed in Article 76(a) as the furtherance of 'international peace and security'. The second objective was listed in Article 76(b) as 'self-government'; but the definition struggled to reconcile the Chinese insistence on the inclusion of 'independence' with the British insistence on reference to local 'circumstance'. Administering authorities were exhorted to promote the 'political, economic, social, and educational advancement of the inhabitants of the trust territories, and their progressive development towards self-government or independence as may be appropriate to the particular circumstances of each territory and its peoples and the freely expressed wishes of the peoples concerned'. The third objective of free trade was included in Article 76 (d), and defined as the assurance of 'equal treatment in social, economic, and commercial matters for all Members of the United Nations and their nationals ... without prejudice to the attainment of the foregoing objectives'. Article 76(c) imported the language of human rights into the trusteeship system, defining a fourth objective of trusteeship as the '[encouragement of] respect for human rights and for fundamental freedoms for all'.

Article 79 stipulated the mechanism for accession to the new trusteeship system. It provided that trusteeship terms for each territory were to be agreed between 'states directly concerned'. Terms were then to be approved by the General Assembly – except terms for strategic trusts which, reflecting the concerns of the Soviet Union, had to be approved by the Security Council. Chapter XIII stipulated the functions and powers of the new Trusteeship Council, and itself marked a significant accretion of administrative form. Article 86 provided that the Council would comprise representatives of all UN Members administering trust territories; all remaining Members of the Security Council; and representatives of as many other Members as required to ensure that the Council was comprised of an equal number of non-trust administering states and trust administering states.[164] The Trusteeship Council was thus not only larger than the PMC had been. Whereas the PMC had comprised European 'experts' in imperial administration sitting in a personal capacity, the new Trusteeship Council included representatives of states ideologically opposed to European imperialism, such as the Soviet Union and China; and – albeit in a non-permanent capacity – states that had themselves

[164] Ibid., Art. 86.

been formerly subject to European imperialism.[165] At the same time, the Council had far more extensive powers of oversight than had the PMC. The Trusteeship Council was empowered not only to consider the annual reports of the administering authorities and to accept petitions directly from trust subjects, but also to visit trust territories to review administrative practices on the ground – and to report not to the Security Council but to a rapidly expanding General Assembly.[166]

4.8 Nauru becomes a Trust Territory

New Zealand was the first Mandatory Power to submit a draft Trusteeship Agreement – for Western Samoa – on 1 January 1946.[167] Over the following eighteen months, draft Trusteeship Agreements were submitted by the erstwhile Mandatory Powers for approval – except for Australia and South Africa, which both lagged on proposing agreements for New Guinea and Nauru, and for South West Africa. A year earlier in San Francisco, South Africa had submitted a memorandum to the United Nations, stating its case for territorial incorporation of the C Mandate of South West Africa into the Union of South Africa.[168] The proposal – which directly contradicted the general agreement against territorial aggrandisement – had been rejected. South Africa adopted a different approach. It maintained that despite the demise of the League, existing mandates remained on foot; and that by its own rules, the new United Nations lacked the power to amend terms of mandatory administration without securing the agreement of the Mandatory Power.[169] In the South African Senate after the signing of the Charter, General Jan Smuts made clear that the South African government had no intention of acceding to the trusteeship system. According to Smuts, the white population of the Mandate desired incorporation into the Union of South Africa, and the territory would be more efficiently administered as part of sovereign territory.[170]

---

[165] Hall, *Mandates, Dependencies and Trusteeship*, 278–9.
[166] Charter of the United Nations, Art. 86.
[167] Chowdhuri, *International Mandates and Trusteeship Systems*, 72.
[168] Solomon Slonim, *South West Africa and the United Nations: An International Mandate in Dispute* (Baltimore and London: Johns Hopkins University Press, 1973), 75–78.
[169] United Nations, Summary of Fourth Meeting of Committee II/4, UNCIO Docs, vol. 10, 439.
[170] Chowdhuri, *International Mandates and Trusteeship Systems*, 44.

The Australian government delayed in submitting draft Trusteeship Agreements for New Guinea and Nauru as it worked to devise legal means of incorporating the erstwhile protectorate of Papua and the C Mandate of New Guinea into a single administrative unit – Papua and New Guinea, to cover the entire eastern half of the island, plus the islands in the Bismarck Sea to the north.[171] Both Australian administrations had been severely disrupted during Japanese occupation of the New Guinea Mandate. The Commonwealth government adopted a plan: it would orchestrate the administrative union of the former Mandate with the adjacent Protectorate, whilst seeking to limit the application of expanded trusteeship obligations to the former Mandate only. The same move was attempted by the United Kingdom for the Togos, and France for the Cameroons. Australia's longer term gambit was to accept as inevitable the eventual independence of New Guinea, which it had ceded begrudgingly to German control sixty years earlier in 1886; and attempt – for a third time – to incorporate the Territory of Papua into the State of Queensland.[172]

The Commonwealth's plan was to agree at the international level to trusteeship obligations for New Guinea, and then move towards legislative incorporation of Papua into New Guinea. The Trusteeship Agreement for New Guinea was approved by the UN in December 1946; and three years later, in 1949, territory and protectorate were incorporated via domestic legislation into the singular Territory of Papua and New Guinea.[173] The western half of the island – divided by the European empires with a blunt vertical slash in the late nineteenth century, demarcating Dutch New Guinea to the west, and the British and German claims to the southeast and northeast – had also been occupied by Japan during the war. After the Japanese withdrawal in 1945, the Netherlands never regained administrative control of the western part of the island. Indonesia claimed the west as sovereign territory following its declaration of independence in 1945. The international status and boundary delimitation of the West Papuan region remain violently contested to this day.[174]

---

[171] The Commonwealth government had contemplated the joinder of the two administrations from at least as early as 1939. The West Australian, 'Papua and New Guinea: Joint Administration Question', *The West Australian* (Perth), 16 February 1939. The joinder was finalised in the New Papua and New Guinea Act 1949 (Cth).

[172] Chowdhuri, *International Mandates and Trusteeship Systems*, 254; Hall, *Mandates, Dependencies and Trusteeship*, 83.

[173] Commonwealth of Australia, Papua and New Guinea Act (No. 9 of 1949).

[174] The United Nations Temporary Executive Authority in West Irian administered the region from 1962 to 1963, after which administrative control was handed to the

4.8 NAURU BECOMES A TRUST TERRITORY

In September 1947 – a month after the legal partition of British India into the Union of India and Dominion of Pakistan – Australia submitted the draft Nauru Trusteeship Agreement to the Trusteeship Council for approval.[175] Expressed as a continuation of the Mandate for Nauru, the draft Agreement was the only one to nominate a group of three states as Administering Authority. Article 4 of the draft then sought to incorporate the tripartite 1919 Nauru Island Agreement into the new Trusteeship Agreement, in order to maintain the exemption of the BPC's phosphate operation from administrative – and thus international – oversight:

> (t)he Administering Authority will be responsible for the peace, order, good government and defence of the Territory, and for this purpose, in pursuance of an Agreement made by the Governments of Australia, New Zealand and the United Kingdom, the Government of Australia will on behalf of the Administering Authority and except and until otherwise agreed by the Governments of Australia, New Zealand and the United Kingdom continue to exercise full powers of legislation, administration and jurisdiction in and over the Territory.[176]

In answer to the administrative obligation, reformulated in Article 76(b) of the UN Charter, to promote the 'progressive development towards self-government or independence', Article 5 of the draft Trusteeship Agreement relied heavily on the caveat of local circumstance Churchill had insisted on including in the definition of self-government. It referred neither to self-government nor independence, instead placing on the Administering Authority the obligation only to 'assure the inhabitants of the Territory, as may be appropriate to the particular circumstances of the Territory and its peoples, a progressively increasing share in the administrative and other services of the Territory'.

Indonesian government. The Free Papua Movement or Organisasi Papua Merdeka, formally established in 1965 to seek Indigenous independence, remains banned by the Indonesian government. In 2003 the Indonesian government separated the territory into Papua and West Papua. See generally Richard Chauvel, *Essays on West Papua: Volume One* (Working Paper Series 120, Monash University, 2003); and Jim Elmslie, Camilla Webb-Gannon and Peter King, *Anatomy of an Occupation: The Indonesian Military in West Papua* (Sydney: West Papua Project at the Centre for Peace and Conflict Studies, 2011).

[175] United Nations Department of Public Information, 'Trusteeship for Nauru Debated: Fourth Committee Examines Draft Agreement' (October 1947) 16 *United Nations Weekly Bulletin*, 492–4.

[176] Trusteeship Agreement for the Territory of Nauru, signed and entered into force 1 November 1947, 138 UNTS 4, art. 4.

The Trusteeship Council sub-committee formed to review Australia's draft was chaired by Awni Khalidy of Iraq, and included representatives of India and Yugoslavia.[177] Australian Deputy Prime Minister and Minister for Foreign Affairs H. V. 'Doc' Evatt, a renowned champion of the new UN regime, presented the draft.[178] Evatt framed the unusual arrangement between the Administration and the tripartite BPC as in the interests not only of the three partner governments, but also of the Nauruan people, and the world at large.[179] On Evatt's logic, the agricultural sectors of Australia and New Zealand were dependent on BPC phosphate and, in turn, Australia and New Zealand exported wheat and dairy to the world: '(t)hus Nauru under Australian administration is making an important contribution to the world's greatest need. This is being done not only without prejudicing the native people but under conditions which assure them an entirely satisfactory standard of living, adequate social services, and an assured future'. The 'conditions' Evatt lauded as providing an 'entirely satisfactory standard of living' were the existing education and health programs established by the Australian Administrator on Nauru. The 'future' of the Nauruan people, Evatt submitted, was 'assured' by the Nauru Landowners Phosphate Royalty Trust, into which the BPC paid a third of the royalties the Administration continued to calculate according to its summation of Nauruan 'need', rather than the world phosphate price.

Professor Boris Stein, the Soviet representative on the Council, was unimpressed with Evatt's rosy pitch. Stein retorted that Australia's proposed Trusteeship Agreement for Nauru amounted to a 'backwards step' towards resuscitation of the mandate system.[180] Firstly, it failed to articulate clear obligations on how Nauruan involvement in administration would be increased. Secondly, in specifying in Article 7 that 'matters of international peace and security' could be taken into account in interpreting trusteeship obligations, it opened the door to the military instrumentalisation of Nauru in the Pacific. With the United States now in control of both its existing naval base on Guam and Japan's base on

---

[177] United Nations Department of Public Information, 'Trusteeship for Nauru Debated', 492.
[178] Evatt was subsequently appointed President of the United Nations General Assembly in 1948. John Murphy, *Evatt: A Life* (Sydney: NewSouth Publishing, 2016).
[179] United Nations Department of Public Information, 'Trusteeship for Nauru Debated', 493.
[180] United Nations Department of Public Information, 'Committee Approves Trusteeship for Nauru: Draft Agreement Calls for Three-Power Administration' (November 1947) 19 *United Nations Weekly Bulletin*, 589–90.

Chuuk Atoll as part of its 'strategic' Trust Territory of the Pacific Islands, Stein's concern was reasonable. Aligning with the Soviet position, the Yugoslav and Ukrainian representatives on the Nauru sub-committee raised related objections. In disclosing no concrete measures for the political advancement of the Nauruan people towards self-government or independence, the draft Trusteeship Agreement was 'static', not progressive, which contradicted the spirit of Chapter XII. When the draft Agreement went for approval before the General Assembly, however, it was passed by forty-six votes to six.[181] The same day the Nauru Agreement was approved, the General Assembly called on South Africa to submit a draft Trusteeship Agreement for South West Africa, the final C Mandate to remain outside the new trusteeship regime.[182] No draft, however, was to prove forthcoming.

4.9 Conclusion

During the mandate period, the ambivalent international status of the C Mandates became a juridical and diplomatic problem, adding to the burdened scale of discontent with the 1919 settlement. At the administrative level, the Nauru District Office of German New Guinea was replaced by the new Australian Administrator of Nauru, authorised by the intra-imperial Nauru Island Agreement to exercise the international mandatory power granted by the Allied Powers in the Mandate for Nauru. The new British Phosphate Commission replaced the Pacific Phosphate Company, acquiring not only its assets, but also the autonomous legal and financial dominance the Jaluit Gesellschaft had first negotiated for itself on the establishment on the company protectorate. With little power over the BPC but unfettered executive power around it, the Australian Administration incorporated and then elaborated on the skeletal order established during the German protectorate period, gradually accreting a set of executive ordinances that purported to regulate life on Nauru. Whilst Nauruan real property rights continued to be recognised as had been the case in the protectorate period, the exercise of those rights was strictly regulated by the new Administration. In 1922 the Nauruan people, now with a clear legal designation of 'native' status, were prohibited from disposing of their land other than via lease to the

---

[181] Ibid., 590.
[182] United Nations Department of Public Information, 'Trusteeship and Non-Self-Governing Areas' (December 1947) 24 *United Nations Weekly Bulletin*, 767.

BPC, and in exchange were paid a nominally increased royalty, part of which was paid directly in the new Nauru Landowners Phosphate Royalty Trust. Under the tripartite BPC monopoly operation, itself dependent on indentured labour, the rate of phosphate extraction from Nauru boomed. The weak response of the PMC to the Nauruan arrangement reflected both its limited powers under the terms of Article 22 of the Covenant, and the staggered collapse of both the mandate system and the League itself over the 1930s.

Nauruan phosphate fed the boom in primary industry in Australia and New Zealand which came to define the nationalist self-image of both new states, seeking to define themselves in the new world order. Guaranteed supply of Nauruan superphosphate at cost price enabled the conversion of inland regions of the Australian continent to farmland, and insulated the flourishing Australian agricultural industry from the worst effects of the Depression over the late 1920s and 1930s. The ideology of white subimperialism that had developed in Australia during the 1880s took a Malthusian turn, as the relation between phosphate supply, food production and global population discourse was framed as a justification for the White Australia policy. Tensions between Australia and Japan, which had emerged explicitly at Paris over Japan's racial equality proposal, deteriorated rapidly in the interwar period, as the two 'new' international subjects shared a mandatory border along the equator between their respective C Mandates. The Mandates of Nauru and New Guinea were occupied during Japan's offensive in the Pacific from 1941, launched from Chuuk Atoll in Japan's Pacific Islands Mandate. As over a thousand Nauruans were interned at Chuuk, the Allies negotiated the reconstitution of the League as the United Nations, and the expansion of Article 22 of the Covenant into three chapters of the new Charter of the United Nations. The transition from mandate to trusteeship status for Nauru was finalised in 1947 with the approval by the Trusteeship Council of the Trusteeship Agreement for Nauru.

The transition in international status from mandate to trust territory required no major alterations in the administrative form through which the Australian Administrator governed the island. The Nauru Island Agreement that had established the tripartite monopoly over the Nauruan phosphate industry and insulated it from administrative oversight in 1919 was indirectly incorporated into the Trusteeship Agreement approved by the Trusteeship Council. However, as will be seen in Chapter 5, the Soviet bloc's challenges to Australia's interpretation of its international obligations in Nauru in the Trusteeship Council in 1947 illustrated two fundamental differences between the mandate and trusteeship regimes, which together rendered the Trusteeship Council a platform for the Nauruan people and their supporters to push for political independence. The first was the dissolution of the C Mandate category, and the transformation of the vague mandatory principle into a juridified regime of trusteeship obligations, which included the promotion of 'self-government or independence'. The second was the expanded membership of the Trusteeship Council with significantly increased powers of review, reporting directly to the General Assembly.

5

From Trust Territory to Sovereign State, 1968

5.1 Introduction

This chapter traces the shift in Nauru's international status from UN Trust Territory to sovereign statehood as the Republic of Nauru in 1968, and the accretions in local administrative form that attended this shift. From 1947 the juridification of the regime of international trusteeship and its reorientation around the end of 'self-government or independence' provided the institutional apparatus and conceptual vocabulary through which the Nauruan people, led by Hammer DeRoburt, prosecuted their case for political independence from Australia in the UN Trusteeship Council. In a protracted series of negotiations brokered by the Trusteeship Council over the 1960s between the Australian Department of Territories and the Nauru Local Government Council led by DeRoburt, Australia begrudgingly ceded administrative control of the island. The Nauruan people celebrated their first Independence Day on 31 January 1968, the anniversary of the return of interned Nauruans from Chuuk Atoll after World War II. Nauru's peaceful accession to sovereign status, supported by the UN Trusteeship Council and the General Assembly, was both a profound political achievement for the Nauruan people, and an effect of the extraordinary gravitational pull of the decolonisation movements of the 1950s and 1960s. The chapter concludes, however, that the shift from trusteeship to sovereign status was beset from the outset by irony. Firstly, it was assumed at international level that the island itself would soon be uninhabitable on the exhaustion of its phosphate. Nauruan independence was supported as a means of allowing the Nauruan people to decide for themselves how to respond to that uninhabitability. Secondly, as this book has sought to trace, the recasting of the existing Nauruan administration as a constitutional republic did not dismantle so much as further expand upon the existing structure of relations first established in the late nineteenth century to facilitate corporate resource extraction.

5.1 INTRODUCTION

The juridification of the concept of international trusteeship after World War II and the removal of differentiated international status for the C Mandates rapidly altered the international context of Australia's administration of Nauru. Firstly, as Administering Authority, Australia was from 1947 charged with meeting the expanded obligations of trusteeship stipulated in the UN Charter and the Nauru Trusteeship Agreement, which had replaced the ambiguous terms of Article 22 and the Mandate for Nauru.[1] Secondly, in contrast to the mandate system, the trusteeship system did not classify a hierarchy of status designations, instead applying the same Charter-based trusteeship principles to all trust territories. As such, the object of self-government – now defined as 'self-government or independence', rather than as the right to choose which imperial power to be governed by, as US President Woodrow Wilson had articulated almost twenty years previously in his Fourteen Points speech – was rendered common to all externally administered territories.[2] The sudden removal of differentiated status for the C Mandates placed their administering powers of the United Kingdom, South Africa, Australia and New Zealand out of step with the global movement towards political self-determination. Over the trusteeship period, their attempts to maintain administrative control over the former C Mandates of South West Africa, Nauru, New Guinea and Western Samoa attracted international opprobrium, particularly from the Soviet Union and the growing body of decolonising states. South Africa's refusal to bring its administration of South West Africa into the new UN trusteeship system prompted a protracted series of cases in the International Court of Justice that drew international attention to the maintenance of imperial control in the former C Mandates. The ICJ's decisions in the South West Africa Cases marked a diplomatic fault line in the United Nations regime between the old European imperial powers and the decolonising states, supported by the Soviet Union and China.[3]

---

[1] Charter of the United Nations, opened for signature 26 June 1945 (entered into force 24 October 1945), Chapter XII 'International Trusteeship System'. United Nations, Trusteeship Agreement for the Territory of Nauru (entered into force 1 November 1947) 1947 ATS 8.

[2] See Chapter 3, Part 3.10 'Internationalisation, the Mandatory Principle and the Peace Treaty'.

[3] The series of Advisory Opinions and preliminary hearings in the South West Africa Cases came to a head in the International Court of Justice, South West Africa Cases, Second Phase (Judgment), ICJ Rep 6, 51 (18 July 1966). For a detailed historical account of the South West Africa Cases, see Solomon Slonim, South West Africa and the United Nations: An International Mandate in Dispute (Baltimore and London: Johns Hopkins University Press, 1973).

Thirdly, the new UN Charter codified principles of external administration applicable not just to the former mandates and to territory confiscated by the Allies during World War II but to all 'non-self-governing territories' – including colonies, protectorates and other territories that had been under European imperial administration since the nineteenth century. As the UN General Assembly assumed to itself the power to scrutinise the administration of all 'non-self-governing territories', the differentiation between 'internationalised' and imperial forms of rule tilted towards collapse.[4] Fourthly, the new Trusteeship Council, the Fourth Committee of the new UN, wielded more powers in the structure of international organisation than its predecessor, the Permanent Mandates Council, had done in the League. The PMC's powers had been limited to receiving reports, issuing questionnaires to mandatory authorities and making recommendations to the Council of the League. The UN Charter expanded upon this base, delegating powers of territorial visitation to the Trusteeship Council.[5] Furthermore, the Trusteeship Council reported to the General Assembly, not to the Security Council. This change in the line of reporting became diplomatically significant as the General Assembly grew in size, incorporating ever more post-imperial and post-colonial states. Over the 1950s and 1960s the administering powers' justifications of their continued deviations from Charter principles of trusteeship met with increasingly open critical response in the General Assembly as well as the Trusteeship Council.

Nauru's shift from mandate to trusteeship status, and the development of the concept of international trusteeship, prompted a new wave of local bureaucratic expansion that was to continue over the following twenty years. As Administering Authority reporting annually to the Trusteeship Council, Australia was now under pressure to formalise Nauruan participation in the administrative structure that a succession of imperial administrations had established around the extraction of resources. Whereas Article 22 of the Covenant of the League had named the object of international administration as native 'well-being and development', the expanded objects of international administration in Chapter XII of the UN Charter reformulated this as 'self-government or independence, as may be appropriate to the particular circumstances of each territory'. Australia's initial move to satisfy this shift was to formalise the Nauruan

---

[4] Charter of the United Nations, 'Chapter XI: Declaration regarding Non-Self-Governing Territories'.
[5] Ibid., 'Chapter XIII: Trusteeship Council'.

5.1 INTRODUCTION

'Council of Chiefs', established under German administration as a pragmatic convention of consultation, and to introduce an electoral mechanism to replace the Administrator's ad hoc nomination of Chiefs. In 1951 the Council was renamed the Nauru Local Government Council (NLGC), and the first elections were held. However, the NLGC lacked administrative power, remaining subordinate to the Administrator. Australia continued to insist that greater political autonomy was inappropriate given the circumstances. Nevertheless, under the leadership of Timothy Detudamo and then Hammer DeRoburt, the NGLC came to function over the trusteeship period as a vehicle through which the Nauruan people could relay their demands for control over phosphate and land disposition, and ultimately full political independence, to the Trusteeship Council and the General Assembly.

Over the 1950s the Trusteeship Council noted that the tripartite monopoly arrangement in Nauru did not conform to the spirit of Chapter XII, but did not challenge either Australia's rationale against Nauruan independence, or the inevitability of strip-mining the island. The Trusteeship Council's approach, however, was to change after the 1960 Declaration on the Granting of Independence to Colonial Countries and Peoples.[6] Owing largely to sustained efforts from the Soviet bloc and delegates from decolonising African states, and in particular the Liberian Permanent Representative to the UN, Angie Brooks, the Trusteeship Council began to push Australia to commit to a clear plan for Nauruan independence. The negotiations between the Australian Department of Territories and the NLGC that came to be known as the Nauru Talks commenced in the mid-1960s. The issue that catalysed the negotiations was the calculation of royalty rates. But between 1965 and 1968 the Nauru Talks moved to address in turn land and phosphate ownership, public administrative control and the environmental rehabilitation of mined-out land.[7] During the German protectorate period, when Nauruan property in land had been recognised, the Nauruan people had been paid a nominal 'half-penny' royalty from the Pacific Phosphate Company's profits. Under mandatory administration, the Australian Administration had instigated a practice of fixing royalty rates on a 'needs' basis, an arbitrary executive measure that continued throughout the trusteeship

---

[6] Declaration on the Granting of Independence to Colonial Countries and Peoples, United Nations General Assembly Resolution 1514(XV), General Assembly Official Records, 15th session, 947th plenary meeting (14 December 1960).

[7] Nancy Viviani, *Phosphate and Political Progress* (Canberra: Australian National University Press, 1970), 132–3.

period. In the Trusteeship Council, the NLGC repeatedly requested that the phosphate royalty rate be calculated with respect to the world phosphate price instead.[8]

Over the 1950s and the 1960s, the jurisprudence on international trusteeship came to draw more directly from private law notions of trust than had been the case during the mandate period. As the obligations of Administering Authorities to trust territory populations were increasingly understood as akin to that of trustee to beneficiary, the NLGC's demands for fairer royalty payments developed into calls for recognition of the Nauruan people's property in phosphate itself, rather than nominal recognition of land ownership. At the same time, the NGLC intensified its calls for rehabilitation of the island's central plateau at the tripartite governments' expense. Throughout the Nauru Talks, Australia rejected the assertion of Nauruan property in phosphate, relying on the 1888 Agreement between the Jaluit Gesellschaft and the Reich, and the 1919 Transfer Agreement between the Pacific Phosphate Company and the British Phosphate Commission. The prospect of rehabilitation was debated from the early 1950s, and repeatedly rejected by Australia, both legally on the basis of an absence of any positive obligation in international or Australian law, and pragmatically on the basis of cost. Whilst continuing to refuse to yield BPC accounts to Trusteeship Council oversight, instead reporting BPC returns in the Administering Authority's Annual Reports, Australia offered to resettle the entire the Nauruan population on Curtis Island off the coast of Queensland, as an alternative to rehabilitation. Australia's proposal envisaged the political assimilation as the Nauruan people as Australian citizens, leaving the island to the BPC.

The NLGC's ultimate refusal of the resettlement and assimilation proposal was supported by the UN. However, both the Trusteeship Council and the General Assembly shared Australia's presumption that the resettlement of the Nauruan people on the exhaustion of phosphate was a foregone conclusion. Nevertheless, in the international political climate of the mid-1960s, the institutional push towards political independence for Nauru as a sovereign state gradually overwhelmed Australian objections. By the mid-1960s what remained to be decided was not whether Nauru would become a sovereign state. What remained

---

[8] On royalty payments under German rule, see Chapter 3, Part 3.6, 'The Pacific Islands Company and its Agreement with the Jaluit Gesellschaft'; and under British rule, see Chapter 4, Part 4.2, 'Administration of Nauru as a C Mandate'.

to be decided was the manner and extent to which control of the administrative structure on the one hand, and the BPC's phosphate rights on the other, would be transferred into Nauruan hands. The Department of Territories adopted aggressive negotiation tactics on both fronts, refusing to permit the Nauruan delegation recourse to independent advice.[9] Until 1967 Australia attempted to satisfy international demands for Nauruan political independence through the creation of a Legislative and Executive Council sitting under the Australian Administrator, but was eventually forced to cede administrative control entirely and accept the Nauruan delegates' date of 31 January 1968 for independence. The matter of BPC rights was even more sharply fought. Australia originally refuted any obligation to relinquish control of the phosphate operation. But as New Zealand and then the United Kingdom backed away from insistence on retention of BPC assets, Australia retreated to demanding market compensation for the BPC's assets from the Nauruan people, to be taken from the royalty trust funds. The issues of historical royalty calculations and liability for rehabilitation were left unresolved.

This chapter argues that, given Australia's diplomatic recalcitrance and the gross asymmetries of power during the Nauru Talks between the Department of Territories and the NGLC, political independence was an extraordinary achievement for the Nauruan people, under the leadership of Hammer DeRoburt. However, an exclusive focus on the shift from trusteeship to sovereign status in international law works to obscure the fact that the administrative structure of the new Republic of Nauru was not a displacement but a further accretion of an imperial bureaucratic form instantiated in the 1880s. Once a date for accession to independence had been brokered by the Trusteeship Council, a Constitution for the new Republic was rapidly drafted by Australian consultants headed by Pacific historian Professor James Wight Davidson, providing for a Westminster-style parliamentary system.[10] In both its provisions and its silences, the 1968 Constitution codified an administrative structure that risked conflation of executive and legislative power; excluded the commercial phosphate operation from public administrative oversight; and failed to establish financial transparency regarding the phosphate operation itself, and the disposal of phosphate royalty trust funds. The chapter concludes that the international status of sovereign statehood attached to a fundamentally imperial administrative form, first

---

[9] Viviani, *Phosphate and Political Progress*, 143.
[10] Ibid., 168–9.

sketched out in an 1888 agreement between a Hanseatic trading company and the Bismarckian Reich.

5.2 Administration of Nauru as a Trust Territory

The re-establishment of Australian administration on Nauru after Japan's occupation of the island during World War II focused almost exclusively on the restoration of the BPC's phosphate operation.[11] The Nauruan community, who had suffered the death of almost a quarter of their number whilst interned on Chuuk Atoll, was critical of the Authority's administrative priorities. The Nauruan Council of Chiefs, first established by German officer Fritz Jung as an ad hoc body and formalised during the mandate period, included many of the 'Geelong boys' sent to Australia for secondary education during the mandate period. Led by Head Chief Timothy Detudamo, the Council objected to the Administration's prioritisation of repair of the phosphate plant over repair of Nauruan homes and villages, which had been bombarded by Germany and then by the United States during the war.[12] This post-war tension between Nauruan and Australian perspectives on the best interests of the Nauruan people characterised the trusteeship period. From the late 1940s the concept of international trusteeship was increasingly interpreted as analogous to a private law trust relationship, eliminating the ambiguity that had characterised the C Mandate in theory and in practice. The juridification of trusteeship obligations undermined the British government's default position of defining its relationship with all 'non-self-governing territories' as political, rather than legal.

Yet despite the expansions in bureaucratic practice implemented by the Administering Authority in response to defined obligations of trusteeship, the legal basis on which the Nauruan administration had accretively developed remained in place. The tripartite Nauru Island Agreement that established the BPC remained on foot. As Administering Authority, Australia continued to wield executive, legislative and judicial power,

---

[11] Parliament of the Commonwealth of Australia, Report to the General Assembly of the United Nations on the Administration of the Territory of Nauru from 1st July 1947 to 30th June 1948 (Canberra: L. F. Johnson, Government Printer, 1948), 1.

[12] Maslyn Williams and Barrie Macdonald, *The Phosphateers: A History of the British Phosphate Commissioners and the Christmas Island Phosphate Commission* (Melbourne: Melbourne University Press, 1985), 344; Christopher Weeramantry, *Nauru: Environmental Damage under International Trusteeship* (Oxford: Oxford University Press, 1992) 113–14. On the Geelong education program, see Chapter 4, Part 2, 'Administration of Nauru as a C Mandate'.

whilst administration of Nauru continued to be funded exclusively from the profits of the BPC, which was officially insulated by the Nauru Island Agreement from administrative interference with its operations. Throughout the trusteeship period, the Trusteeship Council had no direct access to BPC financial records, only secondary summaries of the BPC's annual totals as included in the Administering Authority's annual reports. The BPC continued to claim property in phosphate under the German chain of title, paying fixed rate royalties to the Nauruan people. Over the 1950s and 1960s, as the anti-colonial movements gathered momentum, the BPC accelerated the rate of phosphate extraction, exporting phosphate primarily to Australia and New Zealand.

However, the shift from mandate to trusteeship status did mark two significant differences, which combined to propel the Nauru arrangement towards an ironic denouement. The first was that the strengthened powers of the Trusteeship Council rendered it a focal point for international criticism of Australia's stance against Nauruan independence, particularly after the UN General Assembly's 1960 Declaration on the Granting of Independence to Colonial Countries and Peoples. The second was that from the early 1950s, a general presumption nevertheless coloured international debate over Nauruan independence: that whoever was in control of the island, it would soon be rendered uninhabitable by mining. Throughout the trusteeship period, there was no query at the international level that phosphate extraction would continue until there was no more phosphate to extract, and that the Nauruan people would inevitably be forced to leave their island.

In 1948 Australia submitted its first Annual Report on the Administration of the Trust Territory of Nauru to the United Nations.[13] All pre-war laws and ordinances had been re-established, and '(f)ull powers of legislation, administration and jurisdiction' were restated as vesting in the Administrator.[14] Australia's Trusteeship Reports were longer and more comprehensive than had been the case under the mandate system, reflecting the expansion of trusteeship obligations. Organised as a response to the provisions of Article 76 of Chapter XII of the UN Charter, each Report contained sections on political, social, educational and economic advancement, on international peace and security, and fundamental rights and freedoms. The Trusteeship Report, submitted for the 1948–9 year, struggled to shift in tone from the

---

[13] Parliament of the Commonwealth of Australia, Report to the General Assembly of the United Nations on the Administration of the Territory of Nauru from 1st July 1947 to 30th June 1948 (Canberra: L. F. Johnson, Government Printer, 1948).
[14] Ibid., 12.

paternal logic of the C Mandate, and articulated for the first time the Authority's strategy of endorsing the general principles of UN trusteeship and the specific obligation of promoting self-government or independence, whilst implying an indefinite deferral in the Nauruan case:

> (t)he principles outlined in the Charter are strongly rooted in the Territory, although in a physical sense some are in embryo form only. The chief tasks of the Administration are to adapt the indigenous inhabitants in a changing environment, to educate them to accept responsibility and to show them predominance of reason over instinctive modes of thought. The Administration by sowing these seeds is developing the political, economic, social and educational advancement of the Nauruan people and paving the way for their self-determination.[15]

The Authority went on to report that the objective of 'self-government or independence' stated in Article 76(b) of the Charter would be interpreted as 'ultimately to train these people for administrative positions in their own Territory'.[16] A new organisation chart of the 'Administrative Structure of Government' made the racial point visually. Under the office of Administrator in a band marked 'Europeans' was a tier of managerial offices – including 'Director of Public Health', 'Native Affairs Officer', 'Supervisor of Works' and 'Director of Police'. Under each managerial office was a list of administrative offices – including 'Store Keeper', 'Clerk Typist', 'House Orderly', 'Senior Postal Clerk' and 'Labourer' – grouped together in a band marked 'Nauruans'.[17] The Council of Chiefs appeared outside the hierarchy in the bottom right of the chart, reporting directly to the Administrator.

The 1948 Report appended an expanded list of statistics on health, justice, and expenditure, as well as updating phosphate extraction statistics which had last been made public in 1940.[18] The presentation of the data made clear the BPC's intention to strip-mine Nauru. Of the island's total area of 5,263 acres, 4,116 acres or 78 per cent was estimated to be phosphate-bearing; prior to the war, 459 acres had already been mined out, producing 11,000,000 tons of phosphate; as such, the Report concluded, on the basis of a rate of extraction of 1,000,000 tons per year, Nauru's phosphate industry would 'continue for at least another 70 years'. In the section on 'Economic Advancement', the Report declared with an air of self-congratulation that the total royalty payable on each

[15] Ibid., 1.
[16] Ibid., 59.
[17] Ibid., appendix II.
[18] Ibid., 9.

ton of phosphate had been increased after the war from three pence to thirteen pence – of which a third was paid directly to the landowner, a third quarantined into the Nauru Phosphate Royalty Trust (established during the mandate period in response to questioning by the Permanent Mandates Commission) and the remaining third paid into a new Long Term Investment Fund.[19]

The stated purpose of the Long Term Investment Fund was to provide for the inevitable resettlement of the Nauruan people on the exhaustion of the island's phosphate.[20] In a section entitled 'Conservation of Natural Resources', the Report stated that the mined-out areas were converted into 'waste land', but that conservation was not necessary as the central plateau of the island was 'not, and has never been, arable land'.[21] It went on to assert that in any event, it was 'not practicable to level the worked-out fields as part of a land reclamation project'. Two years later, in 1951, the Administering Authority reported to the Trusteeship Council that possibilities for eventual resettlement of the Nauruan population were being explored: 'when the deposits are exhausted Nauru may not provide sufficient space or opportunity for the Nauruan population to continue there, and it may be necessary to transfer them elsewhere'.[22]

By the early 1950s the Trusteeship Council's responses to Australia's Reports on Nauru had begun to focus on two Article 76(b) obligations: firstly, the obligation to promote political advancement via progressive development toward 'self-government or independence as may be appropriate'; and secondly, the obligation to promote economic advancement. In 1949 the General Assembly had passed resolutions calling for Administering Authorities of all Trust Territories to adopt measures to 'hasten the advancement... toward self-government or independence' in accordance with Article 76(b).[23] But the Council's focus also reflected a growing attentiveness in the UN General Assembly to conditions in the former C Mandates of Nauru, New Guinea, South West Africa and the

---

[19] Ibid., 24.
[20] Barrie Macdonald, *In Pursuit of the Sacred Trust: Trusteeship and Independence in Nauru* (New Zealand: New Zealand Institute of International Affairs, 1988), 38.
[21] Parliament of the Commonwealth of Australia, Report to the General Assembly of the United Nations on the Administration of the Territory of Nauru from 1st July 1947 to 30th June 1948, 29.
[22] Ibid., 38.
[23] Political Advancement of Trust Territories, General Assembly Resolution 320, United Nations General Assembly Official Records, 240th plenary meeting (15 November 1949); and Economic Advancement in Trust Territories, General Assembly Resolution 322, United Nations General Assembly Official Records, 40th plenary meeting (15 November 1949).

former Japanese Mandated Islands. Addressing the former C Mandates specifically – all established by trading companies and formerly exempt from obligations of open-door trade during the interwar period – the General Assembly expressed 'concern that the lack of budgetary autonomy' of Administering Authorities 'did not allow the Trusteeship Council to make a thorough examination' of the financial status of the Territories, and called for the promotion of 'greater participation of indigenous inhabitants in the profits and management of entities, public and private, engaged in the exploitation of mineral and other natural resources ... basic to the economy of Trust Territories'. The resolution seemed to apply clearly to Nauru. In the same resolution, however, the General Assembly held Nauru up as a model of economic advancement: it 'noted with satisfaction' the 'excellent financial situation' in Nauru, and called only for 'formulation of plans laying down a sound economic foundation' for the Territory. This seeming contradiction reflected growing diplomatic tensions between the British imperial bloc and the coalescing anti-imperial cohort in the General Assembly, which was to come to a head over South West Africa and the C Mandates as the decade progressed.

Over the 1950s and 1960s Australia came to deploy bureaucratic expansion and restatement as a means of maintaining control over its sub-empire in the face of growing international criticism. In 1951 the Australian Commonwealth under Prime Minister Robert Menzies created the Department of Territories. The new department was charged with oversight of the UN Trust Territories of Nauru, Papua and New Guinea, as well as Australian 'territories' outside the former colonies' state borders, including the Northern Territory in the central continent, and Norfolk Island and the Cocos Islands in the Western Pacific.[24] Menzies appointed the West Australian historian Paul Hasluck as the Minister for Territories.[25] Hasluck had served as Australia's Permanent Representative to the UN in the years after the war. The addition of an

---

[24] Commonwealth of Australia, *The Progress of the Australian Territories 1950–1956* (Canberra: A. J. Arthur, Commonwealth Government Printer, 1957). The Cocos Islands were transferred from British control as part of the Colony of Singapore to Australian control in 1955.

[25] On the role of Paul Hasluck in Australian policy on Aboriginal and Torres Strait Islander peoples and on external affairs, see Geoffrey Bolton, *Paul Hasluck: A Life* (Crawley: University of Western Australia Publishing, 2014); and Anna Haebich, 'The Formative Years: Paul Hasluck and Aboriginal Issues during the 1930s' in Tom Stannage, Kay Saunders, Richard Nile (eds.) *Paul Hasluck in Australian History: Civic Personality and Public Life* (St Lucia: Queensland University Press, 1998), 95–105.

intervening layer of Australian bureaucratic oversight in the new era was matched by a renovation of the Nauruan Council of Chiefs. In 1951 the Administering Authority passed the Nauru Local Government Council Ordinance, which formalised the existing ad hoc arrangement into a publicly elected municipal council with its own secretariat.[26] The Ordinance delegated a limited set of administrative powers to the renamed NLGC, including powers of appointment of Nauruan district constables, and managerial control of the Nauru Cooperative Store. It stipulated rules of procedure for the Council, and provided that it would be funded not by the Administration but from the Nauru Landowners Phosphate Royalty Trust.[27] Throughout the 1950s the Trusteeship Council repeatedly queried the Administration's annual refrain that the limited powers of the NLGC represented progress towards political advancement. However, the NLGC's role with respect to all decisions of the Administrator remained advisory only, and subject to disallowance. When the matter was questioned in the Trusteeship Council, Australia responded that the NLGC Ordinance provided for substantive administrative powers; but the members of the NLGC lacked the capacity to understand or fully exercise them.

In response to Trusteeship Council questions on economic advancement, the Administering Authority settled into an annual practice of reporting incremental increases in the royalty payable by the BPC to Nauruan landowners and into the two Trust Funds, whilst at the same time insisting that the royalties had to be calculated according to the Administrator's discretionary assessment of the Nauruan peoples' 'needs', as a world market price for Nauruan phosphate was not calculable due to the tripartite monopoly.[28] Throughout the 1950s the Trusteeship Council did not dispute Australia's assertion that independence was inappropriate for the Nauruan people, despite its annual questioning on the sufficiency of administrative actions promoting political and economic advancement. At a number of points it openly endorsed Australia's stance on the inappropriateness of independence in the Nauruan case, as well as

---

[26] Nauru Local Government Council Ordinance No. 2 of 1951, cited in Parliament of the Commonwealth of Australia, Report to the General Assembly of the United Nations on the Administration of the Territory of Nauru from 1st July 1951 to 30th June 1952 (L. F. Johnson, Government Printer, 1952), 12.

[27] Nauru Local Government Council Ordinance No. 2 of 1951; also Viviani, *Phosphate and Political Progress*, 104–6.

[28] Report of the Trusteeship Council 1952–53, United Nations General Assembly Official Records, 8th session, supplement no 4, 112–13.

the inevitability of wholesale resettlement.[29] The 1953 Trusteeship Council Visiting Mission to the Territory of Nauru, for example, reported that there was 'no alternative to resettlement of the population elsewhere'; and that it was 'imperative to observe that the Nauruan people cannot be regarded as more than a small community, and in no case as a potential state'.[30]

However, the coordinates of international oversight of the Nauruan case changed rapidly over the 1950s. As global anti-colonial momentum gathered pace and found institutional expression in the UN, the Australian strategy of reading down its trusteeship obligations on political and economic advancement in Nauru through reference to local circumstance gradually lost legitimacy. In 1956 Hammer DeRoburt of Boe district was elected Head Chief of the NLGC. DeRoburt had attended the Gordon Institute of Technology in Geelong in the 1930s and had been interned on Chuuk Atoll by the Japanese during the war.[31] On his return, he had worked in the Nauruan administration under the Director of Education and was appointed to the NLGC in 1951. DeRoburt had a history of political activism. In 1953 he had led a four-month strike of the Nauru Workers Organisation and succeeded in securing increased wages and training for Nauruans working in the Administration.[32] As Head Chief, DeRoburt set about making good use of the Trusteeship Council's power to accept petitions directly under Article 87(b) of the UN Charter, and formally raised issues with the Administering Authority with each Trusteeship Council Visiting Mission. These ranged from the calculation of phosphate royalties, to the absence of secondary education on Nauru and the lack of Administration investment in subsidiary industries.[33] In 1957 DeRoburt sent a letter directly to the BPC in his capacity as Head Chief of the NLGC, openly disputing the tripartite governments'

---

[29] United Nations Visiting Mission to Trust Territories in the Pacific 1953: Report on Nauru, UN Trusteeship Council Official Records, 12th session, UN Doc T/1054 (26 May 1953) 2; also Macdonald, *In Pursuit of the Sacred Trust*, 41.

[30] Trusteeship Council Report 1953 on Nauru, 2; also Macdonald, *In Pursuit of the Sacred Trust*, 41.

[31] For colloquial accounts of DeRoburt's place in Nauruan politics, see Don Chambers, *'Boss' Hurst of Geelong and Nauru* (Melbourne: Hyland House, 1994), 150-1, 167-8.

[32] Macdonald, *In Pursuit of the Sacred Trust*, 38.

[33] Petition 324 ('Petitions from the Nauruan Council of Chiefs concerning Nauru'), Trusteeship Council Report 1951 on Nauru, United Nations Trusteeship Council Official Records, 342nd meeting, UN Doc T/877 (15 March 1951) 25-7, and Petition 325 ('Petition from the Chiefs of Yarren and Boe concerning Nauru'), Trusteeship Council Report 1951 on Nauru, UN TCOR, 342nd meeting, UN Doc T/878 (15 March 1951) 27-8; Macdonald, *In Pursuit of the Sacred Trust*, 38.

longstanding assertion that the interests of the Nauruan people were not affected by the strip-mining of the island's central plateau:

> (t)here is a prevailing belief which is born of distorted facts remaining unchallenged for many years concerning the hinterland area that the Nauruans never used this land ... It was from this area that half his normal foods were grown: pandanus and almond trees; roots and greens he obtained mostly from this area ... He turned to this area for preserved foods for drought. Materials for a house were from the hinterland (Tomano and pandanus) ... In short, it was this area which afforded him and his children their means of livelihood. You removed his and his posterity their means of living, when you deprived him of this area.[34]

With this letter, DeRoburt struck at the heart of official arguments as to why the BPC's exploitation of Nauruan phosphate did not contravene mandatory or trusteeship obligations.

5.3 Trusteeship, Decolonisation and the South West Africa Cases

The trusteeship regime provided the NGLC and DeRoburt with an expanded platform for formally articulating Nauruan protest against the Administration and the BPC's aggressive exploitation of the island. The Nauruan peoples' push for political independence and control over phosphate profits reflected the global post-war momentum towards official decolonisation.[35] As had been the case in the western half of the island of Papua, where the Dutch had failed to regain administrative control after Japan's occupation during World War II, the European empires had struggled to re-establish control in many of their pre-war territories, where administration had either been ousted by hostile occupation, or heavily stripped back during the war. Independence movements in Indonesia, French Indochina, Iran and Egypt had moved against weakened rule to declare independence and resist the re-establishment of European administrative control. At the same time, the geopolitical hegemony of the European imperial powers was eroded by the growing power of the United States, the Soviet Union and China.[36]

---

[34] Letter from the Nauru Local Government Council to the British Phosphate Commissioners dated 30 May 1957, reproduced in Macdonald, *In Pursuit of the Sacred Trust*, 40.

[35] R. P. Anand, 'Role of the "New" Asian-African Countries in the Present International Order' (1962) 56 *American Journal of International Law*, 383–406. Yassin Al-Ayouty, *The United Nations and Decolonization: The Role of Afro-Asia* (The Hague: Martinus Nijhoff, 1971).

[36] See Melvyn P. Leffler, 'The Emergence of an American Grand Strategy, 1945–1952' and Shu Guang Zhang, 'The Sino-Soviet Alliance and the Cold War in Asia, 1954–1962' in

Over the 1950s, the tension between the juridification of principles of 'self-government or independence' in the UN Charter, and the 'political fact' of continued imperial administration in a patchwork of the old imperial territories came to a head in the protracted dispute between South Africa and the United Nations over the post-war status of South West Africa. From 1947 South Africa began to articulate its refusal to recognise the shift from mandate to trusteeship regimes in procedural terms, and moved to perfect the annexation that Smuts had first attempted in 1919. South Africa submitted a final report on South West Africa to the United Nations in 1947. The report claimed to meet the obligations listed under Article 73 of the Charter, which applied to non-self-governing territories – not trust territories, which all of the former mandates were expected to become.[37] Echoing submissions made in 1945 by the South African delegation to the General Assembly, the report insisted that the Mandate for South West Africa, as a treaty between South Africa and the Allied Powers made in December 1920, continued on foot and could not be revoked without South African consent.[38] At the same time, South Africa insisted that as it had not voluntarily submitted to the trusteeship system, the United Nations wielded no powers of oversight over its administration of South West Africa.[39] Despite South Africa's refusal to acknowledge trusteeship obligations, in 1948 the General Assembly resolved to submit South Africa's report to the Trusteeship Council for review.[40] The Trusteeship Council's report on South West Africa was strongly critical of South Africa's administration, even after moderation at the insistence of the Australian representative.[41] It criticised the absence of a franchise or any administrative representation of the indigenous population; minimal expenditure on indigenous education; state-supported monopolisation of arable land by the European population of the territory; and the physical segregation of indigenous Africans in 'native reserves'.[42] In a barely veiled criticism of

---

Melvyn P. Leffler and Odd Arne Westad (eds.), *Cambridge History of the Cold War* (Cambridge: Cambridge University Press, 2010), 67–89 and 353–75.

[37] For a South African nationalist perspective, see Gail-Maryse Cockram, *South West African Mandate* (Cape Town: Juta and Company Limited, 1976), 233–5.
[38] T. D. Gill, *South West Africa and the Sacred Trust 1919–1972* (The Hague: TMC Asser Institut, 1984), 24–5.
[39] Ibid., 24–5.
[40] Slonim, *South West Africa and the United Nations*, 86–90.
[41] Ibid., 94–5.
[42] Cockram, *South West African Mandate*, 236–7.

South African domestic policy, the Trusteeship Council insisted that racial segregation was 'to be deplored in principle'.[43]

From the late 1940s the international response to South Africa's continued occupation of South West Africa was thus strongly related to the statutory institutionalisation of apartheid in South Africa by the right-wing National Party coalition following its election in 1948.[44] Unable to achieve legal annexation of South West Africa at the international level, the National Party executive legislated domestically for representation of the 'white' population of South West Africa in the South African Parliament, and the extension of apartheid legislation to the territory.[45] In July 1949 the government sent a letter to the United Nations advising that no further reports on South West Africa would be submitted, as the Trusteeship Council's critical response to its 1947 report had had 'deleterious effects of the maintenance of the harmonious relations which had hitherto existed and were so essential to successful administration' in the territory.[46] Five months later, the General Assembly resolved to submit the question of the international status of South West Africa to the International Court of Justice with a request for an advisory opinion.[47]

The 1950 Advisory Opinion on the Status of South-West Africa was the first of a pivotal series of ICJ treatments of the dispute that spanned over the 1950s and 1960s into the 1970s. The South West Africa Cases straddled fundamental fault lines in the post-war order, not only between the old imperial powers and the newly decolonising states, but also between the diplomatic and judicial arms of the UN system. In the 1950 Advisory Opinion, the ICJ held eight to six that the Charter created no positive legal obligation for Mandatory Powers to submit a draft Trusteeship Agreement, as required to bring mandates within the trusteeship system.[48] However, according to the Joint Opinion, the

---

[43] Ibid., 236.
[44] Deborah Posel, 'The Apartheid Project, 1948–1970' in Robert Ross, Anne Kelk Nager and Bill Nasson (eds.), *Cambridge History of South Africa*, vol. 2 (Cambridge: Cambridge University Press, 2011), 319–68.
[45] South West Africa Affairs Amendment Act No. 23 of 1949 (SA); Gill, *South West Africa and the Sacred Trust*, 26.
[46] Cockram, *South West African Mandate*, 238.
[47] Question of South West Africa: Request for an Advisory Opinion of the International Court of Justice, General Assembly Resolution 338(IV), United Nations General Assembly Official Records, 4th session, 269th plenary meeting, UN Doc A/RES/338(IV) (6 December 1949).
[48] International Status of South-West Africa (Advisory Opinion) [1950] ICJ Rep 128, 140 ('Advisory Opinion on the International Status of South-West Africa'). The Court was comprised of Judges Basdevant of France, Guerrero of El Salvador, Alvarez of Chile,

international obligations assumed by South Africa with respect to South West Africa were 'of two kinds'. The first arose from the 'sacred trust of civilisation' 'referred to' – as opposed to created – in Article 22 of the Covenant and the text of the Mandate. The second concerned the 'machinery for implementation' by which 'performance of the trust' was secured.[49] The Opinion held twelve to two that uncertainty with respect to the correct procedure for succession of international oversight did not affect the first order of mandatory obligation South Africa had assumed in 1920 – a position South Africa had itself adopted in its 1947 report to the UN.[50] As such, in the majority's opinion South Africa lacked the power unilaterally to alter the international status of South West Africa without the consent of the UN; and the UN was competent to exercise oversight of mandatory obligations by receiving reports as contemplated in the Covenant of the League.[51]

Unsurprisingly, South Africa rejected the 1950 Advisory Opinion. As the Cold War deepened and ideological divisions over the form and substance of 'decolonisation' began to emerge, debates over whether and how the UN should take further action on South West Africa occupied the General Assembly for the following decade.[52] Over the course of the 1950s the UN divided into two loose blocs on the issue. One comprised the USSR, the new African and Asian states, India, Brazil, Syria and Uruguay, and called for UN intervention in support of South West African independence against South African occupation.[53] The second comprised the former imperial powers including Britain, France, the United States, the Netherlands, Australia and New Zealand, and called for a UN-negotiated transition from mandate to trusteeship.[54] Attempts to negotiate UN supervision of the territory via an ad hoc

---

Hackworth of the United States, Winiarski of Poland, Zoricic of Yugoslavia, De Visscher of Belgium, McNair of the United Kingdom, Klaestad of Norway, Read of Canada, Hsu Mo of China, and Azevedo of Brazil. Judges McNair and Read gave Separate Opinions, and Judges Alvarez, de Visscher and Krylov gave Dissenting Opinions.

[49] Ibid., 133.
[50] Advisory Opinion on the International Status of South-West Africa, 134–5; also Faye Carroll, *South West Africa and the United Nations* (Lexington: University Press of Kentucky, 1967), 52.
[51] Advisory Opinion on the International Status of South-West Africa, 134–44.
[52] Boris N. Mamlyuk, 'Decolonization as a Cold War Imperative' in Luis Eslava, Michael Fakhri and Vasuki Nesiah (eds.), *Bandung, Global History and International Law: Critical Pasts and Pending Futures*(Cambridge: Cambridge University Press, 2017), 196–214.
[53] Slonim, *South West Africa and the United Nations*, 126.
[54] Ibid., 126; Cockram, *South West African Mandate*, 259–63.

Committee on South West Africa failed, and after a further two ICJ Advisory Opinions in 1955 and 1956 on procedural questions, in November 1959 the General Assembly adopted a Resolution that 'drew attention' to the capacity of Member States to bring direct legal action against South Africa in the ICJ under the terms of the 1920 Mandate.[55]

In November 1960 Ethiopia and Liberia filed Applications in the ICJ instituting proceedings against South Africa – six months after the Ovamboland People's Congress was reconstituted as the South West Africa People's Congress, or SWAPO; and one month before the UN General Assembly passed Resolution 1514, the Declaration on the Granting of Independence to Colonial Countries and Peoples.[56] The Applications submitted that South Africa had violated its obligations under Article 22 and the Mandate instrument to 'promote the well-being and development' of the indigenous population of South West Africa – first, through the refusal to subject the administration to UN oversight; and secondly, through the formal institutionalisation of apartheid in the territory. With respect to standing, the Applications submitted that Ethiopia and Liberia, as Members of the UN (and Ethiopia, of the League before it), had a legal interest in South Africa's 'proper exercise' of the Mandate.[57] In May 1961 South Africa voted by referendum to leave the British Commonwealth and become a republic, the first of the Dominions to sever all formal ties with the British empire.[58] In December 1961 the new Republic of South Africa submitted its Preliminary Objections to the ICJ.[59] South Africa argued that the Mandate was no longer in force due to the dissolution of the League; that if it was, it could not be enforced by Ethiopia or Liberia, as neither

---

[55] Legal Action to Ensure the Fulfilment of the Obligations Assumed by the Union of South Africa in Respect of the Territory of South West Africa, General Assembly Resolution 1361(XIV), United Nations General Assembly Official Records, 14th session, 838th plenary meeting, UN Doc A/RES/1361(XIV) (17 November 1959).

[56] 'Application Instituting Proceedings', *South West Africa Cases (Ethiopia v. South Africa; Liberia v. South Africa)*, International Court of Justice, General List, filed 4 November 1960, 4–18 et seq. ('*South West Africa Cases*'). On the history of SWAPO, see SWAPO of Namibia Department of Information and Publicity, *To Be Born a Nation: The Liberation Struggle for Namibia* (London: Zed Books, 1981); and Roger Southall, *Liberation Movements in Power: Party and State in Southern Africa* (South Africa: University of KwaZulu-Natal Press, 2013), 29–43.

[57] 'Application Instituting Proceedings', *South West Africa Cases*, International Court of Justice, General List, filed 4 November 1960, 4–18 et seq. See also Ernest A. Gross, 'The South West Africa Case: What Happened?' (October 1966), *Foreign Affairs*, 36–48.

[58] Republic of South Africa Constitution Act 1961 (SA).

[59] *South West Africa Cases (Preliminary Objections)* [1961] ICJ Rep 212 (30 November 1961).

continued to be a 'Member of the League' and were therefore incapable of enforcing the Mandate terms; and that both states otherwise lacked standing to bring the action, as neither had established a sufficient material interest in the dispute.[60] The ICJ decided eight to seven against South Africa in its 1962 Judgment on the Preliminary Objections.[61] Consisting of Judges Alfaro (Panama), Badawi (United Arab Republic), Moreno Quintana (Argentina), Wellington Koo (China), Koretsky (Soviet Union), Bustamante (Peru), Jessup (United States) and the Applicants' Judge ad hoc Mbanefo (Nigeria), the 1962 majority held that despite the dissolution of the League, the dispute resolution provision of the Mandate was still in force, and the ICJ Statute confirmed the Court's jurisdiction to hear the matter.[62] In the minority, Judges Percy Spender of Australia and Gerald Fitzmaurice of the United Kingdom delivered a joint dissenting opinion holding that the Mandate had expired on the dissolution of the League; and that even if mandatory obligations remained on foot, Liberia and Ethiopia were not 'members of the League' given its dissolution, and thus did not have standing to enforce the terms of the Mandate.[63]

After five years, more than a hundred hearings, and over six thousand pages of testimony, in 1966 the ICJ delivered its judgment on the 1960 Applications. Whereas in 1962 the Court had held that it had jurisdiction to hear the merits, the 1966 majority declined to decide on the merits of the case, holding that Ethiopia and Liberia had not established standing.[64] The Court had divided evenly on the issue; however, in a notorious intervention, the Australian Judge Percy Spender, now President of the Court, used his casting vote to reject the Applicants' case. Spender cited the same reasons given in his joint dissent with Fitzmaurice in 1962. In the joint Judgment, the Court applied a strict interpretive approach to the 'judicial function' of the ICJ, holding that – contrary to the 1962 Judgment – the principle of the 'sacred trust of civilisation' could not in and of itself generate binding rights and

---

[60] Ibid.
[61] *South West Africa Cases (Judgment)* [1962] ICJ Rep 319 (21 December 1962).
[62] Ibid., 329–35.
[63] *South West Africa Cases (Judgment)* [1962] ICJ Rep 319, 465 (Joint Dissenting Opinion of Sir Percy Spender and Sir Gerald Fitzmaurice) (21 December 1962). In addition to Judges Spender and Fitzmaurice, the remainder of the minority comprised Basdevant of France, Judge Winiarski of Poland, Morelli of Italy, Spiropoulos of Greece, and Judges ad hoc van Wyk of South Africa, Morelli of Italy.
[64] *South West Africa Cases, Second Phase (Judgment)*, ICJ Rep 6 (18 July 1966); also Gross, 'The South West Africa Case', 44–5.

obligations, particularly given that its scope was 'highly controversial'.[65] Rights and obligations could be created positively only through the text of legal instruments, and on a strict reading of the terms of the Covenant and the Mandate, neither Ethiopia nor Liberia had evinced sufficient interest to establish standing.[66] President Spender attached a Declaration to the Judgment, stating that the minority judges in their dissents should not opine on matters not dealt with in the majority judgment – namely, whether the Mandate for South West Africa continued to exist, and if so, whether South Africa had breached its mandatory obligations.[67]

Notwithstanding Spender's disciplinary Declaration, strident dissenting opinions were given by Judges Wellington Koo of China, Jessup of the United States, Padilla Nervo of Mexico, Forster of Senegal, Tanaka of Japan, Koretsky of the USSR and Mbanefo of Nigeria.[68] The common arguments in the dissents ranged from the technical to the interpretive to the political. According to Judge Koretsky, the majority judgment had breached the principle of *res judicata* in reaching a contradictory conclusion on the same questions of jurisdiction and standing that had come before it in 1962.[69] According to Judge Wellington Koo, the intention of the mandate system – namely to uphold the 'sacred trust of civilisation' – was directly relevant to the interpretation of the text of the Mandate.[70] Judge Jessup explicitly addressed the broader consequences of the ICJ's record on South West Africa: the fact that the Court had proceeded to lengthy hearings on the merits only to uphold South Africa's Preliminary Objections on the Applicants' standing undermined the political legitimacy of the Court, and suggested the 'utter futility' of the ICJ itself.[71] Writing on the 'jurisprudential implications' of the 1966 decision, Wolfgang Friedmann echoed Judge Tanaka's assessment of the split between the majority and the minority as reflecting a split between 'strict

---

[65] Ibid., 48–9.
[66] Ibid.
[67] Ibid., 51–7 (Declaration of President Spender). See also Victor Kattan, '"There Was an Elephant in the Court Room": Reflections on the Role of Judge Sir Percy Spender (1897–1985) in the *South West Africa Cases* (1960–1966) After Half a Century' (2018) 31 *Leiden Journal of International Law*, 147–70.
[68] Ibid. Also Wolfgang Friedmann, 'The Jurisprudential Implications of the South West Africa Case' (1967) 6 *Columbia Journal of Transnational Law* 1, 7–8; and Gill, *South West Africa and the Sacred Trust*, 70–3.
[69] *South West Africa Cases, Second Phase (Judgment)* [1962] ICJ Rep 6, 239 (Dissenting Opinion of Judge Koretsky).
[70] Ibid., 216 (Dissenting Opinion of Vice-President Wellington Koo).
[71] Ibid., 325 (Dissenting Opinion of Judge Jessup).

juristic formalism' and a 'sociological' approach to judicial function.[72] Friedmann then moved to consider the political impact of the case on the international reputation of the Court:

> the fact is that the International Court of Justice is on record as having rejected the claim of Ethiopia and Liberia. This is what will be remembered by the great majority of nations and especially the African states ... the division of representatives (on the Court) between the older and newer countries, or, in a different perspective, between the 'developed' and the 'less-developed' countries that inevitably will be analysed and remembered.[73]

From August 1966 SWAPO and the South African Defence Force were in open armed conflict in South West Africa.[74] In October 1966 the United Nations General Assembly resolved to determine politically what the ICJ had so controversially declined to determine legally. Opening with an affirmation of the 'inalienable right of the people of South West Africa to freedom and independence' as declared in Resolution 1514, the General Assembly resolved to declare the Mandate for South West Africa terminated, and to revert the power of administration to the UN in order to prepare the 'people of the Territory' for independence.[75] The Security Council took three more years to reach consensus on the matter. In March 1969, with Britain and France abstaining, Security Council Resolution 264 recognised the General Assembly's 1966 termination of the Mandate, declared the continued presence of South Africa in Namibia to be an illegal occupation and called upon South Africa to withdraw from the territory.[76] It took twenty-one more years of armed conflict between SWAPO and SADF for the international status of the former South West Africa to be finally settled. In March 1990 the Republic of Namibia officially gained independence as a sovereign state – 106 years after Chancellor Bismarck's declaration of the first German protectorate in Angra Pequeña, in response to the demands of Bremen tobacco merchant F. A. E. Lüderitz.[77]

---

[72] Ibid., 278 (Dissenting Opinion of Judge Tanaka).
[73] Friedmann, 'Jurisprudential Implications of the South West Africa Case', 2.
[74] Lauren Dobell, *Swapo's Struggle for Namibia, 1960–1991: War by Other Means* 2nd ed. (Basel: P. Schlettwein Publishing, 2000).
[75] *Question of South West Africa*, General Assembly Resolution 2145(XXI), General Assembly Official Records, 21st session, 1454th plenary meeting, UN Doc A/RES/2145/(XXI) (27 October 1966).
[76] *The Situation in Namibia*, Security Council Resolution 264, United Nations Official Records, 24th session, 1465th meeting, UN Doc S/RES/264(1969) (20 March 1969).
[77] See Chapter 2, Part 2.12, 'The Establishment of the German Protectorates'.

5.4 The Nauru Talks: Resettlement, Political Independence and Phosphate

In drawing international attention to the status of the former C Mandates, the South West Africa Cases sharpened the political isolation of Australia in its attempt to maintain paternalistic control over Nauru, an isolation which had steadily deepened following the 1960 Declaration on the Granting of Independence to Colonial Countries and Peoples. The Declaration undermined the legitimacy of Australia's repeated claims to the Trusteeship Council that its Chapter XII obligations of promoting political and economic advancement in Nauru were satisfied by participation of Nauruan officials in the lower levels of administration, and the maintenance of the two phosphate royalty funds. In stating plainly that the '(i)nadequacy of political, economic, social or educational preparedness should never serve as a pretext for delaying independence', the Declaration directly repudiated the logic of Article 22 that had grounded the three-tiered mandate system, as well as Australia's continued argument that 'local circumstance' rendered independence inappropriate in the Nauruan case. Furthermore, the Declaration insisted that 'peoples may, for their own ends, freely dispose of their natural wealth and resources without prejudice to any obligations arising out of international economic co-operation'. Even with its capacious caveat, this principle was difficult to reconcile with the Administering Authority's practice of calculating phosphate royalties on a needs- as opposed to market-based rate. The Declaration also effectively contradicted the Trusteeship Council's 1953 position that independence would not be appropriate for the Nauruan people due to the community's size. Asserting a 'belief' that the 'process of liberation' was 'irresistible and irreversible', the Declaration called for 'immediate steps' to be taken to 'transfer all powers to the peoples of those territories, without any conditions or reservations, in accordance with their freely expressed will and desire'.

Between 1960 and 1968 the Trusteeship Council and the General Assembly made periodic resolutions in support of Nauruan independence, becoming more and more specific as to terms.[78] By 1965 Australia

---

[78] Question of the Trust Territory of Nauru, General Assembly Resolution 211(XX), General Assembly Official Records, 20th session, 1407th plenary meeting, UN Doc A/RES/211(XX) (21 December 1965); and Question of the Trust Territory of Nauru, General Assembly Resolution 2226(XXI), General Assembly Official Records, 21st session, 1500th plenary meeting, UN Doc A/RES/2226(XXI) (20 December 1966).

had accepted that it could not maintain formal administrative control over Nauru, and turned its focus to maintaining effective control over BPC's phosphate operation. In stark contrast to the protracted armed conflict that preceded the recognition of the independence of Namibia, the shift in the international status of Nauru towards sovereign statehood occurred via a series of business-like negotiations between the Australian Department of Territories and the NLGC, under the oversight of the Trusteeship Council. The 'Nauru Talks' focused on two main issues: the terms of transfer of administrative power on one hand; and ownership and control of phosphate on the other.

Yet Nauru's negotiated transition to political independence occurred in paradoxical context. Both the Australian Department of Territories and the Trusteeship Council itself continued to presume that, whether or not Nauru became a sovereign state in the meantime, the need for resettlement of the Nauruan people on the exhaustion of the island's phosphate was inevitable.[79] In October 1960 – a few months prior to Resolution 1514 – the Minister for Territories Paul Hasluck had proposed to the NLGC that the Nauruan population be resettled via a fully funded immigration scheme to any of the three BPC partner states, leaving the island of Nauru under BPC control.[80] The NLGC had refused.[81] In 1962 Head Chief Hammer DeRoburt and Councillors Raymond Gadabu and Joseph Detsimea Audoa attended the Trusteeship Council meeting that followed that year's Visiting Mission to Nauru. The delegation's submissions walked a difficult line between tolerating the shared presumption of the inevitability of resettlement, and invoking the 1960 Declaration to support Nauru's case for political independence. Tabling a document called 'Nauruan Proposals for Resettlement', the NGLC delegation put forward a plan for the administrative transition from Australian to Nauruan control, making their claim to sovereignty clear:

> We believe that the sovereignty of the Nauruan people lies in the Nauruan race and our government should be answerable to that power. We have not yet determined how the person is brought to his high office in whom the sovereign power, for the time being, will be vested. Nevertheless it can be stated clearly that we desire the Nauruan nation to be sovereign and free to govern itself.[82]

[79] Williams and Macdonald, *The Phosphateers*, 464.
[80] Macdonald, *In Pursuit of the Sacred Trust*, 41.
[81] Ibid., 41.
[82] United Nations, Trusteeship Council, Summary Records of Meetings, 29th session (1962), 10–14.

After lengthy negotiations – during which the Soviet representative, Vladimir Brykin, accused Australia of displaying 'contempt for the UN in general and the Trusteeship Council in particular' – the Trusteeship Council proposed a pale compromise: resettlement of the Nauruan population as a distinct community within Australia, with some level of local administrative control over their own affairs.[83]

In 1962 the Department of Territories proceeded to propose a plan for resettlement of the Nauruan people on one of a number of islands in the state of Queensland, which were already under federal control as national parks. The Assistant Director of the Northern Territory in Australia, Reginald Marsh, was appointed as Director of Nauruan Resettlement, to negotiate terms with the NLGC.[84] The choices presented included Fraser Island, Hinchinbrook Island, Prince of Wales Island, Curtis Island and Great Palm Island.[85] An NLGC Resettlement Sub-Committee was formed to tour the islands. Initial Nauruan interest in Fraser Island, preferred by the Nauruan Sub-Committee for its distance of six kilometres from the coast of Australia which would allow for relative seclusion, was rejected by Minister Hasluck for the same reason. In February 1963 the Sub-Committee relayed an interest in Curtis Island to Marsh; and in August, terms of resettlement to Curtis Island were negotiated on Nauru. However, the Department of Territories' Curtis Island resettlement plan included political assimilation of the Nauruan people into Queensland as Australian citizens, with Nauruan control of a local government council for Curtis Island.[86] In Marsh's view, this proposal satisfied the end of 'self-government' required under the Trusteeship Agreement. The NLGC countered with a two-part proposal: full Nauruan sovereignty over Curtis Island; or full sovereignty over Nauru. Minister Hasluck rejected the proposal of Nauruan sovereignty over Curtis Island. The NLGC resolved to reject resettlement altogether, and push for sovereign independence on Nauru – including rehabilitation of the island's central plateau at the expense of the tripartite governments.[87]

Over the course of 1965, any ground Australia had for refusing sovereign independence for the Nauruan people on Nauru finally dissolved.

---

[83] International Organization, 'Trusteeship Council' (1964) 18(1) *International Organization* 120, 122; United Nations, Trusteeship Council, Summary Records of Meetings, 29th session (1962), supplement nos. 2, 8–9.

[84] Viviani, *Phosphate and Political Progress*, 143.

[85] Ibid., 143–7.

[86] Macdonald, *In Pursuit of the Sacred Trust*, 46.

[87] Williams and Macdonald, *The Phosphateers*, 475.

The former C Mandate of Western Samoa had been recognised as independent by New Zealand three years earlier, in January 1962, after which New Zealand had accepted the inevitability of Nauruan independence, and distanced itself in the Trusteeship Council from Australia's intransigence on the question.[88] Following the April 1965 Trusteeship Council Visiting Mission to Nauru, the General Assembly took note of the failed resettlement talks between the NGLC and the Department of Territories, and resolved to support the Nauruan request for independence on Nauru, and for rehabilitation of the island's central plateau.[89] The independence negotiations now known as the Nauru Talks that took place between 1965 and 1967 focused on four points of contention between the NLGC and the Department of Territories: ownership of phosphate and control over the phosphate industry; responsibility for rehabilitation of mined-out land; the legal relationship between Nauru and Australia that was to replace that of UN trusteeship; and a timeline for transition of administrative control to the Nauruan people.

The Department of Territories' strategy throughout the Nauru Talks was to negotiate on devolution of public administrative power from the Administering Authority to the NLGC, whilst insisting on continued BPC control of the mining operation. To that end, the Department of Territories adopted a corporate bargaining strategy of offering slight increases to the phosphate royalty and in Nauruan participation in BPC operations, whilst flatly rejecting Nauruan requests for legal transfer of phosphate ownership, and managerial control of the BPC.[90] At the same time, the BPC itself responded to repeated NLGC requests to slow the rate of phosphate extraction during the Nauru Talks by significantly increasing it, declaring that an increased extraction rate under BPC control was to Nauruan benefit, given the increase in royalties proffered by the Department.[91] By 1966 the Department of Territories had moved only as far as offering a phosphate royalty based on a world phosphate price in substitution of the fixed rate set by the Nauruan Administrator, and a 'partnership' arrangement of joint

---

[88] Ibid., 476–7.
[89] Question of the Trust Territory of Nauru, General Assembly Resolution 211(XX), General Assembly Official Records, 20th session, 1407th plenary meeting, UN Doc A/RES/211(XX) (21 December 1965); and Question of the Trust Territory of Nauru, General Assembly Resolution 2226(XXI), General Assembly Official Records, 21st session, 1500th plenary meeting, UN Doc A/RES/2226(XXI) (20 December 1966).
[90] Williams and Macdonald, *The Phosphateers*, 481.
[91] Ibid., 480.

5.1 Nauru Legislative Council on a visit to Australia during the Nauru Talks. J. A. Bop (chairman), Agoko Doguape, Edwin Tsitsi and Roy Degoreore. Credit: John Patrick O'Gready/Fairfax Media via Getty Images.

ownership of Nauruan phosphate, under the control of the BPC for at least five years after independence.[92] The Nauruan delegation rejected the partnership deal. Insisting on sole Nauruan ownership of the phosphate, Head Chief DeRoburt put forward a counterproposal: a gradual buy-out of the BPC operation and assets over a ten-year period by the new Nauruan state.[93]

On the question of rehabilitation, the Department responded to NLGC demands by appointing a Nauru Lands Rehabilitation Committee in 1965, charged with 'examining the practicability, costs and usefulness of rehabilitating the mined out areas of the phosphate island of Nauru'.[94] In 1966 the Rehabilitation Committee issued its report, concluding that whilst 'technically feasible', rehabilitation was 'impracticable' due to

---

[92] Ibid., 47–8.
[93] Ibid., 486.
[94] Minister for Territories of Nauru, 'Nauru Lands Rehabilitation Committee' (media release, 24 January 1966).

prohibitive cost.[95] The Committee further commented on the absence of legal responsibility for rehabilitation, reporting that 'it would seem inconsistent with the general trend in regulatory policies for extractive industries to require such treatment to be a responsibility of the phosphate-extractive industry'. The NLGC rejected the findings of the Rehabilitation Committee, arguing that it had gone beyond its terms of reference in commenting on legal responsibility, and reiterated yet again the Nauruan position: responsibility for rehabilitation of lands mined from 1919 onward lay with the governments party to the Nauru Island Agreement.[96] From 1966 with mounting pressure on all three governments in the UN General Assembly, New Zealand made clear that it preferred full political independence for Nauru, and immediate cessation of all trusteeship responsibilities.[97] In the Trusteeship Council, the United Kingdom indicated that it was open to political independence for Nauru; but elsewhere expressed concern over the repercussions of Nauruan independence for the Gilbert and Ellice Islands, Fiji and the Solomon Islands, over which it maintained territorial administrative control.[98]

On the matter of the nature of Nauru's future legal relationship with Australia, the Department of Territories moved over the course of the Nauru Talks from refusing to entertain any prospect of sovereign independence, to proposing an arrangement whereby Nauru would gain administrative control over internal affairs, and Australia would retain control over Nauru's external affairs – a strong echo of both the classic protectorate form, and Australia's own erstwhile status as a self-governing Dominion.[99] The NLGC's response was that any such arrangement could only be negotiated after full political independence, on the basis of sovereign equality.[100] Regarding a timeline for transition of administrative power, from 1965 the NLGC insisted upon 31 January 1968 as the date for official independence, on the anniversary of the return in 1945 of those Nauruans interned by Japan on Chuuk

---

[95] Nauru Lands Rehabilitation Committee, 'Report by Committee appointed to investigate the Possibilities of Rehabilitation of Mined Phosphate Lands' (Sydney, 1966) ('Nauru Lands Rehabilitation Committee Report'). Also Merze Tate, 'Nauru, Phosphate and the Nauruans' (1968) *Australian Journal of Politics and History* 177, 186-7.
[96] Weeramantry, *Nauru*, 274-6; Viviani, *Phosphate and Political Progress*, 149.
[97] Macdonald, *In Pursuit of the Sacred Trust*, 49-50.
[98] Ibid., 49-50.
[99] On the classical form of the protectorate, see Chapter 2, Part 2.7, 'The Concept of the Protectorate'.
[100] Williams and Macdonald, *The Phosphateers*, 488.

Atoll during the war. The Department of Territories initially responded that a date for independence should not be fixed but the NLGC should be gradually prepared for 'political responsibility'.[101] To that end, the Department agreed to the formation of a new Legislative Council and Executive Council, to be added to the existing administrative structure.[102] The Legislative Council would consist of the nine members of the NLGC, plus the five Australian heads of department on Nauru, to be chaired by the Administrator. In accordance with the Nauru Island Agreement, matters concerning the BPC's phosphate operation would be excluded from the Legislative Council's remit.[103] An Executive Council consisting of two Nauruan and two 'official' members would be drawn from the Legislative Council, and would also be chaired by the Administrator.[104] The NLGC agreed to the creation of the new Legislative and Executive Councils, yet continued to insist that full control be devolved to the expanded administration by 31 January 1968.

In December 1965 the Nauru Act was passed in the Australian federal Parliament, establishing the Nauru Legislative and Executive Councils.[105] The Nauru Act 1965 left the Administrator's role largely intact, providing for appointment by the Australian Governor-General, and stipulating that the Administrator was answerable to the Minister of Territories.[106] The Australian Governor-General was vested with the power to make ordinances under heads of power that reconfigured those divided between the Jaluit Gesellschaft and the Reich in 1886, amounting in effect to a juridified notion of the nineteenth-century notion of external sovereignty, coupled with total ownership and control over the phosphate operation: 'defence, internal security and the maintenance of peace and order'; 'external affairs'; 'the phosphate industry (including the operation, ownership and control of that industry)'; 'phosphate royalties'; and 'ownership and control of phosphate-bearing land'.[107] The Legislative Council was vested with the power to make Ordinances excluding those matters so reserved to the Governor-General. All actions of the Legislative Council were subject to

---

[101] Viviani, *Phosphate and Political Progress*, 151–2.
[102] Parliament of Australia, *Parliamentary Debates*, 'Bill 1965', 2 December 1965 (Minister for Territories Charles Barnes MP, second reading speech).
[103] Minister for Territories Charles Barnes MP, 'Nauru Talks' (media release, 10 June 1965).
[104] Charles Barnes MP, 'Nauru Talks'.
[105] Nauru Act 1965 (Cth).
[106] Ibid., s. 6.
[107] Ibid., s. 34.

disallowance by the Governor-General, and by the Administrator, nominated as President.[108] The Executive Council was delegated an advisory role on matters referred to it by the Administrator.[109] Part VII of the Nauru Act 1965 also juridified the existing Nauruan judicial structure, which had developed over time via a series of executive ordinances from an implied power exercised unilaterally by the Administrator, into a three-tiered court hierarchy of District Court, Central Court (formerly the Supreme Court) and Court of Appeal, with a further right of appeal to the High Court of Australia.[110] The Nauruan Legislative and Executive Councils were inaugurated on 31 January 1966. However, the Department of Territories continued its strategy of deferring a date for full independence, maintaining that full sovereignty should not be exercised until the new Legislative Council gained 'practical experience' of administration, and its 'political progress' could be appreciably observed.[111] With respect to phosphate, the Department of Territories continued to maintain that ownership and control of Nauruan phosphate remained legally vested in the BPC, and refused to negotiate on any phosphate matter except royalty calculations.[112]

In the face of Australian intransigence on full sovereign independence, transfer of ownership and control of phosphate, and the question of rehabilitation, in December 1966 the UN General Assembly resolved to support the NLGC's position on all points of contention.[113] Whilst the Nauruan delegation had been denied legal representation during the Nauru Talks on the island and in Canberra, Hammer DeRoburt had insisted that all documentation be submitted to the Trusteeship Council for review, effectively subjecting Australia's negotiated outcomes to international oversight.[114] Two months after it resolved to terminate the Mandate for South West Africa, the General Assembly acted on the advice of the Trusteeship Council, and recommended that the Administering Authority fix a date for full political independence for Nauru, not later than 31 January 1968. The General Assembly further

[108] Ibid., ss. 26–33.
[109] Ibid., s. 43.
[110] Ibid., Part VII 'The Judicial System'.
[111] Report of the Trusteeship Council 1964–1965, United Nations General Assembly Official Records, 20th session, supplement no. 4, 37–8.
[112] Minister for Territories, 'Nauru Talks'.
[113] Question of the Trust Territory of Nauru, General Assembly Resolution 2226(XXI), General Assembly Official Records 21st session, 1500th plenary meeting, UN Doc A/RES/2226(XXI) (20 December 1966).
[114] Williams and Macdonald, *The Phosphateers*, 483–4.

resolved that ownership in phosphate and control over the phosphate industry should then be transferred to the Nauruan people; and that the Administration take 'immediate steps, irrespective of the cost involved, towards restoring the island of Nauru for habitation by the Nauruan people as a sovereign nation'.[115] By the end of 1966, the Department of Territories' protracted attempt to maintain BPC ownership and control of Nauruan phosphate by trading off increased royalties and increased Nauruan participation in the island's expanding administrative structure had failed. A date for Nauruan independence had been set.

In April 1967, four months after the General Assembly's resolution in favour of Nauru, another round of negotiations was held in Canberra – this time attended not only by the Department of Territories and the new Nauru Legislative Council, but also by representatives of the New Zealand government and the UK Foreign Office.[116] Also in attendance for the first time was New Zealand historian James Wightman Davidson, Chair in Pacific History at the Australian National University in Canberra, whom the Department appointed as constitutional adviser to Nauru. Davidson – who had completed his PhD at Cambridge and began his academic career there as lecturer in colonial studies, later becoming an expert on constitution making in the British Commonwealth – had acted into similar roles for the Cook Islands and Western Samoa during their negotiated transitions to independence from New Zealand.[117] The Department of Territories proposed a final agreement. Full political independence would be transferred to the Nauru Legislative Council and Executive Council; property in phosphate would vest in Nauruan landowners; and ownership and control of the BPC operation would be bought by the Nauruan administration progressively over a three-year transition period, to be vested in a substitute entity, the Nauru Phosphate Corporation.

In return, Nauru would be required to guarantee phosphate supply to the BPC at 1967 levels for at least three years. It would further be required to indemnify Australia and the partner governments from any future claims for rehabilitation of the island.[118] Having lost its attempt to

---

[115] *Question of the Trust Territory of Nauru*, GA Res 2226(XXI).
[116] Viviani, *Phosphate and Political Progress*, 167–9; Williams and Macdonald, *The Phosphateers*, 488–90.
[117] Donald Denoon, 'Davidson, James Wightman (Jim) (1915–1973)', *Australian Dictionary of Biography*, vol. 13 (Melbourne: Melbourne University Press, 1993).
[118] Macdonald, *In Pursuit of the Sacred Trust*, 55; Viviani, *Phosphate and Political Progress*, 165–6.

234   5 FROM TRUST TERRITORY TO SOVEREIGN STATE, 1968

maintain control over the phosphate industry, the Department of Territories focused its energy on arguing that legal responsibility for rehabilitation was not owed as a matter of mining law; and that the Long Term Investment Fund established in 1947 by the Administering Authority and funded entirely by sequestered Nauruan phosphate royalties was sufficient to meet both the cost of rehabilitation, and any trusteeship obligations owed. The Nauruan delegation agreed to the substantive terms of the proposal, agreeing to buy out the BPC between 1968 and 1971 at a cost of AUD$21 million, in exchange for full ownership and control over phosphate and BPC assets. However, they refused to accept that such agreement implied indemnity of Australia, or the United Kingdom or New Zealand, from future claims for rehabilitation.[119] At the time of independence, one-third of island's land mass had been excavated by the BPC, and left as open-cut mine.[120]

5.5 Independence Day: Nauru becomes a Republic

On 15 June 1967 the Nauru Island Phosphate Industry Agreement was signed by the NLGC and the Department of Territories, transferring control of the BPC's phosphate operation.[121] The 1967 Agreement provided that the NLGC would purchase the assets of the BPC over a three-year period on an agreed basis of valuation; and that ownership of phosphate, the phosphate mining right, and property in plant and equipment would vest in a new Nauruan entity, the Nauru Phosphate Corporation. Phosphate would continue to be supplied exclusively to the BPC at an agreed volume and price, rather than on the open market, with cessation of supply requiring twelve months' notice. On its terms, the Phosphate Industry Agreement did not deal with the question of rehabilitation. Still, the Australian government maintained that the settlement represented in the Agreement was sufficient to meet the costs of rehabilitation, and therefore released the partner governments from liability. After the 1967 Agreement was signed, Hammer DeRoburt again expressly rejected Australia's claim that it somehow constituted an indemnity against a future rehabilitation claim.[122]

---

[119] Weeramantry, *Nauru*, 274–5.
[120] International Court of Justice, *Nauru v. Australia* ('Certain Phosphate Lands Case'), Memorial of the Republic of Nauru, ICJ Rep (20 March 1990).
[121] Nauru Phosphate Industry Agreement, 15 June 1967; Minister for Territories, 'Nauru Phosphate Agreement' (media release, 15 June 1967).
[122] Weeramantry, *Nauru*, 274–80.

5.5 INDEPENDENCE DAY: NAURU BECOMES A REPUBLIC

That same day of 15 June 1967, the Nauruan delegation released the 'Statement on the Constitutional Future of Nauru', drafted in collaboration with Professor Davidson to sketch out the administrative form an independent Nauru would take.[123] Davidson had acted as constitutional adviser to Western Samoa prior to independence from New Zealand in 1962, and to the Cook Islands, a New Zealand Trust Territory that had opted for self-government within New Zealand.[124] The Statement proposed that Nauru become a republic with a form of government 'based on the British parliamentary system', as had occurred in Western Samoa on the former C Mandate's independence from New Zealand.[125] The Statement sketched out a basic constitutional structure that expanded on the existing administrative form, with brief sections on the President, the Executive, the Legislature, the Judiciary, and the Public Service, and a preceding section on Fundamental Rights. The Statement outlined a governmental form consisting of a Legislative Assembly of 'around fifteen', with members elected by each of the nine constituencies represented in the NLGC, replaced in 1965 by the Legislative Council; a President, elected by the Legislative Assembly, to take over from the Administrator; an Executive, consisting of the President as Chief Minister, and a Cabinet of three or four Ministers appointed by the President – a reframing of the 1965 Executive Council; a Judiciary, consisting of a District Court, a Supreme Court and a right of appeal to the High Court of Australia, with the Magistrates of the District Court and the Judge of the Supreme Court to be appointed by the President; and a public service, overseen by a Head of Department, appointed by the President. The public service itself would arrange the existing administration into four ministerial portfolios, to be overseen by the Ministers of the Executive.

The Statement on the Constitutional Future of Nauru explicitly addressed the risk inherent in the marked concentration of power in the new office of President, which would comprise both head of state and head of government, and exercise powers of appointment with respect to both the judiciary and the public service, as had its preceding office of

---

[123] Department of Territories, 'Documents relating to the Constitutional Future of Nauru' (22 June 1967); Minister for Territories, 'Constitutional Development in Nauru' (media release, 15 June 1967).
[124] Macdonald, *In Pursuit of the Sacred Trust*, 52–3; Viviani, *Phosphate and Political Progress*, 168–69.
[125] Department of Territories, 'Documents relating to the Constitutional Future of Nauru', 10.

Administrator.[126] The Statement reasoned that given the size of Nauru, a stronger separation of powers would be excessive. To balance the risk of abuse of office, however, the Statement proposed a mechanism of executive accountability to the Legislative Assembly, whereby the Assembly would be empowered to remove the President and the Cabinet from office via a motion of no confidence. Noting the potential for 'an undue number of changes in the tenure of the Presidency', the Statement reasoned somewhat opaquely that 'due to the circumstances of Nauru, it seems unlikely that there will be violent or rapid changes of political opinion'.

On the issue of control over Nauru's external affairs, the Statement reiterated that any prospective treaty relationship with Australia would be negotiated as sovereign equals, after the devolution of full political independence to Nauru.[127] On the question of rights, the Statement envisaged protection of fundamental rights and freedoms of Nauruan citizens in the new constitution; but that citizenship should be 'largely' restricted to those of Nauruan descent, to limit the prospect of acquisition of citizenship rights by emigrant workers in the phosphate industry. Finally, the Statement strongly advocated that the proposed constitutional structure be adopted by a Constitutional Convention elected from the Nauruan people, rather than by an instrument of the Australian Parliament.

The administrative form of the new Republic was finalised rapidly over the following months. In October 1967 the Nauru Independence Act was passed in the Australian federal Parliament. Consisting of just four sections, the Independence Act vested in the Nauru Legislative Council the power to make 'an Ordinance establishing a convention for the purpose of establishing a constitution for Nauru'.[128] It provided that on the 'expiration of the day preceding' 31 January 1968, the Nauru Act that only two years previous had established the Legislative and Executive Councils would cease to operate; and that 'on and after' 31 January 1968, 'Australia shall not exercise any powers of legislation, administration or jurisdiction in and over Nauru'.[129]

With the transition of control over the phosphate industry and control over the administration of Nauru in place, what remained was for the shift in Nauru's international status to sovereign state to be approved by

[126] Ibid., 3–4.
[127] Ibid., 2–3.
[128] Nauru Independence Act 1967 (Cth), s. 2.
[129] Ibid., ss. 3, 4.

5.5 INDEPENDENCE DAY: NAURU BECOMES A REPUBLIC 237

the United Nations. In November 1967 a special session of the Trusteeship Council was called to assess the terms of Nauruan independence provided in the Phosphate Industry Agreement and the Nauru Independence Act, in order to decide whether the 1947 Trusteeship Agreement had been determined in accordance with Chapters XII and XIII of the UN Charter.[130] During the session, the Australian delegate to the Trusteeship Council, Patrick Shaw – Permanent Australian Representative to the UN, and a former adviser to H. V. Evatt – did not mention the rehabilitation issue, instead implying that the Nauruan people's assumption of control over Nauruan phosphate and the trust fund was more than enough of a generous concession on Australia's behalf:

> since January 1946 the indigenous population of Nauru had risen from 1,280 to approximately 3,100 and the standard of living was now one of the highest in the world, the per capita income being higher than that in Australia. If the price paid for the phosphate and the cost of production remained in approximately the same relationship as at present and the Nauruan people put aside the same proportion of their funds as they had the previous year, their long-term fund would stand at approximately US$400 million when the phosphate deposits were exhausted.

Hammer DeRoburt, however, explicitly addressed the rehabilitation issue, reporting that full agreement had been reached with the Department of Territories on all matters except rehabilitation of land mined out during the mandate and trusteeship periods. DeRoburt stated his wish to 'place on record that the Nauruan Government would continue', after independence, to 'seek what was, in the opinion of the Nauruan people, a just settlement of their claims':

> There was one subject, however, on which there was still a difference of opinion – responsibility for the rehabilitation of phosphate lands. The Nauruan people fully accepted responsibility in respect of land mined subsequently to 1 July 1967, since under the new agreement they were receiving the net proceeds of the sale of phosphate. Prior to that date, however, they had not received the net proceeds and it was therefore their contention that the three Governments should bear responsibility for the rehabilitation of land mined prior to 1 July 1967. That was not an issue relevant to the termination of the Trusteeship Agreement, nor did the Nauruans wish to make it a matter for United Nations discussion.[131]

---

[130] United Nations Trusteeship Council, Official Records, 13th special session, 1323rd meeting (22 November 1967), 4.
[131] Ibid.

In the ensuing Trusteeship Council deliberations, only the Soviet representative, P. F. Shlakov, explicitly raised the Nauruans' claim for full rehabilitation at the cost of the partner governments.[132] In contrast to DeRoburt's careful insistence on sustained 'friendship' with Australia after independence, Shlakov delivered a strident anti-colonial statement, describing the Nauruan cause as a result of a worldwide 'decisive attack on the forces of reaction, imperialism and colonialism'. He concluded his intervention with pointed 'confidence' 'that the further development of Nauru as a sovereign nation would not be accompanied by any outside pressure and that the legitimate demands of the Nauruan people for sovereignty over the natural resources of the Territory and for the rehabilitation of the land would be fully met'. The Trusteeship Council resolved to approve the determination of the Trusteeship Agreement and the accession of Nauru to independence on 31 January 1968.[133]

On 19 December 1967 an election was held in Nauru to appoint three members of each of the island's nine constituencies to the Constitutional Convention, to join with the nine sitting members of the Legislative Council.[134] The Convention met in January 1968 to settle the text of the new Constitution, drafted by Professor Davidson and Victorian lawyer Rowena Armstrong as sketched out in the Statement on the Constitutional Future of Nauru released in June 1967. Elections for the eighteen positions on the new Legislative Assembly were held on 26 January 1968, consisting of two positions for each of the nine represented constituencies. All nine members of the Legislative Council were elected as members of the new Legislative Assembly. On 29 January 1968 the Convention unanimously adopted a text for the Constitution. Two days later, on 31 January 1968, the Republic of Nauru celebrated its Independence Day. The day's ceremonies were attended by the UN Under-Secretary, General Issoufou Saidou-Djermakoye of Niger, and the Australian Governor-General, Baron Richard Casey.[135] Hammer DeRoburt was voted Nauru's first President by the new Legislative Assembly; DeRoburt and Casey signed

---

[132] Ibid.
[133] Trusteeship Council Resolution 2149(S-XIII), United Nations Trusteeship Council Official Records, 13th Special Session, 1323rd meeting, 22 November 1967.
[134] Viviani, *Phosphate and Political Progress*, 173.
[135] Australian Associated Press, 'Guns Boom and People Grave as Nauru is "Born"', *Canberra Times* (Canberra) 1 February 1968; Macdonald, *In Pursuit of the Sacred Trust*, 60.

5.2 The British Phosphate Commissioners (D. J. Carter (NZ) C. E. Barnes (Aus) and Sir Charles Johnston (UK)) with President Hammer De Roburt and the flag of the Republic of Nauru, Independence Day, 31 January 1968. Credit: Image courtesy of the National Archives of Australia. NAA: A1200, L69077.

a Proclamation of Independence; and the island, with an area of four by five kilometres, and a Nauruan population of just over 3,000, became a sovereign state.[136]

5.6 The Constitution of the Republic of Nauru

In May 1968 the Constitution of the Republic of Nauru came into effect through an Act of the new Legislative Assembly.[137] Subject to the express terms of the new Constitution, transitional provisions preserved the existing administrative and legal structure. As had happened with the transition from protectorate to mandate, and from mandate to trust territory, Article 85(1) provided that all existing laws remained in force; and Article 86 provided that any reference in an existing law to the

---

[136] Australian Associated Press, 'Guns Boom and People Grave as Nauru is "Born"'.
[137] Constitution of Nauru 1968 (incorporating the alterations made by the Constitutional Convention of Nauru under Article 92 on 17 May 1968).

Australian Administrator, Minister of Territories, or Governor-General or should be read as a reference to the President, unless the context required otherwise. Article 87 provided that, with the exception of the Administrator, all other administrative officeholders remained in their positions. The powers of the Legislative Assembly, Executive and President were codified as proposed a year earlier in the 1967 Statement. Article 24 empowered the Legislative Assembly to remove a Cabinet including the President by a vote of no confidence, the mechanism proposed to temper the concentration of power in the presidential office. Such no confidence votes, however, were required to be passed not by a majority but an even half of the Legislative Assembly of eighteen.

The new Constitution dealt sparingly with the new Republic's economic structure. Article 62(1) codified the existence of the Long Term Investment Fund established in the early years of the trust period, and provided for investments from the fund. Article 63 empowered the Legislative Assembly to create a royalty trust fund, but did not codify the terms of management of the Nauru Landowners Phosphate Royalty Fund, established in the early years of the mandate, and shielded from international oversight during both mandate and trusteeship periods. Article 58 provided that all revenue raised and not payable into another fund was to be paid into a Treasury Fund, accessible in 'accordance with law'. With respect to phosphate operations, Article 93 provided that the Phosphate Industry Agreement entered into with Australia in 1967 was binding on the Republic. Beyond this, the Constitution provided only minimal codification of the phosphate operation on which the island's economy wholly depended. Article 83(1) vested the right to mine phosphate, previously held by the BPC, in the Republic of Nauru; but the new Nauru Phosphate Corporation formed to take over from the BPC was omitted from constitutional purview, as had been the case with the BPC. The rehabilitation issue, however, was explicitly addressed: Article 83(2) exempted the Republic of Nauru from liability for rehabilitation of land mined prior to the enactment of the Phosphate Industry Agreement.

In this way the 1968 Constitution codified central elements of the administrative structure that had developed in Nauru since the establishment of the German protectorate in 1888. The Constitution maintained the basic concentration of executive power in the Presidential office, whilst providing for further bureaucratisation in the delineation of official powers and functions, in the expanded Legislative Assembly, the addition of an Executive Cabinet, and codification of administrative appointment processes. Legislative and judicial powers, devolved to a nominal degree to the NLGC and the District and Supreme Courts on the insistence of the Trusteeship Council, remained subject to significant executive influence. The Constitution included no express provision for financial transparency of the phosphate operation, nor of disposition of trust fund moneys, which together constituted the entire revenue base of the new Republic. The body of domestic law developed by executive ordinance over the preceding eighty-year period, and the legal rights and obligations it had created, remained in effect. As Nauru celebrated its first year of sovereign independence, the Nauruan people moved to occupy an administrative structure that had accreted through the protectorate, mandate and trust periods around the primary purpose of facilitating the outward flow of natural resources from the island.

5.7 Conclusion: The Ironies of Nauruan Independence

The transition in international status from trust territory to statehood was an astounding achievement of the Nauruan people under the leadership of Hammer DeRoburt. The recognition of Nauruan ownership and control of phosphate was perhaps a greater achievement still, given the aggressive negotiation strategy of the Australian Department of Territories on the issue during the Nauru Talks, even as it conceded the inevitability of formal political independence. However, international recognition of Nauruan independence, as urged by the Trusteeship Council and the General Assembly, was in many respects profoundly ironic. The presumption of the inevitable uninhabitability of the island on the exhaustion of phosphate was widely shared. Nauru's accession to sovereign statehood was regarded at the international level less as the inauguration of a viable state, than as a principled means by which the Nauruan people would be free to determine for themselves how to respond to that uninhabitability.

The push towards international recognition of Nauruan sovereignty was to a large extent a result of the juridification of the obligations of trusteeship in the UN Charter, propelled by the insistence of post-colonial and anti-imperial states in the Trusteeship Council, the General Assembly and the International Court of Justice that those obligations be interpreted in good faith. But in the Nauruan case at least, the language of trusteeship proved a far more effective tool for negotiating devolution of political control than it did for protecting the territory from vigorous economic and environmental exploitation. Since independence, the environmental harm wrought on the island of Nauru has become an infamous fable of unsustainable resource exploitation.[138] That exploitation of Nauru correlated directly with the immense financial and industrial benefit of monopoly access to cost-price superphosphate that flowed under the 1919 Nauru Island Agreement to Australia, and to a lesser extent to New Zealand and the United Kingdom. The full extent of the benefit to Australia of stable agricultural growth over the twentieth century is difficult to quantify. Yet the aggression with which a series of Australian governments from the Paris Peace Conference onward sought to establish and maintain that benefit was telling. As historian David Goldsworthy has noted of Australian attitudes to Nauru, 'the principle of cheap [phosphate] was embedded in the political and economic order, and threats to it were not to be countenanced'.[139]

Yet as striking as the recognition of Nauruan sovereignty was, the administrative structure codified in the 1968 Constitution of the Republic of Nauru was not a novel institution but a palimpsest of administrative forms that had accreted under eighty years of imperial rule. The Constitution of the Republic of Nauru was drafted, adopted and ratified in less than twelve months. Despite further expansion of the legislature and judiciary, the concentration of executive power in the office of President echoed the concentration of power in the office of Administrator, mitigated only by a blunt mechanism of no confidence motions passable by a simple half of the Legislative Assembly. Despite the phosphate industry comprising the only planned source of revenue, the structure of the Nauru Phosphate Corporation was left outside the purview of the Constitution, leaving the issue of financial transparency between the administration and the phosphate industry to legislative control. The management and disposition of royalty trust funds was similarly left to legislative control, and thus left susceptible to significant executive intervention. All existing laws were left on foot until repealed or amended by the Legislative Assembly; all existing administrative offices were left in place, to be occupied by Nauruans; and all references to the Administering Authority were replaced by references to the President. In 1968 the Nauruan people secured their

---

[138] See for example Carl N. McDaniel and John M. Gowdy, *Paradise for Sale: A Parable of Nature* (Berkeley: University of California Press, 2000); and Naomi Klein, *This Changes Everything: Capitalism vs The Climate* (London: Allen Lane, 2014), 161–70.

[139] David Goldsworthy, 'British Territories and Australian Mini-Imperialism in the 1950s' (1995) 41 *Australian Journal of Politics and History*, 356–72 at 357.

5.7 CONCLUSION: IRONIES OF NAURUAN INDEPENDENCE

sovereign independence, and the international status of Nauru shifted from trust territory to sovereign state, a moment customarily associated with clean beginnings and political promise. Yet a focus on the story of international status at the expense of attentiveness to administrative form works to obscure a far more burdened transition. The administrative structure to which Nauru's sovereign status attached was built on the foundations of an improvised arrangement struck eighty years previous between a Hanseatic trading company and a reluctant German empire.

6

After Independence: Sovereign Status and the Republic of Nauru

6.1 Introduction

In January 1968, at the height of the decolonisation movements, the island of Naoerō became the Republic of Nauru, the third smallest state in the world after the Vatican and the principality of Monaco. This book has offered a critical redescription of the transitions in Nauru's international status from German protectorate, to League of Nations C Mandate, to UN trust territory, to sovereign state, mapped against corresponding changes in local administrative form. It argues that this final shift to sovereign status, accompanied by the expansion of the existing Australian administration into a 'British-style parliamentary system', did not dismantle the forms of relation that had developed under eighty years of imperial then international rule. Rather, it further expanded upon them. The implication is that the shift from UN trust territory to sovereign state in 1968 was not a departure from but a stage in the bureaucratisation of an imperial administrative form instantiated in the late nineteenth century.

The intention in drawing this conclusion is absolutely not to undermine the political achievement of the Nauruan people in their accession to sovereign status in 1968. Through Hammer DeRoburt and the Nauru Local Government Council, the Nauruan people exercised deft diplomacy in negotiating their way to political independence from Australia, in an international institutional context that prescribed statehood as the only means of achieving that independence, despite the ill-fit of the statist paradigm of decolonisation to the Nauruan context. They further negotiated their way to control over their island's phosphate, in an international legal context that insisted such control had to be bought. Australia's official attitude was that the Nauruan people's gaining control over Nauruan phosphate, the phosphate industry and the two Trust Funds was somehow a mark of Australian magnanimity. That attitude

6.1 INTRODUCTION

still finds unofficial expression even now. But the reality was much darker. Australia – and with it, Britain and New Zealand – refused to accept any responsibility for environmental rehabilitation of the island; for under-calculation of phosphate royalties for over four decades; or for the entrenchment of an administrative regime that had for three of those four decades prioritised phosphate profits over every possible function of government. As Weeramantry wrote in 1992, after four decades of exploitation the withdrawing administrators effectively 'gave' the Nauruan people nothing at all:

> (t)here were two principal benefits the Nauruans received at Independence – independence and control over the phosphate industry. Neither of these was any more than what they were entitled to in law. It would not be unfair to say that over and above these the Nauruans received *nothing* from the partner governments at the time of Independence.[1]

That refusal left the new Republic on the brink of a widely predicted economic and environmental crisis, with a constitutionalised administration that functioned only to perpetuate the state of affairs that had brought that crisis about.

This historical continuity dispels any notion that the now notorious 'failures' of the Republic of Nauru – the concentration of executive power in a single office; the imbrications of public and private control of state power; the financial dependence on royalties and rent; and the lack of financial transparency or accountability around public funds – originated with Nauruan mismanagement of state following the withdrawal of Australian control. Those issues are directly continuous with imperial forms of relation entrenched under German, then British, then Australian rule. The entrenchment of those relations over eighty years, coupled with Australia's refusal at the time of independence to accept responsibility for addressing the political, economic and environmental effects of sustained exploitation, left the new Republic of Nauru facing ruin from its first day.[2]

Once the last shift in Nauru's international status in 1968 towards sovereignty is no longer treated as an historical erasure, the continuities between imperial administration and the island's post-independence trajectory become clear. This book has sought to trace that continuity from the imperial side, constructing an account of the administration of

---

[1] Weeramantry, *Nauru: Environmental Damage under International Trusteeship* (Oxford: Oxford University Press, 1992), 267.
[2] Katerina Teaiwa, 'Ruining Pacific Islands: Australia's Phosphate Imperialism' (2015) 46 *Australian Historical Studies*, 374–91.

Nauru up to the moment of political independence. As such, it does not seek to offer a comprehensive account of the Republic's post-1968 history, or a comprehensive analysis of Nauru's contemporary political situation, both of which are properly told by Nauruan voices. Still, some reflections on the post-independence implications of the narrative constructed in this book are warranted, if only to counteract the 'riches to rags' clichés that now circulate in popular renderings of the island's situation.[3] Since the rejection of constitutional change in 2010, the recommencement of Australia's offshore processing regime in 2012 and the election of the Waqa government in 2013, Nauru has listed towards autocracy, with the tacit support of the Australian Commonwealth.[4] The story of the Republic is habitually recounted in international affairs as a parable, whether of environmental destruction, of exile, or of corruption and predation.[5] As Teaiwa has noted, Nauru is now 'one of the most maligned countries in mainstream and popular media', with the most negative criticisms coming from Australian sources.[6] As detailed in Chapter 1, tropes of Nauruan irresponsibility and corruption are habitually invoked on both sides of the policy debate over offshore detention in Australia. When severed from the imperial history revisited in this book, these tropes work to reinscribe much older ideologies of Australian regional supremacy.

Given the circumstances of its creation, however, the story of the Republic is just as readily understood as one of survival as one of failure. Ratuva has observed that the experience of sustained exploitation under imperial administration had both traumatic and galvanising effects on the Nauruan people's determination to survive on their island as a community: 'instead of permanently fracturing the Nauruan notion of place, colonial experience had actually reconfigured it, made it more resilient and durable as a means of self-preservation'.[7] In the two decades after independence, Nauru gained an international reputation as an

---

[3] Helen Hughes, *From Riches to Rags: What are Nauru's Options and How Can Australia Help?* (Canberra: Centre for Independent Studies, 2004).

[4] Stewart Firth, 'Australia's Detention Centre and the Erosion of Democracy in Nauru' (2016) 51 *Journal of Pacific History*, 286–300. In Nauruan parliamentary elections in August 2019, President Baron Waqa lost his seat, and Lionel Aingimea was elected President by the new Parliament.

[5] See Chapter 1, Part 1.2, 'Nauru as Symptom Versus Nauru as Parable'.

[6] Teaiwa, 'Ruining Pacific Islands', 377.

[7] Steven Ratuva, 'The Gap Between Global Thinking and Local Living: Dilemmas of Constitutional Reform in Nauru' (2011) 20 *The Journal of the Polynesian Society*, 241–68 at 244.

economic marvel.[8] The world phosphate price spiked in the 1970s and, for a time, Nauru had the second highest GDP per capita in the world, due to its small population and high return on phosphate. But the inevitability of the exhaustion of phosphate loomed, as it had since the 1950s. With financial advice from an Australian firm, the Republic sought to create an additional future revenue stream by investing trust funds in foreign real estate, in Australia, the United States and neighbouring Pacific Islands. From the 1980s onward the Republic has navigated an ever-more erratic path around the conditionalities of its independence: economic dependence on a single source of revenue; a rapidly drafted constitutional structure that converted an imperial administration into a British parliamentary system, with little to no reference to the political structures of the Nauruan community; and fundamental tension between the concept of its international status as a sovereign state, and the forms of legal, economic and administrative relation under which the island is in fact governed. That disjuncture between international status and administrative form has existed since the declaration of German protection in 1888.

6.1 His Excellency Hammer DeRoburt, President of Nauru (right) and Queen Elizabeth II. Credit: John Shelley Collection/Avalon/Getty Images.

[8] Robert Trumbull, 'World's Richest Little Isle', *The New York Times*, 7 March 1982.

6.2 *Nauru* v. *Australia* and the Unresolved Question of Rehabilitation

Within international law, the history of imperial administration in Nauru is usually refracted through the case brought by Nauru against Australia in the International Court of Justice in 1989. In *Nauru* v. *Australia* ('Certain Phosphate Lands in Nauru'), the Republic sought final resolution of the rehabilitation issue that had remained outstanding following Nauru's Trusteeship Council-brokered transition to independence in 1968.[9] The Certain Phosphate Lands Case is now famous for being the first brought by a former dependent territory against its administrators for breach of trusteeship obligations, and for breach of general international legal principles of self-determination and permanent sovereignty over natural resources.[10] In 1987 the Nauruan government established the Commission of Inquiry into the Rehabilitation of Worked Out Phosphate Lands of Nauru. Christopher Weeramantry, then an international legal scholar at Monash University, was appointed as Chair, with the support of three Commissioners: senior Nauruan Gideon Degidoa, Australian mining executive Robert Challen and Australian legal academic Barry Connell. The Commission worked for two years to assess the viability of bringing a case for compensation in international law, with the research assistance of Deborah Cass and Antony Anghie. It examined the records of the League of Nations and the United Nations; the records of Britain, Australia and New Zealand; the available records of the British Phosphate Commission; and applicable laws – German, British, Australian and international – from the commencement of the mandate in 1920 through to independence in 1968.

In May 1989, twenty-one years after independence, Nauru lodged an Application Instituting Proceedings against Australia in the International Court of Justice, seeking resolution of the issues that remained outstanding in 1968. The first was liability for rehabilitation of lands on the central plateau of the island, mined out during the mandate and trusteeship periods. The second was the historical calculation of royalty payments as owed within the legal framework of phosphate exploitation established during the German protectorate period. Flowing from the original 1886 protectorate declaration, that framework imposed a European tripartite distribution of rights and obligations over

---

[9] Ratuva, 'Gap Between Global Thinking and Local Living', 241–68.
[10] Antony Anghie, '"The Heart of My Home": Colonialism, Environmental Damage and the Nauru Case' (1993) 34 *Harvard International Law Journal*, 445–506 at 447–8.

the island and its natural resources, establishing Nauruan property rights in land, the Reich's radical ownership over natural resources and the Jaluit Gesellschaft's mining concession.[11] The Phosphate Lands Case therein relied on foundational substrates of imperial law to hold Australia and the partner governments to account.[12]

In a section entitled 'Background to the Dispute', the Application summarised in fourteen paragraphs a version of the story presented in this book – a version which, to borrow from Craven, exemplified the 'use of history in international law'.[13] That account was expanded upon in Nauru's Memorial filed in 1990.[14] Running through the protectorate, mandate and trust territory periods, and ending with independence in 1968, the Memorial listed the principal legal instruments and events of war that have affected the international status of Nauru, and traced the claimed chain of title of Nauruan phosphate: the agreement between the Bismarckian Reich and the Jaluit Gesellschaft, which included a concession to mine guano; the transfer of the concession from the Jaluit Gesellschaft to the Pacific Phosphate Company under German administration; the occupation of Nauru by Australian forces in 1914; the creation of the Mandate for Nauru under Article 22 of the Covenant of the League, conferred upon 'His Britannic Majesty', frustrating Australia's gambit for annexation; the Nauru Island Agreement, in which Britain, Australia and New Zealand agreed on terms of the tripartite state monopoly over Nauruan phosphate and the 'provision for exercise of the said Mandate' by an Administrator with executive powers limited only by the right of the new British Phosphate Commissioners (BPC) to mine phosphate without administrative intervention; the occupation of Nauru by Japanese forces in 1942; the resumption of Australian administration immediately after the war, and accession to UN trusteeship oversight in the Trusteeship Agreement for Nauru of 1947; the creation under trusteeship of the Nauru Local Government Council and then the Legislative and Executive Councils of Nauru, and the limited power exercised by them; the resolutions of the Trusteeship Council and the General Assembly on the satisfaction of trusteeship

---

[11] Application Instituting Proceedings, *Nauru v. Australia* ('*Certain Phosphate Lands in Nauru*'), International Court of Justice, General List, 19 May 1989.
[12] See Chapter 1, Part 1. 5, 'Situating this Book in the Field'.
[13] Matthew Craven, 'Introduction: International Law and its Histories' in Matthew Craven, Malgosia Fitzmaurice and Maria Vogiatzi (eds.), *Time, History and International Law* (Leiden and Boston: Martinus Nijhoff Publishing, 2007), 7.
[14] Memorial of Nauru, *Certain Phosphate Lands in Nauru*, vol. 1, April 1990.

obligations; the Nauru Phosphate Industry Agreement of 1967; and the independence of Nauru in 1968.[15]

Nauru's Application rested on the submission that the 1967 Phosphate Industry Agreement did not include settlement of the issue of liability for rehabilitation, and that repeated attempts in the interim to secure an admission of liability from Australia had failed.[16] As such, Nauru requested a declaration of Australian liability for rehabilitation, and an order for restitution.[17] In its Preliminary Objections, Australia repeated its decades-old position that all claims relating to the administration of Nauru during the mandate and trusteeship periods were settled in the 1967 Agreement.[18] Australia also contested the jurisdiction of the Court and admissibility of the case on various grounds.[19] In its judgment on the Preliminary Objections, the ICJ held there was no evidence that the pre-independence Nauruan authorities had waived the claim for rehabilitation, and rejected Australia's alternative arguments.[20]

The case, however, never reached decision on the merits. Following the submission of exhaustive memorials, Australia and Nauru settled in August 1993 for a sum of AUD$107 million.[21] The 'Nauru Australia Compact of Settlement' (NACOS) provided that the settlement was made 'without prejudice to Australia's long-standing position that it bears no responsibility for the rehabilitation of the phosphate lands worked out before 1 July 1967'.[22] The financial settlement was to be paid by Australia in a series of upfront payments, with the balance paid in instalments over a twenty-year period – from 1993 to 2012. In exchange, Nauru agreed to discontinue its ICJ action, and indemnify Australia, New Zealand and the United Kingdom from any future action 'arising out of or concerning the administration of Nauru during the period of the Mandate or Trusteeship or the termination of that administration, as well as any

---

[15] Ibid., 4–12.
[16] Ibid., 24–8.
[17] Ibid., 30–2.
[18] Preliminary Objections, *Nauru* v. *Australia* ('*Phosphate Lands Case*') International Court of Justice, General List, December 1990.
[19] Ibid.
[20] *Nauru* v. *Australia* ('*Phosphate Lands Case*'), (*Judgment on the Preliminary Objections*) [1992] ICJ Rep 240, 247–50.
[21] *Nauru* v. *Australia* ('*Phosphate Lands Case*'), (*Order of 13 September 1993*) [1993] ICJ Rep 322.
[22] 'Agreement between Australia and the Republic of Nauru for the Settlement of the Case in the International Court of Justice concerning Certain Phosphate Lands in Nauru', *Nauru* v. *Australia* ('*Phosphate Lands Case*') [1993] ICJ Pleadings, vol. III, 511, art. 1 ('*NACOS*').

matter pertaining to phosphate mining, including matters pertaining to the British Phosphate Commissioners, their assets or the winding up thereof.[23] The NACOS further provided that the annual payment of AUD$2.5 million would be disposed of by agreement between the parties.[24] With that, the possibility of any further accounting in international law for Australia's conduct in Nauru from 1920 to 1968 was effectively to laid to rest.

In addition to the indemnification and reassertion of Australian control over disposition of funds, the longer term outcomes of the NACOS mitigate against regarding the Certain Phosphate Lands Case as any kind of break with imperial relations between the two states. In a revealing indication of the Commonwealth's attitude towards the case in general, NACOS payments were included in Australia's annual reports of development aid paid to Nauru from 1993 to 2012.[25] The Department of Foreign Affairs and Trade's categorisation of NACOS payments as 'aid' – as opposed to damages owed – is an almost poetic indictment of the post-independence paradigm of development.[26] Yet the potential poetry of this observation is blunted by an appreciation of the purposes to which NACOS funds were put. The Nauru Rehabilitation Corporation set up after the settlement has nominal responsibility for rehabilitation. Its primary function is now mining phosphate.[27] In 2012–13, at the end of the twenty-year settlement period, the Australian Department of Foreign Affairs and Trade produced its annual Aid Program Performance Report for Nauru, which reported that NACOS funds had been largely dedicated to phosphate mining, and that progress on rehabilitation had been

[23] Ibid., art. 3.
[24] Ibid., art. 1(d).
[25] Department of Foreign Affairs and Trade, 'Australian Agency for International Development Annual Reports 1998–2013' (Commonwealth of Australia); and Department of Foreign Affairs and Trade, 'Nauru Aid Program Performance Reports 2012–2016' (Commonwealth of Australia). From 2001 to 2007, payments made to Nauru in relation to offshore detention were described as 'additional aid' and 'development assistance' and included in total aid funds. See for example, Department of Foreign Affairs and Trade, 'AusAID Annual Report 2001–2002' (Commonwealth of Australia), 44, 54.
[26] On the continuities between imperialism and the post-independence development paradigm, see Balakrishnan Rajagopal, *International Law from Below: Development, Social Movements and Third World Resistance* (Cambridge: Cambridge University Press, 2003); and Sundhya Pahuja, *Decolonising International Law: Development, Economic Growth and the Politics of Universality* (Cambridge: Cambridge University Press, 2011).
[27] Republic of Nauru, 'National Sustainable Development Strategy 2005–2025' (Revised 2009) 24, available at adb.org/sites/default/files/linked-documents/cobp-nau-2016-2018-nsds.pdf.

'limited'.[28] The DFAT report sought to put a sheen on this irony, asserting that the long-term failure of the rehabilitation programme was mitigated by the short-term benefits to Nauru of continued mining:

> (t)his is balanced to some extent by the economic and social benefits provided by Nauru's more prosperous mining industry, including higher dividends for land owners and government and increased employment opportunities. Funds provided under NACOS represent a significant proportion of the operational budget for the Nauru Rehabilitation Corporation's work on mining and land rehabilitation. It is as yet unclear how the corporation plans to fund these operations once the final payment due under the NACOS treaty is made in 2013–14.[29]

6.3 After Independence: Deployments of Sovereign Status and the Future of Nauru

The Memorandum of Understanding that re-established Australia's 'Regional Processing Centre' in Nauru for the detention of asylum seekers who arrive in Australian waters by sea was signed in August 2012, the year of the final NACOS payment.[30] The Memorandum described its objective as 'combating People Smuggling and Irregular Migration in the Asia-Pacific region', reinscribing a much older Australian racial narrative established in the early twentieth century of the threat of 'Asian' immigration via the Pacific Islands.[31] The agreement provided that Australia would 'transfer' detained persons to Nauru and bear all costs related to the re-establishment of the Regional Processing Centres and assessment of asylum claims under the 1951 Refugee Convention. Nauru, for its part, would 'host' the Centres and undertake assessment of asylum claims.

The current Nauruan government was elected in 2013, just after the recommencement of offshore processing on the island, following three years of parliamentary deadlock.[32] The full extent of the

---

[28] Department of Foreign Affairs and Trade, 'Aid Program Performance Report 2012–13 Nauru', Commonwealth of Australia, 19.
[29] Ibid.
[30] 'Memorandum of Understanding between the Republic of Nauru and the Commonwealth of Australia, Relating to the Transfer to and Assessment of Persons in Nauru, and Related Issues', signed 29 August 2012.
[31] See Chapter 4, Part 4.3, 'Phosphate, Agriculture, Population and Race in the Australian Interwar Period'.
[32] Le Roy, Katy, 'Nauru's Parliament in Crisis' (2010) 91 *The Parliamentarian*, 240–3 at 242. Firth, 'Australia's Detention Centre', 289–90.

6.3 SOVEREIGN STATUS AND THE FUTURE OF NAURU 253

6.2 Satellite image of Australia's Regional Processing Centre, topside, Nauru. Credit: DigitalGlobe via Getty Images.

financial agreement between Australia and Nauru has never been made public. It is known, however, that direct payments to the Nauruan government include an initial per-head visa processing fee, and per-head per-month fees.[33] Between mid-2012 and mid-2015, at least AUD$27 million was paid to the Nauruan government for its role in Australia's offshore detention regime.[34] On DFAT's own statistics in its 'Aid Investment Plan' for Nauru, the Republic's revenue has increased by over 500 per cent due to the re-opening of the Regional Processing Centre, from AUD$20 million in 2010–11 to

[33] Firth, 'Australia's Detention Centre', 290.
[34] *Plaintiff M68/2015* v. *Commonwealth of Australia* (2016) 257 CLR 42.

AUD$115 million in 2015–16.[35] DFAT's assessment of the impact of this rapid increase in revenue to the government on the political situation in Nauru is an unabashed exercise in euphemism: 'Nauru continues to face capacity challenges to utilise those resources to achieve human development outcomes and build economic resilience in the medium to longer term'.[36]

This DFAT statement illustrates a broader Commonwealth practice of speaking around – and thus tacitly supporting – the Nauruan government's progressive abandonment of the rule of law since 2013, the year this project began. Since then, the Nauruan executive has sacked foreign judicial officers who have pursued official actions contrary to the executive's personal interests.[37] It has effectively prevented international media access to the island, moved to shut down civic debate over national policy and disposition of public funds, and suspended a group of opposition MPs, revoking their passports and pursuing heavy criminal penalties for political protest.[38] It has also severed the right of appeal to the High Court of Australia in the 1968 Constitution, seemingly to avoid the constitutionality of its actions being reviewed by independent judicial officers. The Nauruan executive defends all of these actions as legitimate exercises of Nauru's sovereignty that have brought political stability and economic growth to the country after a decade of escalating parliamentary crisis.[39] For opposition MPs and their supporters, those actions constitute blatant abuses of executive power, and a progressive slide towards autocracy.[40] The Australian government has responded with a mantra of non-interference in the domestic affairs of a sovereign state, all the whilst

---

[35] Department of Foreign Affairs and Trade, 'Aid Investment Plan: Nauru 2015–16 to 2018–19', Commonwealth of Australia, 2.

[36] Ibid.

[37] Firth, 'Australia's Detention Centre', 291 et seq.; Melissa Clarke, 'Nauru Expels Australian Magistrate Peter Law, Bars Chief Justice Geoffrey Eames from Returning to Country', Australian Broadcasting Corporation, 20 January 2014.

[38] Firth, 'Australia's Detention Centre', 291 et seq.; Australian Associated Press, 'Nauru Suspends Two More Opposition MPs Ahead of Budget Hand Down', *The Guardian*, 5 June 2014.

[39] Republic of Nauru Government Information Office, 'Nauru Government Sets the Record Straight' (media release, 25 January 2014); 'Supreme Court has Deemed Suspension of MPs Lawful' (media release, 11 December 2014); 'Opposition False Claims Show Election Eve Desperation' (media release, 7 July 2016).

[40] Eleanor Ainge Roy, 'Nauru Opposition MP Secretly Granted NZ Citizenship Flees to Wellington', *The Guardian*, 12 July 2016. Richard Ewart, 'Nauru Officials Accused of 'Persecutory Conduct' as Judge Throws Out Long-Running Protest Case', *Australian Broadcasting Corporation*, 14 September 2018. Stephen Lawrence and Felicity Graham, 'Former President of Nauru Pursued to the Last', *The Australian*, 15 May 2019.

providing around 30 per cent of the Republic's revenue in direct payments related to offshore processing.[41] This position has left the Australian government open to the charge of supporting increasing autocracy in Nauru.[42] The current situation limits the potential for successful legal challenge to Australia's offshore detention regime and effectively prevents media scrutiny of that regime in practice.

At the time of writing, Australia's refugee processing regime is still in operation in Nauru, although the number of asylum seekers detained on the island has been reducing steadily since 2016. Despite serious logistical and political difficulties, legal challenges to the offshore processing regime have been mounted on a number of fronts. In international law, the argument that the regime breaches Australia's obligations as a signatory to the Refugee Convention continues to be rejected by the government, despite six years of repeated findings to the contrary by the United Nations High Commission for Refugees.[43] In Australian constitutional law, the strongest challenge to the regime was brought in 2016, in the case of *Plaintiff M68* v. *Minister for Immigration and Border Protection*. In *Plaintiff M68*, a Bangladeshi asylum seeker submitted that the Australian executive's entry into the 2012 Memorandum of Understanding lacked a valid legislative basis, as did its private contractual arrangements with the major corporate contractor managing the regime, Transfield (now Broadspectrum).[44] The plaintiff further submitted that her detention on Nauru fell outside the Australian executive's constitutional power to detain non-citizens, and that the High Court had original jurisdiction to review that detention. The Minister and second respondent Transfield submitted that the executive's actions were valid under legislative amendments to Australia's byzantine Migration Act 1958 – the Act that replaced the Immigration Restriction Act of 1901, which formally inaugurated the White Australia policy. They further argued that the Australian government did not detain the plaintiff on Nauru, because any such detention was attributable to the Nauruan government under its own sovereign jurisdiction, and therefore fell outside the jurisdiction of the Australian High Court. The High Court itself

---

[41] Roland Rajah, 'Securing Sustainability: Nauru's New Intergenerational Trust Fund and Beyond', Asian Development Bank (2017), 6.
[42] Commonwealth of Australia, Foreign Policy White Paper (2017), 2.
[43] United Nations High Commissioner for Refugees, 'United Nations Observations on Australia's Transfer Arrangements with Nauru and Papua New Guinea (2012-present)' (2018) available at www.unhcr.org/en-au/5bb364987.pdf.
[44] *Plaintiff M68/2015* v. *Minister for Immigration and Border Protection*.

upheld the validity of the regime. The majority accepted the respondents' arguments that despite being wholly designed and funded by the Commonwealth, the regime established via the Memorandum fell wholly under Nauruan sovereign jurisdiction.[45]

Within fifty years of Nauru's accession to political independence, then, Australia has devised a means of refiguring Nauruan sovereignty as a legal justification for a new era of imperial relation. But the Nauruan government, too, has learned to leverage its international status for its own interests, which do not always align with Australia's. In an era of renewed geopolitical competition in the Pacific, Australia is not the only erstwhile empire with which the Republic has quid pro quo arrangements. Under its Non-Project Aid Program, Japan supplies Nauru with the diesel fuel required to run the island's electricity plant, and Nauru votes with Japan in the International Whaling Commission.[46] In 2009 Nauru recognised the independence of the Georgian provinces of Abkhazia and South Ossetia, announcing at the same time an estimated US$50 million aid deal with the Russian Federation.[47] Nauru maintains a shifting web of diplomatic alliances, including with the Republic of China (Taiwan) and the Republic of Cuba. Furthermore, the Nauru Local Government Council's experience with the United Nations Trusteeship Council throughout the 1950s and 1960s laid the foundations for a culture of strategic engagement with international institutions. In 2015 Nauru voted with Israel and the United States in the United Nations against a set of resolutions protecting the non-member observer status of Palestine.[48]

After the decline in phosphate revenue and the draining of trust funds, international status itself has become the resource the Republic seeks to rent. The ICJ case against Australia is only one of the revenue

---

[45] One dissenting judge, Justice Gordon held that the arrangement was invalid, finding that arrangement was not supported by a head of executive power, and that the Commonwealth had by its acts, conduct and agents effectively detained the plaintiff. *Plaintiff M68/2015*, Gordon J. (dissent).

[46] 'Early Win for Anti-Whaling Lobby at IWC', *Australian Broadcasting Corporation*, 20 June 2005; 'Japan "Bullying" Countries to Back Whaling', *Sydney Morning Herald*, 20 June 2005.

[47] Luke Harding, 'Tiny Nauru Struts World Stage by Recognising Breakaway Republics', *The Guardian*, 15 December 2009. 'Tiny Nauru Recognises Georgia's Other Rebel Enclave', *Reuters*, 16 December 2009.

[48] United Nations, 'Traditional Voting Pattern reflected in General Assembly's Adoption of Drafts on Question of Palestine, Broader Middle East Issues' (media release, 24 November 2015).

sources the Republic has pursued. In the early 1990s the Nauruan government enacted legislation to attract offshore financial services, quickly becoming a haven for tax avoidance and money laundering. Nauru was blacklisted by the United States and the OECD for its lack of action against organised crime. The Russian Central Bank later reported that US$92 billion was laundered through Nauru from the USSR in the two years following its collapse.[49] The initial phase of Australia's 'Pacific Solution' of offshore processing began in September 2001, and ran until 2007. Increased international interest in Nauru's economic precarity over this period contributed to the establishment with UNDP funding of the Constitutional Review Commission in 2004, the year the Nauru Phosphate Royalties Trust went into receivership. In 1990 when the ICJ case against Australia was underway, the NPRT had an estimated value of $1.5 billion.[50] By 2004 its value had dropped to $100 million. Parables of corruption and mismanagement became staples in media coverage of the island's post-independence trajectory.

How Nauru will survive both economically and politically when Australia's offshore detention regime is inevitably shut down remains an open question at the time of writing. In 2005 the Republic prepared a National Sustainable Development Strategy, which identified rehabilitation of the island's central plateau, commercialisation of fish stocks, the establishment of a new national Trust Fund and improved access for Nauruans to overseas labour markets as imperative to the island's economic future. Nauru subsequently expanded its commercial fishery licensing programme. Revenue raised from licence fees now comprises around a third of the Republic's revenue base. A new Nauru Trust Fund was established in 2014, with the support of the Asian Development Bank, Australia and Taiwan.[51] Management of the new Fund is to be governed by an Advisory Committee comprising representatives of the Nauruan, Australian and Taiwanese governments. But strict provisions around the Trust Fund, designed to avert the fate of the NPRT, restrict use of the Fund by the incumbent government to address any short-term liquidity problems.

---

[49] *Washington Post*, 'Russians Use Tiny Island to Hide Billions', *Washington Post*, 28 October 1999; and Jack Hitt, 'The Billon-Dollar Shack', *New York Times Magazine*, 10 December 2000.
[50] Rajah, 'Securing Sustainability', 5.
[51] Ibid.

6.3 DeepGreen CEO Gerard Barron and Kenyan delegate Pauline Mcharo, International Seabed Authority, February 2019. Credit: IISD/Diego Noguera (enb.iisd.org/oceans/isa/2019-1/26feb.html).

Nauru's economic vulnerability has repeatedly attracted new corporate suitors looking to leverage the island's international status – and its economic precarity – to their own ends. In late July 2018 the Republic announced that it had entered into a 'partnership' with mining company DeepGreen Metals, to make use of an exploration licence granted by the International Seabed Authority (ISA) for an area covering around 75,000 square kilometres of seabed in the Clarion-Clipperton Zone between Hawai'i and Mexico.[52] Under the ISA regime contained in Chapter XI of the United Nations Convention on the Law of the Sea, companies must partner with 'sponsoring States' to obtain exploration licences for the international seabed.[53] At the ISA Council meeting in March 2019, DeepGreen CEO Gerard Barron addressed the meeting

---

[52] Government of the Republic of Nauru, 'Nauru Partners with Deep Sea Mining Company on Quest for Sustainable Future' (media release, 28 July 2018). Isabel Feichtner, 'Mining for Humanity in the Deep Sea and Outer Space: The Role of Small States and International Law in the Extraterritorial Expansion of Extraction' (2019) 32 *European Journal of International Law*, 255–74.

[53] Surabhi Ranganathan, 'Ocean Floor Grab: International Law and the Making of an Extractive Imaginary' (2019) 30 *European Journal of International Law*, 573–600.

from Nauru's chair.[54] One hundred and thirty years after the establishment of a German company protectorate in Nauru on the request of the Jaluit Gesellschaft, and the subsequent shifts in Nauru's international status from protectorate to mandate to trust territory to sovereign state, the conflation of public and private authority around which the administrative form of Nauru accreted over the long twentieth century continues to find new expression, now couched in contemporary concepts of partnership and development.

6.4 Conclusion

This book began with the premise that the Republic of Nauru is not anomalous to the contemporary international order but deeply symptomatic of it. Drawing on theories of jurisdiction and Weber's account of bureaucratisation, it has placed the administration of Nauru at the centre of a critical redescription of the transition from imperial ordering of the late nineteenth century through to the international ordering of the twentieth century. Tracing four shifts in Nauru's international status – from the declaration of German protectorate status in 1888, to C Mandate of the League of Nations in 1920, to UN trust territory in 1947, to sovereign state in 1968 – it has mapped those shifts onto corresponding changes in administrative form. The argument that emerges from this redescription is that as international status shifts, imperial form accretes: as Nauru's status shifted across the late nineteenth and twentieth centuries, the administrative form through which the island was governed underwent a process of internal bureaucratisation and external restatement according to the prevailing concepts of the period. The final shift to sovereign status in 1968 is therein refigured not as a rupture with that history of imperial administration but as a stage in the bureaucratisation of an administrative form instantiated in the late nineteenth century to facilitate the extraction of resources from the island and its people. The argument contributes to a vibrant post-Marxist tradition of critical engagement with the imperial legacies of international law, a tradition that has long challenged the presumption that sovereign territorial statehood is the natural or final vehicle for decolonisation. To argue that administrative form itself – often normalised as necessary or neutral, but which for Weber was as pivotal to European

---

[54] Gerard Barron, CEO and Chairman of DeepGreen Metals, 'Address to ISA Council', 27 February 2019.

modernity as capital accumulation and democratisation – realises and entrenches imperial relations, is not to suggest that the attainment of sovereign status, whether for Nauru or for any post-imperial or post-colonial state, is a hollow achievement. Rather, it suggests that recognition of sovereign status in international law can only mark a beginning of decolonisation, and not an end. The dismantling of imperial forms of relation – administrative and economic, public and private – constitutes a distinct field of post-independence challenges.

This argument emphasises the distinction between the history of international law as a mode of conceptual reasoning or an ideal framework for governing the world, and the histories of international law as a set of administrative forms and practices established and maintained in place. Fixing the administration of Nauru at the centre of an account of the transition from imperialism to international law reconfigures what might otherwise seem a familiar story in an unfamiliar way. Habitually marginalised aspects of that transition are thereby recovered, and all point towards further areas of research. The first is the legacy of German imperialism in the Pacific, for the peoples and places that came under German rule, and for the legal and geographical contours of imperial competition that came to structure the region over the twentieth century. This book offers a new engagement with German imperialism of the late nineteenth century, and in particular with the relationship between the old Hanseatic firms and the imperial policies of the new Reich, and the relationship between German commercial presence in the Pacific and the federation movement in the Australasian colonies.

A second aspect of the transition from imperial to international ordering that this book recasts is the slow disintegration of the British empire. Focus is pulled towards the changing relationship between the British self-governing Dominions and the Imperial government over the late nineteenth and early twentieth centuries. Chapters 2 and 3 reveal the extent to which Australian claims for greater autonomy and control over external affairs and defence powers were closely related to sub-imperial aspirations for dominance in the Pacific. Drawing on the Monroe Doctrine, those aspirations conflated late nineteenth and early twentieth-century ideologies of white supremacy and economic protectionism. Along with the Union of South Africa, the Commonwealth's pursuit of that aspiration during the Paris Peace Conference was instrumental both in the subsequent recognition of its international personality, and in the creation of the C Mandate.

6.4 CONCLUSION

A third aspect of the transition from imperial to international ordering emphasised by the focus on Nauru is the significance of phosphate in the development of the world economy in the later nineteenth and early twentieth centuries. This account reinstates the place of phosphate, not only at the heart of the island itself, but also as a geological phenomenon and a finite global natural resource. The commodification of phosphate had a significant impact not only on modes of imperial expansion into the Pacific, but also on the rapid industrialisation of agricultural production across the world. The use of phosphate as a fertiliser dramatically altered patterns of food production and land use over the nineteenth and twentieth centuries – with often devastating impact on the landscapes from which it is removed, and on the ecosystems in which it has been extensively used. It is not only the Nauruan natural environment that has been irrevocably altered by the aggressive mining practices of the BPC. Subsidised access to superphosphate, insulated entirely from world price fluctuations for over sixty years, facilitated the rapid development of Australia's wheat, sugar and dairy industries in regions of the continent that would otherwise not have been arable. The long-term effects of the exploitation of Nauruan phosphate on Australian land-use practices could constitute an additional chapter of the story told in this book, as could the importance of phosphate to colonial economies more generally.[55]

Whatever it might reveal of the transition from imperial to international ordering from the late nineteenth through to the later twentieth century, the account this book has offered is a highly partial one, constructed by an Australian scholar from pre-independence imperial sources. In tracing the way that still-evolving imperial projects have worked through forms of law and administration that might otherwise be presumed as neutral or inevitable, the book is a counterbalance to external perspectives that locate the origins of the Republic's notorious post-independence trajectory with the Nauruan community, rather than with the empires, old and new, that have sought to exploit the island for their own purposes. Retracing those imperial continuities into the present is a small but necessary step towards dismantling them. That task remains as urgent now as it was in 1968.

---

[55] Stuart White and Dana Cordell, 'Peak Phosphorus: Clarifying the Key Issues of a Vigorous Debate about Long-Term Phosphorus Security' (2011) 3(10) *Sustainability*, 2027–49.

BIBLIOGRAPHY

Books and Articles

Abrams, Lynn, *Bismarck and the German Empire 1871–1918*, 2nd ed. (London and New York: Routledge, 2006)

Alam, Shawkat, Atapattu, Sumudu, Gonzalez, Carmen G., and Razzaque, Jona (eds.), *International Environmental Law and the Global South* (Cambridge: Cambridge University Press, 2015)

Alatas, Syed Hussein, *The Myth of the Lazy Native* (London: Frank Cass, 1977)

Alford, Charles J., *Mining Law of the British Empire* (Charles Griffin and Company, 1906)

Anderson, Kevin B., *Marx at the Margins: On Nationalism, Ethnicity and Non-Western Societies* (Chicago: University of Chicago Press, 2016)

Anghie, Antony, *Imperialism, Sovereignty and the Making of International Law* (Cambridge: Cambridge University Press, 2005)

Anghie, Antony, '"The Heart of My Home": Colonialism, Environmental Damage and the Nauru Case' (1993) 34 *Harvard International Law Journal*, 445–506

Anghie, Antony, 'Race, Self-Determination and Australian Empire' (2019) 19 *Melbourne Journal of International Law*, 1–39

Anson, Sir William Reynell, *The Law and Custom of the Constitution*, vol. 2 (Oxford: Clarendon Press, 1886)

Arista, Noelani, *The Kingdom and the Republic: Sovereign Hawai'i and the Early United States* (Pennsylvania: University of Pennsylvania Press, 2018)

Aydelotte, William Osgood, *Bismarck and British Colonial Policy: The Problem of South West Africa 1883–1885*, 2nd ed. (London: Russell and Russell, 1970)

Baker, P. J. Noel, *The Present Juridical Status of the British Dominions in International Law* (New York: Longmans, Green and Co, 1929)

Barbour, Charles and Pavlich, George (eds.), *After Sovereignty: On the Question of Political Beginnings* (London: Routledge Cavendish, 2011)

Bashford, Alison, *Global Population: History, Geopolitics, and Life on Earth* (New York: Columbia University Press, 2014)

Bateson, Charles, *The Convict Ships 1787-1868*, 2nd ed. (Glasgow: Brown, Son and Ferguson, 1969)
Baty, Thomas, 'Protectorates and Mandates' (1922) 2 *British Yearbook of International Law*, 109-21
Bean, C. E. W. (ed.), *Official History of Australia in the War 1914-1918*, 1941 ed. (Canberra: Australian War Memorial, 1941)
Bedjaoui, Mohammed, *Towards a New International Economic Order* (New York and London: UNESCO, 1979)
Benton, Lauren and Ross, Richard J. (eds.), *Legal Pluralism and Empires, 1500-1850* (New York: New York University Press, 2013)
Benton, Lauren, *A Search for Sovereignty: Law and Geography in European Empires 1400-1900* (Cambridge: Cambridge University Press, 2010)
Billings, Peter, 'Irregular Maritime Migration and the Pacific Solution Mark II: Back to the Future for Refugee Law and Policy in Australia' (2013) 20 *International Journal on Minority and Group Rights*, 279-306
Blakeslee, George H., 'The Mandates of the Pacific' (September 1922) *Foreign Affairs* 98-115
Boers, P. C. M., Cappenberg, Th E., and Raaphorst, W. (eds.), *Proceedings of the Third International Workshop on Phosphorus in Sediments* (Netherlands: Springer Netherlands, 1993)
Bollard, A. E., 'The Financial Adventures of J C Godeffroy and Son in the Pacific' (1981) 16 *Journal of Pacific History*, 3-19
Bolling, John Randolph, *Chronology of Woodrow Wilson* (New York: Frederick A. Stokes Company, 1927)
Bolton, Geoffrey, *Paul Hasluck: A Life* (Crawley: UWA Publishing, 2014)
Brailsford, Henry Noel, *A League of Nations* (London: Headley Bros, 1917)
Brandenburg, Erich, *From Bismarck to the World War: A History of German Foreign Policy 1870-1914*, trans. Annie Elizabeth Adams (Oxford: Oxford University Press, 1927)
Breuning, E. C. M. and Chamberlain, Muriel Evelyn, *Studies in German Thought and History*, 3rd ed. (New York: Edwin Mellen Press, 1998)
Brookes, Jean Ingram, *International Rivalry in the Pacific Islands 1800-1875* (Berkeley: University of California Press, 1941)
Bruun, Hans Henrik and Whimster, Sam (eds.), *Max Weber: Collected Methodological Writings* (London: Routledge, 2012)
Burkman, Thomas W. *Japan and the League of Nations: Empire and World Order 1914-1938* (Honolulu: University of Hawai'i Press, 2008)
Burnett, Christina Duffy, 'The Edges of Empire and the Limits of Sovereignty: American Guano Islands' (2005) 57 *American Quarterly*, 779-803
Busch, Moritz, *Bismarck: Some Secret Pages of His History* (London: Macmillan, 1898)
Carey, Jane and McLisky, Claire (eds.), *Creating White Australia* (Sydney: University of Sydney Press, 2009)

Carroll, E. Malcolm, *Germany and the Great Powers 1866-1914: A Study in Public Opinion and Foreign Policy* (London: Archon Books, 1966)

Carroll, Faye, *South West Africa and the United Nations* (Lexington: University Press of Kentucky, 1967)

Carr-Saunders, Alexander Morris, *The Population Problem: A Study in Human Evolution* (Oxford: Clarendon Press, 1922)

Cecil, Robert, *A Great Experiment: An Autobiography of Viscount Cecil* (London: Jonathan Cape, 1941)

Chakrabarty, Dipesh, *Provincialising Europe: Postcolonial Thought and Historical Difference*, 2nd ed. (Princeton: Princeton University Press, 2008)

Chambers, Don, *'Boss' Hurst of Geelong and Nauru* (Melbourne: Hyland House, 1994)

Charteris, A. H., 'The Mandate over Nauru Island' (1923-1924) 4 *British Yearbook of International Law*, 137-52

Chauvel, Richard, *Essays on West Papua: Volume One* (Working Paper Series 120, Monash University, 2003)

Chimni, B. S., 'Capitalism, Imperialism, and International Law in the Twenty-First Century' (2012) 14 *Oregon Review of International Law*, 17-46

Chimni, B. S., 'Third World Approaches to International Law: A Manifesto' (2006) 8 *International Community Law Review*, 3-27

Chowdhuri, R. N., *International Mandates and Trusteeship Systems: A Comparative Study* (The Hague: Martinus Nijhoff, 1955)

Clark, Dymphna and Sack, Peter (eds.), *German New Guinea: The Annual Reports* (Canberra: Australian National University Press, 1979)

Cockram, Gail-Maryse, *South West African Mandate* (Cape Town: Juta and Company Limited, 1976)

Cochrane, Glynn, *Max Weber's Vision for Bureaucracy* (St Lucia: Palgrave Macmillan, 2018)

Colvin, Ian D., *The Germans in England 1066-1598* (London: The National Review, 1915)

Commonwealth Scientific and Industrial Research Office, *The Australian Environment*, 3rd ed. (Melbourne: Melbourne University Press, 1960)

Connell, John, 'Nauru: The First Failed Pacific State?' (2006) 95 *The Round Table*, 47-63

Conrad, Sebastian, *German Colonialism: A Short History* (Cambridge: Cambridge University Press, 2012)

Corris, Peter, '"White Australia" in Action: The Repatriation of Pacific Islanders from Queensland' (1972) 15 *Historical Studies*, 237-50

Corris, Peter, '"Blackbirding" in New Guinea Waters, 1883-84: An Episode in the Queensland Labour Trade' (1968) 3 *Journal of Pacific History*, 85-105

Council of the League of Nations, 'The Mandates Question' (Jan-Feb 1921) 2 *League of Nations Official Journal*, 84-95

Council of the League of Nations, '*Proces-Verbal* of the First Meeting of the Council of the League of Nations' (Feb 1920) 1 *League of Nations Official Journal*, 1–27

Craven, Matthew, 'Between Law and History: The Berlin Conference of 1884–1885 and the Logic of Free Trade' (2015) 3 *London Review of International Law*, 31–59

Craven, Matthew, Fitzmaurice, Malgosia and Vogiatzi, Maria (eds.), *Time, History and International Law* (Leiden and Boston: Martinus Nijhoff Publishing, 2007)

Craven, Matthew, 'What Happened to Unequal Treaties? The Continuities of Informal Empire' (2005) 74 *Nordic Journal of International Law*, 335–82

Crawford, James, *The Creation of States in International Law*, 2nd ed. (Oxford: Oxford University Press, 2007)

Crawford, James, Koroma, Abdul G., Pellet, Alain & Mahmoudi, Said, *The International Legal Order: Current Needs and Possible Responses. Essays in Honour of Djamchid Momtaz* (Leiden and Boston: Brill Nijhoff, 2017)

Cumpston, I. M., 'Sir Arthur Gordon and the Introduction of Indians into the Pacific: The West Indian System in Fiji' (1956) 25 *Pacific Historical Review*, 369–88

Cushman, Gregory T., *Guano and the Opening of the Pacific World: A Global Ecological History* (Cambridge: Cambridge University Press, 2013)

d'Aspremont, Jean and Singh, Sahib (eds.), *Concepts for International Law: Contributions to Disciplinary Thought* (UK: Edward Elgar Publishing, 2019)

Dawson, Robert MacGregor (ed.), *The Development of Dominion Status 1900–1936* (Oxford: Oxford University Press, 1937)

Denoon, Donald with Firth, Stewart, Linnekin, Jocelyn, Meleisea, Malama and Nero, Karen (eds.), *Cambridge History of the Pacific Islanders* (Cambridge: Cambridge University Press, 2008)

Dobell, Lauren, *Swapo's Struggle for Namibia, 1960–1991: War by Other Means*, 2nd ed. (Basel: P. Schlettwein Publishing, 2000)

Dollinger, Phillippe, *The German Hansa* (London: Routledge, 1999)

Dorsett, Shaunnagh and Hunter, Ian (eds.), *Law and Politics in British Colonial Thought: Transposition of Empire* (Basingstoke: Palgrave Macmillan, 2010)

Dorsett, Shaunnagh, and McVeigh, Shaun, *Jurisdiction* (Abingdon and New York: Routledge, 2012)

Drayton, Richard and Motadel, David, 'Discussion: The Futures of Global History' (2018) 13 *Journal of Global History*, 1–21

Dunbabin, Thomas, *The Making of Australasia: A Brief History of the Origin and Development of the British Dominions in the South Pacific* (London: A. & C. Black Ltd, 1922)

Duve, Thomas (ed.), *Entanglements in Legal History: Conceptual Approaches* (Frankfurt: Max Planck Institute for European Legal History, 2014)

Dziedzic, Anna, 'The Use of Foreign Judges on Courts of Constitutional Jurisdiction in Pacific Island States' (2018), PhD thesis, University of Melbourne
East, Edward, *Mankind at the Crossroads* (New York: Scribners, 1923)
El-Ayouty, Yassin, *The United Nations and Decolonization: The Role of Afro-Asia* (The Hague: Martinus Nijhoff, 1971)
Elden, Stuart, *The Birth of Territory* (Chicago: Chicago University Press, 2013)
Ellis, Albert, *Mid-Pacific Outposts* (Auckland: Brown and Stewart Limited, 1946)
Ellis, Albert F., *Ocean Island and Nauru: Their Story* (Sydney: Angus and Robertson, 1935)
Elmslie, Jim, Webb-Gannon, Camilla and King, Peter, *Anatomy of an Occupation: The Indonesian Military in West Papua* (Sydney: West Papua Project at the Centre for Peace and Conflict Studies, 2011)
Eric White Associates, *Republic of Nauru: Independence Day, January 31, 1968* (Sydney and Melbourne Publishing Co Pty Ltd, 1968)
Eslava, Luis, Fakhri, Michael and Nesiah, Vasuki (eds.), *Bandung, Global History and International Law: Critical Pasts and Pending Futures* (Cambridge: Cambridge University Press, 2017)
Evans, Luther Harris, 'Are "C" Mandates Veiled Annexations?' (1927) 7 *Southwestern Political and Social Science Quarterly*, 381–400
Evatt, H. V., *The British Dominions as Mandatories* (Melbourne: Melbourne University Press, 1934)
Fabricius, Wilhelm, *Nauru 1888–1900: An Account in German and English Based on Official Records of the Colonial Section of the German Foreign Office Held by the Deutsches Zentralarchiv in Potsdam*, trans. Dymphna Clark and Stewart Firth (Canberra: Research School of Pacific Studies, Australian National University, 1992)
Fassbender, Bardo and Peters, Anne (eds.), *Oxford Handbook of the History of International Law* (Oxford: Oxford University Press, 2012)
Feichtner, Isabel, 'Mining for Humanity in the Deep Sea and Outer Space: The Role of Small States and International Law in the Extraterritorial Expansion of Extraction' (2019) 32 *European Journal of International Law*, 255–74
Fenwick, Charles G., *Wardship in International Law* (Washington, DC: Government Printers Office, 1919)
Feuchtwanger, Edgar, *Bismarck: A Political History*, 2nd ed. (London and New York: Routledge, 2014)
Firth, Stewart, 'German Firms in the Western Pacific Islands 1857–1914' (1973) 8 *Journal of Pacific History*, 10–28
Firth, Stewart, 'German Labour Policy in Nauru and Angaur 1906–1914' (1978) 13 *Journal of Pacific History*, 36–52
Firth, Stewart, *New Guinea under the Germans* (Melbourne: Melbourne University Press, 1983)

Fitzhardinge, L. F., 'Hughes, Borden and Dominion Representation at the Paris Peace Conference' (1968) 49 *Canadian Historical Review*, 160-9

Fitzhardinge, L. F., *William Morris Hughes: A Political Biography* (Sydney: Angus and Robertson, 1964)

Fitzmaurice, Andrew, 'Context in the History of International Law' (2018) 20 *Journal of the History of International Law*, 5-30

Fitzmaurice, Andrew, *Sovereignty, Property and Empire, 1500-2000* (Cambridge: Cambridge University Press, 2014)

Fitzpatrick, Peter, *Law and State in Papua New Guinea* (London and New York: Academic Press, 1980)

Ford, Lisa and Rowse, Tim (eds.), *Between Indigenous and Settler Governance* (United States and Canada: Routledge, 2013)

Förster, Stig, Mommsen, Wolfgang J. and Robinson, Ronald (eds.), *Bismarck, Europe, and Africa: The Berlin Africa Conference 1884-1885 and the Onset of Partition* (Oxford: Oxford University Press, 1988)

Foucault, Michel, *The Order of Things: An Archaeology of the Human Sciences*, reissue ed. (London: Vintage Books, 1994)

Friedmann, Wolfgang, 'The Jurisprudential Implications of the South West Africa Case' (1967) 6 *Columbia Journal of Transnational Law*, 1-16

Galbraith, John S., *Crown and Charter: The Early Years of the British South Africa Company* (London: University of California Press, 1977)

Gann, L. H., and Duignan, Peter, *The Rulers of German Africa 1884-1914* (Stanford: Stanford University Press, 1977)

Gathii, James Thuo, 'TWAIL: A Brief History of its Origins, Its Decentralized Network, and a Tentative Bibliography' (2011) 3 *Trade, Law and Development*, 26-64

Gerth, H. H., and Mills, C. Wright (eds.), *From Max Weber: Essays in Sociology* (Abingdon and New York: Routledge, 2009)

Gevers, Christopher, 'An Intellectual History of Pan-Africanism and International Law', PhD thesis in progress at Melbourne Law School

Ghandour, Zeina B., *A Discourse on Domination in Mandate Palestine: Imperialism, Property and Insurgency* (London: Routledge, 2009)

Gilchrist, Huntington, 'The Japanese Islands: Annexation or Trusteeship?' (1944) 22 *Foreign Affairs*, 635-42

Gill, T. D., *South West Africa and the Sacred Trust 1919-1972* (The Hague: TMC Asser Instituut, 1984)

Giordani, Paolo, *The German Colonial Empire: Its Beginning and Ending*, trans. Gustavus W. Hamilton (London: G Bell and Sons, 1916)

Goldsworthy, David, 'British Territories and Australian Mini-Imperialism in the 1950s' (1995) 41 *Australian Journal of Politics and History*, 356-72.

Gong, Gerrit, *The Standard of 'Civilization' in International Society* (Oxford: Oxford University Press, 1984)

Gribetz, Louis J., *The Case for the Jews: An Interpretation of their Rights under the Balfour Declaration and the Mandate for Palestine* (New York: Block Publishing Company, 1930)

Gross, Ernest A. 'The South West Africa Case: What Happened?' (October 1966) *Foreign Affairs* 36

Grotke, Kelly L. and Prutsch, Markus J. (eds.), *Constitutionalism, Legitimacy and Power: Nineteenth Century Experiences* (Oxford: Oxford University Press, 2014)

Grove, Richard, *Green Imperialism: Colonial Expansion, Tropical Island Edens and the Origins of Environmentalism, 1600–1860* (Cambridge: Cambridge University Press, 1996)

Grovogui, Siba N'Zatioula, *Sovereigns, Quasi Sovereigns, and Africans: Race and Self-Determination in International Law* (Minneapolis: University of Minnesota Press, 1996)

Hage, Ghassan *White Nation: Fantasies of White Supremacy in a Multicultural Society* (NSW: Pluto Press, 1998)

Hall, H. Duncan, *Mandates, Dependencies and Trusteeship* (Stevens & Sons Limited, 1948)

Hall, H. Duncan, *The British Commonwealth of Nations: A Study of its Past and Future Developments* (London: Methuen & Co Ltd, 1920)

Hambruch, Paul, *Nauru: Ergebnisse der Südsee-Expedition, 1908–1910* (Hamburg: L. Friedrichsen, 1914)

Hamerow, Theodore S., 'Guilt, Redemption and Writing German History' (1983) 88 *The American Historical Review*, 53–72

Hamerow, Theodore S. (ed.), *The Age of Bismarck: Documents and Interpretations* (New York: Harper & Row, 1973)

Hamerow, Theodore S., *Social Foundations of German Unification 1858–1871, Volume I: Ideas and Institutions* (Princeton: Princeton University Press, 1969)

Harreld, Donald J. (ed.), *Companion to the Hanseatic League* (Leiden: Brill, 2015)

Harris Foundation, *Great Britain and the Dominions* (Chicago: Chicago University Press, 1928)

Hartmann, Wolfram, 'Making South West Africa German? Attempting Imperial, Juridical, Colonial, Conjugal and Moral Order' (2007) 2 *Journal of Namibian Studies* 51

Haskins, Charles Homer, *Some Problems of the Peace Conference* (Cambridge, MA: Harvard University Press, 1920)

Hasluck, Paul, *Shades of Darkness: Aboriginal Affairs 1925–1965* (Melbourne University Press, 1988)

Hattori, Anne Perez, 'Textbook Tells: Gender, Race, and Decolonizing Guam History Textbooks in the 21st Century' (2018) 14 *AlterNative: An International Journal of Indigenous Peoples*, 173–84

Headlam, James Wycliffe, *Bismarck and the Foundation of the German Empire* (New York: G. P. Putnam's Sons, 1899)

Hempenstall, Peter J., *Pacific Islanders under German Rule: A Study in the Meaning of Colonial Resistance* (Canberra: Australian National University Press, 1978)

Henderson, Mary, *Origins of Modern German Colonialism* (New York: Howard Fertig, 1974)

Henderson, W. O., *The German Colonial Empire 1884-1919* (London: Frank Cass & Co, 1993)

Hennis, Wilhelm, *Max Weber's Central Question*, trans Keith Tribe, 2nd ed. (Newbury: Threshold Press, 2000)

Hezel, Francis X. *Strangers in Their Own Land: A Century of Colonial Rule in the Caroline and Marshall Islands* (Honolulu: University of Hawai'i Press, 1995)

Hickford, Mark, 'Sovereignties Viewed Through Anomalies: A Search for Sovereignty. Law and Geography in European Empires 1400-1900, Lauren Benton' (2013) 15 *Journal of the History of International Law*, 103-15

Hiery, Hermann, *The Neglected War: The German South Pacific and the Influence of World War I* (Honolulu: University of Hawai'i Press, 1995)

Hobsbawm, Eric, *The Age of Empire: 1875-1914* (London: Weidenfeld and Nicolson, 1987)

Hobson, John Atkinson, *Towards International Government* (G. Allen and Unwin, 1915)

Hohlfeld, Johannes (ed.), *Deutsche Reichsgeschichte in Dokumenten 1849-1926*, vol. 1 (Berlin: Deutsche Verlagsgesellschaft für Politik und Geschichte, 1927)

House, Edward Mandell and Seymour, Charles (eds.), *What Really Happened at Paris: The Story of the Peace Conference by American Delegates* (London: Hodder and Stoughton, 1920)

Howe, K. R., 'Tourists, Sailors and Labourers: A History of Early Labour Recruiting in Southern Melanesia' (1978) 13 *Journal of Pacific History*, 22-35

Hughes, Helen, *From Riches to Rags: What are Nauru's Options and How Can Australia Help?* (Canberra: Centre for Independent Studies, 2004)

Hughes, The Right Hon W. M., *The Splendid Adventure: A Review of Empire Relations Within and Without the Commonwealth of Britannic Nations* (Ernest Benn Limited, 1929)

Hymans, Paul, 'Obligations Falling Upon the League of Nations under the Terms of Article 22 of the Covenant (Mandates)' (1920) *League of Nations Official Journal*, 334-41

Ienaga, Saburo, *Japan's Last War: World War II and the Japanese, 1931-1945*, trans. Frank Baldwin (London: Blackwell, 1979)

Immerwahr, Daniel, *How to Hide an Empire: A History of the Greater United States* (London: Random House, 2019)

International Organization, 'Trusteeship Council' (1964) 18 *International Organization*, 120

Jarrett, Mark, *The Congress of Vienna and its Legacy: War and Great Power Diplomacy after Napoleon* (London: I.B. Tauris & Co, 2013)

Jenks, Stuart, and Wubs-Mrozewicz, Justyna (eds.) *The Hanse in Medieval and Early Modern Europe* (Leiden: Brill, 2012)

Jenkyns, Sir Henry, *British Rule and Jurisdiction Beyond the Seas* (Oxford: Clarendon Press, 1902)

Johns, Fleur and Skouteris, Thomas, 'The League of Nations and the Construction of the Periphery – Introduction' (2011) 24 *Leiden Journal of International Law*, 797

Johnston, W. Ross, *Sovereignty and Protection: A Study of British Jurisdictional Imperialism in the Late Nineteenth Century* (Durham: Duke University Press, 1973)

Jones, Henry, 'Property, Territory, and Colonialism: An International Legal History of Enclosure' (2019) 39 *Legal Studies*, 187–203

Jung, Fritz, 'Aufzeichnungen über die Rechtsanschauungen der Eingeborenen von Nauru' ['Notes on the Legal Concepts of the Natives of Nauru'] (1897) 10 *Mittheilungen aus den deutschen Schutgebieten*, 64

Kaczorowska-Ireland, Alina, *Public International Law*, 4th ed. (London: Routledge, 2010)

Kattan, Victor, 'There Was an Elephant in the Court Room': Reflections on the Role of Judge Sir Percy Spender (1897–1985) in the South West Africa Cases (1960–1966) After Half a Century' (2018) 31 *Leiden Journal of International Law*, 147–70

Keith, Arthur Berriedale, *The Sovereignty of the British Dominions* (London: Macmillan and Co Limited, 1929)

Keith, Arthur Berriedale, 'The Imperial Conference 1926' (1927) 9 *Journal of Comparative Legislation and International Law*, 68–94

Keith, Arthur Berriedale, 'Notes on Imperial Constitutional Law' (1924) 6 *Journal of Comparative Legislation and International Law*, 193–209

Kendall, David, 'Doomed Island' (2009) 35 *Alternatives Journal*, 34–7

Kennedy, Duncan, 'The Disenchantment of Logically Formal Legal Rationality, or Max Weber's Sociology in the Genealogy of the Contemporary Mode of Western Legal Thought' (2004) 55 *Hastings Law Journal*, 1031–76

Keynes, John Maynard, *The Economic Consequences of the Peace* (New York: Harcourt, Brace and Howe Inc, 1920)

Kingsbury, Benedict, 'The Concept of "Law" in Global Administrative Law' (2009) 20 *European Journal of International Law*, 23–57

Kingsbury, Benedict, Krisch, Nico, and Stewart, Richard B., 'The Emergence of Global Administrative Law' (2005) 68 *Law and Contemporary Problems*, 15–61

Klabbers, Jan, 'The Emergence of Functionalism in International Institutional Law: Colonial Inspirations' (2014) 25 *European Journal of International Law*, 645–75

Kleeberg, John Martin, 'The *Disconto-Gesellschaft* and German Industrialization: A Critical Examination of the Career of a German Universal Bank 1851–1914', PhD thesis, University of Oxford (1988)

von Kolisch, Otto, *Die Kolonialgesetzgebung des deutschen Reichs mit dem Gesetze über die Konsulergerichtsbarkeit* (Hanover: Helwing, 1896)
Koskenniemi, Martti, Rech, Walter and Fonseca, Manuel Jimenez (eds.), *International Law and Empire: Historical Explanations* (Oxford: Oxford University Press, 2017)
Koskenniemi, Martti, 'Colonial Laws: Sources, Strategies and Lessons?' (2016) 18 *Journal of the History of International Law*, 248-77
Koskenniemi, Martti, 'Less is More: Legal Imagination in Context – Introduction' (2018) 31 *Leiden Journal of International Law*, 469-72
Koskenniemi, Martti, *From Apology to Utopia: The Structure of International Legal Argument* (Cambridge: Cambridge University Press, 2005)
Koskenniemi, Martti, *Gentle Civilizer of Nations: The Rise and Fall of International Law 1870-1960* (Cambridge: Cambridge University Press, 2001)
Klein, Naomi, *This Changes Everything: Capitalism versus the Climate* (London: Penguin Group, 2014)
Knoll, Arthur J. and Hiery, Hermann J. (eds.), *The German Colonial Experience: Select Documents on German Rule in Africa, China and the Pacific 1884-1914* (Maryland: University Press of America, 2010)
Knop, Karen, *Diversity and Self-Determination in International Law* (Cambridge: Cambridge University Press, 2008)
Knox, Rob, 'Strategy and Tactics' (2012) 21 *Finnish Yearbook of International Law*, 193-229
Lake, Marilyn and Reynolds, Henry, *Drawing the Global Colour Line: White Men's Countries and the International Challenge of Racial Equality* (Cambridge: Cambridge University Press, 2012)
Lal, Brij V., *Girmitiyas: The Origins of the Fiji Indians* (Canberra: Journal of Pacific History, 1983)
Lenin, V. L., *Imperialism: The Highest Stage of Capitalism, A Popular Outline*, 1970 ed. (Moscow: Progress Books, 1970)
Liebig, Justus, *Chemistry in its Application to Agriculture and Physiology* (Cambridge: John Owen, 1842)
Lindley, Mark Frank, *Acquisition and Government of Backward Territory in International Law* (New York: Longmans Green, 1926)
Le Roy, Katy, 'Nauru's Parliament in Crisis' (2010) 91 *The Parliamentarian*, 240-3
Leffler, Melvyn P. and Westad, Odd Arne (eds.), *Cambridge History of the Cold War* (Cambridge: Cambridge University Press, 2010)
Lloyd George, David, *The Truth about the Peace Treaties*, vol. I (London: Victor Gollanz Ltd, 1938)
Locke, John, *Two Treatises of Government*, ed. Peter Laslett, 17th ed. (Cambridge: Cambridge University Press, 2005)
Lorca, Arnulf Becker, *Mestizo International Law: A Global Intellectual History 1842-1933* (Cambridge: Cambridge University Press, 2015)

Lorimer, James, *Institutes of the Law of Nations* (Edinburgh: William Blackwood and Sons, 1883)

Louis, William Roger, *Ends of British Imperialism: The Scramble for Empire, Suez, and Decolonization* (London: I.B. Tauris, 2006)

Louis, William Roger, *Great Britain and Germany's Lost Colonies 1914–1919* (Oxford: Clarendon Press, 1967)

Luard, Evan, *A History of the United Nations, Volume 2: The Years of Decolonisation 1955–1965* (London: Macmillan, 1982)

Lucas, Charles Prestwood (ed.), *George Cornewall Lewis: An Essay on the Government of the Dependencies* (Oxford: Clarendon Press, 1891)

Luckau, Alma, *The German Delegation at the Peace Conference* (New York: Columbia University Press, 1941)

Lugard, Frederick, *The Dual Mandate in British Tropical Africa* (Edinburgh and London: William Blackwood and Sons, 1922)

Lyne, Charles, *New Guinea: An Account of the Establishment of the British Protectorate over the Southern Shores of New Guinea* (London: Sampson Low, 1885)

McDaniel, Carl N. and Gowdy, John M., *Paradise for Sale: A Parable of Nature* (Berkeley and London: University of California Press, 2000)

McGill, Sarah M. '"Peak" Phosphorous? The Implications of Phosphate Scarcity for Sustainable Investors' (2012) 2 *Journal of Sustainable Finance and Investment*, 222

McSporran, Peter H., 'Land Ownership and Control in Nauru' (1995) 2 *Murdoch University Electronic Journal of Law*

McVeigh, Shaun (ed.), *Jurisprudence of Jurisdiction* (Oxford: Routledge Cavendish, 2007)

Macaulay, Neil, *Mandates: Reasons, Results, Remedies* (London: Methuen and Co Ltd, 1937)

Macdonald, Barrie, *In Pursuit of the Sacred Trust: Trusteeship and Independence in Nauru* (New Zealand: New Zealand Institute of International Affairs, 1988)

Macmillan, Margaret, *Peacemakers: The Paris Conference of 1919 and its Attempt to End War* (London: J. Murray, 2001)

Maischak, Lars, *German Merchants in the Nineteenth Century Atlantic* (Cambridge: Cambridge University Press, 2013)

Mar, Tracey Banivanua, *Violence and Colonial Dialogue: The Australian-Pacific Indentured Labour Trade* (Honolulu: University of Hawai'i Press, 2007)

Mar, Tracey Banivanua, *Decolonisation and the Pacific: Indigenous Globalisation and the Ends of Empire* (Cambridge: Cambridge University Press, 2016)

Margalith, Aaron, *The International Mandates* (Baltimore: Johns Hopkins Press, 1930)

Margolies, Daniel, Özsu, Umut, Pal, Maia and Tzouvala, Ntina (eds.), *The Extraterritoriality of Law: History, Theory, Politics* (London: Routledge, 2018)

Marks, Susan, 'Empire's Law (The Earl A. Snyder Lecture in International Law)' (2003) 10 *Indiana Journal of Global Legal Studies*, 449–66

Marks, Susan, *International Law on the Left* (Cambridge: Cambridge University Press, 2009)

Marks, Susan, *The Riddle of All Constitutions: International Law, Democracy, and the Critique of Ideology* (Oxford: Oxford University Press, 2003)

Marks, Susan, 'Three Concepts of Empire' (2003) 16 *Leiden Journal of International Law*, 901

Marschner, Petra (ed.), *Marschner's Mineral Nutrition of Higher Plants*, 3rd ed. (UK: Elsevier Ltd, 2012)

Martinez, Jenny S., *The Slave Trade and the Origins of International Human Rights Law* (Oxford: Oxford University Press, 2012)

Marx, Karl, *Capital: A Critical Analysis of Capitalist Production*, ed. Frederick Engels, trans. Samuel Moore and Edward Aveling (New York and London: Appleton & Co, 1889)

Marx, Karl and Engels, Frederick, *Collected Works: Volume 16, 1858–1860*, trans. Richard Dixon, Henry Mins and Salo Ryazanskaya (Chadwell Heath: Lawrence & Wishart, 2010)

Massey, Doreen, *For Space* (London: SAGE Publications, 2005)

Mathew, W. M., *The House of Gibbs and the Peruvian Guano Monopoly* (London: Royal Historical Society, 1981)

Mazower, Mark, *Governing the World: The History of an Idea* (Penguin Press, 2012)

Mazower, Mark, *No Enchanted Palace: The End of Empire and the Ideological Origins of the United Nations* (Princeton University Press, 2009)

Merry, Sally Engle and Brenneis, Donald (eds.), *Law and Empire in the Pacific: Fiji and Hawai'i* (New Mexico: School of American Research Press, 2003)

Metcalfe, Susan, *The Pacific Solution* (Melbourne: Australian Scholarly Publishing, 2010)

Minkkinen, Panu, 'The Legal Academic of Max Weber's Tragic Modernity' (2010) 19 *Social and Legal Studies*, 165–82

Minohara, Tash, Dawley, Evan and Hon, Tze-ki (eds.), *The Decade of the Great War: Japan and the Wider World in the 1910s* (Leiden and Boston: Brill, 2014)

Mommsen, W. J., and de Moor J. A. (eds.), *European Law and Expansion: The Encounter of European and Indigenous Law in 19th and 20th Century Africa and Asia* (Oxford and New York: Berg, 1992)

Morel, E. D., *Africa and the Peace of Europe* (London: National Labour Press, 1917)

Moreton-Robinson, Aileen, *The White Possessive: Property, Power and Indigenous Sovereignty* (Minneapolis: University of Minnesota, 2015)

Moses, John A. and Kennedy, Paul M. (eds.), *Germany in the Pacific and the Far East, 1870–1914* (St Lucia: University of Queensland Press, 1977)

Muller, Sven Oliver, and Torp, Cornelius (eds.), *Imperial Germany Revisited: Continuing Debates and New Perspectives* (New York: Berghahn Books, 2011)

Munro, Doug, and Firth, Stewart, 'Towards Colonial Protectorates: The Case of the Gilbert and Ellice Islands' (1986) 32 *Australian Journal of Politics and History*, 63–71

Murphy, John, *Evatt: A Life* (Sydney: NewSouth Publishing, 2016)

Nash, E. Gee, *The Hansa: Its History and Romance* (London: Bodley Head, 1929)

Natarajan, Usha, Reynolds, John, Bhatia, Amar and Xavier, Sujith, 'Introduction: TWAIL – On Praxis and the Intellectual' (2016) 37 *Third World Quarterly*, 1946

Natarajan, Usha, 'Creating and Recreating Iraq: Legacies of the Mandate System in Contemporary Understandings of Third World Sovereignty' (2011) 24 *Leiden Journal of International Law*, 799–822

Nathan, Manfred, *Empire Government: An Outline of the System Prevailing in the British Commonwealth of Nations* (Cambridge: Harvard University Press, 1930)

Nesiah, Vasuki, 'Placing International Law: White Spaces on a Map' (2003) 16 *Leiden Journal of International Law*, 1–35

Nish, Ian, *Japan's Struggle with Internationalism: Japan, China and the League of Nations, 1931–1933* (London and New York: Kegan Paul International, 1933)

Nkrumah, Kwame, *Neo-Colonialism: The Last Stage of Capitalism* (USA: International Publishers, 1965)

Noel-Baker, Philip J., *Present Juridical Status of the Dominions in International Law* (New York: Longmans Green and Co, 1929)

Oppenheim, Lassa, *International Law: A Treatise*, 2nd ed. (New York: Longman Green and Co, 1905)

Oppenheim, Lassa, *International Law: A Treatise*, ed. Ronald F. Roxburgh, 3rd ed. (New York and London: Longmans, Green and Co, 1920)

Orford, Anne, 'From Promise to Practice? The Legal Significance of the Responsibility to Protect Concept' (2011) 3 *Global Responsibility to Protect*, 400–24

Orford, Anne, 'In Praise of Description' (2012) 25 *Leiden Journal of International Law*, 609–25

Orford, Anne, 'International Territorial Administration and the Management of Decolonization' (2010) *International and Comparative Law Quarterly*, 227–49

Orford, Anne, 'Jurisdiction Without Territory: From the Holy Roman Empire to the Responsibility to Protect' (2009) 30 *Michigan Journal of International Law*, 981–1015

Orford, Anne and Hoffmann, Florian (eds.) *Oxford Handbook of the Theory of International Law* (Oxford: Oxford University Press, 2016)

Orford, Anne, 'The Past as Law or History? The Relevance of Imperialism for Modern International Law' (Institute for International Law and Justice Working Papers, History and Theory of International Law Series, 9 September 2011)

Osterhammel, Jürgen, 'Global History in a National Context: The Case of Germany' (2009) 20 *Global History*, 40–58
Pahuja, Sundhya, 'Laws of Encounter: A Jurisdictional Account of International Law' (2013) 1 *London Review of International Law*, 63–98
Pahuja, Sundhya, *Decolonising International Law: Development, Economic Growth and the Politics of Universality* (Cambridge: Cambridge University Press, 2011)
Parfitt, Rose, 'Empire des Nègres Blancs: The Hybridity of International Personality and the Abyssinia Crisis of 1935–36' (2011) 24 *Leiden Journal of International Law*, 849–72
Pedersen, Susan, *The Guardians: The League of Nations and the Crisis of Empire* (Oxford: Oxford University Press, 2015)
Perraudin, Michael and Zimmerer, Jürgen with Heady, Katy (eds.), *German Colonialism and National Identity* (London: Routledge, 2011)
Pitts, Jennifer, 'Political Theory of Empire and Imperialism' (2010) 13 *Annual Review of Political Science*, 211–35
Pope, Harold B., *Nauru and Ocean Island: Their Phosphate Deposits and Workings* (Melbourne: Albert J. Mullett, Government Printer, 1921)
Press, Steven, *Rogue Empires: Contracts and Conmen in Europe's Scramble for Africa* (Cambridge, MA: Harvard University Press, 2017)
Rajagopal, Balakrishnan, *International Law from Below: Development, Social Movements and Third World Resistance* (Cambridge: Cambridge University Press, 2003)
Ranganathan, Surabhi, 'Ocean Floor Grab: International Law and the Making of an Extractive Imaginary' (2019) 30 *European Journal of International Law*, 573–600
Rappard, William, 'The Mandates and the International Trusteeship Systems' (1946) 61 *Political Science Quarterly*, 408–19
Rasulov, Akbar, 'Writing About Empire: Remarks on the Logic of a Discourse' (2012) 23 *Leiden Journal of International Law*, 449–71
Ratuva, Steven, 'The Gap Between Global Thinking and Local Living: Dilemmas of Constitutional Reform in Nauru' (2011) 20 *The Journal of the Polynesian Society*, 241–68
Reynolds, John, 'Anti-Colonial Legalities: Paradigms, Tactics & Strategy' (2016) 18 *Palestine Yearbook of International Law*, 8–52
Rheinstein, Max (ed.), *Max Weber on Law in Economy and Society* (Cambridge, MA: Harvard University Press, 1954)
Roberts, Stephen H., *Population Problems of the Pacific* (London: George Routledge and Sons, Ltd, 1927)
Robertson, George Scott, *Basic Slags and Rock Phosphates* (Cambridge: Cambridge University Press, 1922)
Roberts-Wray, Kenneth, *Commonwealth and Colonial Law* (London: Stevens & Sons, 1966)

Röhl, John C. G., 'Goodbye to All That (Again)? The Fischer Thesis, the New Revisionism and the Meaning of the First World War' (2015) 91 *International Affairs*, 153–66

Röhl, John C. G., *Wilhelm II: The Kaiser's Personal Monarchy, 1888-1900* (Cambridge: Cambridge University Press, 2004)

Ross, Robert, Nager, Anne Kelk and Nasson, Bill (eds.), *Cambridge History of South Africa* (Cambridge: Cambridge University Press, 2011)

Rotberg, Robert I., *The Founder: Cecil Rhodes and the Pursuit of Power* (Oxford: Oxford University Press, 1988)

Royal Institute of International Affairs, 'British Policy in Palestine, 1937–8' (1938) 15 (23) *Bulletin of International News*, 3–7

Royal Institute of International Affairs, *The British Empire: A Report on its Structure and Problems* (Oxford University Press, 1937)

Royal Institute for International Affairs, *United Nations Documents 1941-1945* (London and New York: Broadwater Press, 1946)

Sack, Peter and Clark, Dymphna (eds. and trans.), *Eduard Hernsheim: South Sea Merchant* (Boroko: Institute of Papua New Guinea Studies, 1983)

Sack, Peter G. and Clark, Dymphna (eds. and trans.), *Albert Hahl: Governor in New Guinea* (Canberra: Australian National University Press, 1980)

Schildhauer, Johannes, *The Hansa: History and Culture* (Leipzig: Edition Leipzig, 1985)

Schmitt, Carl, *The Nomos of the Earth in the International Law of the Jus Publicum Europaeum* (USA: Telos Press Publishing, 2006)

Schnee, Heinrich, *German Colonization Past and Future: The Truth about the German Colonies* (London: George Allen and Unwin, 1926)

Schnee, Heinrich, 'The Mandate System in Germany's Lost Colonies' (April 1930) 32 *Current History*, 76–80

Scott, David, 'Colonial Governmentality' (1995) 43 *Social Text*, 191–220

Secretariat of the League of Nations, *The Aims, Methods and Activity of the League of Nations* (League of Nations Office de Publicité, 1935)

Shahabuddin, Mohammad, 'The "Standard of Civilisation" in International Law: Intellectual Perspectives from Pre-War Japan' (2019) 32 *Leiden Journal of International Law*, 13–32

Shimazu, Naoko, *Japan, Race and Equality: The Racial Equality Proposal of 1919* (London and New York: Routledge, 1998)

Simpson, Gerry, *Great Powers and Outlaw States: Unequal Sovereigns in the International Legal Order* (Cambridge: Cambridge University Press, 2004)

Sinclair, Guy Fiti, *To Reform the World: International Organizations and the Making of Modern States* (Oxford: Oxford University Press, 2017)

Sinclair, Guy Fiti, 'Towards a Postcolonial Genealogy of International Organizations Law' (2018) 31 *Leiden Journal of International Law*, 841–69

Skaggs, Jimmy M., *The Great Guano Rush: Entrepreneurs and American Overseas Expansion* (New York: St Martin's Press, 1994)

Slonim, Solomon, *South West Africa and the United Nations: An International Mandate in Dispute* (Baltimore and London: Johns Hopkins University Press, 1973)

Sluga, Glenda and Clavin, Patricia (eds.) *Internationalisms: A Twentieth Century History* (Cambridge: Cambridge University Press, 2016)

Smith, Linda Tuiwai, *Decolonizing Methodologies: Research and Indigenous Peoples* (London: Zed Books, 2012)

Smith, Woodruff D., *The German Colonial Empire* (North Carolina: University of North Carolina Press, 1978)

Smuts, J. C., *A League of Nations: A Practical Suggestion* (Hodder and Stoughton, 1918)

Snow, Alpheus Henry, *The Question of Aborigines in the Law and Practice of Nations* (New York: Putnam and Sons, 1921)

Snyder, Louis L. (ed.), *Documents of German History* (Rutgers University Press, 1958)

Southall, Roger, *Liberation Movements in Power: Party and State in Southern Africa* (South Africa: University of KwaZulu-Natal Press, 2013)

Speedy, Karin, 'The Sutton Case: The First Franco-Australian Foray into Blackbirding' (2015) 50 *Journal of Pacific History*, 344–64

Spennemann, Dirk H. R., 'A Hand List of Imperial German Legislation regarding the Marshall Islands (1886–1914)' (2007) 3 *Studies in German Colonial Heritage*, 1

Spoehr, Florence Mann, *White Falcon: The House of Godeffroy and its Commercial and Scientific Role in the Pacific* (California: Pacific Books, 1963)

Spruyt, Henrik, *The Sovereign State and its Competitors: An Analysis of Systems Change* (Princeton: Princeton University Press, 1994)

Stannage, Tom, Saunders, Kay and Nile, Richard (eds.) *Paul Hasluck in Australian History: Civic Personality and Public Life* (St Lucia: Queensland University Press, 1998)

Steinberg, Jonathan, *Bismarck: A Life* (Oxford: Oxford University Press, 2011)

Steinmetz, George, 'Decolonizing German Theory: An Introduction' (2006) 9 *Postcolonial Studies*, 3–13

Steinmetz, George, *The Devil's Handwriting: Precolonial Ethnography and the German Colonial State in Qingdao, Samoa, and Southwest Africa* (Chicago: University of Chicago Press, 2007)

Steer, G. L., *Judgment on German Africa* (London: Hodder and Stoughton Ltd, 1939)

Stevens, E. V., 'Blackbirding: A Brief History of South Sea Islands Labour Traffic and the Vessels Engaged in It' (1950) 4 *Historical Society Journal*, 361–403

Stevenson, Robert Louis, *A Footnote to History: Eight Years of Trouble in Samoa* (New York: Charles Scribner's Sons, 1895)

Stockwell, Sarah E. (ed.), *The British Empire: Themes and Perspectives* (Wiley-Blackwell, 2008)

Stoecker, Helmuth (ed.), *German Imperialism in Africa: From the Beginnings until the Second World War*, trans. Bernd Zöllner (London: C. Hurst & Company, 1986)

Storr, Cait, '"Imperium in Imperio": Sub-Imperialism and the Formation of Australia as a Subject of International Law' (2018) 19 *Melbourne Journal of International Law*, 335–68

SWAPO of Namibia Department of Information and Publicity, *To Be Born a Nation: The Liberation Struggle for Namibia* (London: Zed Books, 1981)

Swedberg, Richard, 'The Changing Picture of Max Weber's Sociology' (2003) 29 *Annual Review of Sociology*, 283–306

Tabucanon, Gil and Opeskin, Brian, 'The Resettlement of Nauruans in Australia: An Early Case of Failed Environmental Migration' (2011) 46 *Journal of Pacific History*, 337–57

Takeuchi, Taksuji, *War and Diplomacy in the Japanese Empire* (Doubleday, Doran and Company, 1935)

Tan, Shao-Hwa, 'The Legal Status of the Japanese Mandate for the Ex-German Islands and the Question of Japan's Withdrawal from the League' (1933) 6 *China Law Review*, 296–317

Tanaka, Yuki, 'Japanese Atrocities on Nauru during the Pacific War: The Murder of Australians, The Massacre of Lepers and the Ethnocide of Nauruans' (2010) 45 *The Asia-Pacific Journal*, 1–19

Tarring, Charles James, *Chapters on the Law Relating to the Colonies*, 3rd ed. (London: Stevens and Haynes, 1906)

Tate, Merze, 'The Australasian Monroe Doctrine' (1961) 76 *Political Science Quarterly*, 264–84

Tate, Merze, 'Nauru, Phosphate and the Nauruans' (1968) *Australian Journal of Politics and History*, 177–92

Taylor, A. J. P., *Germany's First Bid for Colonies 1884–1885* (London: Macmillan, 1938)

Taylor, Savitri, 'The Pacific Solution or a Pacific Nightmare: The Difference between Burden Shifting and Responsibility Sharing' (2005) 6 *Asian-Pacific Law and Policy Journal*, 1–43

Teaiwa, Katerina Martina, *Consuming Ocean Island: Stories of People and Phosphate from Banaba* (Bloomington: Indiana University Press, 2014)

Teaiwa, Katerina, 'Ruining Pacific Islands: Australia's Phosphate Imperialism' (2015) 46 *Australian Historical Studies*, 374–91

Temperley, H. W. V. *History of the Peace Conference of Paris* (Oxford: Oxford University Press, 1924)

Thomas, Chantal, 'Max Weber, Talcott Parsons and the Sociology of Legal Reform: A Reassessment with Implications for Law and Development' (2006) 15 *Minnesota Journal of International Law*, 383–424

Thompson, Roger C. *Australian Imperialism in the Pacific: The Expansionist Era 1820-1920* (Melbourne: Melbourne University Press, 1980)

Thompson, Warren S. *Danger Spots in World Population* (New York: Alfred A. Knopf, 1930)

Toussaint, Charmian Edwards, *The Trusteeship System of the United Nations* (London: Stevens & Sons Limited, 1956)

Toynbee, Arnold, 'Peaceful Change or War? The Next Stage in the International Crisis' (1936) 15 *International Affairs*, 26–56

Twiss, Travers, *Law of Nations Considered as Independent Political Communities – On the Rights and Duties of States in Time of Peace*, 2nd ed. (Oxford: Clarendon Press, 1884)

Upthegrove, Campbell L. *Empire by Mandate: A History of the Relations of Great Britain with the Permanent Mandates Commission of the League of Nations* (New York: Bookman Press, 1954)

van Maanen-Helmer, Elizabeth, *The Mandates System in Relation to Africa and the Pacific Islands* (London: P. S. King and Son Ltd, 1929)

Veracini, Lorenzo, "Settler Colonialism': Career of a Concept' (2013) 41 *Journal of Imperial and Commonwealth History*, 313–22

Viviani, Nancy, *Nauru: Phosphate and Political Progress* (Canberra: Australian National University Press, 1970)

Voeltz, Richard A. *German Colonialism and the South West Africa Company, 1894-1914* (Ohio: Ohio University Center for International Studies, 1988)

Vogl, Anthea, 'Over the Borderline: A Critical Inquiry into the Geography of Territorial Excision and the Securitisation of the Australian Border' (2015) 38 *UNSW Law Journal*, 114–45

Wadham, S. M. and Wood, G. L. *Land Utilization in Australia* (Melbourne: Melbourne University Press, 1939)

Waller, Bruce, *Bismarck at the Crossroads: The Reorientation of German Foreign Policy after the Congress of Berlin 1878-1880* (London: Athlone Press, 1974)

Watt, Robert D. *Romance of the Australian Land Industries* (Sydney: Angus and Robertson, 1955)

Weber, Marianne, *Max Weber: A Biography*, trans. Harry Zohn (New York: John Wiley, 1975)

Weber, Max, *Protestant Ethic and the Spirit of Capitalism*, trans. Talcott Parsons (London: Routledge, 1992)

Weeramantry, Christopher, *Nauru: Environmental Damage under International Trusteeship* (Oxford: Oxford University Press)

Wehler, Hans-Ulrich, *The German Empire 1871-1914*, trans. Kym Traynor (Leamington Spa: Berg Publishers, 1985)

Wells, H. G., *In the Fourth Year: Anticipations of a World Peace* (London: Macmillan Company, 1918)
Wemper, Sean Andrew, 'From Unfit Imperialists to Fellow Civilizers: German Colonial Officials as Imperial Experts in the League of Nations, 1919–1933' (2016) 34 *German History*, 21–48
White, Stuart and Cordell, Dana, 'Peak Phosphorus: Clarifying the Key Issues of a Vigorous Debate about Long-Term Phosphorus Security' (2011) 3 *Sustainability*, 2027–49
Whittaker, J. L., Nash, N. G., Hookey, J. F., and Lacey, R. L. (eds.), *Documents and Readings in New Guinea History: Pre-History to 1899* (Milton: Jacaranda Press, 1975)
Wilde, Ralph, *International Territorial Administration* (Oxford: Oxford University Press, 2008)
Williams, Maslyn and Macdonald, Barrie, *The Phosphateers: A History of the British Phosphate Commissioners* (Melbourne: Melbourne University Press, 1985)
Willoughby, W. W. and Fenwick, C. G., *Types of Restricted Sovereignty and of Colonial Autonomy* (Washington, DC: Government Printers Office, 1919)
Wilkinson, H. L., *The World's Population Problems and A White Australia* (London: P. S. King and Son Ltd, 1930)
Winichakul, Thongchai, *Siam Mapped: A History of the Geo-Body of a Nation* (Honolulu: University of Hawai'i Press, 1994)
Woolf, L. S., *International Government: Two Reports prepared for the Fabian Research Department* (London: Brentano's, 1916)
Wright, Quincy, 'Sovereignty of the Mandates' (1923) 17 *American Journal of International Law*, 691–703
Zimmerman, Alfred, *Geschichte der deutschen Kolonialpolitik* [History of German Colonial Policy] (Mittler, 1914)
Zimmerman, Andrew, 'Decolonizing Weber' (2006) 9 *Postcolonial Studies*, 53–79
Zimmern, Helen, *The Hansa Towns* (London: T. Fisher Unwin, 1891)

Cases, Treaties, Legislation and Other Legal Instruments

Agreement between His Most Gracious Majesty King George V and Others and The Pacific Phosphate Company, Westminster, 25 June 1920
Arbitration under the Timor Sea Treaty (Timor-Leste v. Australia), Permanent Court of Arbitration (Case 2015-42)
Certain Phosphate Lands in Nauru Case (Nauru v. Australia), Order of 13 September 1993, ICJ Rep 1993, 322
Application Instituting Proceedings, ICJ General List, 19 May 1989
Memorial of Nauru, Vol. 1, April 1990
Preliminary Objections of Australia, ICJ General List, December 1990

Judgment on the Preliminary Objections, ICJ Rep 1992, 240
International Status of South-West Africa (Advisory Opinion) [1950] ICJ Rep 128, 140
South West Africa Cases (Ethiopia v. South Africa; Liberia v. South Africa), Second Phase (Judgment), ICJ Rep 6 (18 July 1966)
Application Instituting Proceedings, ICJ General List, 4 November 1960
Preliminary Objections, ICJ Rep 212 (30 November 1961)
Judgment, ICJ Rep 319 (21 December 1962)
Phosphates in Morocco (Italy v. France) (Judgment) [1938], PCIJ, ser A/B74, 4
Plaintiff M68/2015 v. Commonwealth of Australia (2016) 257 CLR 42
Timor-Leste v. Australia (Questions relating to the Seizure and Detention of Certain Documents and Data), International Court of Justice, Summary of Judgments and Orders (2014)

Legislation and Regulations

Allerhöchster Erlaß, betreffend die Errichtung des Reichs-Kolonialamts [Decree on the Establishment of the Reich Colonial Office], 17 May 1907
British Settlements Act 1887 (UK) 50 & 51 Vict. ch. 54
Constitution of Nauru 1968
Deutsche Bundesakte [German Federal Act] 8 June 1815
Gesetz, betreffend die Kaiserliche Schutztruppe für Deutsch-Ostafrika [Law concerning the Imperial Colonial Forces for German East Africa], 22 March 1891
Gesetz, betreffend die Rechtsverhältnisse der deutschen Schutzgebiete [Law Governing the Legal Status of the German Protectorates], 17 April 1886
Gesetz über die Konsulargerichtsbarkeit [Law on Consular Jurisdiction], 10 July 1879
Gesetz wegen Abänderung des Gesetzes, betreffend die Kaiserliche Schutztruppe für Deutsch-Ostafrika und des Gesetzes, betreffend die Kaiserlichen Schutztruppen für Südwestafrika und für Kamerun [Law amending the Laws on the Imperial Colonial Forces for German East Africa, South West Africa and Cameroon], 7 July 1896
Guano Islands Act of 1856 (USA) 48 USC § 1411
Immigration Restriction Act (Cth), 17 of 1901
Interpretation Act 1889 (UK) 52 & 53 Vict, c. 63
Migration Amendment (Excision from Migration Zone) Act 2001 (Cth)
Movement of Natives Ordinance (No. 12 of 1921) (Cth)
Native Administration Ordinance (No. 17 of 1922) (Cth)
Nauru Independence Act 1967 (Cth)
Nauru Island Agreement Act 1919 (Cth)
Nauru Lands Ordinance (No. 12 of 1921) (Cth)
Nauru Local Government Council Ordinance No. 2 of 1951

Pacific Island Labourers Act (Cth) No. 16 of 1901
Papua Act 1905 (Cth)
Papua and New Guinea Act 1949 (Cth)
Public Acts of New Zealand 1908–1931 (Wellington: Butterworths, 1933)
Die Reichsverfassung [German Imperial Constitution of 1871]
Republic of South Africa Constitution Act 1961 (SA)
South West Africa Affairs Amendment Act No. 23 of 1949 (SA)
Verordnung betreffend die anderweitige Regelung der Verwaltung und der Rechtsverhältnisse im Schutzgebiet der Marshall-, Brown und Providence Inseln [Ordinance regarding the Changed Execution of the Administration and the Jurisdiction in the Protectorate of the Marshall, Brown and Providence Islands], 17 January 1906
Verordnung, betreffend die Rechtsverhältnisse in dem Schutzgebiete der Marschall-, Brown- und Providence-Inseln [Law governing Legal Relations in the Marshall, Brown and Providence Islands Protectorates], 17 September 1886

Treaties and International Instruments

Atlantic Charter, opened for signature 14 August 1941, ATS 1942(4)
Charter of the United Nations, opened for signature 26 June 1945, entered into force 24 October 1945
Council of the League of Nations, British Mandate for Palestine, signed and entered into force on 24 July 1922
Council of the League of Nations, Mandate for Nauru, 17 December 1920 (London: His Majesty's Stationery Office, 1921)
Declaration by United Nations (Subscribing to the Principles of the Atlantic Charter), opened for signature 1 January 1942, ATS 1942(4)
Declaration on the Granting of Independence to Colonial Countries and Peoples, UN Doc A/RES/1514(XV) (14 December 1960)
General Act of the Conference of Berlin concerning the Congo (entered into force 26 February 1885)
Economic Advancement in Trust Territories, GA Res 322, UN GAOR, 40th plen. mtg (15 November 1949)
League of Nations, 'Report of the Council under Article 15, Paragraph 4 of the Covenant submitted by the Committee of the Council on October 5th and adopted by the Council on October 7th, 1935' (November 1935) *League of Nations Official Journal*, 1605
League of Nations Permanent Mandates Commission, 'Minutes of the Second Session held in Geneva August 1st–11th, 1922'
League of Nations Permanent Mandates Commission, 'Minutes of the Third Session held in Geneva July 20th–August 10th, 1923'

League of Nations Permanent Mandates Commission, 'Report of the Permanent Mandates Commission on the Work of its Eleventh Session' (October 1927), 8 *League of Nations Official Journal*, 1118–21

League of Nations Secretariat, 'Notification by the German Government of its Intention to Withdraw from the League of Nations' (January 1934) *League of Nations Official Journal*, 16

League of Nations Secretariat, 'Notification by the Japanese Government of its Intention to Withdraw from the League of Nations' (May 1933) *League of Nations Official Journal*, 657

League of Nations Secretariat, 'Fifth Meeting (Private, then Public)' (December 1932) *League of Nations Official Journal*, 1870

League of Nations Secretariat, 'Report from the Executive Committee of the Arab Palestine Congress' (June 1921) *League of Nations Official Journal*, 331

Legal Action to Ensure the Fulfilment of the Obligations Assumed by the Union of South Africa in Respect of the Territory of South West Africa, GA Res 1361 (XIV), UN Doc A/RES/1361(XIV) (17 November 1959)

Memorandum of Understanding between the Republic of Nauru and the Commonwealth of Australia, Relating to the Transfer to and Assessment of Persons in Nauru, and Related Issues, signed 29 August 2012

Moscow Conference Declarations, 19–30 October 1943

Political Advancement of Trust Territories, GA Res 320 (15 November 1949)

Question of South West Africa: Request for an Advisory Opinion of the International court of Justice, GA Res 338(IV), UN Doc A/RES/338(IV) (6 December 1949)

Question of the Trust Territory of Nauru, GA Res 2226(XXI), UN Doc A/RES/2226(XXI) (20 December 1966)

Question of the Trust Territory of Nauru, GA Res 211(XX), UN Doc A/RES/211(XX) (21 December 1965)

The Situation in Namibia, Security Council Resolution 264, UN Doc S/RES/264(1969) (20 March 1969)

Treaty of Friendship between the Marshallese Chiefs and the German Empire, Germany–Marshall Islands, signed 1 November 1885 (trans. Dirk Spennemann)

Treaty of Peace between the Allied and Associated Powers and Germany, opened for signature 28 June 1919, 2 USTS 43, entered into force 10 January 1920

Trusteeship Agreement for the Territory of Nauru, 138 UNTS 4, signed and entered into force 1 November 1947

United Nations, Revised and Updated Report on the Question of the Prevention and Punishment of the Crime of Genocide prepared by Mr. B. Whitaker ('Whitaker Report'), E/CN.4/Sub.2/1985/6, 2 July 1985

United Nations Visiting Mission to Trust Territories in the Pacific 1953: Report on Nauru, UN Trusteeship Council Official Records, 12th sess, UN Doc T/1054 (26 May 1953)

Government Papers, Reports and Speeches

Australian Delegation to the United Nations Conference on International Organization, 1945, *United Nations Conference on International Organization, held at San Francisco, USA, from 25th April to 26th June, 1945: Report by the Australian Delegates* (Canberra: Commonwealth Government Printer, 1945)

Commonwealth of Australia, *Foreign Policy White Paper*, November 2017

Commonwealth of Australia, House of Representatives Official Hansard, 'Ministerial Statement made by the Prime Minister with Reference to the Administration of Nauru', 8 September 1922

Commonwealth of Australia, *Parliamentary Debates*, House of Representatives, Thursday 18 September 1919

Commonwealth of Australia, *Parliamentary Debates*, House of Representatives, 24 September 1919

Commonwealth of Australia, *Parliamentary Debates*, House of Representatives, 16 June 1920

Commonwealth of Australia, *Parliamentary Debates*, House of Representatives, 2 July 1920

Commonwealth of Australia, *Parliamentary Debates*, House of Representatives, 29 July 1920

Commonwealth of Australia, *Parliamentary Debates*, House of Representatives, 25 June 1941

Commonwealth of Australia, *Parliamentary Debates*, House of Representatives, 20 July 1944

Commonwealth of Australia, *Parliamentary Debates*, House of Representatives, 10 May 1945

Commonwealth of Australia, *Papers Laid before the Colonial Conference, 1907* (London: His Majesty's Stationery Office, 1907)

Commonwealth of Australia, *Progress of the Australian Territories 1950–1956* (A. J. Arthur, Commonwealth Government Printer, 1957)

Department of Foreign Affairs and Trade, 'Aid Investment Plan: Nauru 2015–16 to 2018–19' (Commonwealth of Australia, 2015)

Department of Foreign Affairs and Trade, 'Aid Program Performance Report 2012–13 Nauru' (Commonwealth of Australia, 2013)

Department of Foreign Affairs and Trade, 'AusAID Annual Report 2001–2002' (Commonwealth of Australia, 2002)

Department of Foreign Affairs and Trade, 'Australian Agency for International Development Annual Reports 1998–2013' (Commonwealth of Australia, 2013)

Department of Foreign Affairs and Trade, 'Nauru Aid Program Performance Reports 2012–2016' (Commonwealth of Australia, 2016)

Department of Territories, 'Documents relating to the Constitutional Future of Nauru' (22 June 1967)

Great Britain Colonial Office, *Proceedings of the Imperial Conference 1911 presented to both houses of Parliament by the command of His Majesty* (London: His Majesty's Stationery Office, 1911)

Great Britain Colonial Office, *Correspondence respecting Military Operations against German Possessions in the Pacific, presented to both Houses of Parliament by Command of His Majesty* (London: His Majesty's Stationery Office, 1915)

Great Britain Colonial Office, *Imperial War Conference 1917: Extracts from Minutes of Proceedings Laid Before the Conference* (London: His Majesty's Stationery Office, 1917)

Great Britain Foreign and Commonwealth Office, *British and Foreign State Papers*, vol. 91 (1898–1899), 1272–3

Government of the Republic of Nauru and United Nations Development Programme, 'Nauru Constitutional Reform Project', 2008

Lloyd George, David, 'Speech delivered to Trades Union Congress', Caxton Hall, London, 5 January 1918

Minister for Territories of Nauru, 'Nauru Lands Rehabilitation Committee' (media release, 24 Jan. 1966)

Minutes of Proceedings of the Imperial Conference 1911 (London: His Majesty's Stationery Office, 1911)

Nauru Constitutional Review Commission, '"*Naoero Ituga*": Report', 28 February 2007

Nauru Lands Rehabilitation Committee, 'Report by Committee Appointed to Investigate the Possibilities of Rehabilitation of Mined Phosphate Lands' (Sydney, 1966)

Parliament of the Commonwealth of Australia, *Report to the General Assembly of the United Nations on the Administration of the Territory of Nauru from 1st July 1951 to 30th June 1952* (Canberra: L. F. Johnson, Commonwealth Government Printer, 1952)

Parliament of the Commonwealth of Australia, *Report to the General Assembly of the United Nations on the Administration of the Territory of Nauru from 1st July 1947 to 30th June 1948* (Canberra: L. F. Johnson, Commonwealth Government Printer, 1948)

Parliament of the Commonwealth of Australia, *Report to the Council of the League of Nations on the Administration of the Island of Nauru during the Year 1937* (Canberra: L. F. Johnson, Commonwealth Government Printer, 1938)

Parliament of the Commonwealth of Australia, *Report to the Council of the League of Nations on the Administration of the Island of Nauru during the Year 1931* (Canberra: Commonwealth Government Printer, 1932)

Parliament of the Commonwealth of Australia, *Report to the Council of the League of Nations on the Administration of the Island of Nauru during the Year 1924* (H. J. Green, Government Printer)

Parliament of the Commonwealth of Australia, *Report on the Administration of Nauru during the Year 1922, prepared by the Administrator for Submission to the League of Nations* (Melbourne: Albert J. Mullett, Government Printer, 1923)

Parliament of New Zealand, *Intercolonial Convention 1883: Report of the Proceedings of the Intercolonial Convention held in Sydney, in November and December 1883*, Parliamentary Paper A-3 (Wellington: George Didsbury, Government Printer, 1883)

Parliament of Victoria, *German Interests in the South Sea: Abstracts of White Books Presented to the Reichstag, December 1884 and February 1885*, Parliamentary Paper No. 36 (Melbourne: John Ferres, Government Printer, 1885)

Parliament of Victoria, *Western Pacific Orders in Council: Report of a Royal Commission Appointed by the Imperial Government to Inquire into the Working of the Western Pacific Orders in Council and the Nature of the Measures Requisite to Secure the Attainment of the Objects for which those Orders in Council Were Issued*, Parliamentary Paper No. 42 (Melbourne: John Ferres, Government Printer, 1884)

Parliament of Victoria, *Australasian Convention on the Annexation of Adjacent Islands and the Federation of Australasia*, Parliamentary Paper No. 48 (Melbourne: John Ferres, Government Printer, 1883)

Republic of Nauru, *Nauru National Assessment Report for the Third International Conference on Small Island Developing States (SIDS)* (Report, 17 May 2013)

Republic of Nauru Government Information Office, 'Supreme Court has Deemed Suspension of MPs Lawful' (media release, 11 December 2014)

Republic of Nauru Government Information Office, 'Nauru Government Sets the Record Straight' (media release, 25 January 2014)

Republic of Nauru Government Information Office, 'Opposition False Claims Show Election Eve Desperation' (media release, 7 July 2016)

Republic of Nauru, 'National Sustainable Development Strategy 2005–2025' (Revised 2009), available at www.adb.org/sites/default/files/linked-documents/cobp-nau-2016-2018-nsds.pdf

Wilson, President Woodrow, Speech delivered to the Congress of the United States, Washington, DC, 2 April 1917

Media Articles and Press Releases

The Age, 'Melbourne, Wednesday, 12th August 1914', *The Age*, 12 August 1914

Australian Broadcasting Corporation, 'Early Win for Anti-Whaling Lobby at IWC', *ABC News*, 20 June 2005

Australian Broadcasting Corporation, 'How Nauru Threw it All Away', ABC Radio National, 11 March 2014

Australian Broadcasting Corporation, 'Nauru Gives Reasons for Sacking Magistrate', *ABC News*, 21 January 2014

BIBLIOGRAPHY

Australian Broadcasting Corporation, 'Nauru Media Visa Fee Hike to 'Cover up Harsh Conditions at Australian Tax-payer Funded Detention Centre', *Australian Broadcasting Corporation*, 9 January 2014

Albany Advertiser, 'Good News: Early Occupation of Nauru', *Albany Advertiser* (Western Australia), 9 March 1944

The Argus, 'Charter of the German New Guinea Company', *The Argus* (Melbourne), 24 July 1885

The Argus, 'A Great Conference', *The Argus* (Melbourne), 13 May 1944

The Argus, 'Nauru Boys' Progress', *The Argus* (Melbourne), 22 December 1938

Australian Associated Press, 'Nauru Suspends Two More Opposition MPs Ahead of Budget Hand Down', *The Guardian*, 5 June 2014

Australian Associated Press, 'Guns Boom and People Grave as Nauru is "Born"', *Canberra Times*, 1 February 1968

Australian Worker, 'Raider Shells Nauru Island', *The Australian Worker*, 1 January 1941

Barron, Gerard, CEO & Chairman of DeepGreen Metals, 'Address to ISA Council', 27 February 2019

Brisbane Courier, 'The Annexation of the Marshall Islands by Germany', *The Brisbane Courier*, 17 February 1886

British Labour Party, 'Memorandum of War Aims', 28 December 1917

Callick, Rowan, 'Conmen's Paradise', *The Australian*, 19 January 2007

Charles, Stephen, 'Our Detention Centres are Concentration Camps and Must be Closed', *The Sydney Morning Herald*, 4 May 2016

Clarke, Melissa, 'Nauru Expels Australian Magistrate Peter Law, Bars Chief Justice Geoffrey Eames from Returning to Country', Australian Broadcasting Corporation, 20 January 2014

Courier Mail, 'Evacuation of Nauru and Ocean I.', *Courier Mail*, 10 March 1942

The Cumberland Argus, 'On the Sheep's Back', *The Cumberland Argus*, 3 May 1934

The Economist, 'Paradise Well and Truly Lost', *The Economist*, 20 December 2001

Ewart, Richard, 'Nauru Officials Accused of 'Persecutory Conduct' as Judge Throws Out Long-Running Protest Case', *Australian Broadcasting Corporation*, 14 September 2018

Gray, A. N., 'Phosphate Rock: The World's Output', *Perth Western Mail*, 11 August 1932

Henley, Jon, 'Pacific Atoll Paradise for Mafia Loot', *The Guardian*, 23 June 2001

Hitt, Jack, 'The Billon-Dollar Shack', *New York Times Magazine*, 10 December 2000

Koziol, Michael and Gordon, Michael, 'UN Slams Australia's Regional Processing Centres in Nauru', *Sydney Morning Herald*, 7 October 2016

The Land Sydney, 'Farmers Urge Local Search for Phosphate', *The Land Sydney*, 13 March 1942

Lawrence, Stephen and Graham, Felicity, 'Former President of Nauru Pursued to the Last', *The Australian*, 15 May 2019

Mackay Daily Mercury, 'Backbone of the Nation: Farmers' Difficulties', *Mackay Daily Mercury* 28 September 1935

Murray, Martin McKenzie, 'The Dysfunction of Offshore Detention on Nauru', *The Saturday Paper*, 27 August 2016

Nuzzo, Luigi, 'Colonial Law' *European History Online*, 16 April 2012, available at www.ieg-ego.eu/en/threads/europe-and-the-world/european-overseas-rule/luigi-nuzzo-colonial-law

Rajah, Roland, 'Securing Sustainability: Nauru's New Intergenerational Trust Fund and Beyond', Asian Development Bank (2017)

Reuters, 'Pacific Island Recognises Georgian Rebel Region', *Reuters*, 15 December 2009

Roy, Eleanor Ainge, 'Nauru Opposition MP Secretly Granted NZ Citizenship Flees to Wellington', *The Guardian*, 12 July 2016

Simpson, Glenn R. 'Tiny Island Selling Passports Is Big Worry for U.S. Officials', *The Wall Street Journal* (USA), 16 May 2003

Su, Joy, 'Nauru Switches its Allegiance back to Taiwan from China', *Taipei Times*, 15 May 2005

The Sun, 'Triangular Battle between Milner, Hughes and Massey', *The Sun*, 17 March 1919

The Sunday Times, 'Nauru Island – Great Wealth in Phosphatic Rock', *The Sunday Times*, 20 May 1917

Sydney Morning Herald, 'Japan "Bullying" Countries to Back Whaling', *Sydney Morning Herald*, 20 June 2005

Thomas, Tony, 'The Naughty Nation of Nauru' (Jan.–Feb. 2013) Quadrant, 30–4

Trumbull, Robert, 'World's Richest Little Isle', *The New York Times*, 7 March 1982

Tweed Daily, 'Large Fires at Nauru', *Tweed Daily*, 14 December 1943

United Nations Department of Public Information, 'Trusteeship and Non-Self-Governing Areas' (December 1947) 24 *United Nations Weekly Bulletin* 767

United Nations Department of Public Information, 'Committee Approves Trusteeship for Nauru: Draft Agreement Calls for Three-Power Administration' (November 1947) 19 *United Nations Weekly Bulletin* 589

United Nations Department of Public Information, 'Trusteeship for Nauru Debated: Fourth Committee Examines Draft Agreement' (October 1947) 16 *United Nations Weekly Bulletin* 492

United Nations, 'Traditional Voting Pattern Reflected in General Assembly's Adoption of Drafts on Question of Palestine, Broader Middle East Issues' (media release, 24 November 2015) available at: www.un.org/press/en/2015/ga11732.doc.htm

United States Agricultural Research Service, *Superphosphate: Its History, Chemistry and Manufacture* (Washington, DC: Government Printers Office, 1964)

The Week, 'Germans in the Pacific', *The Week*, 29 December 1888

The Week, 'Pacific Islands Company', *The Week*, 28 May 1897

The West Australian, 'Australian Agriculture: None Better in the World', *The West Australian*, 10 November 1934

The West Australian, 'Papua and New Guinea: Joint Administration Question', *The West Australian*, 16 February 1939

Waqa, Baron, 'Media Mudslingers Distort the Image of Nauru', *The Australian*, 22 August 2016

Washington Post, 'Russians Use Tiny Island to Hide Billions', *Washington Post*, 28 October 1999

INDEX

Abyssinia, 96, 185
administrative form, 99, 159, 259
  bureaucratic authority, 23
  bureaucratic management, 19
  definition, 23
  democratisation compared, 19
  interwar years, 179–82
  jurisdictional thinking, 9–44
  legitimacy, 18
Advisory Opinion on the Status of South-West Africa (1950), 219
agriculture, 121, 148, *see also* industrial agriculture
  Australia, 175, 202
  British, 148
  guano, 122–4
  industrialisation, 68, 69, 70
  labour, 120–1
  phosphate, 121–5, 175–6
  United States, 122
American Guano Company, 127
Anghie, Antony, 28, 38
annexation, 62, 68, 73, 100, 116, 143, 170
  dominion annexation of the German colonies, 100, 101, 139–40
  internationalisation concept compared, 140–8
  Nauru, 142, 148, 149, 157
  New Guinea, 34, 72, 73
anti-imperialist movements, 182
Arundel, John T
  Jaluit Gesellschaft, agreement with, 125–9, 130
  Pacific Phosphate Company, 154
Asian Development Bank
  Nauru Trust Fund, 257
asylum seekers, 252

financial agreement between Australia and Nauru, 253
offshore processing, 252
Pacific solution, 3, 252–4, 255–6, 257
Atlantic Charter, 191–2, 194
Australia. *See also* Nauru Island Agreement (1919)
  agriculture, 121, 151, 202
  asylum seeker policy, 3
  Australian Commonwealth, 118, 120, 167, 190
  civilian administration, 167
  Department of Territories, 2
  Immigration Restriction Act 1901, 120
  industry, 121
  military occupation of Nauru, 163, 167
  Nauruan phosphate, 13, 99, 134, 139, 149, 150, 151, 161, 163–4, 176, 188, 202–3, 232
  offshore detention regime, 3, 252–4, 255
  Pacific Island Labourers Act (1901), 120
  sub-imperialism, 135–6, 149, 157, 179, 197, 202
  'White Australia' policy, 120, 144
Australia/NewZealand
  disputed colonial claims, 149
authority
  definition, 23

Balfour Declaration (1917), 186
Balfour, Arthur James, 148, 149, 154
Banaba
  phosphate operations, 129, 130, 137, 154, 175
Benton, Lauren, 16

INDEX

Berlin Conference (1884), 39, 46, 47, 59–62, 76, 93
  General Act, 94, 141
Bismarck, Otto von,
  appointment, 46
  imperial expansion, 50, 55, 59–62, 66, 67, 68
  resignation, 110
Bismarckian Reich, 45, 46, 48, 50, 55, 67, 70, 71
Board of Commissioners, 100, *see also* British Phosphate Commission
Bretton Woods Agreement (1944), 192
British Commonwealth of Nations, 181
British Foreign Office
  German imperial expansion, 73
British imperial forms, 114
  administrative arrangements, 117
  colonies, 117, 119
  condominiums, 116
  Crown colonies, 116
  dependencies, 116
  dominions, 116, 119
  international status of the colonies, 115
  levels of self-rule, 118
  protectorates, 115
  self-governing colonies, 117
  sovereignty, 116
British Phosphate Commission, 24, 100, 154, 159, 161–2, 164, 167, 175, 201, 249, 251
Brooks, Angie, 207
bureaucracy. *See also* administrative form
  theoretical law, 15–24

C Mandate status, 24, 99, 100, 152, 161, 201, 202
  mandatory principle, 140–7
  categories of mandate, 147–8
  Nauru, 154–7, 163–75
  removal of differentiated status, 205
  sovereignty, 172
  territorial annexation compared, 171
Certain Phosphate Lands Case, 29, 204–43

Charter of the United Nations. *see* United Nations Charter
Churchill, Winston
  Atlantic Charter, 191–2, 194
  League of Nations, 192
  self-government, 193, 195
  United Nations, 193
co-existence of mandates and protectorates, 179–82
colonial appeasement, 182
Colonial Department, 111
colonial protectorates, 65
colonies
  common law, 117
Committee of Imperial Defence, 119
Compulsory Education Ordinance (1921), 174
condominiums, 116
consent
  legitimate rule, 18
  self-determination, 142–8, 191
Constitution of the Republic of Nauru, 236, 239–41
constitutional referendum (2010), 1, 8
  public awareness campaign, 1
Constitutional Review Commission, 1, 12
  recommendations, 2
consular jurisdiction
  British, 77, 78
  German, 76, 103
contemporary international order
  Nauru's place within, 9–44
Cook, Joseph, 136, 167, 168
copra trade, 77, 89, 109, 126–7, 159
  Godeffroy & Sohn, 45, 55–7
Covenant of the League of Nations, 146, *see also* United Nations Charter
  Article 15, 186
  Article 22, 40, 101, 146–8, 158, 160, 161–2, 193, 202
  incorporation of Nauru, 151–3
  criticisms, 182
criminal jurisdiction, 105
Crown colonies, 114–16
Curtis Island (Queensland)
  resettlement, 2, 208, 227
customary law of Nauru, 2, 107

de Roburt, Hammer, 3, 207, 216, 217, 226, 229, 234, 237, 238, 241, 244
decolonisation, 16–17, 25, 27, 125–50, 204, 206, 260
Demarcation Agreement (1886), 114
Australian Commonwealth, 118
Department for Foreign Affairs and Trade, Australia (DFAT)
Nauru land rehabilitation, 252
dependencies, 116
Deutsche Handels- und Plantagen-Gesellschaft der Südsee-Inseln. *See* German Trading and Plantation Company of the South Sea Islands (DHPG)
Deutsche Kolonial Gesellschaft für Südwest-Afrika. *See* German South West Africa Company
Deutsch-Ostafrikanische Gesellschaft. *See* German East Africa Company
DHPG. *See* German Trading and Plantation Company of the South Sea Islands (DHPG)
direct administration, 46, 65, 110, 112, 114
direct representation
Committee of Imperial Defence, 119
direct rule, 107–14
dominion annexation of the German colonies, 139
dominions, 116, 181
international status, 181
Dorsett, Shaunnagh, 15, 16
Dumbarton Oaks, 192, 194
Dutch New Guinea, 72, 198

economy and Pacific trade, 13, 119–20
Guano Islands Act, 124
interwar years
food production, 178
phosphate, 175–7, 178
racialised anxieties, 177
labour, 120–1
phosphate, 35, 121–5, 178, 247
education, provision of, 173–5, 212
compulsory primary education, 173, 174

Compulsory Education Ordinance, 174
secondary education, 174, 175, 216
trust territories, 196
Ellis, Albert, 127, 129, 163, 175, 191
Ethiopia, 221–4

First World War
Australia, opportunities for, 137
British declaration of war, 136
Nauru, occupation of, 138
New Guinea, 138
pre-war preparations, 135–6
Fisher, Andrew, 136–8, 139
Foreign Jurisdiction Act (1843), 60, 77
Foreign Jurisdiction Acts
consolidation, 116
Foreign Jurisdiction Bill (1888), 115
free trade, 142
mandate agreements, 169
Royal Institute of International Affairs, 182
Treaty of Versailles, 179
United Nations Charter, 191, 196

General Act (1885), 47, 59, 60, 94, 141
Geographical and Colonial Definitions in Future Acts, 117
geography of Nauru, 13
German Colonial Society, 67
German Confederation, 54, 67
German East Africa Company, 80, 109–10
German Foreign Office, 36, 73
German imperialism, 32, 45, 47, 110, 260
Bismarck's changing attitude, 67, 71
direct colonial administration, 115
economic considerations, 69
imperial expansion, 66–8
concerns, 72–6
jurisdictional issues, 76
political considerations, 69, 70–2
Schutzgebiet, 69
German New Guinea, 45, 47, 67, 100, 113, 119, 130, 132, 155, 183, *see also* New Guinea Company
Australia, 149, 201

C Mandate status, 147
  phosphate rights, 150
  surrender, 138, 144
German Protectorate of the Marshall Islands, 13, 24, 45, 48
  administration of Nauru, 102–7
  establishment, 80–2, 84
    administration of Nauru, 102–7
    incorporation of Nauru, 89–92
    legal incorporation of Nauru, 93–7
    protectorate status, 80–2
    Treaty between the Marshallese Chiefs and the Reich, 81
German Samoa
  C mandate status, 147, 155
  New Zealand, 149
German South West Africa Company, 110, 111
German Trading and Plantation Company of the South Sea Islands (DHPG), 46–8, 58–9
Gesellschaft für Deutsche Kolonisation, 67, 109
Godeffroy & Sohn, 24, 45, 48–50, 55–9, 66, 71, 113
  copra trade, 45, 55
Godeffroy, Johann Cesar, 55, 57–9, 90
Gordon, Arthur, 121, 126, 148, 160
government structure of Nauru, 231
guano
  expansion of trade, 125
  global trade, 122
  Guano Islands Act, 88, 122, 123, 124, 125
  Jaluit Gesellschaft agreement, 86, 87, 88, 89
  regulation, 123
  right to mine, 85, 87, 88
  rock guano, 127
  United States, 88
Guano Islands Act (USA), 88, 122–4, 125

Hansa
  background, 50–4
  Hanseatic authority, 52
  Hanseatic companies, 55–9, 66
Hanseatic authority, 52, 159

Hanseatic companies, 55–9, *see also* Godeffroy & Sohn, German Trading and Plantation Company of the South Sea Islands (DHPG)
Hansemann, Adolph von, 48–50, 58–9, 71–2, 73–6
  Neuguinea Kompagnie, 79, 112, 119
  New Guinea, 77, 79–80, 112, 119
Hansemann, David, 49
Henderson & McFarlane, 126, 127, 129
  copra exports, 127
Hernsheim & Kompagnie, 76, 77, 80, 84, 88, 98, 107
Hernsheim, Franz, 77, 80
Hitler, Adolf, 183
Hughes, Billy, 40, 139, 144, 147, 157, 168, *see also* Australia, Nauru Island Agreement (1919)
  Appropriations Bill, 154

Immigration Restriction Act (1901), 120
Imperial Commissioner, 103, 108
Imperial Conferences, 180
  Imperial Conference (1907), 135
  Imperial Conference (1911), 135
  Imperial Conference (1917), 139
  Imperial Conference (1923), 180
  Imperial Conference (1926), 181
imperial expansion. See German imperialism
imperialism defined, 28
independence (Nauru), 13, 25, 33, 42, 234–9
  international recognition, 241, 244
Independence Day (Nauru), 238
Indigenous peoples
  conscription, 111
  criminal jurisdiction, 105
  land ownership, 87
  property rights, 95, 96–7, 106, 126, 159, 165–6, 201
  'sham' agreements, 45
  sovereignty, 87
  treaties, 81
industrial agriculture, 68, 69, 70, 121, *see also* agriculture

Inquiry into the Rehabilitation of
    Worked Out Phosphate Lands
    of Nauru, 248
Institut de droit international, 46, 93,
    94, 98
territorium nullius, 96
International Bank for Reconstruction
    and Development, 192
International Court of Justice (ICJ), 192
    Advisory Opinion on the Status of
        South-West Africa, 219
    Certain Phosphate Lands Case,
        29, 248
    Ethiopia and Liberia, 224
    proceedings against South
        Africa, 221
    South West Africa Cases, 205, 219
International Monetary Fund, 192
international status, 24–6, 158, 159,
    180, 241, see also independence
    (Nauru), trust territory,
    C Mandate status, protectorate
    status
    imperial form, relationship to, 25
    Nauru, 25, 99, 100, 204
internationalisation, 140
    mandatory principle, 146
    national self-determination, 141
Interpretation Act (1889), 117
interwar years, 175
    Australia
        agriculture, 177
        phosphate, 175
        racial policy, 177
    global politics, 179
        administrative form, 179–82
    phosphate, 178

Jaluit Gesellschaft, 46, 84–6, 98,
    249, 259
    administrative powers, 150
    administrative responsibilities, 102
    guano clauses, 86, 88, 89, 128
    indigenous peoples, 87
    legal framework, 86
    Pacific Islands Company, agreement
        with, 125–9
    phosphate rights, 130, 150
    property clauses, 86, 89
    termination of Nauru arrangement,
        107, 109, 113
Japan, 185
    Nauru, occupation of, 162,
        187–91
    Non-Project Aid Program, 256
John T. Arundel and Company,
    125, 127
Jung, Fritz, 106–7, 108, 173
jurisdiction. See also consular
    jurisdiction
    jurisdictional divisions within
        protectorates, 64
    theoretical law, 15–17
jurisdictional thinking, 9–44

Kaiserlicher Kommissar. See Imperial
    Commissioner
Kennedy, Duncan, 23
Klabbers, Jan, 17

labour, 133
    agriculture, 120–1
    blackbirding, 57, 120–1, 134, 159,
        166, 202
    immigrant labour, 121, 172
    indentured labour, 57, 120–1, 134,
        159, 166, 202
    labour shortages, 121, 189
    Pacific Island Labourers Act, 120
    regulation, 51, 121
land ownership, 97, 106, 126, 159, 165,
    see also property rights of
    Indigenous peoples
Landowners Phosphate Royalty Trust,
    2, 166, 200, 202
law enforcement, 77, 104
Law on Consular Jurisdiction (1879),
    76, 83, 102, 103
League of Nations. See also Covenant of
    the League of Nations
    Council, 155
        mandatory allocations, 155
    Germany, 183
    Italy, 185
    Japan, 184
    legitimacy, 182–7

INDEX

Permanent Mandates Commission, 155
legality. *See* legitimacy
legitimacy, 18
League of Nations, 182–7
Liberia, 221–3
limitations of the book, 36–9
literary contribution, 26
Lloyd George, David, 140, 142, 143, 148, 152, 191

Mandate (1920), 100, *see also* C Mandate status
mandatory obligations, 174
mandatory principle, 143, 146, *see also* C Mandate status
categories of mandate, 147
criticisms, 184
resource exploitation, 171
Marshall Islands. *See* German Protectorate of the Marshall Islands
Martitz, Ferdinand de, 95
territorium nullius, 94–5, 97
Massey, William, 140, 145, 146, 149, 150, *see also* New Zealand, Nauru Island Agreement (1919)
McVeigh, Shaun, 15, 16, 23
mineral deposits, 89, 176, 214, *see also* phosphate deposits
money laundering, 257
Monroe Doctrine for the Pacific, 135, 136, 137
Moscow Declarations, 192, 196

Namibia, 33, 224, 226
Native Administration Ordinance (1922), 166
Native Status Ordinance (1921), 166, 201
natural resource commodification, 35, 40, 121–5
Nauru Act (1965), 231, 236
Nauru Australia Compact of Settlement (NACOS), 250–2
Nauru Constitution. *See* Constitution of the Republic of Nauru

Nauru Independence Act (1967), 236, 237
Nauru Island Agreement (1919), 13, 41, 100, 148–51, 161, 163, 201
Article 22 Covenant of the League of Nations, 151–3
Australian administration, 148, 164
incorporation
Australia, 151
Britain, 153
League of Nations, 152
Nauru Talks, 228
Paris Peace Conference, 148
phosphate industry, 231
rehabilitation of mined land, 230
Trusteeship Agreement, 199, 202
Nauru Lands Ordinance, 165, 169, 170
Nauru Lands Rehabilitation Committee, 229
Nauru Local Government Council (NLGC), 226, 244
Nauru Phosphate Agreement, 234, 250
United Nations Trusteeship Council, 225, 256
Nauru Phosphate Agreement (1967), 234, 237, 250
Nauru Phosphate Corporation, 24, 233, 234, 240, 242
Nauru Rehabilitation Corporation, 251
Nauru Talks, 228
administrative form of independence, 232
future legal relationship with Australia, 119
phosphate ownership, 228
rehabilitation of mined out land, 228, 229, 232
Nauru Trust Fund (2014), 257
Nauru v. Australia. *See* Certain Phosphate Lands Case
Nauruan 'Council of Chiefs', 108
Neuguinea Kompagnie. *See* New Guinea Company
New Guinea, 67
annexation, 72, 73, 157
Australian administrative control, 157

New Guinea (cont.)
  British protectorate, 76
  German imperialism, 79, 82
  Hanseatic authority, 72, 77
  Hansemann, 77, 79
  labour supply, 57
  Marsall Island status compared, 80
  Neuguinea Kompagnie, 79, 112, 119
  occupation by Japan, 157
  Schutzbrief, 80
New Guinea Company, 79, 112, 119
new Reich. *See* Bismarckian Reich
New Zealand, 228, *see also* Nauru Island Agreement (1919)
  Cook Islands, 235
  disputes with Australia, 149
  independence of Nauru, 230
  Nauru Island Agreement, 148–9, 150–1, 153, 163, 242
  Nauru Talks, 233
  Nauruan phosphate, 13, 134, 149, 151, 161, 163, 176, 200, 202
  sub-imperialism, 135, 140
  Trusteeship Agreement, 197, 199
  Trusteeship Council, 194, 211
  Western Samoa, 29, 171, 184, 197, 235

obligations of trusteeship, 29, 69, 161, 174, 198, 200, 203, 208, 216, 225
open-door trade, 141–4, 146, 153, 162, 167, 184, 191, *see also* self-determination
Orford, Anne, 16
organised crime, 257
Ormsby-Gore, William, 153
ownerless land, 85, 87, 106

Pacific Island Labourers Act 1901, 120
Pacific Islands Company, 101
  Jaluit Gesellschaft, agreement with, 125–9
Pacific Phosphate Company, 40, 99, 128, 149, 150, 191
  commencement of phosphate operations, 131–4
  Jaluit Gesellschaft, relationship with, 129–31, 150, 201, 249

labour, 132, 133
mining rights, 129
Nauru Island Agreement, 149
Transfer Agreement, 154, 163
Palestine, 186–7, 256
Papua, 119, 180, 198
  incorporation into New Guinea, 198
Papua New Guinea
  asylum seekers, 3
  Hansemann, 86
  sovereignty, 35
Paris Peace Conference, 40, 101, 145–6, 148, 158, 161, 163
Permanent Court of International Justice
  Phosphates in Morocco Case, 178
Permanent Mandates Commission, 29, 148, 155, 161, 162, 167, 171, 187
  concerns, 168
  education, 173–5
  limited powers, 165, 183, 202
  Ormsby-Gore, 153
  Palestine, 186
  social, moral and material welfare of the natives, 173
phosphate deposits, 35, 88, 113, 124, 202, 247, 261
  Banaba, 129, 130, 137, 154, 175
  commencement of operations, 131–4
  declining revenue, 256
  inland deposits, 124
  Nauruan phosphate, 129, 130
    exports, 131
    German administration, 132
    labour, 133
  ownership, 228
  Pacific phosphate trade, 125
  seabed deposits, 124
phosphate mining rights, 88, 99, *see also* rehabilitation of mined-out land
  acquisition of mining rights by Pacific Phosphate Company, 129–31
  Board of Commissioners, 150
  Jaluit Gesellschaft, 150
  Nauruan phosphate, 149
  Phosphates in Morocco Case, 178

Plaintiff M68 v. Minister for Immigration and Border Protection, 255–6
Pleasant Island (Nauru), 89–90
political status, 9–16, 24, 260, *see also* independence (Nauru), trust territory, C Mandate status, protectorate status
   C Mandate status, 24
   German protectorate, 24
   Nauruan national administration, 25
   trust territory status, 25
Pope, Harold, 163, 175
population, 9
   global population growth, 161, 176, 177
   post-independence, 25, 36, 261
property rights of Indigenous peoples, 95, 96–7, 106, 126, 159, 165–6, 201, 249, *see also* land ownership
Protectorate Law (1886), 82–4, 87, 102, 103, 109, 114
   Schutzgewalt, 93
protectorate status, 24, 39, 45–6, 62–5, 97–8, 201
   colonial protectorates, 65–6
   colony distinguished, 65, 69
   concept, 62–3, 69
   consular jurisdiction, 76–80
   German protectorates
      Bismark's attitude to imperial expansion, 66–72
      collapse, 107–10
      establishment, 66–72
   German Trading and Plantation Company of the South Sea Islands, 46–8
   Hanseatic authority, 50–4
   Jaluit Gesellschaft, 84–9
   jurisdiction over non-Europeans, 83
   jurisdictional divisions between protector and protected, 64
   legal basis of declarations of protectorate status, 63
   legal establishment (German protectorate regime), 82–4
   legal framework, 82, 93, 101, 103

mandates, co-existence, 180
Marshall Islands, 80–2
incorporation of Nauru, 93–7

Queensland
   annexation of New Guinea, 34, 72, 73
   Nauru as a municipality of, 3
   resettlement of Nauruan people Curtis Island, 2, 14, 208, 227
   self-government, 72

Radack chain. *See* German Protectorate of the Marshall Islands
Ralick chain. *See* German Protectorate of the Marshall Islands
rehabilitation of mined out land, 228, 229, 232, 233, 234
Reich, 158
   armistice, 145
   Australian colonial unrest, 73
   authority over Nauru, 94, 98, 158
   Consular law, 102
   direct colonial administration, 101
   direct colonial rule, 113, 158
   direct, militarised colonial rule, 134
   economic difficulties, 112
   incorporation of Nauru, 13
   Jaluit Gesellschaft, agreement with, 84–6, 100, 102, 104, 106, 108, 113, 127, 159, 173
      administrative powers, 150
      guano clauses, 39, 86, 88, 130
      phosphate rights, 150
      property clauses, 86
   jurisdiction, 83, 116
   law enforcement, 92
   legal framework for its protectorate regime, 96
   New Course, 114, 134
   New Guinea, 119
   other protectorates, 82
   phosphate mining, 130, 131–4, 149
   Protectorate Law, 102, 103
   Samoa, 112
   Schutzgewalt, 93
   sovereignty arrangements, 79, 82
   trading interests, 46, 77, 109, 110, 134
   trading tax, 108

Reich (cont.)
   Treaty between the Marshallese Chiefs and the Reich, 81
Reich Colonial Office, 40, 46, 85, 112
relationship between imperialism and international law, 38, 238
Republic of Nauru, 238, 244, *see also* independence (Nauru)
   autocracy, 246
   changing international status, 9–12
   Constitution
      administrative structure, 239, 240
      failures, 1–2, 245
         abandonment of the rule of law, 254
         authoritarianism, 254–5
resettlement, 2–8, 14, 208, 226
resource exploitation, 10, 171, 245, *see also* phosphate deposits, phosphate mining rights
Roosevelt, Franklin D.
   Atlantic Charter, 191–2, 194
   League of Nations, 192
rule of law, 254

Samoa, 112
Samoan Tripartite Convention (1899), 112
Schnee, Heinrich, 183
Schutzgebiet. *See* protectorate status
Schutzgebiet der Marshall-Inseln. *See* German Protectorate of the Marshall Islands
seabed deposits, 257–8
   exploration licenses, 258
   phosphate, 124
Second World War, 187–91
self-determination, 142–8, 167, *see also* open door trade
self-governing colonies, 116, 118, 119
self-governing dominions, 101, 119, 153, 155, 158
self-government principle, 2–3, 117, 118, 193
   League of Nations, 186, 187, 206
   trusteeship, 193, 196, 199, 203, 205, 206, 217–18, 227
   United Nations Charter, 193, 195, 196, 199, 203, 205, 206, 212, 218

separation of powers, 2
Smuts, Jan, 139–40, 142–3, 147, 197
   mandatory principle, 143–6
Sonnenschein, Franz, 92, 94, 97
South Africa, 101, 140, 218
   South West Africa, 171, 197, 205, 218–21
   sovereignty, 197
   sub-imperialism, 157, 197
South African Defence Force, 224
South West Africa
   decolonisation, 220–4
   South African Defence Force, 224
   trusteeship, 218–21
sovereignty. *See* independence (Nauru)
Soviet Union
   trusteeship, 205
   Trusteeship Council, 194–5, 196–7
Statement on the Constitutional Future of Nauru, 232–9
   new constitution
      administrative structure, 242
Stein, Boris, 200
sub-imperialism, 34, 134–40, 149, 157, 179, 194, 202
substantive rights, 102

tax avoidance, 257
territorium nullius, 95, 97
textual sources, 24
trade and traders, 104, 159
   trading tax, 108
Transfer Agreement
   Pacific Phosphate Company, 154
   phosphate rights, 154
treaties with Indigenous peoples
   'sham' agreements, 45
Treaty between the Marshallese Chiefs and the Reich, 81
Treaty of Versailles (1919), 101, 142, 145, 146, 150, 166, 179
tripartite agreement. *See* Nauru Island Agreement (1919)
trust territory, 25, 161–3, 193, 202
   Nauru, 13, 197–201, 206
      administration, 210–11
      obligation to promote political advancement, 213

phosphate operations, 210
trusteeship, 193, 205
Trusteeship Council, 162, 194, 256
  functions and powers, 196

United Kingdom. *See also* British
    Phosphate Commission, Nauru
    Island Agreement (1919)
  Certain Phosphate Lands Case,
    248–51
  consular jurisdiction, 77–8
  imperial forms, 114–19
  Moscow Declarations, 192
  Nauruan phosphate, 151, 161
United Nations, 192
  mandates, 194
  trusteeship system, 193, 195–7
United Nations Charter, 193, 195
  Declaration Regarding Non-Self-
    Governing Territories, 195, 206
  external administration
    principles, 206
  International Trusteeship
    System, 195
  obligations of trusteeship, 199,
    205, 241
United Nations Development
    Programme (UNDP)
  constitutional review process, 3,
    see also Constitutional Review
    Commission

United States
  administrative form, 194
  agriculture, 122
  Eastern Samoa, 112
  Eastern Somoa, 112
  Guano Islands Act, 88, 122–4,
    178
  Pacific islands, 185, 194, 200
  Second World War, 189–91, 192
  trust territories, 194

Weber, Max, 22
  democratisation, 19, 259
  Protestant ethic, 22
Weeramantry, Christopher, 28,
    245
Western Pacific
  consular jurisdiction, 76–80
Western Samoa
  independence, 228
White Australia policy, 120, 135
Wilhelm I, 54, 81, 91, 93, 102,
    109
Wilhelm II, 111, 119
  centralisation of colonial policy, 111
  New Course, 111, 158
  Samoa, 112
  Schutztruppe, 134
Wilson, Woodrow, 142

Yalta conference, 192, 193

CAMBRIDGE STUDIES IN INTERNATIONAL AND COMPARATIVE LAW

Books in the Series

151 *Marketing Global Justice: The Political Economy of International Criminal Law*
Christine Schwöbel-Patel

150 *International Status in the Shadow of Empire*
Cait Storr

149 *Treaties in Motion: The Evolution of Treaties from Formation to Termination*
Edited by Malgosia Fitzmaurice and Panos Merkouris

148 *Humanitarian Disarmament: An Historical Enquiry*
Treasa Dunworth

147 *Complementarity, Catalysts, Compliance: The International Criminal Court in Uganda, Kenya, and the Democratic Republic of Congo*
Christian M. De Vos

146 *Cyber Operations and International Law*
François Delerue

145 *Comparative Reasoning in International Courts and Tribunals*
Daniel Peat

144 *Maritime Delimitation as a Judicial Process*
Massimo Lando

143 *Prosecuting Sexual and Gender-Based Crimes at the International Criminal Court: Practice, Progress and Potential*
Rosemary Grey

142 *Capitalism as Civilisation: A History of International Law*
Ntina Tzouvala

141 *Sovereignty in China: A Genealogy of a Concept Since 1840*
Adele Carrai

140 *Narratives of Hunger in International Law: Feeding the World in Times of Climate Change*
Anne Saab

139 *Victim Reparation under the Ius Post Bellum: An Historical and Normative Perspective*
Shavana Musa

138 *The Analogy between States and International Organizations*
Fernando Lusa Bordin

137 *The Process of International Legal Reproduction: Inequality, Historiography, Resistance*
Rose Parfitt

136 *State Responsibility for Breaches of Investment Contracts*
Jean Ho

135 *Coalitions of the Willing and International Law: The Interplay between Formality and Informality*
   Alejandro Rodiles
134 *Self-Determination in Disputed Colonial Territories*
   Jamie Trinidad
133 *International Law as a Belief System*
   Jean d'Aspremont
132 *Legal Consequences of Peremptory Norms in International Law*
   Daniel Costelloe
131 *Third-Party Countermeasures in International Law*
   Martin Dawidowicz
130 *Justification and Excuse in International Law: Concept and Theory of General Defences*
   Federica Paddeu
129 *Exclusion from Public Space: A Comparative Constitutional Analysis*
   Daniel Moeckli
128 *Provisional Measures before International Courts and Tribunals*
   Cameron A. Miles
127 *Humanity at Sea: Maritime Migration and the Foundations of International Law*
   Itamar Mann
126 *Beyond Human Rights: The Legal Status of the Individual in International Law*
   Anne Peters
125 *The Doctrine of Odious Debt in International Law: A Restatement*
   Jeff King
124 *Static and Evolutive Treaty Interpretation: A Functional Reconstruction*
   Christian Djeffal
123 *Civil Liability in Europe for Terrorism-Related Risk*
   Lucas Bergkamp, Michael Faure, Monika Hinteregger and Niels Philipsen
122 *Proportionality and Deference in Investor-State Arbitration: Balancing Investment Protection and Regulatory Autonomy*
   Caroline Henckels
121 *International Law and Governance of Natural Resources in Conflict and Post-Conflict Situations*
   Daniëlla Dam-de Jong
120 *Proof of Causation in Tort Law*
   Sandy Steel
119 *The Formation and Identification of Rules of Customary International Law in International Investment Law*
   Patrick Dumberry
118 *Religious Hatred and International Law: The Prohibition of Incitement to Violence or Discrimination*
   Jeroen Temperman

117 *Taking Economic, Social and Cultural Rights Seriously in International Criminal Law*
   Evelyne Schmid
116 *Climate Change Litigation: Regulatory Pathways to Cleaner Energy*
   Jacqueline Peel and Hari M. Osofsky
115 *Mestizo International Law: A Global Intellectual History 1842–1933*
   Arnulf Becker Lorca
114 *Sugar and the Making of International Trade Law*
   Michael Fakhri
113 *Strategically Created Treaty Conflicts and the Politics of International Law*
   Surabhi Ranganathan
112 *Investment Treaty Arbitration As Public International Law: Procedural Aspects and Implications*
   Eric De Brabandere
111 *The New Entrants Problem in International Fisheries Law*
   Andrew Serdy
110 *Substantive Protection under Investment Treaties: A Legal and Economic Analysis*
   Jonathan Bonnitcha
109 *Popular Governance of Post-Conflict Reconstruction: The Role of International Law*
   Matthew Saul
108 *Evolution of International Environmental Regimes: The Case of Climate Change*
   Simone Schiele
107 *Judges, Law and War: The Judicial Development of International Humanitarian Law*
   Shane Darcy
106 *Religious Offence and Human Rights: The Implications of Defamation of Religions*
   Lorenz Langer
105 *Forum Shopping in International Adjudication: The Role of Preliminary Objections*
   Luiz Eduardo Salles
104 *Domestic Politics and International Human Rights Tribunals: The Problem of Compliance*
   Courtney Hillebrecht
103 *International Law and the Arctic*
   Michael Byers
102 *Cooperation in the Law of Transboundary Water Resources*
   Christina Leb
101 *Underwater Cultural Heritage and International Law*
   Sarah Dromgoole
100 *State Responsibility: The General Part*
   James Crawford

99 *The Origins of International Investment Law: Empire, Environment and the Safeguarding of Capital*
Kate Miles

98 *The Crime of Aggression under the Rome Statute of the International Criminal Court*
Carrie McDougall

97 *'Crimes against Peace' and International Law*
Kirsten Sellars

96 *Non-Legality in International Law: Unruly Law*
Fleur Johns

95 *Armed Conflict and Displacement: The Protection of Refugees and Displaced Persons under International Humanitarian Law*
Mélanie Jacques

94 *Foreign Investment and the Environment in International Law*
Jorge E. Viñuales

93 *The Human Rights Treaty Obligations of Peacekeepers*
Kjetil Mujezinović Larsen

92 *Cyber Warfare and the Laws of War*
Heather Harrison Dinniss

91 *The Right to Reparation in International Law for Victims of Armed Conflict*
Christine Evans

90 *Global Public Interest in International Investment Law*
Andreas Kulick

89 *State Immunity in International Law*
Xiaodong Yang

88 *Reparations and Victim Support in the International Criminal Court*
Conor McCarthy

87 *Reducing Genocide to Law: Definition, Meaning, and the Ultimate Crime*
Payam Akhavan

86 *Decolonising International Law: Development, Economic Growth and the Politics of Universality*
Sundhya Pahuja

85 *Complicity and the Law of State Responsibility*
Helmut Philipp Aust

84 *State Control over Private Military and Security Companies in Armed Conflict*
Hannah Tonkin

83 *'Fair and Equitable Treatment' in International Investment Law*
Roland Kläger

82 *The UN and Human Rights: Who Guards the Guardians?*
Guglielmo Verdirame

81 *Sovereign Defaults before International Courts and Tribunals*
Michael Waibel

80 *Making the Law of the Sea: A Study in the Development of International Law*
    James Harrison

79 *Science and the Precautionary Principle in International Courts and Tribunals: Expert Evidence, Burden of Proof and Finality*
    Caroline E. Foster

78 *Transition from Illegal Regimes under International Law*
    Yaël Ronen

77 *Access to Asylum: International Refugee Law and the Globalisation of Migration Control*
    Thomas Gammeltoft-Hansen

76 *Trading Fish, Saving Fish: The Interaction between Regimes in International Law*
    Margaret A. Young

75 *The Individual in the International Legal System: Continuity and Change in International Law*
    Kate Parlett

74 *'Armed Attack' and Article 51 of the UN Charter: Evolutions in Customary Law and Practice*
    Tom Ruys

73 *Theatre of the Rule of Law: Transnational Legal Intervention in Theory and Practice*
    Stephen Humphreys

72 *Science and Risk Regulation in International Law*
    Jacqueline Peel

71 *The Participation of States in International Organisations: The Role of Human Rights and Democracy*
    Alison Duxbury

70 *Legal Personality in International Law*
    Roland Portmann

69 *Vicarious Liability in Tort: A Comparative Perspective*
    Paula Giliker

68 *The Public International Law Theory of Hans Kelsen: Believing in Universal Law*
    Jochen von Bernstorff

67 *Legitimacy and Legality in International Law: An Interactional Account*
    Jutta Brunnée and Stephen J. Toope

66 *The Concept of Non-International Armed Conflict in International Humanitarian Law*
    Anthony Cullen

65 *The Principle of Legality in International and Comparative Criminal Law*
    Kenneth S. Gallant

64 *The Challenge of Child Labour in International Law*
    Franziska Humbert

63 *Shipping Interdiction and the Law of the Sea*
    Douglas Guilfoyle

62 *International Courts and Environmental Protection*
   Tim Stephens
61 *Legal Principles in WTO Disputes*
   Andrew D. Mitchell
60 *War Crimes in Internal Armed Conflicts*
   Eve La Haye
59 *Humanitarian Occupation*
   Gregory H. Fox
58 *The International Law of Environmental Impact Assessment: Process, Substance and Integration*
   Neil Craik
57 *The Law and Practice of International Territorial Administration: Versailles to Iraq and Beyond*
   Carsten Stahn
56 *United Nations Sanctions and the Rule of Law*
   Jeremy Matam Farrall
55 *National Law in WTO Law: Effectiveness and Good Governance in the World Trading System*
   Sharif Bhuiyan
54 *Cultural Products and the World Trade Organization*
   Tania Voon
53 *The Threat of Force in International Law*
   Nikolas Stürchler
52 *Indigenous Rights and United Nations Standards: Self-Determination, Culture and Land*
   Alexandra Xanthaki
51 *International Refugee Law and Socio-Economic Rights: Refuge from Deprivation*
   Michelle Foster
50 *The Protection of Cultural Property in Armed Conflict*
   Roger O'Keefe
49 *Interpretation and Revision of International Boundary Decisions*
   Kaiyan Homi Kaikobad
48 *Multinationals and Corporate Social Responsibility: Limitations and Opportunities in International Law*
   Jennifer A. Zerk
47 *Judiciaries within Europe: A Comparative Review*
   John Bell
46 *Law in Times of Crisis: Emergency Powers in Theory and Practice*
   Oren Gross and Fionnuala Ní Aoláin
45 *Vessel-Source Marine Pollution: The Law and Politics of International Regulation*
   Alan Khee-Jin Tan
44 *Enforcing Obligations* Erga Omnes *in International Law*
   Christian J. Tams

43 *Non-Governmental Organisations in International Law*
    Anna-Karin Lindblom

42 *Democracy, Minorities and International Law*
    Steven Wheatley

41 *Prosecuting International Crimes: Selectivity and the International Criminal Law Regime*
    Robert Cryer

40 *Compensation for Personal Injury in English, German and Italian Law: A Comparative Outline*
    Basil Markesinis, Michael Coester, Guido Alpa and Augustus Ullstein

39 *Dispute Settlement in the UN Convention on the Law of the Sea*
    Natalie Klein

38 *The International Protection of Internally Displaced Persons*
    Catherine Phuong

37 *Imperialism, Sovereignty and the Making of International Law*
    Antony Anghie

35 *Necessity, Proportionality and the Use of Force by States*
    Judith Gardam

34 *International Legal Argument in the Permanent Court of International Justice: The Rise of the International Judiciary*
    Ole Spiermann

32 *Great Powers and Outlaw States: Unequal Sovereigns in the International Legal Order*
    Gerry Simpson

31 *Local Remedies in International Law* (second edition) Chittharanjan Felix Amerasinghe

30 *Reading Humanitarian Intervention: Human Rights and the Use of Force in International Law*
    Anne Orford

29 *Conflict of Norms in Public International Law: How WTO Law Relates to Other Rules of International Law*
    Joost Pauwelyn

27 *Transboundary Damage in International Law*
    Hanqin Xue

25 *European Criminal Procedures* Edited by Mireille Delmas-Marty and J. R. Spencer

24 *Accountability of Armed Opposition Groups in International Law*
    Liesbeth Zegveld

23 *Sharing Transboundary Resources: International Law and Optimal Resource Use*
    Eyal Benvenisti

22 *International Human Rights and Humanitarian Law*
    René Provost

21 *Remedies against International Organisations*
    Karel Wellens

20 *Diversity and Self-Determination in International Law*
    Karen Knop
19 *The Law of Internal Armed Conflict*
    Lindsay Moir
18 *International Commercial Arbitration and African States: Practice, Participation and Institutional Development*
    Amazu A. Asouzu
17 *The Enforceability of Promises in European Contract Law*
    James Gordley
16 *International Law in Antiquity*
    David J. Bederman
15 *Money Laundering: A New International Law Enforcement Model*
    Guy Stessens
14 *Good Faith in European Contract Law*
    Reinhard Zimmermann and Simon Whittaker
13 *On Civil Procedure*
    J. A. Jolowicz
12 *Trusts: A Comparative Study*
    Maurizio Lupoi and Simon Dix
11 *The Right to Property in Commonwealth Constitutions*
    Tom Allen
10 *International Organizations before National Courts*
    August Reinisch
9   *The Changing International Law of High Seas Fisheries*
    Francisco Orrego Vicuña
8   *Trade and the Environment: A Comparative Study of EC and US Law*
    Damien Geradin
7   *Unjust Enrichment: A Study of Private Law and Public Values*
    Hanoch Dagan
6   *Religious Liberty and International Law in Europe*
    Malcolm D. Evans
5   *Ethics and Authority in International Law*
    Alfred P. Rubin
4   *Sovereignty over Natural Resources: Balancing Rights and Duties*
    Nico Schrijver
3   *The Polar Regions and the Development of International Law*
    Donald R. Rothwell
2   *Fragmentation and the International Relations of Micro-States: Self-Determination and Statehood*
    Jorri C. Duursma
1   *Principles of the Institutional Law of International Organizations*
    C. F. Amerasinghe

CPSIA information can be obtained
at www.ICGtesting.com
Printed in the USA
LVHW081908270721
693842LV00006B/501